D1297376

VALUING ENVIRONMENTAL GOODS

AN ASSESSMENT OF THE CONTINGENT VALUATION METHOD

R.G. Cummings
D.S. Brookshire
W.D. Schulze

Contributors
Richard Bishop, Don L. Coursey,
A. Myrick Freeman, Thomas A. Heberlein,
Alan Randall, V. Kerry Smith

Commentators
Kenneth Arrow, Daniel Kahneman,
Sherwin Rosen, Vernon Smith

ROWMAN & ALLANHELD
PUBLISHERS

ROWMAN & ALLANHELD

Published in the United States of America in 1986
by Rowman & Allanheld, Publishers
(a division of Littlefield, Adams & Company)
81 Adams Drive, Totowa, New Jersey 07512

Library of Congress Cataloging in Publication Data

Cummings, Ronald G.
   Valuing Environmental Goods: An Assessment of the
Contingent Valuation Method

Bibliography: p. 247
Includes index.
   1. Public goods—Cost effectiveness.   I. Brookshire,
David S.   II. Schulze, William D.   III. Bishop, Richard C.
IV. Arrow, Kenneth Joseph, 1921–   .   V. Title.
HB846.5.C86   1986   363   85–14298
ISBN 0-8476-7448-7

86 87 88 / 10 9 8 7 6 5 4 3 2 1
Printed in the United States of America

Contents

Tables and Figures   ix

Preface and Acknowledgments   xi

Part I   The Contingent Valuation Method   *1*

1   Introduction   *3*
     The Contingent Valuation Method *3*; The CVM Has Achieved Acceptability *4*; But on the Other Hand *5*; The Need for a State of the Arts Assessments of the CVM *6*; Notes *9*

2   A Historical Perspective for the CVM Assessment   *10*
     Overview *10*; Social Welfare: What Is It and How Is It Measured? *11*; Benefit-Cost Analysis and the General Possibilities Theorem *11*; Market Prices as Measures of Social Welfare *12*; Valuing Public Goods *13*; Developing the CVM *15*; Related Research in Other Disciplines *17*; The Structure for a CVM Assessment *19*; Notes *20*

3   Applications of the CVM: An Overview of Issues   *21*
     Overview *21*; Strategic Bias and The CVM *21*; Axiomatic Behavior and CVM Valuations *27*; Bias Issues Related to the Design of CVM Questionnaires *28*; Starting Point Bias *28*; Vehicle Bias *31*; Information Bias *33*; Willingness to Pay vs. Willingness to Accept *35*; Concluding Remarks *36*

4   Experimental Economics: Implications for the CVM   *37*
     Introduction *37*; Methodological Development in Experimental Economics *38*; Recent Applications of Laboratory Methods Related to CVM Developments *41*; Valuations Under Uncertainty Conditions: Relevant Results from Laboratory Experiments *44*; An Example: Revelation of Compensating Income Variation *45*; Solicited Compensating Variations *46*; Tatonnement Version of the Second-Price Auction *46*; Conclusions *48*; Notes *48*

5   Imputing Actual Behavior From Choices Made Under Hypothetical Circumstances   *49*
     The Issues *49*; Hypothetical Payment: An Incentive for Accuracy? *50*; Hypothetical Biases Related to Time *50*;

Perceptions, Framing and the CVM 56; Perceptions 56; Framing 60; Attitudes vs. Intended Behavior 65; Concluding Remarks 67; Notes 69

6   Comparison Studies: What is Accuracy?   71
Introduction 71; Value Comparisons: The CVM and the TCM 72; Knetsch and Davis 73; Bishop and Heberlein 74; Desvousges, Smith and McGivney 76; Seller, Stoll and Chavas 81; Thayer 87; Fisher 89; Value Comparisons: The CVM and the HPM 89; Brookshire et al. 90; Cummings et al. 92; Brookshire et al. (1984) 93; What Is Accuracy? 95; Implications for Assessments of the CVM 102; Final Remarks 106; Notes 109

Part II   The Assessment Conference and Conclusions:
          The State of the Arts of the CVM   111

7   The Assessment Conference: Overview   113

8   The Possibility of Satisfactory Benefit Estimation with
    Contingent Markets   114
ALAN RANDALL
A Theory of CVM-Participant Behavior 115; Value Formation 115; Value Reporting 116; Implications 119; "Information Bias" and Policy Evaluation 120; Concluding Comments 121; Notes 121

9   Does Contingent Valuation Work?   123
RICHARD C. BISHOP AND THOMAS A. HEBERLEIN
Experimental Results 124; Goose Study Design 124; Goose Study Analysis 124; Goose Study Interpretation 126; Deer Study Design 128; Preliminary Results 129; Deer Study Interpretation and Plan for Further Research 131; Implications for CBS 133; Is Contingent Valuation Biased? 133; Do CBS Deal Adequately with Accuracy Issues? 134; Does Iterative Bidding Improve Accuracy? 135; Are Experimental Approaches the Key to Assessing and Improving CVM? 137; Should Willingness to Accept be Abandoned in CVM Applications? 138; Will the Application of Vickrey Auctions Improve the Accuracy of CVM? 139; Is Attitude-Behavior Research Relevant to CVM Research? 141; Our Assessment of CVM 146; Notes 147

10 On Assessing the State of the Arts of the Contingent Valuation
    Method of Valuing Environmental Changes   148
A. MYRICK FREEMAN III
Introduction 148; Criteria 149; Bias 151; Strategic Bias 152; Starting Point Bias 153; Information Bias 153; Vehicle Bias 154; Summary 154; Random Error 155; Assessment 157; Two Miscellaneous Comments 159; Conclusions 160; Notes 160

11 To Keep or Toss the Contingent Valuation Method   *162*
    V. KERRY SMITH
    Introduction *162*; Non-CVM Data: How Objective Are They?
    164; Tasks Requested of Survey Respondents *170*; The
    Problems with Hypothetical Questions *172*; The Bottom Line
    174; Notes *176*; Appendix: Some Quibbles on the Cummings,
    Brookshire, Schulze Summary of CVM Research *177*

12 The Review Panel's Assessment   *180*
    Introduction *180*; Comments by Professor Kenneth Arrow
    180; Comments by Professor Danial Kahneman *185*; ROC
    #5; The CVM should be used only for problems that have
    a "purchase structure": *186*; ROC #6: The use of CVM
    should be restructed to user values, rather than to ideological
    values *190*; ROC #7: Accurate description of payment mode
    is essential to the CVM *193*; Comments by Professor Sherwin
    Rosen *194*; Comments by Professor Vernon Smith *197*

13 Summary and Conclusions   *205*
    Overview *205*; Structural Biases in the CVM *206*; Strategic
    Bias *206*; Starting Point Bias *207*; Information Bias *208*;
    Vehicle Bias *209*; Conclusions *210*; Hypothetical Biases in the
    CVM *211*; Preference Research Issues *211*; The Comparability
    of WTP and WTA Measures *217*; Attitudes vs. Intended
    Behavior *221*; Hypothetical Biases in the CVM: Conclusions
    223; The Accuracy of CVM Measures of Value *226*; Overview
    of the "Accuracy" Issue *226*; What Is Accuracy? *227*;
    Reference Accuracy and Public Good Values *229*; The Need
    for Accuracy or Calibration Research *229*; The Reference
    Operating Conditions *230*; The State of the Arts of the
    Contingent Valuation Method *231*; The CVM Without
    Apology *232*; Conclusions Concerning Accuracy *233*; Final
    Remarks *234*; Critical Issues for Future CVM Research *235*

*Appendix: Some Comments on the State of the Arts Assessment
of the Contingent Valuation Method Draft Report*   *237*
    ROBERT CAMERON MITCHELL AND RICHARD T. CARSON

References   *247*

Index   *259*

Tables and Figures

TABLES

3.1	Iterative Bidding and the Payment Card Approach	*30*
3.2	Measures of WTP and WTA	*35*
6.1	Summary of Results	*75*
6.2	Comparison of Benefit Estimates for Water Quality Improvements	*77*
6.3	A Comparison of Contingent Valuation and Generalized Travel Cost Benefit Estimates	*80*
6.4	A Comparison of Contingent Valuation and Contingent Ranking Benefit Estimates	*82*
6.5	Results of the TCM	*84*
6.6	Results of the Open-Ended CVM	*85*
6.7	Results of the Close-Ended CVM	*86*
6.8	Logit Analysis of the Close-Ended Form of the Contingent Valuation Method	*87*
6.9	Bidding Game and Site Substitution Results	*88*
6.10	Tests of Hypotheses from the BTSd Study	*91*
6.11	Elasticity Measures	*93*
6.12	Summary of Results from Comparison Studies	*101*
6.13	Reference Operating Conditions and Implied Reference Accuracy	*105*
6.14	ROC Satisfied in Selected Applications of the CVM	*105*
9.1	Regression Analysis of Simulated and Contingent Markets for Willingness-to-Sell Goose Hunting Permits	*125*
9.2	Willingness to Accept Compensation for Sandhill Deer Hunting Permits	*130*
9.3	Willingness to Pay for Sandhill Deer Hunting Permits	*131*
11.1	Selected Sample of Sources for Non-CVM Economic Data	*167*
13.1	Alternative Reference Operating Conditions	*231*

FIGURES

3.1	Examples of Bid Distributions	25
4.1	Overall Average Experimental Responses	43
4.2	Group Willingness to Pay Function	46
4.3	Vickrey Auction of N Units	47
6.1	Order of Magnitude Estimates	98
6.2	ROCs and Market, Non-Market Commodities	108
9.1	Schematic of Attitude-Behavior Relationships	143
12.1	A Hypothetical Value Function	187
12.2	Expressed Willingness to Pay Tax for Cleanup to Preserve Fishing in Muskoka, Haliburton, and All Ontario	191
12.3	WTA – WTP Relationships 200	200
12.4	Tentative Results from University of Arizona Experiments	202
12.5	Change in Seller Surplus Relative to Total Surplus	203

Preface and Acknowledgments

This book has as its goal the perhaps ambitious task of assessing the state of the art of the Contingent Valuation Method (CVM) for estimating benefits attributable to public goods in general, and environmental goods in particular. Given the controversy surrounding the issue of CVM viability as a tool for benefit estimation, and the wide latitude for individual judgement and interpretation in considering any of the characteristics of the method, efforts by any group of authors to set out the state of the art for the CVM might at the outset be viewed as pretentious and, therefore, doomed to failure. Who is to say that the judgements/interpretations of any one set of authors is in any way definitive with regard to the state of the art of the CVM?

The authors' concern with this issue, coupled with their conviction that there exists a critical need for a profession-wide assessment of the CVM, is reflected in the somewhat curious structure of this book. Thus, in part I, the authors develop their tentative assessment of the strengths and weaknesses of the CVM as a method for deriving credible, accurate estimates for public goods. Part I, particularly chapter 6, sets the stage for what the authors hope will be regarded as representative of a profession-wide debate as to the state of the art of the CVM. This "debate," reported in the book's part II, takes the following form. A draft of part I was made available to two groups of people: a group of contibutors and a group of commentators. The contributors consisted of scholars actively involved in efforts to develop and assess the CVM and included Professors Richard Bishop and Thomas Heberlein (University of Wisconsin), A. Myrick Freeman (Bowdoin College), Alan Randall (University of Kentucky), and V. Kerry Smith (Vanderbilt University). These contributors prepared papers wherein they address two questions: what is their critique of part I as a state of the art assessment of the CVM?; and, what is *their* assessment of the state of the art of the CVM? The commentators consisted of an outstanding group of scholars from the economics and psychology professions and included Professors Kenneth Arrow (Stanford University), Daniel Kahnman (University of British Columbia), Sherwin Rosen (University of Chicago) and Vernon Smith (University of Arizona).

The commentators and contributors were brought together at an "Assessment Conference" held in Palo Alto, California on July 2, 1984. The commentators, who had access to part I of the book prior to the conference, listened to the contributors' papers during the morning of the conference. During the afternoon, each commentator discussed *his* reactions to part I's assessment of the CVM, as well as to the presentations by the contributors and his assessment of the state of the art of the CVM. The contributors' papers and the commentators' comments are given in part II, chapters 8–12, in this book.

The reader can now appreciate the substance of the authors' efforts to develop a broad, professionally representative view of the state of the art of the CVM. The culmination of (1) the authors' initial efforts to assess the CVM, part I of the book; (2) refinements and extensions of these assessments by other scholars in the field; and (3) critical assessments by leading scholars in the economics and psychology professions is seen in the book's concluding chapter—chapter 13—wherein the authors bring together these diverse views to the end of attempting to describe the state of the art of the CVM.

From the above it should be obvious that, in this book, the reader will not be offered "truths" concerning the feasibility, or lack thereof, of the CVM. Rather, as he/she proceeds through chapters 1–13, the reader essentially participates in the intellectual *process* of searching for critical issues relevant for assessing the CVM and the professional exchange as to the relative weights, and the strengths and weaknesses, of these issues. Thus, the reader will find problems identified as important issues by the authors in part I treated as *non*-issues after their discussion at the Assessment Conference. Similarly, problems either ignored or given superficial treatment by the authors in their initial (part I) assessment became recognized as substantive and important issues in the collective judgements of conference participants (as reported in chapter 13). The book then has something of a different structure. Our hope is that the reader will enjoy and benefit from the difference.

As is obvious from the above description of commentators and contributors who have heavily contributed to the development of ideas used in the authors' ultimate efforts to set out the state of the art of the CVM, this book results from a group effort to address important questions concerning the valuation of public goods. The group whose efforts are reflected in the pages of this book extend well beyond the individuals named above, however. There are three other individuals whose contributions form an integral part of the line of intellectual debate threading its way throughout the book. Professor Don L. Coursey, University of Wyoming, played a major role in assisting the authors in recognizing the importance of and contributions from the field of Experimental Economics for assessments of the CVM; a substantial part of chapter 4's discussions of laboratory experiments and their relevance for the CVM were written by Professor Coursey.

In response to our request for comments on the first draft of part I, the depth and perceptiveness of comments offered by Robert C. Mitchell (Resources for the Future, Inc.) and Richard T. Carson (University of California–Berkeley) were such that we requested, and received, their permission to include them as a part of the book. The contribution by these two scholars is therefore included as an appendix to chapter 13.

Given the critical importance of the Assessment Conference for the substance of intellectual exchanges reported in this book, the role of Professor Ralph C. d'Arge in arranging the conference, and his role as chairman of the afternoon session, is gratefully acknowledged by the authors. It goes without saying that such acknowledgements do not adequately reflect the cumulative impact of Professor d'Arge's intellectual contributions to the development of environmental economics in general, and the public good valuations issue in particular.

Professor d'Arge's long-standing position as a peer in our profession is well known.

There are many other members of the group whose efforts are reflected in the book. Professor Mark Walbert, then a graduate research assistant at the University of New Mexico and now an Assistant Professor of Economics at Illinois Normal University, played an important role in the intensive and extensive literature research and analysis for assessments of the CVM given in part I of the book. Professor Walbert's participation in the project extended well beyond that normal for a research assistant; his creative suggestions in early efforts to assess comparative studies involving the CVM were particularly important in the ultimate shaping of those assessments.

Others who contributed substantially by providing critiques of early drafts of the book or in shaping the Assessment Conference include Professor Shelby Gerking, Director, Institute for Policy Research, University of Wyoming; and Alan Carlin and Ann Fisher, United States Environmental Protection Agency.

Financial support for the research required for the preparation of the book, and for the Assessment Conference, was provided by the Office of Policy, Planning and Evaluation, United States Environmental Protection Agency. We gratefully acknowledge not only the financial support from this office of the E.P.A., but also the intellectual support and encouragement offered by the office's Director, Dr. Ralph Luken and the grant monitors, Drs. Alan Carlin and Ann Fisher.

Finally, among the many who have assisted the authors in one way or another whose help they wish to explicitly acknowledge are the three people who barely survived the frenzied logistical process of preparing the many drafts of the manuscript: our secretarial staff: Ema Shenefelt at the University of Wyoming, and Ingrid Martin and Gwyn Byers at the University of New Mexico,

November, 1985   Ronald G. Cummings
                                                        Albuquerque, New Mexico

                                                          David S. Brookshire
                                                            Laramie, Wyoming

                                                          William D. Schulze
                                                            Boulder, Colorado

Part I
The Contingent Valuation Method

1
Introduction

THE CONTINGENT VALUATION METHOD

The purpose of this book is to assess the state of the arts of the contingent valuation method (CVM) as this method is used to estimate values for public goods in general and for environmental goods in particular. The CVM is a survey method, the essence of which is succinctly expressed by Randall et al. (1983) as follows:

> Contingent valuation devices involve asking individuals, in survey or experimental settings, to reveal their personal valuations of increments (or decrements) in unpriced goods by using contingent markets. These markets define the good or amenity of interest, the status quo level of provision and the offered increment or decrement therein, the institutional structure under which the good is to be provided, the method of payment, and (implicitly or explicitly) the decision rule which determines whether to implement the offered program. Contingent markets are highly structured to confront respondents with a well-defined situation and to elicit a circumstantial choice contingent upon the occurence of the posited situation. Contingent markets elicit contingent choices. (p. 637)

The use of surveys as a means for obtaining values from individuals elicits in many a feeling of uneasiness. This may be attributable in part to the association of surveys with opinion polls and the general awareness that such polls may not be reliable: in 1948, opinion polls "elected" Mr. Dewey, but voters elected Mr. Truman. As is discussed later, psychologists would generally support the notion that opinion polls may be unreliable; their research demonstrates that opinions, or *attitudes*, may be poor predictors of actual behavior.

In the CVM, however, individuals are asked neither about their opinions nor about their attitudes: they are asked about their *contingent valuation* (if "this" happens, what would you be willing to pay?). While questions posed in the CVM are (arguably) not attitudinal, however, the "market," the commodity and the payment, as they appear in the CVM, are hypothetical. As will be seen, a large part of the criticisms of the CVM, in terms of the reliability or accuracy of value measures drawn therefrom, arise from the hypothetical nature of the CVM.

The CVM has strengths and it has weaknesses. Experimental efforts to develop the method—devise ways to mitigate or eliminate weaknesses and enhance strengths—began but a decade ago; prior to 1978, only a handful of scholars were involved in its development. As interest in applications of the CVM increased, and its presence became more broadly recognized in the research community, more and more scholars have entered the debate as to the efficacy of the CVM, in real and potential terms, as a means for valuing public goods. At this point in time, a substantial literature has developed concerning the issue, in the most general terms, as to whether one can hope to derive meaningful measures of individual values from a method wherein all aspects "relevant" to value decisions are artifical or hypothetical. A brief overview of this literature will provide the reader with some flavor for this controversy and, therefore, with an appreciation for the major objectives of this book—a topic that will be discussed below. Thus, in the following two sections we consider arguments related to the proposition: "The CVM has achieved acceptability..., but on the other hand."

THE CVM HAS ACHIEVED ACCEPTABILITY...

Randall and others argue that research to date has established the acceptability of the CVM as a method for non-market benefit estimation and that the current task "is to identify and explain systematically the relationship between the structure and performance of contingent markets." (Randall et al. 1983, p. 642) Thus, Randall et al. assert:

> At the outset, the research agenda in contingent valuation sought to establish, in the face of considerable skepticism, contingent valuation as an acceptable method of non-market benefit estimation (acceptable in the sense that it works about as well as available alternative techniques and is adaptable to at least some valuation tasks that alternative methods cannot handle). That objective has been attained. In addition, the experimental work of others has blunted traditional fears that strategic responses would inevitably dominate data sets of stated personal valuations.

Other authors, despite their critique of some CVM studies, suggest cautious optimism for the promise of the CVM. For example:

> CVM studies are a promising approach for the estimation of non-market environmental values. There has been steady progress in minimizing biases, just as there has been progress with problems in other techniques; nevertheless, we are far from being out of the woods. (Rowe and Chestnut 1983, p. 408)

Since the relatively recent beginning of empirical experiments with the CVM,[1] progress of sorts has undeniably been made in the development of the CVM. As pointed out by Randall et al. (1983), bids obtained in CVM studies are generally shown to be significantly related to income, availability of substitute and complementary commodities, and demographic characteristics; i.e., CVM bids "not radom numbers." (p. 639–40) Bids have been shown to be consistent with actual behavior. (Randall et al. pp. 1983, 639–40) As is discussed in some detail in a later chapter of this book, maximum willingness to pay measures derived from CVM studies have been shown to be consistent with market-demand-based values. Within this context, a basis exists for Randall et al.'s assertion (p. 639) that "several kinds of evidence generated by CVM studies support contingent valuation methods." Moreover, in a recent study by Schulze et al. (1981c), selected CVM studies were reviewed to the end of assessing the extent of various biases in CVM measures. The authors conclude that "Biases do not appear to be an overriding problem" (p. 170), although they point out that "to establish a precise contingent market—the 'good' must be well-defined." (p. 170)[2]

BUT ON THE OTHER HAND

Notwithstanding the "progress" noted above, others within the economics profession, and many outside the profession, reject the above described notion that the CVM has attained anything near the level of "acceptability" ascribed to the method. In reviewing estimation methods, including the CVM, for valuing non-market goods, Feenberg and Mills (1980) offer the dreary conclusion that "In the absence of market data, demand or willingness to pay estimation would appear to be hopeless." (p. 58)[3] Referring specifically to survey methods such as the CVM, Feenberg and Mills seemingly presume to speak for the economics profession in offering the following conclusion:

> Economists are biased against such surveys because they believe crucial contrary-to-fact questions are unlikely to be answered accurately. People lack the incentive and ability to answer accurately questions such as, 'How much more often would you swim in lake L if ambient pollution concentrations were reduced 10%?' Most people presumably experiment and talk to others to ascertain the effect of pollution abatement on their utility-maximizing behavior. Thus, economists doubt the accuracy of survey responses regarding effects of pollution abatement. (p. 169)

Interestingly enough, the "incentives" criticism of measures drawn from the CVM, as couched above, is inextricably related to a second criticism of the CVM, that is, biases resulting from strategic behavior on the part of survey participants. Essentially, the strategic behavior hypothesis—discussed in detail below in chapter 2 – posits behavior by survey respondents whereby false responses are given when such respones may result in a gain to the individual; i.e., "it is in the selfish interest of each person to give false signals, to pretend to have less interest in a given collective comsumption activity than he really has." (Samuelson 1954, p. 389) From empirical efforts to test the strategic behavior hypothesis, it is shown that the more hypothetical the question in a survey, the less the incentive for strategic behavior—the use of hypothetical questions could be a means of avoiding biases from strategic behavior. (Freeman 1979a, pp. 97–99) Herein lies the potential dilemma: the more hypothetical the question, the less the incentives for strategic behavior but, also, the less the incentives for accurate responses.

In addition to the above, two related sets of considerations that pose questions as to the efficacy of the CVM emanated from outside of the profession per se, that is, from the branch of psychology referred to as "cognitive psychology". The first of these (noted above) questions the extent to which responses derived in CVM studies are expressions of attitudes as opposed to intended behavior (as is presupposed in CVM studies) and a related controversy in the discipline of psychology concerning the extent to which attitudes are reliable predictors of behavior (Bishop and Heberlein 1979). A second set of considerations received from psychology which is of potential relevance for the CVM strikes at one of the most basic concepts in economic analysis: the concept of rational behavior. A number of recent studies point to stark discrepancies between actual decision-making behavior and the postulates of rationality, particularly in circumstances involving uncertainty.[4] Arrow (1982) notes that "these failures of the rationality hypothesis are in fact compatible with some of the specific observations of cognitive psychologists." (p.5) The "observations" referred to by Arrow will receive considerable attention in later sections of this book. For present purposes, two of these observations from psychological research are germane. In direct contrast to expected utility theory wherein subjective probabilities based on prior information play a major role, cognitive psychologists argue that individuals, in evaluating uncertain events, tend to ignore *both* prior information and the quality of present evidence. (Tversky and Kahneman, 1974, 1981) Second, also in direct contrast with the rationality precepts underlying expected utility theory, cognitive psychologists essentially argue that an individual's valuation of a commodity, along with many other commodities, is not simply dependent on the commodity set (prices, income and commodities), but on *how the set is described*—different descriptions of the *same* commodity space may yield different values for specific commodities. (Tversky and Kahneman, 1981)

Implications of these observations for potential biases in results from CVM studies are obviously a matter of some concern. For example the first issue—excessive reaction to current information—may imply that obtained CVM values are susceptible to the influence of (often) temporary "media events"; in terms of efforts to value environmental quality, the Three-Mile Island incident and the furor over Love Canal—a popular media topic in 1980—come to mind. Moreover, the applicability of CVM values obtained in one "current information" climate to values relevant for a different climate is questionable. The second issue—the dependence of commodity values on how commodities are described—implies potential biases arising from the framing of willingness-to-pay questions in the CVM questionnaire; thus, for any given public/environmental commodity to be valued via the CVM, different descriptions of the same basic commodity could yield different estimates of values of the commodity.[5]

It is important that the reader understand the context for which the controversy described above is relevant. President Reagan's Executive Order 12,291 (46 Fed. Reg. 13, 193, Feb. 17, 1981) requires that federal agencies such as the EPA consider the benefits and costs of federal regulations/actions prior to their implementation. For EPA regulations, such as air and/or water quality standards and regulations on hazardous waste disposal pratices, costs may be amenable to estimation, but benefits attributable to a large part of these regulations are non-market, "public goods" in nature: cleaner air and water, a safer environment. Agencies such as the EPA then have strong incentives and interests in identifying and developing means by which benefits attributable to public goods—such as environmental improvements—may be assessed.

Methods other than the CVM exist for valuing public goods, primarily the Travel Cost Method (TCM)[6] and the Hedonic Price Method (HPM)[7] The environmental (and other public good) "commodities" for which the TCM or HPM might be used for valuation purposes are very limited, however.[8] For the broad range of air quality and environmental safety issues of potential regulatory concern to the EPA, the CVM is, metaphorically, the only game in town for estimating relevant benefits. Obviously, the fact that the CVM is no worse than other methods or is the only game in town is not a sufficient reason for the use of CVM values as "acceptable" economic measures of social benefits in policy assessments. However, one sees rationales like these suggested as justifications for the continued development of the method. For example, Burness et al. (1983) conclude their discussion of caveats relevant for reported CVM results with the observation:

> Continued interest and research in this (the CVM) area are clearly warranted given, first, the importance of the public goods issue and, second, the lack of apparent alternatives to some form of the survey method in deriving valuations for large classes of public (environmental) goods. (p. 682)

On the other hand, the fact that the CVM is "the only game in town" for providing information of relevance to critical policy issues of the day is a powerful incentive for scholars to meet the intellectual challenge to devise means by which the CVM (or other methods) can be effectual in responding to society's needs.

Within this millieu (chapter 2 traces the character of historical efforts to develop the CVM), it seems fair to say that all scholars—whatever their predilection towards the CVM—who are directly or indirectly involved with the method appreciate the immediate need for a reflective pause in CVM experiment/application activities. Such a pause is required for thinking through the many (again, intuitive) propositions that have been posed as indicative of sources for bias in CVM measures, as well as related (again, often intuitive) counter-arguments. Most importantly, a reflective pause is required for a re-examination of means by which we can effectively apply the scientific method in our efforts to assess the CVM. In this regard, Joan Robinson's (1962) polemic concerning the difficulty in social sciences of applying the scientific method, is relevant for our discussions:

> [Referring to why economics is a branch of theology] ". . . the process of science . . . consists in trying to *disprove* theories . . . The great difficulty in social sciences . . . of applying scientific method, is that we have not yet established an agreed standard for the disproof of an hypothesis (pp. 22–3) (theories become religions in the social sciences because) first, the subject matter has much greater political and ideological content, so that other loyalties are . . . involved . . . (and secondly) it has been sometimes remarked that economists are more queazy and ill-natured than other scientists. The reason is that, when a writer's personal judgement is involved in an argument, disagreement is insulting." (pp. 23–24)

As will be seen in later discussions, it is not rare to find one writer questioning the judgement of other writers in the CVM literature and there exists considerable disagreement, if not confusion, as to standards for proving or disproving hypotheses relevant for important aspects of the method. Thus, developments with the CVM have reached an important watershed at which a state of the arts assessment of the method is timely. The purpose of this book is to provide such an assessment.

The critical assessment of the literature relevant for the CVM is the substance of the remaining five chapters in part I of this book. Given that the intent of this literature review is to go beyond a simple description of literature to an *assessment* of the strengths and weaknesses of the CVM, we begin in chapter 2 with the development of an historical setting for the CVM within which an assessment framework for evaluating the state of the arts of the method is promulgated. Arguments developed in chapter 2 will set the stage for the central thrust of remaining chapters in part I.

The arguments developed by the authors in these five chapters are intended to serve as a point of departure for a critical examination of the state of the arts for the CVM. Obviously, the author's assessment of the CVM is in no way "the profession's" assessement and, as noted above, what is needed at this point in time is a profession-wide evaluation of the CVM. An effort to obtain something akin to a broader, profession-wide assessment is accomplished via an Assessment Conference, which has the following form.
"A Conference on Valuing Environmental Improvements: A STATE OF THE ARTS ASSESSMENT OF THE CVM" was held in Palo Alto, California, on July 2, 1984. The purpose of the Conference was to elicit a review panel's judgements as to the promise of the CVM as a means for valuing public/environmental goods. The panel consisted of leading scholars in the economics profession and included:

Kenneth Arrow, Stanford University
Daniel Kahneman, University of British Columbia
Sherwin Rosen, University of Chicago
Vernon Smith, University of Arizona

The review panel's consideration of the CVM was based, in addition to their general knowledge and expertise in the science of public goods valuation, upon two sets of information. The first information set was the author's critical assessment of the CVM as set out in part I of this book; part I was made available to Panel members well in advance of the Conference. The second information set was papers and presentations provided by four leading scholars involved in research related to the CVM. Paper/presentations by these scholars focused first on the critical assessment of part I of this book and secondly on their individual assessments of the promise, strengths, and weaknesses of the CVM. The four scholars offering presentations at the conference were:

Richard Bishop, University of Wisconsin
A. Myrick Freeman, Bowdoin College
Alan Randall, University of Kentucky
V. Kerry Smith, Vanderbilt University

Results from the conference are reported in part II of this book. The authors' assessment of the CVM—the substance of part I—and a more general, profession-wide assessment of the CVM—part II of the book—allow us to conclude with what the authors hope will be regarded as an objective, benchmark evaluation of the CVM. Drawing from the diverse sources described above, in chapter 13 the authors will offer final conclusions as to the current state of the arts for the CVM.

NOTES

1. As examples, see Davis (1963a) and Bohn (1971).

2. These conclusions are challanged, however, in Rowe (1983).

3. As part of the authors' context for the cited conclusion, the authors also assert that "almost no empirical work has been based on careful theoretical analysis" (p.58). Excepting the use of surveys, this conclusion is softened somewhat in their Chapter 10 however.

4. As examples, see S. Lichtenstein and P. Slovic (1971); D. Grether and C. Plott (1979); Kunreuther et al. (1978); H. Simon (1979).

5. For related discussions, see M.C. Weinstein and R.J. Quinn, (1983). Furthermore, it may be tempting to set this source of bias aside as one which can be readily eliminated through questionnaires with alternative question frames. A careful consideration of the example given in Arrow (1982, p. 7) belies the ease by which this problem may be mitigated by questionnaire design or administration.

6, See R. Mendelsohn and G.M Brown, Jr. (1983).

7. See S. Rosen (1974).

8. See Freeman (1979a), Chapters 4–6; particularly pp. 85–87.

2
A Historical Perspective for the CVM Assessment

As stated above, the CVM is a method for estimating values attributable to non-market, or public, goods. The intent of this chapter is to provide the reader with some flavor for how and why interest in the CVM was initiated, the rationale for and nature of early experimental efforts to develop the method and the evolution of our current understanding of the strengths and weaknesses imputed to the method. These discussions then serve to define the necessary scope of our inquiry as to the state of the arts of the CVM.

In establishing an historical perspective for an assessment of the CVM, we must begin by recognizing the ultimate ends sought in applications of the method. As noted above, the need for benefit measures arises from the need for benefit-cost assessments related to environmental (more broadly, public) goods/commodities—commodities which are "public good" in nature; of course, market prices (and their use in deriving measures for consumer surplus) are not available for such goods. Implicitly, market prices are appropriate measures of the "benefits" (social welfare) of concern in benefit-cost assessments and, therefore, represent a standard for accuracy, or "appropriateness", against which CVM measures are often compared.

Our historical perspective must therefore begin with a consideration of the benefit-cost analysis (BCA) framework *per se* in terms of its efficacy as a structure for processing information in ways that are meaningfully reflective of social welfare consequences associated with social actions; this topic is considered in sections below. We then consider the extent to which market prices, as they are commonly used in BCA, are "appropriate" measures of social welfare, as social welfare is implicitly *defined* in the BCA. We will then have established some basis (which will be later expanded) for appreciating the nature of the valuation institution—the market—which is (arguably) a standard for assessing measures derived by the CVM. At this point, we will be prepared to begin our inquiry as to the public goods valuation issue. We begin by describing the general valuation issue. We then describe relevant, related research in the field of psychology. The chapter concludes with an effort to focus on related questions as to the necessary scope and structure of a comprehensive assessment of the state of the arts of the CVM.

SOCIAL WELFARE: WHAT IS IT AND HOW IS IT MEASURED?

Economists have long been concerned with questions concerning how one might define and measure economic, or social "welfare".[1] In early years, a good deal of this concern focused on the debate as to the dependence of any notion of social welfare on value judgments, a dependence argued by Robbins (1932) as out of place in scientific, objective analysis. Bergson's (1938) "social welfare function provided the profession with a mechanism wherein the role of value judgments in welfare economics could be isolated and clarified: such "non-economic" factors could be entered in the welfare function as variables just as we include 'economic factors' such as goods, services and factors of production. "

While Bergson's economic welfare function provided a context for tracing implications that arise from any given set of value judgments, two major problems remained. First, some guide was required as to how one might define/delineate alternative sets of values which might lead to a useful social ordering of alternatives; secondly, how might we choose from among these alternative sets of values? These were the questions addressed by Arrow (1951). Based on five general conditions, including the condition that the social welfare function is not to be imposed or "dictatorial"—i.e., individual preferences count—Arrow derives the renowned General Possibility Theorem which says, in essence, that one cannot structure a meaningful social welfare function without violating one or more of his five conditions—particularly those related to "counting" individual preferences. (Arrow 1951, pp. 46-60). While the general relevance of Arrow's theorem to welfare economics has been criticized, particularly in terms of its relevance to Bergson's welfare function[2] the bulk of such criticisms has been dismissed by later analysis.[3]

The necessarily brief, and admittedly incomplete, sketch of early controversy concerning value judgments in a social welfare function given above is intended to set the stage for a theme which will recur throughout this book and which will be particularly important for efforts to suggest conclusions regarding the state of the arts for the CVM—the task of the Assessment Conference. This theme is set out in the form of two questions, developed below, and is framed within the context of benefit-cost analysis (BCA). This context is used given that the *raison d'être* for our interest in the CVM is its use in generating estimates of value (benefits) for use in benefit-cost analysis related to the provision of public goods in general, and environmental commodities in particular. The questions of interest in this regard are: (a) how are value judgments treated in BCA; i.e., how does use of the BCA square with the General Possibilities Theorem? (b) to what extent are market prices, commonly used in applications of the BCA, "appropriate" measures of social welfare (or benefits)?

BENEFIT-COST ANALYSIS AND THE GENERAL POSSIBILITIES THEOREM

While well-understood by most economists, it is useful to briefly review a basic inconsistency underlying BCA as it relates to the General Possibilities Theorem (GPT). The relevant issue is succinctly expressed by Dasgupta and Pearce (1978) as follows:

> From the point of view of BCA the main lesson of this discussion seems to be the following. BCA has been generally interpreted as a method of aggregating individual preferences so as to provide a basis for social

choice. The Impossibility Theorem claims to show that no such aggregation is possible without introducing ethical judgements of a more specialized kind than requiring simply that individual preferences should count. The explicit introduction of ethical judgements into BCA thus appears inevitable. (p. 90)

Thus, since a social welfare function involves value judgements, the question becomes how such judgements are to be treated by BCA practitioners. Under the worst conditions, this question is simply begged. Under the best (and most common) conditions, economists simply rely on efficiency criteria, arguing that such things as distributional effects will either cancel out or can be addressed by other means.[4] In this case, the economist prepares the BCA which follows from alternative sets of value judgements and leaves to the decision-maker the choice of appropriate value judgments.

The central issue here is that, first, the idea of consumer sovereignty supposedly underlies the logic of BCA wherein values (discussed below), or preferences, are aggregated across consumers. But, following the GPT, such aggregation cannot occur without violating one or more of Arrow's reasonableness criteria. We should note that even if such aggregation were justifiable, substantive *ethical* issues would attend the BCA result when interpreted as a measure of social welfare.[5] Thus, BCA "proceeds in a fashion which is at odds with its apparent philosophy." *(Dasgupta and Pearce 1978, p. 94)* From this we conclude the following which will be relevant for later discussions: in using BCA for assessments of benefits/welfare accruing to society as a result of (e.g.) the adoption of an environmental policy, measures used therein are appropriately assessed within a context which *includes* consideration of implied judgements as to the substance of social value.

MARKET PRICES AS MEASURES OF SOCIAL WELFARE

As implied in the above, the maximization of net benefits derived via BCA is typically used for assessing a projects' implications for social welfare. It is typically assumed that market prices for outputs and inputs serve, at least as a first approximation, as proper measures for socially relevant benefits and costs. We will not further belabor the point that appropriate prices must reflect an appropriate objective (social welfare) function[6]; "proper", in this regard, is generally taken to refer to the Pareto criterion.

It is generally appreciated that market prices are identical to the shadow prices implicit to Pareto Optimality under conditions which include: equality between market prices and marginal production costs; and equality between marginal production costs and the social opportunity costs of resources. (Dasgupta and Pearce 1978, pp. 97–105) It is also generally appreciated that these two conditions are seldom, if ever, satisfied in the real world due to, among other reasons, the existence of externalities, imperfect competition in product and factor markets and unemployed resources. (Dasgupta and Pearce 1978, pp. 105-109) In terms of the public sector, we note the unresolved controversy as to whether or not movements *toward* Pareto Optimality might result from marginal social cost pricing, notwithstanding distortions in the private sector.[7] In the end, one sees in the debate over the extent to which market prices may serve as "adequate" proxies for Pareto-like shadow prices, our earlier-cited lament by Joan Robinson regarding the absence in the social sciences of standards by which hypotheses can be disproved; e.g., after reviewing this debate, Dasgupta and Pearce observe " The role of personal judgement is the real source of criticisms of imputed price estimates, since it would appear to lend a large element of 'subjectivity' to a discipline which purports to be objective . . .

(referring to market prices) . . . using them for the purposes of CBA might be no less subjective. " (Dasgupta and Pearce 1978, p. 116)

From the above we may conclude the following. Given—accepting—Pareto efficiency as "the" social welfare criterion for ranking and/or assessing the consequences of social actions, market prices serve, at best, as weak approximations for relevant measures of social value.

VALUING PUBLIC GOODS

In the debate surrounding the social welfare function issue, relatively little attention was given to that class of goods which, when made available to one person are made available to all because of joint supply and access to which cannot be denied to individuals via pricing policies, i.e., to "public goods." A formal inquiry as to the relationship between social welfare and levels of provision of public goods was introduced by Samuelson in (1954). Samuelson's conclusions of primary relevance for our discussions are as follows: First, one cannot hope to obtain values/measures of individual preferences for public goods by directly asking people to reveal their preferences: "One can imagine every person (being asked to reveal) . . . his preferences by signalling in response to price parameters . . . to questionnaires, or to other devices" (p. 389), but with such procedures, "any one person can hope to snatch some selfish benefit in a way not possible under the self-policing competitive pricing of private goods." (p. 388) This observation has been interpreted as a rationale for rejecting the possible use of surveys (questionnaires) as a means for valuing non-market, public goods inasmuch as individuals will, when asked to value a public good, behave strategically in efforts to "snatch some selfish benefit"; resulting biases are referred to as "strategic bias." This then leads to a second conclusion, *viz*, that in the absence of market prices reflecting (however imperfectly) individual preferences, "we are unable to define an unambiguously 'best' state" (p. 388) in terms of a level of provision of public goods.

At about this same time, Ciriacy-Wantrup (1952) (hereafter, C-W) considered the question as to how one might obtain values for a particular class of "extra-market"—public—goods, *viz*., public goods related to resource and environmental conservation. In this regard, C-W proposed the use of survey methods for obtaining such values:

> Individuals . . . may be asked how much money they are willing to pay for successive additional quantities of a collective extra-market good . . . The results correspond to a market demand schedule. For purposes of public policy, this schedule may be regarded as a marginal social revenue function. [Ciriacy-Wantrup 1952, pp. 241-42][8]

C-W considered the following five possible objections to this valuation procedure, *all* of which, in his view, could be reasonably overcome with the careful design of questionnaires.[9] First, he considers the interdependence (and, therefore, non-additivity) of individual utilities, an influence which he regarded as minor and correctable by questionnaire design (C-W 1952, p. 242) Second, he mentions the problem of "lumpiness" in the provision of extra-market goods, a potential problem considered by him as (a) not peculiar to extra-market goods and, (b) possibly requiring for its resolution an appeal to *costs* rather than benefits. (C-W 1952, p. 243) Third, he notes the potential for individuals to purposefully bias responses to interrogation. Of course, this objection is an early statement of Samuelson's "strategic behavior" argument noted above. C-W regarded the potential bias from strategic behavior as correctable by questionnaire design and, in any case, small; of course, Samuelson regarded the issue as the "fundamental technical difference (vis-à-vis markets) going to the heart of the whole problem of social economy." (Samuelson 1954, p. 389)

The fourth objection to the use of surveys for valuing public goods considered by C-W relates to potential biases stemming from (a) the fact that other extra-market goods are not considered (in a survey focused on one particular good) and (b) the fact that the marginal utility of money is not likely to remain constant. The "other goods" issue is considered by C-W to be of minor importance and *not* peculiar to extra-market goods: they "apply also to the use of demand functions in analyzing the market." (C-W 1952, p. 243) For "practical" ends sought in the survey, C-W suggests that the assumption of constant marginal utility of money may frequently be realistic "because of compensating variations in the prices of other commodities or in money income." Fifth, and finally, C-W suggests that the survey method might be regarded as too academic: the supply of extra-market goods is determined by political machinery, not by monetary valuation. Without the benefit of President Reagan's Executive Order 12291, however, C-W notes the potential contribution of value information to the decision-making process in a democratic government (p. 244).

As an aside, it is interesting to observe that the notion of "option demand" formally introduced by Weisbrod (1964) has as its precursor C-W's observation that "planning agents may allow for uncertainty by keeping their utilization plan flexible. This means that they may decrease the periods over which costs are sunk, avoiding obligations to pay fixed charges." (p. 113) Indeed, as observed by Krutilla (1967), "It must be acknowledged that with sufficient patience and perception nearly all of the arguments for preserving unique phenomena of nature can be found in the classic on conservation economics by Ciriacy-Wantrup." (p. 778)

Notwithstanding C-W's apparent optimism regarding the use of survey methods for deriving estimates for public goods values, we find no evidence of immediate efforts to develop and apply the idea. Indeed, following Samuelson's 1954 paper one finds little in the literature concerning the public goods valuation issue until the late 1960's-early 1970's. However speculative, it might seem as if Samuelson's arguments were found compelling vis-à-vis the impossibility of deriving value measures for non-market, public goods.

Three distinct lines of inquiry were introduced around the late 1960's-early 1970's, which had the effect of rekindling interest in the public goods valuation issue. First, Clawson and Knetsch (1966) refined and popularized the Travel Cost Method (TCM) for valuing recreation sites.[10] Second, Rosen (1974) introduced the Hedonic Price Method (HPM) as a means for valuing some classes of non-market goods. Third, the question as to the potential efficacy of surveys as a means for valuing public goods was reintroduced as a result of: (a) an experiment wherein C-W's suggestion for using surveys was implemented by Davis (1963a and 1963b) and later by Knetsch and Davis (1965); (b) Bohm's (1971, 1972) experiments with survey methods which tested and rejected Samuelson's strategic bias hypothesis; and (c) refinements in the survey method introduced by Randall et al. (1974a) based on the aggregate "bid curve" suggested by Bradford (1970). The structure for surveys set out by Randall et al. (1974a) provides the essence of contemporary applications of surveys referred to as the CVM.

The resurgence of intellectual interest in the public goods valuation issue alluded to here is by no means attributable solely to the above-cited works. The 1960's and early 1970's were the formative years for what is now the sub-discipline of "resource and environmental economics." Interest in the valuation of the public good, "the environment", was stimulated by the provocative works by Krutilla (1967) and Kneese (1962), to name but two of the imaginative contributors to the air of intellectual excitement that characterized that period. Our focus on *methodological* lines of inquiry initiated during this period simply reflects the methodological nature of the issue of primary concern in this book.

We will not divert attention from the developments of concern regarding the CVM for a discussion of the Travel Cost and Hedonic Price Methods for valuing public goods; these methods have direct relevance for our assessments of the CVM, as is discussed below in chapter 6. At this juncture, we wish to focus attention on developments with the CVM initiated by the works of Davis, Bohm, and Randall et al.

DEVELOPING THE CVM

In two ways, Randall et al.'s (1974a) paper set the use of surveys, in terms of their use for estimating values for public goods, on a distinctively different track from that implied by C-W (and applied by Davis) and/or from that implied by Bohm's work. First, Randall et al. (1974a) attempted to define and impose on the survey a rigorous structure design to differentiate their use of a method whereby values were elicited from individuals (a survey) from "ordinary" surveys. Their survey method was called a "bidding game." Their "structure" was a questionnaire design wherein willingness to pay questions were posed within a context which draws from a market analogy: the context of a contingent market. In terms *now* familiar to those working with the CVM (discussed below), the "structure" was an effort to elicit behavioral, as opposed to attitudinal, revelations of individual preferences. This structure, and its variants, are now referred to as the Contingent Valuation Method—CVM.

Secondly, with the benefit (not afforded Davis in his earlier study) of Bohm's results which weakened Samuelson's strategic bias proposition, Randall et al. suggest the potential applications of the CVM to the task of valuing a wide range of environmental improvements—types of public goods that extend well beyond those amenable to cross-checks via other methods (e.g., the TCM with recreation demands as in the 1966 study by Knetsch and Davis) and relatively "hard" commodities such as Bohm's Public Television commodity. In this regard, witness the "commodity" in Randall et al.'s study: aesthetic benefits from reduced air pollution.

Randall's pursuit of these challenges was quickly joined by other scholars. Efforts to develop the promise (as it was then seen) of the CVM were focused in large part, as one might expect, on methodological problems as they related to the application of the method. In this regard, the specter of Samuelson's strategic bias proposition remained as a concern, notwithstanding Bohm's results, until the appearance of Vernon Smith's (1977) report of experimental evidence that further belied the strategic bias proposition. Thus, a number of earlier CVM studies were focused on tests of the strategic bias proposition. But to *test* the strategic bias proposition, one needed to *apply* the CVM, and in efforts to apply the CVM, an ever-widening range of operational/methodological problems arose: how does one initiate the valuation process?; what is the appropriate mode of payment in which to couch the willingness-to-pay question?; what kind and how much information should be given to survey participants?[11]

As efforts to deal with operational questions of the type posed above continued, applications of the CVM were extended in innovative and imaginative ways. As examples, Daubert and Young (1981) applied the CVM for the estimation of benefits attributable to instream river flows; Walsh et al. (1978b) and others applied the method to estimate option and preservation values attributable to improved water quality in Colorado's Platte River Basin; and Crocker (1984) applied the method to valuing avoided damages to forest stocks from reduced acid depositions.

Operational sorts of problems of the type mentioned above pale in significance in comparison with the problem of "hypothetical bias", however. Regrettably, "hypothetical bias" (HB) seemingly has many different faces—it means different things to different people. As but a few examples, Rowe and Chestnut (1983) view HB as arising "because respondents are predicting what their behavior would be in a hypothetical situation" (p. 408); Schulze et al. (1981, p. 158) see HB as attributable to a respondent's failure to understand all of the ramifications of a posited environmental change; Thayer (1981, p. 32) seemingly views HB as potentially arising because (for unstated reasons) individuals may not behave as they indicate that they will behave (i.e. pay their WTP) in the CVM interviews; Bishop and Heberlein (1979) suggest that HB may result from the fact that the CVM elicits statements of attitudes rather than intended behavior or from the fact that contingent markets are "too artificial to provide a sufficient context for developing accurate values." (Bishop et al. 1983, p. 620) Finally, although certainly not exhaustively, Burness et al. (1983) see HB as resulting from the (asserted) fact that "the CVM market precludes the derivation of values which reliably reflect the interviewee's preferences." (p. 675)

Obviously, from the above, the concept (or concepts) of hypothetical bias is generally intuitive and almost always poorly defined; perhaps understandably in light of the imprecision of the hypothetical bias notion, efforts by researchers to respond, via empirical tests of related hypotheses or otherwise, have been equally imprecise.[12] An exception is found in one form of the hypothetical bias proposition which proposes that choices made under conditions where actual payments are involved will differ from choices involving hypothetical payment. This hypothesis has been stated, tested, and demonstrated as "true" by a number of scholars.[13] We note that this hypothesis is but one possible interpretation of the arguments of Freeman (1979a) and of Feenberg and Mills

(1980) which propose that, with hypothetical payment, individuals lack incentives to incur the disutility associated with time and mental energy required to respond "accurately" to willingness to pay questions. As will be argued later, however, motivators other than actual payment may provide incentives for accurate responses.

Given, unquestionably, that the CVM is hypothetical in character—it involves a hypothetical market for the provision of a commodity which involves hypothetical payment—the persistence of criticisms that CVM measures must be substantively biased is perhaps understandable; this is particularly so given the general failure by scholars working with the CVM to translate posited sources for hypothetical bias into testable hypotheses and *to test them*. Thus, the hypothetical bias issue, with all of its diverse, poorly defined "faces," remains as one of the most important unresolved issues relevant for any assessment of the efficacy of the CVM as a means for estimating values for non-market environmental commodities. As we will see in the following section, the potential intuitive appeal of the hypothetical bias proposition vis-a-vis the credibility of CVM measures is reinforced by research findings in an other sub-discipline.

RELATED RESEARCH IN OTHER DISCIPLINES

As evidenced by an examination of references in the CVM literature, scholars involved in the development of the CVM have only recently become aware of the full implications for their own work of the research ongoing in other areas of economics and in other disciplines. The attitude v. behavior issue which has long been of concern to psychologists was introduced by Bishop and Heberlein (1979). Economists' concern with mechanisms for eliciting "true" preference revelations—e.g., the Vickrey (1961a) "second price" auction—is only recently reflected in the CVM literature (Coursey et al. 1983), and examinations of the potential contributions to the development of the CVM from techniques derived in "experimental economics" are at a relatively infant stage.

Also, in the area of psychology a great deal of empirical research concerning the manner in which individuals make decisions may be relevant for the CVM. As examples of the many anomalies in individual decision-making reported by Tversky and Kahneman (T-K) (1981) their observations concerning "mental accounts" are of particular interest. T-K argue that, in making allocative decisions (regarding income), the individual may focus on *groups* of commodities as opposed to individual commodities. Thus, rather than allocate $15.00 to a night at the movies, $25.00 to an evening at the opera and $10.00 to a day at the beach, an individual may allocate $50.00 to something akin to an "entertainment account." Sub-allocative decisions are then made as the need or opportunity for recreation or entertainment arises. To the extent that individuals do think in terms of "accounts" there may be serious implications for the CVM. In deriving a value, for example, for a specific environmental improvement (e.g., improved air quality in Denver) the obtained value may in fact apply to some more aggregate commodity (account), say environmental quality in general—i.e., the CVM measure may relate to something akin to an "environmental account", as opposed to the specific environmental improvement serving as a "commodity" in the CVM study.

Another related line of argument that is potentially relevant for assessments of the CVM is that developed by researchers at Decision Research (Eugene, Oregon). Of particular interest is the recent work by Slovic et al. (1980). Citing recent research by T-K (see below), they argue that individuals seemingly use inferential rules, called heuristics, to reduce difficult mental tasks to simpler ones. Three characteristics of common heuristics used by individuals are of interest.[14] First, individual judgements of the importance of an event, or the likelihood of its occurence, are affected by the extent to which the event (public good) is easy to imagine or recall—i.e., by information (in the press, T.V., etc.); this "availability" heuristic is related to a second, "representativeness" heuristic which will reappear below in our discussions of risk. Thus, for example, a CVM study focusing on willingness-to-pay for environmental regulations on nuclear waste disposal (more generally, hazardous waste disposal) might result in seriously distorted results given recent, well-publicized events such as the Three Mile Island accident and documentaries on Love Canal. Efforts to value recreation facilities in a nearby National Park could be distorted by recent reports of crowded conditions at any recreational facility. Equally serious, values for public goods related to government actions could be distorted by exposés of official misconduct, reflecting distrust of (or distaste for) the government in general.

Secondly, Slovic points to research suggesting that (a) individuals tend to be overconfident in their heuristics and (b) people's beliefs, once formed, change very slowly—judgements of "fact" are "extraordinarily persistent in the face of contrary evidence." Slovic 1980, p. 189 Thus, to the extent that individual beliefs or perceptions concerning a particular public good are fixed, the task of altering perceptions of the good—communicating the *nature* of, e.g., a specific environmental improvement—may compound the complexities involved in an individual's perception of an *actual* change and their valuation of that change.

Third, Slovic points to what might be referred to as a general aversion to uncertainty by individuals. Evidence from psychological research suggests that, as a means for eliminating the anxiety that attends uncertainty, uncertainty is simply denied—a behavioral pattern vis-à-vis uncertainty noted by other authors as well.[15] Results from survey methods may be seriously distorted if, indeed, individuals generally deny risk and uncertainty, particularly in studies involving public goods affecting such things as mortality and morbidity. Examples include CVM studies designed to value changes in air/water quality and studies designed to value the adoption of any public policy related to health and safety.

Risk and, most prevalently, uncertainty vis-à-vis risk are common dimensions of many of the public-environmental goods of analytical interest in applications of the CVM.[16] The use of the CVM to value public/environmental goods presupposes some understanding as to how individuals form values under conditions of risk and uncertainty. Underlying most analysis is the expected utility hypothesis of behavior under uncertainty combined, in a sense noted by Arrow (1982), with the implicit use of the Bayesian hypothesis wherein individuals consistently use conditional probabilities for changing beliefs on the basis of new information. A recent example of this approach is seen in a paper by Gallagher and Smith (1984) wherein, in valuing (e.g.) improved air quality in a national park, the individual perceives a "change in air quality" as a change in the probability distribution of air quality levels to which he/she has access on any given visitor day. In the Gallagher-Smith model, "to the extent that each individual appreciates the random nature of environmental services" (p. 2) the individual's valuation of a posited environmental quality improvement is then based on the maximization of expected utility (within the context of state-dependent utility functions).

Another area of ongoing research of potential relevance to the CVM concerns the rationality hypothesis so basic to the bulk of economic analysis, and upon which rests the expected utility hypothesis. The rationality hypothesis has long been questioned as to its relevancy vis-à-vis empirical content and there is growing criticism as to its validity, in any operational sense, in explaining or predicting individual behavior under conditions of uncertainty. The degree of complex calculations imputed by the theory to individuals in their efforts to form valuations—witness the weight of such calculations implied in the Gallagher-Smith application—is belied by empirical evidence and, in the authors' minds, by intuition. As observed by Arrow:

> Hypotheses of rationality have been under attack for empirical falsity almost as long as they have been employed in economics. Thorstein Veblen long ago had some choice, sarcastic passages about the extra-ordinary calculating abilities imputed to the average individual in his or her daily economic life by economists. More recently, Herbert Simon and his colleagues have produced much evidence of the difficulties of human beings in arriving at rational choices even in rather simple contexts. (Arrow 1982, p. 1)

Extending Arrow's reference to Simon's work, Simon notes that "When even small complications were introduced into the (decision-making) situations, wide departures of behavior from the predictions of subjective expected utility (SEU) theory soon became evident . . . the conclusion seems unavoidable that SEU theory does not provide a good prediction—not even a good approximation—of actual behavior." (Simon 1979, p. 506)

THE STRUCTURE FOR A CVM ASSESSMENT

As a result of our reflections concerning the thrusts of CVM-related research conducted over the last decade, four issues stand out in terms of encompassing questions of central importance for our efforts to assess the state of the arts of the CVM. These are: (a) questions concerning the degree to which CVM experiments have succeeded in developing questionnaire designs that mitigate, or eliminate, the potential for operational-types of biases (vehicle, information, strategic biases, etc.); (b) questions concerning the extent to which research results outside of the CVM area of research *per se* have been rationalized vis-à-vis their implications for the CVM—in this regard, reference is made particularly to the areas of decision theory, experimental economics and psychology; (c) questions concerning the pervasiveness and magnitude of biases in CVM measures attributable to "hypothetical bias"; and (d) questions concerning the existence of precise standards which serve as a basis for accepting or rejecting hypotheses related to the "accuracy" of CVM measures.

The structure for our assessment of the CVM is, therefore, one which allows sharp focus on these four sets of questions. Thus, chapter 3 focuses on the questions posed in (a): CVM studies are critically reviewed with particular concern being given questionnaire design as it relates to operational biases. A review of research, and its relevance to applications of the CVM, in the area of experimental economics is provided in chapter 4; these discussions focus on a subset of the questions implied by (b). The issue of hypothetical bias is addressed in chapter 5; as a part of our assessments of the many "faces" of hypothetical bias—the substance of question set (c)—we will be required to examine research results from the fields of decision theory and psychology, thereby rounding out our focus on question set (b). Questions related to standards by which the accuracy of CVM measures might be assessed (set (d)) are, in the authors' view, of primary importance. This issue is addressed in chapter 6. As a part of this inquiry, empirical evidence related to comparisons of CVM values with values derived from the TCM and HPM are analyzed and discussed.

Questions posed in (a)-(d) and responses to these questions given in chapters 3 – 6, will hopefully set the stage for discussions at the Assessment Conference concerning the major issue of interest in this book: the state of the arts of the CVM. As noted above, this major issue is the topic of part II of this book.

NOTES

1. See, e.g., J. Rothenberg 1961.

2. I.M.D. Little 1952.

3. See, e.g., J. Rothenberg 1961, pp. 36-41. See also the conclusion in A.K. Dasgupta, and D.W. Pearce 1978, p. 89.

4. See Dasgupta and Pearce 1978, p. 90-93.

5. See W.D. Schulze, D.S. Brookshire and T. Sandler 1981a

6. See Dasgupta and Pearce 1978, Chapters 2 and 4, for a discussion of this point.

7. See, for example, Lipsey and Lancaster (1956).

8. Ciriacy-Wantrup (1952), pp. 241-242. Also, "The psychological mechanism of these subjective evaluations themselves (for example, whether cardinal or ordinal differentiation of utility is involved) are neither accessible nor relevant for the observer—that is, for *objective* evaluation of extra-market goods," Ciriacy-Wantrup (1952), p. 85.

9. "Welfare Economics could be put on a more realistic foundation if a closer cooperation between economics and certain young branches of applied psychology could be established," Ciriacy-Wantrup (1952), p. 244.

10. A letter from Harold Hotelling to the National Park Service wherein Hotelling suggests a method like the TCM is reproduced in Brown, W., A. Singh and E. Castle 1964. See Brown et al. (1964), for an example of competent applications of the TCM prior to Clawson and Knetsch's cited work.

11. For discussions of, respectively, "starting point, vehicle and informational" biases see Schulze et al. 1981c; and R. D. Rowe and L. G. Chestnut 1983.

12. For example, see Burness et al. 1983 and Schulze et al. 1981b.

13. For example, Bohm 1972; D. L. Coursey, W.D. Schulze, and J. Hovis 1983; P. Slovic 1969; and Bishop and Heberlein 1979.

14. Slovic et al.'s arguments focus on decisions involving risk; their arguments would seem to have broader applications however, in substance if not implied magnitudes of importance.

15. For example, Kahneman and Tversky (1979); and Starr, Rudman and Whipple (1976).

16. Given the broad class of environmental "commodities" for which option values may be relevant, it is interesting to note that uncertainty (of purchase or use) lies at the heart of Weisbrod's definition of option value (Weisbrod 1964). Uncertainty vis-à-vis health risks may be relevant for option value as seen in Weisbrod's example of hospitals—a public good "utilized infrequently by most persons and not at all by some; yet . . . (providing) a valuable standby service." (Weisbrod 1964, p. 474). Underlying one's option value for the hospital must be some perception of the probability—risk—of its use at some future date. For related discussions, see B. McNeill et al. 1982 and Lichtenstein and Slovic 1971.

3
Applications of the CVM:
An Overview of Issues

OVERVIEW

In chapter 2 the reader was given some flavor for the setting wherein interest in the potential applications of the CVM was initiated. As a part of those discussions, we noted four sets of questions that have been of primary concern for researchers involved with experimental research related to the development of the CVM. These questions were: (a) the "strategic bias" question; (b) questions concerning the extent to which subjects in CVM experiments understand the "commodity" to be valued, as such understanding is reflected by behavior that is consistent with axioms from received theory; (c) questions related to questionnaire design—starting point, vehicle and information biases; (d) questions concerning the equivalence between willingness-to-pay and willingness-to-accept values derived with the CVM; and (e), more generally, a broad range of questions concerning biases attributable to the hypothetical nature of the CVM's valuation process. In this chapter, we consider research results which are relevant for addressing questions given in (a) – (d). Given the myriad issues relevant to an assessment of hypothetical bias and the need, in responding to related questions, for a review of research results in other disciplines, we defer to chapter 5 the task of considering the hypothetical bias questions referred to in (e).

STRATEGIC BIAS AND THE CVM

Concern with strategic behavior on the part of economic agents can be traced historically to economists' efforts to argue for or against a mechanism or institution that would yield allocations of public goods which parallel in some sense those which would obtain in a competitive market. Wicksell (1896) suggested that:

> provided the expenditure in question holds out any prospect at all of creating utility exceeding costs, it will always be theoretically possible, and approximately so in practice, to find a distribution of costs such that all parties regard the expenditure as beneficial and may therefore approve it unanimously. [Wicksell 1896, p. 90]

Samuelson (1955) notes that Wicksell was careful to separate theoretical from practical solutions; in support of his thoeory of public expenditures, he argues that his theory was:

an attempt to demonstrate how right Wicksell was to worry about the inherent political difficulty of ever getting men to reveal their tastes so as to attain the definable optimum.[p. 355]

Samuelson's categorical rejection of the possibility of obtaining "true" individual valuations of public goods due to "strategic behavior," served as a point of departure for research wherein a variety of theoretical frameworks and a variety of incentive-compatible auction mechanisms were developed in efforts—*a lá* Wicksell's (1896) "approximately so in practice" dictum (p. 89)—to resolve the problem of pricing, and thus of allocating, public goods. Authors involved in these efforts include: Groves (1973), Clarke (1971); Loehman et al. (1979), Groves and Ledyard (1977), Smith (1977, 1979a), Tidemand and Tullock (1976), Bohm (1972) and Scherr and Babb (1975). In what follows, we consider the studies by Bohm (1972); Scherr and Babb (1975); and Smith (1977, 1979a) wherein explicit attention is focused on the strategic behavior hypothesis.

The Bohm (1972) study involved laboratory-type experiments designed to investigate the effects on individual behavior of six alternative approaches for valuing a TV program that had not been previously shown to the public. Four of the six approaches explored by Bohm for determining aggregate willingness-to-pay required that the subject actually, as opposed to hypothetically, pay money for obtaining access to the TV program. If the aggregate stated maximum willingness-to-pay *actually* exceeded the cost of the TV program, the subjects were told that they would have access to the program and that they would actually pay in one of the following modes (pp. 114–15):

(I)   according to his maximum willingness-to-pay as stated,
(II)   the same fraction of the maximum stated, the fraction being equal to costs divided by the stated aggregate maximum willingness to pay,
(III)   according to one of several alternatives, the choice not yet being made,
(IV)   a given amount, the same for all individuals,
(V)   nothing.
(VI)   nothing (this was a hypothetical case).

Incentives for free riding in each of the above payment modes were viewed by Bohm as follows. For approach I, individuals will understate a willingness-to-pay—an expectation based on Samuelson's arguments strategic bias; for approaches II, III, and IV, Bohm argues that subjects will overstate willingness-to-pay. It should be noted that V and VI differed not only in payment modes; subjects given V and VI were also given different definitions of the "commodity" and different amounts of information. Subjects in group VI faced a hypothetical structure quite similar to the standard CVM approach while those in group V did not. Individuals in group V "were simply asked how much they found the program to be worth at a maximum." (p. 119) Approach VI is quite similar to the contingent valuation approach as employed by Mitchell and Carson (1981) and others, which we will take up later in this chapter.

Two of Bohm's results are of interest for our discussions. First, Bohm finds that "none of these (first) five approaches . . . gave an average maximum willingness-to-pay that significantly deviated from that of any other of the approaches" (Bohm 1972, p. 112); from this, Bohm rejects the strategic bias hypothesis. Second, Bohm finds that the sixth approach did produce a hypothetical willingness-to-pay significantly above average valuations obtained in the other five approaches. Such differences lead Bohm to conclude that:

when no payments and/or *formal decisions* (emphasis added to distinguish group VI from V where payments were also not required) are involved . . . this . . . may be seen as still another reason to doubt the usefulness of responses to hypothetical questions, in general, and of *ordinary polls* (emphasis added) to guide political decision making with respect to public goods in particular. [p. 125]

We should note that the weight of Bohm's results at least as regards his conclusions concerning the effects of hypothetical payment, may be diminished somewhat by results reported by Mitchell and Carson (1981). Mitchell and Carson contest Bohm's conclusion in this regard for two reasons. First of all, after deleting an unusually large bid, the authors found the group VI mean bid to drop substantially, to the point where the statistical difference between groups III and VI vanished. Secondly, the authors found that income in group VI was higher than in group III, leading to the possibility of an income effect explaining the differences found by Bohm between the group VI and other group bids.

Scherr and Babb (1975) examined the theoretical pricing system constructs proposed by Clarke (1971) and Loehman, et al. (1979), in a controlled experimental setting for the pricing of two public goods: a concert and a library fund. Scherr and Babb's rationale for testing the Clarke multi-part pricing system and the Loehman-Whinston average incremental cost pricing system was the assertion that:

If the predictions of the theory deviate from the observed behavior in this setting, one may begin to question the possible linkage of the theory to real world behavior. [p. 36]

Scherr and Babb's focus on strategic or free-rider behavior is a bit curious in the following ways.[2] The hypotheses tested by Scherr and Babb were stated in terms of whether the Clarke and Loehman-Whinston systems would *inhibit* free-rider behavior and, implicitly (it would appear; see pp. 45–48), they assume that the subjects could have been free-riding under the voluntary systems. (p. 46) The authors conclude that neither of the proposed pricing systems (neither the Clark nor the Loehman, et al. pricing systems) inhibited free-rider behavior of the subjects. (p. 47) However, as mentioned above, this analysis was predicated on the assumption of free-riding in the voluntary system. Thus, if the voluntary system *did not* lead to free riding by the subjects, then the result that: "There were not significant differences in the demand levels associated with the pricing system" (p. 47) would appear to cloud our attempts to determine whether Scherr and Babb "found" or even "inhibited" free-riding in the experiments utilizing the alternate pricing schemes. This confusion[3] is seen in their assertion that:

The outright offer was the simplest of all situations in that the subjects only had to indicate what part of the 50 cent allotment they wish to donate to sponsor four concerts (books). The opportunity to be a free-rider could not be clearer than in this situation. Yet the outright offers were significantly higher than comparable offers under even the voluntary system, about 45 percent higher. [Scherr and Babb 1975, p. 46]

The authors noted that the proposed "voluntary system closely corresponds to commonly experienced methods of contributing to community projects." (Scherr and Babb 1975, p. 46) Further:

> The proposed pricing systems may not have inhibited free-rider behavior because there was not a great deal of such behavior to inhibit. The debriefing suggested that few subjects attempted to free-ride. [p. 46]

The authors add:

> A different population might contain a larger proportion of people who would attempt to be free-riders and thus improve the chances that the proposed pricing systems would inhibit such behavior. [p. 46]

This last statement is especially interesting in that it suggests only a fraction of a population might free-ride, thus to observe this fraction the sample population must be increased. The experimental arguments set out by Scherr and Babb do not suggest *pervasive* strategic behavior by individuals.

We next briefly consider results from two studies by V. Smith (1977, 1979) which address the strategic bias hypothesis. Smith (1977) reports results obtained in laboratory experiments wherein incentive-compatible auction mechanisms are used in eliciting subject's valuations of public goods. Smith (1979) reports results from a series of experiments utilizing the Groves-Ledyard (G-L) incentive-compatible tax rule for valuing public goods: On the basis of these studies, Smith concludes that:

> What emerged from this paper . . . is that practical decentralized processes exist for the provision of public goods. Some of these processes lead to optimal or approximately optimal allocations. If there are a few such processes there must be thousands—some better, some worse, some cheaper, some dearer. [Smith 1979a, p. 62]

> Why do they not (individuals in the experiments) exhibit the more 'sophisticated,' 'strategic' behavior postulated by Hurwicz and Ledyard-Roberts? I think it is because there are significant direct (and indirect) opportunity costs of thinking, calculating, and signaling which makes strategizing uneconomical. [Smith 1977, p. 1136]

Thus, results from Smith's laboratory experiments belie the notion that individuals behave strategically in response to public good valuation questions.

The studies cited above involve controlled laboratory experiments which focus on the strategic bias question. This question has also been addressed in CVM studies. Results from three of those studies are of particular interest for our discussions—the studies by Brookshire, Ives, and Schulze (1976); Rowe, d'Arge, and Brookshire (1980) and Mitchell and Carson (1981).

Brookshire, et al.'s (1976) study was based upon the following arguments. Consider the individual whose "true" bid is different (either higher or lower) from other subjects. In order to behave strategically, a substantially large false bid (relative to the sample mean bid) that deviates from the individual's "honest" bid would have to be given in order to affect the overall sample mean bid if the strategically-behaving individual is to effectively impose his/her preferences on other subjects. For an "environmentalist", when environmental preservation is at issue, infinity may be the upper bound on his/her bid, while for a "developer" the relevant bid may be zero. Thus, given the assumption that "true" bids are distributed normally, as illustrated by $F(B_1)$ in figure 3.1, the Brookshire, et al. "test" of strategic bias involves the inspection of the actual bid

Figure 3.1
Examples of Bid Distributions

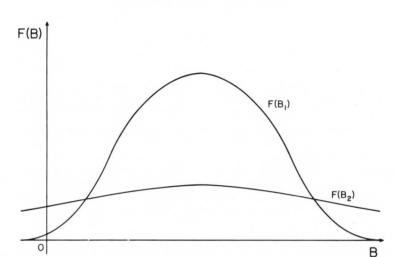

distribution. That is, the greater the occurence of strategic bidding, the flatter the distribution of bids, as illustrated by $F(B_2)$ in figure 3.1. Thus, if CVM bids included a large number of zero and high bids, thereby producing a "flat" distribution of bids, strategic behavior is asssumed to be indicated.

Based upon the argument that bids are distributed normally and that strategic behavior will serve to flatten the distribution, results from the authors' application of the CVM lead them to conclude that "the results of the survey ..., do not lead to the conclusion that strategic behavior was prevalent among the recreators interviewed at Lake Powell." (Brookshire et al. 1976, p. 340)

Rowe et al. (1980) approached the problem of testing for strategic bias differently. Their study involved willingness-to-pay and willingness-to- accept measures for preserving alternative levels of air quality in the Four Corners Region of the Southwest. Subjects from whom CVM valuations were obtained were also asked questions related to their attitudes about environmental issues. Subjects were then classified as: conservationist, semi-conservationist, middle-of-the-road, semi-developer, or developer. Significant correlation between bids and additional dummy variables was interpreted as being indicative of the presence of strategic bias. The authors concluded that:

"the results yielded no significant interactive dummy variables, hence no strategic bias for either the ES or CS bids."

The authors further conclude:

that if zero and very large bids are closely analyzed and possibly rejected, strategic bias, if it exists, has a negligible effect upon the bid distribution. [Rowe et al. 1980, p. 15][6]

Using a bid distribution argument analogous to that used by Brookshire et al. (1976), Mitchell and Carson (1981) investigated the prevalence of strategic bias in CVM bids for improvements in national water quality. Mitchell and Carson's approach differed from that of Brookshire et al., however, in the following way. Mitchell and Carson use average U.S. income distribution (rather than Brookshire et al.'s "normal" distribution) as a "normal" distribution in analyses concerning the flatness of the distribution bids from a CVM. Their analyses result in the following conclusions:

> The overall shape of the (bid) distribution is not flat. It approximates a log normal distribution, a distribution similar to that reported by Brookshire, et al. (1976) in their Lake Powell study, and to the distribution of income in the United States. Since income is a strong predictor of people's willingness to pay for water quality, as we will see in chapter 5, we conclude that the distribution does not suggest strategic bias. [Mitchell and Carson 1981, pp. 4–10]
>
> Eighty-three percent of those who gave amounts greater than zero fall into our 'normal' category. Those in the extreme categories are divided, with 10 percent giving 'high' amounts and 7 percent willing to pay low amounts. We conclude that those at the extremes are relatively few in number and rather evenly balanced. [Mitchell and Carson 1981, pp. 4–13]

Thus, Mitchell and Carson do not find evidence of strategic bias in the results of their application of the CVM.

Results from experimental laboratory and CVM studies concerning efforts to test the strategic bias hypothesis reviewed above do not support the hypothesis. Of course, these results cannot be interpreted as definitive evidence that subjects will not behave strategically in applications of the CVM. As noted earlier, one may criticize structures for questions and information used by Bohm in his experiments. Scherr and Babb's conclusions may be weakened by their basic assumption of free-riding behavior in voluntary exchange systems. The weight of Smith's findings may be challenged by an appeal to the simplified artificial setting of laboratory experiments (an issue discussed below in Chapters 4 and 13). Rowe et al.'s conclusions are not supported by a compelling argument as to why correlation between environmetal attitudes and bids would indicate strategic bias—if strongly conservationist attitudes carry through to budget-related preferences, *lack* of significant correlation between attitudinal variables and bids might be indicative of strategic or other biases (as opposed to their contrary interpretation). Finally, Brookshire, et al. and Mitchell and Carson's studies, which look to "flat" bid distributions as manifestations of strategic bias, may leave some unconvinced as to why "biases" might not be more or less normally distributed across surveyed populations and/or be sufficiently related to incomes so as to result in a distribution of strategically biased bids that approximates the distribution of incomes. These and other questions which might be directed at studies which have focused on the strategic bias issue notwithstanding, the authors find impressive the consistent lack of success in identifying such biases in these studies. Thus, while acknowledging the absence of a basis for categorical conclusions in this regard, we suggest that at a minimum, a basis does exist for diminishing the "priority" position in research agendas that the strategic bias hypothesis has enjoyed for the past decade.

AXIOMATIC BEHAVIOR AND CVM VALUATIONS

The economists' theory of value assumes that individuals have perfect know-ledge over all states of the world, alternative actions and post-action states of the world. In homier terms, the individual is aware of all possible goods/services (and their prices) that he/she might buy, as well as savings alternatives, his/her income and his/her preferences regarding all combinations of purchased goods/services and savings. Based on such perfect knowledge, the individual selects purchases such that equimarginal conditions obtain; i.e., the ratios of marginal utilities to prices for all purchased commodities are equated.

If subjects interviewed in applications of the CVM behave—in terms of their formation of willingness-to-pay responses—as individuals are presumed to behave in market environments, the above-cited axiom from utility theory might be used as a basis for deriving testable hypotheses concerning the extent to which the CVM does, as assumed, "simulate" the market environment. Several authors have taken this tack, testing one or more of the following hypotheses. In what follows, define V as a subjects' stated willingness-to-pay in a CVM study. Let V(y), V(g) and V(b) be values obtained under conditions where the subject is asked to reveal his/her income and monthly expenditure patterns as well as to identify the expenditure category which must be reduced if the subject is to actually pay his/her stated bid for the CVM commodity (V(y)); the subject is "reminded" of "other goods" which he/she might purchase in lieu of the CVM commodity (V(g)); and where a repetitive bidding process is used—"would you pay $1 more?" (V(b)). The following hypotheses are considered.

(a) V = V(y): i.e., bids obtained wherein the individual's "budget constraint" is made explicit, are the same as bids obtained without explicit mention of the budget constraint. Equality in (a) is taken to imply that subjects in CVM experiments *do*, as required by the theory of value, consider income and other goods trade-offs in formulating willingness- to-pay responses.

(b) V = V(g): i.e., bids obtained with and without "reminding" subjects of expenditure alternatives are the same. Equality in (b) is taken to imply that subjects, in valuing the CVM commodity, are cognizant of all states of the world as assumed in value theory.

(c) V = V(b): i.e., the bidding process does not affect bids. Equality in (c) is taken to imply that a subject's initial bid is a preference-researched, *maximum* willingness-to-pay for the CVM commodity.

Studies wherein hypothesis (a) was tested include those by Schulze et al. (1983a), Sorg and Brookshire (1984) and Walbert (1984). For all experiments included in these four studies, the authors fail to reject the hypothesis V = V(y). Thus, the authors of those works conclude that CVM values are indeed formulated within a mental context in which subjects are aware of income trade-offs implied by their stated willingness-to-pay.

Hypothesis (b) is tested in three experiments reported in Schulze et al. (1983a) as well as in Walbert (1984). Generally, the authors' results imply the rejection of the hypothesis V = V(g), i.e., the explicit introduction of other alternative goods (typically other *public* goods) *does* result in a significant change in the subject's willingness- to-pay for the CVM commodity. Curiously, the authors seemingly view this result as "good news" as well as bad news (see Schulze et al. (1983a), Chapter 1). The good news is that, with the introduction of other goods, the reduction in "expenditures" on the CVM commodity (reflecting, one must suppose, the allocaton of expenditures to one or more of the "other" goods) is consistent with the axioms of utility theory. The bad news is that the perfect information assumption is seemingly violated; one must then wonder what the effects on CVM valuations might be of explicit mention of still other alternative goods/services that the subject may not have considered in the CVM valuation process.

Finally, Schulze et al. (1983a), Walbert (1984) and Desvousges et al. (1984) report experiments which include tests of (c). It is generally the case that V = V(g) is rejected—the bidding process resuls in significantly *higher* bids for the CVM commodity. This result, particularly in Schulze et al. (1983a) is interpreted as categorically implying the critical role of the bidding process in inducing preference research on the part of CVM subjects which is required for a subject's formulation of a *maximum* willingness-to-pay for the CVM commodity.

Results from the above-described tests are obviously somewhat mixed vis-à-vis demonstrations that the CVM valuation process approximates "real", market-like behavior. Thus, the comfort that one might take from demonstrations that budget constraints are seemingly operative in a CVM subject's formulation of an offered willingness-to-pay may be dissipated by demonstrations that such subjects are not cognizant of other, possibly competitive, public goods—this issue concerning the range of information considered ("processed") by individuals in forming values, will be pursued at greater length in Chapter 5. In terms of the necessity of including a bidding process in CVM applications, the evidence in this regard appears compelling to the authors. As will be shown, results from experimental work in other areas, especially in experimental economics (chapter 4), support the argument that repetitive bidding-like trials are requred in the CVM as a means for assisting the subject to learn the valuation process and in inducing preference research.

BIAS ISSUES RELATED TO THE DESIGN OF CVM QUESTIONNAIRES

Three sets of potential biases in CVM value measures which may be attributable to the manner in which CVM questionnaires are designed have been dominant in terms of eliciting concern by researchers involved with the development of the CVM. These bias issues, discussed below, are typically described by the rubrics: starting point bias, vehicle bias and information bias.

Starting Point Bias

Randall et al. (1974a) suggested that respondents be asked to respond 'yes' or 'no' to a question of the form: Would you continue to use this recreation area if the cost to you was to increase by X dollars? (p. 135). By varying the amount $X given to different groups of subjects, a demand curve for the recreation area could then be derived. A problem arose, however, concerning the rationale for choosing any value(s) for X and the potential that such choices would result in biased responses (i.e., a "starting point" bias). Two possible sources for starting point bias have been identified. First, the starting bid may suggest (incorrectly) to the individual the approximate range of "appropriate" bids or costs for providing the environmental good. Thus, the individual may respond differently depending on the magnitude of the starting bid. Second, if the subject values time highly, boredom or irritation may set in with any lengthy iterative bidding process. In consequence, if the suggested starting bid is substantially different from actual willingness-to-pay, the subject may be unwilling to go through a lengthy process of searching preferences required for arriving at a maximum willingness-to-pay. It was hypothesized that the effect of these two types of starting point bias would substantially influence the accuracy of contingent valuation measures and, therefore, the usefulness of the approach for the assessment of preferences.

Several studies have explored whether starting point bias exists by examining the effects of alternative starting points. Randall, Grunewald, et al. 1978a,b; Brookshire, D'Arge, Schulze, and Thayer 1981; Brookshire, Randall, and Stoll 1980; Rowe, d'Arge, and Brookshire 1980b. Other studies have explored the effectiveness of alternative valuation mechanisms in avoiding a starting point bias—an example is the payment card, on which a wide range of dollar values is listed. In the case of the payment card, the choice of a starting bid is left up to the subject in that the subject chooses his/her "starting point" from the values given on the payment card. Rowe et al. (1980b) utilized starting bids of $1, $5, or $10, and introduced these values as an independent variable in the estimation of a bid equation as a statistical test for starting point bias. The coefficient was significant and positive, indicating that the choice of a starting bid significantly influenced mean bids. Rowe et al. conclude that "the effect of increasing the starting bid was approximately $0.60/month on a $1.00 increase within the $1.00 to $10.00 range examined." (p. 12) In passing, we note the limited range ($1.00 to $10.00) of starting points used by Rowe et al., a characteristic of their study which has led later writers to question the strength of their conclusions.

Brookshire et al. (1980), in a study of wildlife values, employed starting points of $25, $75, and $200. Brookshire et al. fail to find a significant relationship between starting points and final bids: "the hypothesis that final value data were influenced by the initial bids posited to respondents . . . (is) rejected at the .05 level of significance." (p. 484)

Brookshire, d'Arge, Schulze, and Thayer (1981) explored starting point bias in a contingent valuation study of air quality in Los Angeles. Subjects in twelve communities in the Los Angeles area were surveyed in an attempt to determine willingness-to-pay for improvement in air quality. Three starting points—$1, $10, and $50—were used in the questionnaires. This resulted in three potential comparisons of starting point effects on mean bids: (1) $1 to $10; (2) $1 to $50; and (3) $10 to $50. The authors tested the null hypothesis of equality across bids from each starting format, ignoring all other potential effects on bids. The null hypothesis of equaltiy was rejected Thus the authors found no evidence of starting point biases and concluded that such biases may not be a major problem for applications of the CVM.

Thayer (1981) conducted a contingent valuation experiment wherein starting points of $1 and $10 were used. Three different tests for starting point bias were undertaken: 1) a comparison of mean bids from differing groups of subjects; 2) estimation of a linear bid equation

$$\text{Final Bid} = \alpha + B(s)$$

where B(s) is the starting point; and 3) estimation of a generalized bid equation inclusive of social and economic variables. Thayer's results were as follows. The mean bid comparison indicated "no difference between average bids differentiated by starting point even at the 10 percent significance level." (Thayer 1981, p. 41) The estimated linear equation showed "the coefficient on starting point . . . approximately equal to -0.02, implying that a one dollar increase in the starting bid will cause a two-cent decrease in the bid, an insignificant effect as indicated by the negligible t-statistics." (Thayer 1981, p. 41) Finally, utilizing the generalized regression (which included social and economic variables), "the most noteworthy feature of the equation is that the coefficient on the starting point was not significantly different from zero." (Thayer 1981, p. 42)

While the above-cited studies suggest that starting point biases may be of minimal importance for applications of the CVM, results from a number of other studies suggest otherwise. Thus, significant effects on mean bids from starting bids—i.e. starting point bias—are reported in research conducted by, e.g., Mitchell and Carson (1984) and Boyle et al. (1984). (The authors acknowledge Mitchell and Carson's suggestions in this regard; see appendix to chapter 13 below.)

As noted above, concern over the problem of starting points also led researchers to consider alternative mechanisms for eliciting initial bids, most notably, the use of a payment card. Experiments with payment cards included, in many cases, the use of iterative bidding processes discussed above. The implied rationale for tying iterative bidding to payment cards was seemingly the notion that a subject's initial choice from a payment card may not reflect the subject's *maximum* willingness-to-pay; thus, iterative bidding is assumed to provide incentives for the subject to search his/her preferences for the maximum amount he/she would pay for the CVM commodity.

Sorg and Brookshire (1984) and Schulze et al. (1983a) investigated the relationship of payment card bids and bids obtained with iterative bidding. Mean bids and standard errors from those studies are presented in table 3.1. Examination of table 3.1 indicates that the iterative bidding approach yields measures up to 40 percent higher than initial bids taken from the payment card.

Table 3.1   Iterative Bidding and the Payment Card Approach

Commodity	Average Bid (standard errors) Using		
	Iterative bidding	Payment card	Sample size
Visibility at the Grand Canyon[a]	$9.20 (11.54)	$5.69 (7.21)	64
National water quality[a]	$8.71 (11.11)	$6.50 (8.4)	56
Containment of hazardous waste[a]	$25.85 (36.43)	$16.02 (20.78)	163
Elk wildlife encounters[b]	$65.50 (36.43)	$44.50 (20.78)	20

[a] See Schulze et al. (1983b) for further details.
[b] See Sorg and Brookshire (1984). Their bids are for the situation where the hunter typically sees 10 elk per day.

As noted above, the authors interpret these results as suggesting that iterating initial bids is an important element in the contingent valuation methodology.

Finally, two studies consider interactions between the interviewer and the subject as a possible explanation of the wedge between payment card values and the iterative bidding values noted in table 3.1. Sorg and Brookshire (1984) found no statistical difference between mean bids obtained via payment card (no iteration) in a personal interview format and mean bids obtained via payment card in a mail questionnaire. Schulze, Brookshire et al. (1983a) reach a similar conclusion in a study of ozone effects in Los Angeles. CVM values for reduced ozone concentrations were obtained from in-person interviews (no iterative bidding) and mail responses. Referring to tests of the hypothesis that interview bids equal mail survey bids, the authors conclude that:

> In no case can this hypothesis be rejected at the .05 level, and even at the .10 level the hypothesis can be rejected only in Orange County. [Schulze et al. 1983a, p. 5.41]

Thus results from research to date do not provide a basis for unequivocal conclusions concerning the relevance of starting point bias in CVM studies. Furthermore, we have noted that the use of the payment card format without iterative bidding yields significantly lower values than those derived with an iterative format. Thus, available evidence suggests the desirability of using iterative bidding procedures in CVM applications wherein payment cards are used. the role of iterative bidding procedures in CVM applications is further developed below in chapters 4 and 6.

Vehicle Bias

When willingness-to-pay questions are posed to subjects in an application of the CVM, the questions are typically posed within a context that describes *how* the subject would pay his/her offered payment; as examples, payment via tax payments, entrance fees (to recreation areas), utility bills, or simply higher prices for goods and services. Considerable attention by CVM researchers has been given to potential biases in willingness-to-pay measures that are associated with the choice of a mode of payment or "payment vehicle". For example, if a subject has an aversion to higher taxes, the subject might understate his/her willingness-to-pay for an environmental commodity if such payment must be made through higher taxes. Resulting biases are described as "vehicle biases". Essentially, one finds two possible sources or manifestations of vehicle bias discussed in the literature. First, it is argued that vehicle bias is demonstrated when either mean bids or the recorded number of protest votes varies significantly with the choice of vehicle. Secondly, drawing from economic theory wherein substitution possibilities differ with alternative payment mechanisms, when a payment vehcile allows the individual to substitute over a wider range of current commodity purchases, it is argued that the bid for any given CVM commodity should be higher.

Vehicle bias has been examined by a wide variety of researchers including Randall et al. (1978a,b); Brookshire, Randall and Stoll (1980); Rowe et al. (1980a,b); Brookshire, d'Arge, Schulze, and Thayer (1981); Greenley et al. (1981); Loehman et al. (1981); Cronin and Horzeg (1982); and Daubert and Young (1981). In the wildlife study by Brookshire, Randall and Stoll (1980), the authors utilized hunting license fees and utility bills as bidding vehicles, and tested the null hypothesis that bids were unaffected by the choice of payment vehicle. The results were not conclusive, as is illustrated by the following:

> The hypothesis that final bids . . . were influenced by the choice of bidding vehicle (a component of the bidding scenario) was rejected at the 0.1 level of significance. Nevertheless, it was observed that refusal to bid, with WTP formats, occurred in six of fifty cases with a 'utility bill' vehicle, but in none of fifty-eight cases which used a 'hunting license fee' vehicle. Negative comments in the 'feedback' section occurred more frequently with the 'utility bill' vehicle. [p. 484]

Rowe et al. (1980b) utilized utility bills and payroll deductions as payment vehicles. The payment vehicle was treated as an independent dummy variable in an overall bid regression where a bid based upon a utility bill was designated 0 while a payroll deduction bid was designated 1. For equivalent surplus bids, the coefficient on the dummy variable was positive and significant (i.e., the t-statistic was 3.05). For compensating surplus bids, the coefficient on the dummy (payment vehicle) variable was negative and not significant (i.e., the t-value was -.696). Thus, their results were inconclusive as to the existence of vehicle bias.

Brookshire, d'Arge, Schulze, and Thayer (1981), in an air quality study in Los Angeles, conducted a test of means between bids with a monthly utility bill vehicle and a lump sum payment vehicle. The authors report the following conclusion:

> The null hypothesis of equality of the mean total bids irrespective of the bidding vehicle cannot be rejected for Montebello, Canoga Park, Encino, Huntington Beach, Newport Beach, Pacific Palisades, Palos Verdes, and Redondo Beach. However, for Irvine, Culver City, La Canada, and El Monte, we reject the null hypothesis, at least at the 90% confidence level, for the total bid. The principal reason for these differences seems to stem from the aesthetic bids. [Brookshire et al. 1981, p. 148]

Greenley, Walsh and Young (1981), in a recreation study of the South Platte River Basin in Colorado, utilized a general sales tax and a residential water sewer fee as bidding vehicles. From tests as to the influence of payment vehicles on bids, the authors suggest:

> that willingness to pay for water quality was quite sensitive to the method of hypothetical payment. Residents sampled reported willingness to pay only about one-fourth as much in water-sewer fees as in sales tax for the option value of water quality. Respondents were more reluctant to participate in the water-sewer bill estimation procedure and may have perceived inequities. Everyone, including tourists, pays sales taxes; whereas only property owners and indirectly renters, pay water-sewer bills. Moreover, recent experience with escalating water-sewer fees may have resulted in understatement of willingness to pay for water quality. (p. 671)

Finally, Daubert and Young (1981) conducted a study focusing on recreation demand for maintaining instream flows on the Cache la Poudre River in northern Colorado. The two payment vehicles used in the study were: increments in county sales tax on consumption expenditures; and entrance fees for three recreation activities (fishing, shoreline recreationists, white water kayakers). From tests for vehicle bias, the authors state that "The estimated bid functions for the three recreation activities were statistically different for each repayment obligation; sales tax marginal benefits always exceeded entrance fee values." (p. 672)

Thus, we find rather persistent evidence that supports the vehicle bias proposition—the choice of a payment vehicle would seem to be an important determinant of values derived with the CVM. What is not apparent from the received literature is how one migh go about eliminating such biases—how one identfies a "neutral" or unbiased vehicle. Questions related to his issue will be addressed by participants at the Assessment Conference, described below in Part II of this book.

Information Bias

Information bias is one of the more difficult sources of bias to define with any degree of precision; different researchers have used and explored different notions of such biases. The broadest definition was suggested by Rowe et al. (1980b) as "A potential set of biases induced by the test instrument, inter-viewee, or process, and their effects on the individual's responses." In principle, the different aspects fall into three categories. First, those biases, such as starting point or vehicle bias, which have been discussed earlier. Second, the order in which information is collected or elicited from the respondent is hypothesized to affect the mean bid—a potential bias described by other as a "sequencing bias" (see Brookshire et al. 1981). Third, information bias is argued to result from the quality and quantity of information given to subjects in the CVM.

Rowe et al. (1980b) examined the third view of information bias described above via giving groups of subjects information which differed in quality. Following a subject's bid, the subject was given (randomly chosen) mean bids from other subjects, after which the subject was allowed to alter his/her initial bid. All the subjects were told that they would pay the overall mean bid. This second element allowed the respondents to revise their bid based upon "*new*" information (average bids by others) if they desired to do so. Thus, the reader sees in this aspect of Rowe's test for information bias form of a test for strategic bias. Rowe et al.'s test for information bias involved the construction of a dummy variable where a value of 0 was assigned if the subject was *not* told the mean of other's bids, and 1 if such information was provided. The test result shows the coefficient to be negative and significant (the relevant t-statistic was –4.54). The authors concluded that:

> The effect of prior information concerning previous mean bids, which were stated to have been in the $1.00 to $1.50 range, was equally significant. . . . This result suggests that if the individual is given sufficient information and their true bid exceeds the stated mean bid, they illustrate a form of the classical free-rider behavior by bidding less than their maximum willingness to pay. However, note that the formal structure of the iterative bidding technique need not provide the necessary information to create this incentive. [Rowe et al. 1980b, pp. 12, 14]

Brookshire et al. (1981) obtained bids for the elimination of aesthetic and health (acute and chronic) effects related to air quality. Subjects were asked to value alternative combinations of reduced (a) aesthetic, (b) acute health and (c) chronic health effects. Their analyses focused on the impact on bids for a particular effect, of the sequence in which the effects were introduced. The two alternative sequences used were: (1) aesthetic, aesthetic plus acute, and aesthetic plus acute plus chronic or (2) acute, acute plus chronic, and acute plus chronic plus aesthetic. This allowed for the examination of two hypotheses. First, individuals will bid differently for reduced aesthetics (or acute health effects) depending upon where in the sequential bidding process the aesthetic (or acute) effects are introduced. Second, sequence (1) will result in a cumulative bid (for the reduction of all effects) that differs from sequence (2). The cumulative, or total, bid for all effects assumes additivity with respect to the subject's preference structure related to air quality effects. The authors found that effect-specific bids, as well as total bids, obtained with sequence (1) were significantly different from those obtained with sequence (2). Thus, they conclude that information bias as it relates to the sequence in which information is presented to subjects may be of real concern to those involved with the development of the CVM.

Cronin (1982), in a water quality study conducted along the beaches of the Potomac River designed a survey to examine the effects of different quantities of information on subjects' willingness-to-pay. A subset of subjects was informed that it will help you to know that the average household in the D.C. metropolitan area is paying about $30 per year to maintain the existing water quality. (p. 5.4) All other subjects were not given this information. Cronin concludes:

> While it is difficult a priori to hypothesize the directional bias that additional information might induce on elicited bids, ...comparisons involving the information-no-information situation all indicate substantial differences between respondents provided with cost estimates and those not provided with such estimates. [Cronin 1982, p. 6.11]

As an aside, Cronin also informed one group of subjects that their bid would affect local taxes while others were told that the federal government would bear the costs:

> respondents informed that their bid will impact their local taxes express a willingness to pay significantly lower than do respondents informed that the federal government will bear the costs. [Cronin 1982, pp. 6.10]

Related to our discussions of strategic bias above in sub-section B, Cronin argues that these results are indicative of strategic behavior.

A similar test was conducted by Schulze et al. (1983) in their "Policy Bid Experiment" The authors attempt to discover whether factual information on the current level of expenditures for environmental regulations would affect the initial bid given by subjects for a "new" regulation to control hazardous wastes. Prior to posing willingness-to-pay questions, one half of the sample was informed of the approximate amount they were currently paying in higher taxes and prices for the current state of environmental quality; the other half was not given this information. The authors report a failure to reject the hypothesis of equality between the bids of the two groups—evidence of information bias was not found. They conclude:

> It would appear that, in offering contingent values for our policy commodity, individuals may be, in general terms, cognizant of the existing state of environmental regulations and the cost of maintaining this state. [Schulze et al. 1983, p. VI–49]

WILLINGNESS TO PAY VS. WILLINGNESS TO ACCEPT

Received theory establishes the argument that the amount of money that individuals are willing to pay (WTP) for marginal increases in consumption states available to them should approximately equal the amount of money that they are willing to accept (WTA) for an identical decrement in such consumption states. This argument is developed by Willig (1976) for price changes and by Randall and Stoll (1980) and Takayama (1982) for quantity changes. As a part of these theoretical arguments, income effects, typically viewed as "small" are shown to drive a "small" wedge between measures of WTP and WTA for a given individual.

In contrast with theoretical axioms which predict small differences between WTP and WTA, results from CVM applications wherein such measures are derived almost always demonstrate large differences between average WTP and WTA. Results from fifteen CVM experiments by eight groups of researchers are given in table 3.2. As seen in table 3.2, derived measures of WTA are consistently larger—on the order of three to five times larger—than measures of WTP.

To date, researchers have been unable to explain in any definitive way the persistently observed differences between WTA and WTP measures. Appeal is made to assertion of possible cognitive dissonance (Coursey et al. 1983b), exchange (WTP) as opposed to involuntary exchange (WTA) structures, but we know of no studies wherein posited causes of WTA-WTP differences have been systematically examined. WTP and WTA measures shown in table 3.2 are typically elicited from different groups of subjects—rather than from one subject—but income differences between groups of subjects are generally not sufficiently large to warrant the attribution of WTA-WTP differences to an

---

Table 3.2   Measures of WTP and WTA[a]

Study		WTP	WTA
Hammack and Brown (1974)	(1)	$247.00	$1044.00
Banford, Knetsch and Mauser (1977)	(2)	43.00	120.00
		22.00	93.00
Sinclair (1976)		35.00	100.00
Bishop and Heberlein (1979)[a]		21.00	101.00
Brookshire, Randall and Stoll (1980)	(1)	43.64	68.52
	(2)	54.07	142.60
	(3)	32.00	207.07
Rowe, d'Arge and Brookshire (1980)	(1)	4.75	24.47
	(2)	6.54	71.44
	(3)	3.53	46.63
	(4)	6.85	113.68
Coursey, Schulze and Hovis (1983)	(1)	2.50	9.50
	(2)	2.75	4.50
Knetsch and Sinden (1984)	(1)	1.28	5.18

[a] Carson and Mitchell (1984) reestimated Bishop and Heberlein's results with contrary conclusions.
Note: All figures are in year-of-study dollars. The numbers in parentheses refer either to the number of valuations received or the number of trials (in experiments) conducted.

income effect. Thus, at this point in time all that can be said is first, we have observed differences—large differences—between WTA and WTP measures obtained in applications of the CVM; and secondly, we have little more than intuitive conjectures as to why such differences persist in CVM results. Setting aside such anomalies found in results from CVM applications, some insight as to a rationale for WTA-WTP differences may be gained from ongoing research in experimental economics. An overview of such research is given below in chapter 4; we thus defer further discussion of this issue to chapter 4's review of experimental economics.

Experimental efforts to develop the CVM as a tool for deriving estimated values associated with public/environmental goods have enjoyed substantial progress in many areas. Improvements have been made in some areas of questionnaire design—e.g., in the use of visual aids for communicating to subjects the substance of hypothetical changes in the environment Schulze et al., 1983a —and in the development of imaginative applications of the method to a wide variety of environmental commodities. Walsh et al. 1978a,b Also, as noted above in sub-section B, experimental research with the CVM (and research in other fields) has provided an empirical perspective regarding "strategic bias" in CVM results wherein the potential for such biases is no longer a source of preoccupation for CVM researchers—strategic behavior by subjects in applications of the CVM is no longer considered inevitable nor is the potential for related bias thought to be a matter for primary concern.

Less progress has been made in terms of responding to other questions related to the efficacy of the CVM for its intended uses. While CVM subjects seemingly consider income constraints in their formulation of valuation responses, their valuation of a given CVM commodity may be substantively affected by: "reminders" of *other*, substitute, public goods, which they might wish to "purchase"; alternative modes of payment (payment vehicles); and different (quantitatively and/or qualitatively) sets of information concerning the CVM commodity. When payment cards are used in lieu of starting points, existing evidence points to the necessity of using an iterative bidding process as a part of the CVM application if measures of a subject's *maximum* willingness to pay for a commodity are to be obtained. Finally, large differences between WTA and WTP measures derived from applications of the CVM persist and remain unexplained.

While CVM research specifically directed at questions of the sort described above has not produced definitive results, it would be premature at this point in our discussions to suggest state of the arts *conclusions* as to the implications of research results reviewed in this chapter. Insights relevant to assessing the issues discussed in this chapter are found in results from research in other disciplines and in results from CVM research which is directed at the broader question as to the nature of "hypothetical bias" in values derived with the CVM. These topics are addressed in the following three chapters. Thus, a formulation of our tentative (pre-Conference) conclusions regarding the implications of research reviewed in this chapter for the state of the arts of the CVM must await discussions in chapter 6 where results from our more comprehensive review of multidisciplinary research are used in efforts to suggest state of the arts conclusions.

4
Experimental Economics:
Implications for the CVM

INTRODUCTION

As noted in chapter 3, the contingent valuation approach has been used to generate willingness-to-pay functions for a large and diverse set of consumer goods. The principal concern remains that answers to hypothetical survey questions concerning value may be biased—they may not reveal individual preferences in any meaningful way. As originally expressed by Bohm (1972), the fact that respondents do not actually pay for the provision of the public good in question gives rise to problems in interpreting reported values. As argued above, while not necessarily having an incentive to exhibit free-rider behavior, subjects may simply have no incentive to "tell the truth" and may easily be influenced by spurious, irrelevant factors such as a desire to please the surveyor or the desire to avoid socially unacceptable responses.

Researchers have attempted to reduce the potential for these irrelevant factors in CVM applications by making survey questions as realistic as possible. This has led Davis (1963a,b) and Randall et al. (1974a) to construct so called *bidding game* surveys wherein the valuation process is initiated with the subject's response to an initial starting bid after which the interviewer begins a a process of asking for increasingly higher commitments for payment until the respondent indicates that he or she would not pay more for the public good than the last price quoted by the interviewer; when "high" initial values are used, and initially rejected by the subject, the initial value is incrementally lowered until the subject indicates a willingness-to-pay.

Another approach, described in detail in chapter 3, which has been used by Mitchell and Corson (1981) and Schulze et al. (1983) in the valuation process, involves the use of the *payment card*. In this type of survey, the subject is asked to circle that amount of money from a set of alternatives printed on the payment card which most closely represents his or her maximum willingness-to-pay. Schulze et al. (1983a) used the results of three public goods studies to show that willingness-to-pay obtained from the iterative bidding approach significantly exceeds willingness-to-pay obtained from the payment card approach. For the studies given in table 3.1 the iterative bidding approach yields value measures that are about 40 percent higher than those obtained with the payment card approach. Why would or should we expect these differences? Which is the appropriate technique to employ?

Randall et al. initially used an iterative bidding approach because they hypothesized that such a process might be more "market-like" to subjects and could, therefore, simulate a competitive auction experience. In fact, auction results from laboratory experiments have shown that even when it is theoretically in the *immediate best interest* of an individual subject to reveal his/her maximum willingness-to-pay, the auction process yields values which reflect full willingness-to-pay only after a series of iterative learning periods. (Cox, Roberson, Smith 1982)[1] This would suggest *a priori* that an iterative bidding survey scheme might be expected to outperform the payment card approach.

A second unresolved problem in the contingent valuation approach is the unexpectedly large value difference obtained for both private and public goods in willingness-to-pay (WTP) and in willingness-to-accept (WTA) compensation studies. Theoretically, questionnaires designed to ask an individual for payment to acquire a good should provide similar results as questionnaires designed to ask an individual how much compensation is required to give up the same good. [2] However, results from the studies compiled in table 3.2 of the previous chapter serve to document the large differences between WTP and WTA measures obtained in CVM studies. The questions then arise: should one use WTA or should one use WTP measures of value in contingent valuation studies? Which, if either, corresponds most closely to values which are "true" in the sense of meaningful revelations of preferences? In what follows, we consider results from experimental economics as they provide insights regarding these important questions.

METHODOLOGICAL DEVELOPMENTS IN EXPERIMENTAL ECONOMICS

Contingent valuation surveys are designed to collect field data relevant for social policy analysis using alternative survey instruments (questionaires). Each of the instruments has its own set of rules and therefore causes a specific set of individual messages about the public good whose level of provision is to be increased or decreased. The survey method exercises control over changes in the institutional rules for allocating a public good, but it offers little or no control over the incentives which may affect the subjects' valuation of the good. A researcher may propose a new questionnaire design and test that design in the field. However, lacking control or information concerning preferences, the results of that survey cannot be unambiguously interpreted. Evaluation of each survey's results is complicated by the classic problem of underidentification. Field experiments must be interpreted in terms of prior assumptions regarding individual preferences and behavior as they are implied by the rules of the survey. However, the fundamental objective behind a *laboratory* experiment in economics is to create a manageable "microeconomic environment in the laboratory where adequate control1 can be mandated and accurate measurement of relevant variables guaranteed." Wilde 1980, p. 138 As noted by Smith (1977), control and measurement can only be measured in relative terms, but undoubtedly are much more precise in the laboratory than in the field.

The most important concept in the evaluation of an allocative system, and the concept which has driven institutional theorists, is that of "incentive compatibility." An institution's rules are incentive-compatible if the information and incentive conditions that it provides agents are compatible with the attainment of socially preferred outcomes.... "This means that the *rules* specified in the *institution* in conjunction with the maximizing *behavior* of agents yields a choice of *messages* which constitutes an equilibrium whose *outcomes* are (socially desirable)." (Smith 1982, p. 927)

Vickrey (1961a) published the first article in which a mechanism for achieving optimal allocations in laboratory settings was proposed. His sealed-bid auction mechanism had the property that each participant had a dominant bidding strategy to truthfully reveal demand. Vickrey's fundamental and path-breaking result has recently enjoyed a renaissance and has precipitated considerable attention on the design of demand-revealing mechanisms: Shubik (1975); Dubey and Shubik (1980); Cox, Roberson and Smith (1982); Forsythe and Isaac (1982); and Milgrom and Weber (1982).

Most of this literature analyzes a model in which a single indivisible object is to be sold to one of a group of potential buyers. Each bidder has preferences defined over the object and over risk but not necessarily over the value to other bidders. The auction is assumed to be a noncooperative game played by the bidders.

Two kinds of auction mechanisms have been considered in the theoretical literature, oral auctions and sealed-bid auctions. In oral auctions an exchange of messages occurs between individuals according to a set of rules of negotiation. A contract can then occur. In an *English auction*, bids are announced by the buyers, a bid remains standing until a new higher bid replaces it, and the auction stops when an auctioneer decides that no higher bid will be forthcoming from the buyers. In a *Dutch auction*, price is set initially "high" and then lowered automatically in increments until a price is accepted by one of the buyers; the acceptance terminates the auction. In sealed-bid auctions, individuals submit messages to a seller or a representative of the seller who then determines outcomes based upon a set of pre-announced rules. In a *first price auction* the buyer who submits the highest bid receives the object and must pay his bid. In a *second price auction* the highest bidder also receives the object but only pays what the second highest bidder bid.[3] Several interesting results emerge from the theoretical consideration of these auctions.[4]

1) In first-price auctions the optimal individual bid is less than the value of the auctioned item. That is, an individual has no incentive to reveal demand.
2) The first-price auction does not imply Pareto optimal allocations.
3) Conclusions concerning the first-price auction also apply to Dutch auctions.
4) In second-price auctions the optimal individual bid is equal to the value of the auctioned item. That is, an individual's incentive is to reveal demand.
5) The second-price auction implies Pareto optimal allocations.
6) Conclusions concerning the second-price auction also apply to English auctions.

Based upon the results of 12 experiments conducted by Coppinger, Smith and Titus (1980) and 780 experiments conducted by Cox, Roberson and Smith (1982),[5] the above implications were supported for groups of size four or greater except that first-price and Dutch auctions did not appear to be exactly isomorphic. The deviant results for groups of size less than four were conjectured to be due to a failure in the assumption of noncooperation. An important conclusion from these studies was that not all subjects in a second-price sealed-bid auction realize that their dominant strategy was to offer bids equal to their maximum willingness-to- pay; some subjects never realize this. Others require a period of time over a sequence of bidding games to "learn" the strategy. Coppinger, Smith and Titus question whether any meaningful one-shot observations can (therefore) be made on processes characterized by a dominant strategy equilibrium. (1980, p. 21) It appears that the desirable properties of second-price auctions—elicitation of "true" preference revelations—can be obtained, but sometimes only in a limited sense, after the subject has had time to experience the operation of the valuation mechanism.

Why does the second-price auction have such nice theoretical properties and the first-price auction not have them? Vickrey (1976) has posited the following intuitive explanation:

> The essence of these cases that to admit of the achievement of a Pareto-optimal result seems to be the extent that the participants have a choice as to participating or not, it is an all-or-nothing choice. There can be no strategic holding back (of demand): for an individual to hold back is to achieve a zero gain for himself. [Vickrey 1976, p. 15]

This general result has led researchers to consider the properties of more complex multiple unit auctions. Engelbrecht-Wiggans (1980) has shown that, when more than one unit is auctioned in a single sealed-bid auction, the desirable properties of demand revelation are not achieved. Individuals will tend to understate willingness-to-pay. If each person can only bid on one unit however, the desirable properties of the second-price auction will result. [Vickrey 1976a] The performance of auction mechanisms which include more complex bidding, such as a sealed-bid auction involving a single price for a multiple number of units or a sealed-bid auction in which the individual submits a different bid for each unit, is examined by Dubey and Shubik (1980); Palfrey (1980); Coursey and Smith (1982); and Miller and Plott (1983).

The implications of these results from private good auction theory for the design of contingent valuation surveys are as follows. First, they provide insights concerning how true valuations might be elicited. Individuals must be placed in an "all or nothing" situation in the questionnaire where no strategic holding back can help them. If the questionnaire can be designed in such a manner that a single unit or a single unit per individual is to be hypothetically auctioned off in a second-price fashion, then more demand-revealing behavior, and therefore information about true valuations, should be expected to occur. Secondly, an iterative auction framework is suggested. Because of the "learning period" required for incentive-compatible demand revelations found in experiments with the second-price auction, individuals also should be placed in a survey situation which provides them with tentative information about allocation before results are finalized.[6]

The question as to just how the auction mechanisms develped in experimental economics might be applied to public goods valuations in the CVM setting warrants specific attention. In a series of papers, Smith (1977, 1979a, 1979b, 1980); Ferejohn, Forsythe and Noll (1979a, 1979b); and Ferejohn, Forsythe, Noll and Palfrey (1982) have considered the application of auction mechanisms to the problem of valuing public goods.[7] Such applications involve the design of a process initially suggested by Groves and Ledyard (1977). In a public good auction individuals submit desired quantities of the commodity and the cost share or contribution for the commodity that they would voluntarily accept.

Each individual is told the average group quantity and his or her share of total cost given the contributions of others in the group. Each individual then has the right to veto or agree to the tentative results. Group agreement prevails if and only if each individual agrees upon the outcome and the group covers the cost of the proposed amount of the public good. If agreement is reached, then each individual receives the public good and must pay his or her cost share.

The veto condition means that we have a tatonnement process in the sense that no contracts can occur until all individuals in the group are in equilibrium or agreement. This provides at least a partial solution to the problem of free-riding or the incentive to contribute less than true maximum willingness-to-pay. One individual can veto the results of the auction even if every other individual in the group agrees about a given quantity and distribution of cost shares.

A number of experimental and field applications of auction mechanisms similar to those described above have been conducted. Experimental applications include those by Smith (1979a, 1979b, 1980); Ferejohn et al. (1982); and Coursey and Smith (1982); field applications include those by Bohm (1972); Ferejohn and Noll (1976); and Scherr and Babb (1975).

Results from these studies also suggest how an iterative auction framework can be integrated into a questionnaire framework. An iterative or sequential survey can be combined with a tatonnement voting process. Such a unanimity requirement is used in the London gold bullion market (Jarecki 1976) and has been found to improve efficiency in private as well as collective allocation mechanisms. (Smith 1982; Coursey and Smith 1982; and Miller and Plott 1983)

RECENT APPLICATIONS OF LABORATORY METHODS RELATED TO CVM DEVELOPMENTS

Two recent experiments were motivated at least in part by assessment-related questions in the CVM literature—primarily to WTP-WTA differences discussed above in chapter 3. The first experiment, conducted by Knetsch and Sinden (1984), demonstrated that the large disparity between willingness-to-accept (WTA) and willingness-to-pay (WTP) measures of value is found to exist in cases where actual (as opposed to hypothetical) payments are made in the laboratory. Unfortunately, the Knetsch and Sinden experiment did not use a demand-revealing mechanism such as the Vickrey second-price auction described above. They argue that the large disparity between WTA and WTP measures of value may be due to what psychologists term "cognitive dissonance."

The second experiment, conducted by Coursey, Schulze and Hovis (1983b), (hereinafter referred to as CSH) addressed several questions of concern for CVM developments: issues concerning the large disparity shown to exist between WTA and WTP measures of value and issues concerning the efficacy of payment cards and the iterative bidding process as methods for eliciting hypothetical payments. Given the potential importance of these issues for our later discussions, the CSH experiment is described in some detail as follows. Individuals were assumed to have a state-dependent utility function which included income and also exposure to an unpleasant (bitter) taste experience. The experiment was designed to determine how individuals value this unusual experience from both the perspective of accepting payment to endure the experience and from the perspective of paying to avoid a bitter-tasting experience. The bitter substance used in the experiment, sucrose octa-acetate (SOA), has long been used by psychologists in taste experiments and provides a carefully controlled, safe, but unpleasant experience. (Green 1942 and Linegard 1943)

The CSH experiment consisted of three parts. In part I, each subject was asked to provide either a hypothetical WTA or a WTP for tasting SOA based on a verbal description of the substance. In part II, subjects were allowed to sample a few drops of SOA and were again asked for either WTA or WTP. Respondents were then allowed to change their earlier (part I) bid and an iterative bidding procedure was used to determine maximum WTP (or minimum WTA). In part III, groups of eight, who were originally asked the WTA questions, participated in a Vickrey auction for a fixed supply of four one ounce cups of the SOA. Low bidders were then *actually* compensated to taste the substance. For groups originally asked the WTP questions, a similar Vickrey auction was held for not tasting the substance and high bidders actually paid their offered amounts to avoid tasting SOA. Presumably, the well documented demand-revealing properties associated with the competitive Vickrey auction should have provided "true" values in the form of individual bids.

The results of the CSH experiment are summarized in figure 4.1. First, note that as one moves from left to right across figure 4.1, WTA and WTP move in opposite directions through each and every phase of the experiment. Hypothetical WTA and WTP values (given as average values across individuals) are initially far apart (points α and α', respectively). This result is consistent with the existing literature on field applications of the survey approach for valuing public goods. Bishop and Heberlein 1979 and Rowe et al. 1980b Surprisingly, actual experience with the commodity (tasting SOA) in part II drives hypothetical WTA and WTP values further apart (points β and β'). The iterative bidding process results in WTA and WTP values which converge (points γ and γ'); obviously this suggests that the iterative procedure may be of some value. As the Vickrey auction begins in part III (points δ and δ'), opening bids for WTA and WTP are similar to, but further apart than, the iterated hypothetical bids. In the second auction trial (ε and ε') WTA and WTP diverge, possibly due to efforts by some subjects to employ dynamic trial strategies not addressed in the static Vickrey models. In early trials individuals may not initially understand that the best strategy is to reveal true values but, ultimately, WTA and WTP values do indeed converge (points ω and ω'). This convergence is, however, strongly asymmetrical in that the WTA measure of value "collapses" downward under the competitive market-like experience of the auction while WTP trial values show only modest upward movement.

Final auction measures of WTA (point ω) and WTP (point ω') are statistically similar. However, although hypothetical WTA (e.g., the point γ) is not statistically similar to WTA obtained in the auction (point ω), hypothetical willingness to pay (point γ') is statistically similar to WTP obtained from the auction (point ω').

Results from the CSH experiment suggest the following conclusions. First, the lack of significant differences between WTA and WTP measures in this experiment may be attributable to the demand-revealing nature of, and learning experiences in, the Vickrey auction. This result is consistent with economic

Figure 4.1
Overall Average Experimental Responses

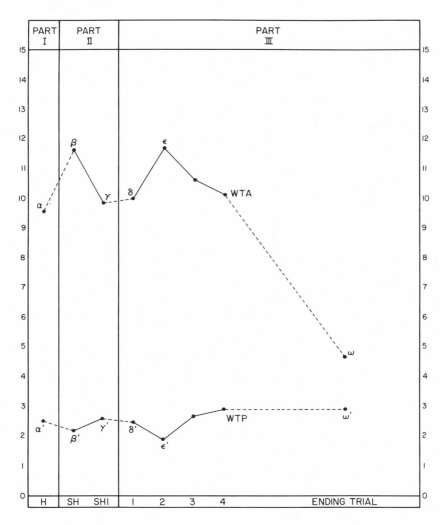

Each point represents overall average of the thirty-two individuals who participated
in each of the WTA and WTP experiments.

theory and suggests that the observed divergences between *hypothetical* measures of WTA and WTP may result mainly from lack of a market-like environment.

Second, hypothetical WTA measures of value are likely to be biased upwards vis-a-vis what we would interpret as true values obtained from a market-like auction. Psychological factors may of course explain this bias. However, economists might argue that opening WTA bids might well be biased upwards for simple strategic bidding reasons.

Third, hypothetical WTP measures of value may correspond more closely to true (final Vickery auction) value than do WTA measures.

VALUATIONS UNDER UNCERTAINTY CONDITIONS: RELEVANT RESULTS FROM LABORATORY EXPERIMENTS

The experimental economics literature provides insights to still another set of issues of relevance for our assessment of the CVM *viz*, issues concerning individual behavior under conditions of uncertainty. In this regard, Grether and Plott (1979) have documented the phenomenon of "preference reversal" for the case in which individuals face a choice between two lotteries. Consider the following example: Lottery A has a high probability of a low monetary reward. Lottery B has a lower probability of a higher monetary reward. Grether and Plott demonstrate convincingly that the same individual will often choose Lottery A over Lottery B but assign a higher monetary value to B than to A. Preferences, as determined by the pattern of choice, are reversed when expressed in monetary terms.

Grether and Plott did not use repetitive trials wherein, as in the CSH experiment, subjects might "learn" dominant strategies. Thus, Pommerhehne, Schneider and Zweifel (1982) argue that since the Grether and Plott study was a "one-shot" experiment and since "judging gambles is cognitively difficult," (p. 570) then in a second trial of an experiment structured similarly to Grether and Plott's, the frequency of preference reversals would be reduced. This in fact did not occur in their experiment to test this hypothesis. As an aside we note that two trials may still have been insufficient for subjects to have "learned" dominant strategies—in the above described experiment by CSH, four non-binding learning trials and up to ten total trials were allowed. In another related experiment conducted by Reilly (1982), it was shown that additional information, including a detailed explanation of expected values and monetary incentives, reduced the frequency of preference reversals. However, such reversals still occurred frequently.

The preference reversal issue relates to the larger question concerning the efficacy of the economists' expected utility (EU) model in describing individual behavior under conditions of uncertainty. Results from research conducted by psychologists (reviewed below in chapter 5) seriously challenge the "rationality" precepts underlying the EU model—a challenge which finds support in the research of decision theorists (Arrow 1982; Simon 1979) and experimental economists. However, one finds in the experimental economics literature reported results which suggest that predictions from the expected utility model may be satisfied *asymptotically* after many experimental trials with subjects. Plott and Sunder (1982), in an experiment examining the rational expectations model, found that:

There seems to be no doubt that variables endogenous to the operation of these markets served to convey accurately the state of nature to otherwise uninformed agents. We can conclude that rational expectations models (based on maximization of expected utility) must be taken seriously as not universally misleading about the nature of human capabilities and markets. [p. 692]

The implications of this result for CVM may be that when individuals are dealing with a new, highly uncertain, commodity; the survey instrument may not be able to supply enough of a learning experience, in a reasonably short time frame, to allow an asymptotic approach to rational expected utility-maximizing behavior.

These experimental results effectively support the psychologists' arguments that serious problems may exist for traditional economic value theory where a high degree of uncertainty is present.[8] Although some progress is being made in developing an alternative model of value under uncertainty (see for example, Chew and MacGrimmon 1979), however, it is premature at this date to adopt a new economic-theoretical perspective.

AN EXAMPLE: REVELATION OF COMPENSATING INCOME VARIATION

In order to illustrate some of the points made in the previous sections we consider the problem of constructing two different survey instruments which attempt to reveal how much individuals are willing to accept in order to have a factory move into their physical environment. The first survey proposed is structured more or less along the lines of current contingent valuation practice. The second is structured along the lines of current experimental economics practice, using a hypothetical Vickrey second-price auction.

Suppose that the environment consists of $i = 1, 2, \ldots$ I individual economic agents who have utility functions defined over income, Y_i, and Q_i, a "bad" commodity such as the smoke produced by the factory. Thus,

$$U_i = U_i (Q_i, Y_i)$$

is individual i's utility function with $U_i / Y_i \geq 0$ and $U_i^2 / Q_i^2 \leq 0$ for all i. Suppose that there exists an income compensation $\triangle Y_i$ which would just make an individual i indifferent to a choice between a smoky environment and extra income and a clean environment with no extra income. Or, $\triangle Y_i$ is implicitly defined by $U_i(Y_i + \triangle Y_i, 1) = U_i(Y_i, 0)$. Thus, $\triangle Y_i$ is i's willingness to accept monetary payment for the smoke produced by a nearby factory.

Suppose now that the Y_i are rank-ordered from $i = 1, 2, \ldots, I$, and that $\triangle Y < \triangle Y \ldots < \triangle Y$. Then this ranking defines a compensating income variation supply function[9] (See figure 4.2). This curve may also be thought of as the supply function for pollutable locations. Assume for simplicity that the factory produces an integer $N < I$ total units of pollution and that the maximum consumption of Q is one unit per individual. Each individual who is affected by the factory consumes one unit of pollutant and each individual who is not affected by the factory consumes zero units of the pollutant. The situation described can be imagined as a cloud of smoke which, as it grows in size (N), envelops more and more homeowners (individuals) who surround the factory which emits the smoke. The problem facing the economist is to conduct a survey

Figure 4.2: Group Willingness to Pay Function
(I = 5 assumed)

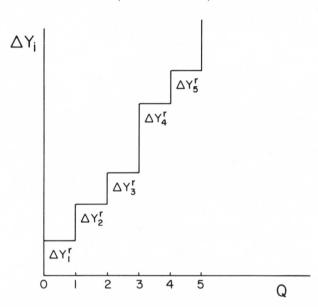

to determine the damages done by a given factory which produces N units of smoke. In what follows, we consider two institutional approaches for estimating such damages.

SOLICITED COMPENSATING VARIATIONS

The first approach in response to this problem might involve the construction of a survey which solicits or asks each i to submit a message mi which is his or her willingness to accept an income compensation offer (Yi) for one unit of Q; i.e., mi = Yi. This would require only one period of data collection and analysis. Allocation of one unit is made to the N individuals who submit the lowest willingness-to-accept offers. For these individuals, Ui = Ui(Yi – mi, 1). All other individuals j receive no units of Q, and for this group Uj = Uj (Yj, 0). The problem with this institution is that a dominant strategy involves the individuals' asking for an *infinite* income compensation.[10] There is no incentive for an individual to provide the surveyor with any accurate information concerning his/her actual willingness-to-accept-payment except perhaps a desire to be honest, which may conflict with any auction-like experience the respondent may have had. This theoretical result is consistent with the large difference between willingness-to-accept and willingness-to-pay previously shown in table 3.2.

Tatonnement Version of the Second-Price Auction

Now consider an alternative iterative survey. During each trial t; t = 1, 2, . . . T, let each individual i submit a message mi which is his or her willingness-to-accept an income compensation offer for one unit of Q. Tentative allocation would then occur according to the following rules: First, the offers mi would be ranked from lowest to highest such that $m_1 \leq m_2 \ldots \leq m_I$. A reigning offer price for all accepted offers m^* would be determined according to rules of second-price auction. Thus, $m^* = m_{N+1}$ (see figure 4.3). For this first trial round, if $mi < m^*$ then an individual would be compensated with a payment of m^* and would have to consume one unit of pollutant; for this group it would be true that $Ui = Ui(Yi + m^*, 1)$. If $mi \geq m^*$ then an individual would receive no compensation and would consume zero units of the pollutant; for this group $Ui = Ui(Yi, 0)$.

These results from the first trial of the survey would then be put to a vote. All members of the group who were allocated one unit of the pollutant would vote on whether to finalize the allocation results for that trial. If all voted "yes" then everyone would realize their allocations. If at least one individual voted "no", thereby vetoing the results of the trial, then a new trial would be conducted. A second survey would be administered. The survey and voting processes would continue until a unanimous agreement occurred or until a maximum number (T) of trials had been conducted. In that case, some terminal (perhaps random) allocation procedure might be invoked.

Notice that this survey instrument incorporates three elements which theoretically and empirically should allow it to outperform the first survey. It is a second-price auction, iterative learning effects are permitted to occur, and it includes a tatonnement process. Its primary disadvantage over the simple survey lies in the cost of performing multiple trials. The two surveys might easily be compared in the laboratory. Monetary values can be induced which reflect the compensating income required for each individual to hypothetically consume a

Figure 4.3: Vickrey Auction of N Units
(N = 4, I = 5 assumed)

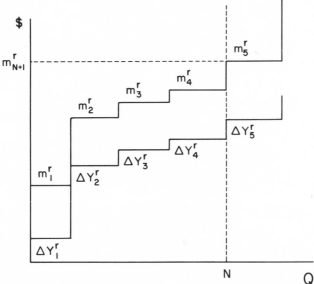

fictitious pollutant. In addition, more complicated allocation mechanisms can be constructed and tested for cases where individuals may consume more than one unit of the pollutant or where the pollutant is a pure public good or externality. Similarly, the performance of the relatively simple hypothetical iterative bidding game and other intermediate mechanisms can be contrasted to the Vickrey second-price auction. Value measures derived from each institution can be assessed for accuracy through laboratory experiments.

CONCLUSIONS

We have argued in this chapter that a dynamic, iterative survey mechanism may well need to be employed in the design of CVM survey instruments in order to improve the accuracy of responses. Furthermore, due to the current inaccuracy of hedonic and travel cost approaches for valuing public goods, the least cost method, in our view, for testing alternative survey instruments is to use laboratory experiments. The objective of these experiments should be the development of the most simple survey design which gives accurate responses in terms of eliciting preference revelations from subjects. Several questions are implied by the discussions in this chapter: is a complex iterative voting procedure required; how fast will such a procedure converge to "true" values; what is the effect on incentives of relaxing the unanimity voting feature for large groups; can a contingent valuation mechanism be constructed which overcomes cognitive difficulties observed when individuals face an uncertain situation for the first time? All of these operational questions can at least qualitatively be answered in an experimental laboratory setting.

NOTES

1. The example cited refers to a second-price Vickrey sealed-bid auction. It is a dominant strategy equilibrium for each individual in such an auction to bid full value or reveal demand for the single unit sold in each period. At best, it usually takes subjects a few periods to realize this. Some individuals *never* totally reveal demand. See Cox, Roberson, Smith (1982) for details.

2. The difference between the two measures in theory is due to an income effect. This income effect is argued to be "small" in most cases. See Willig (1976).

3. These descriptions are meant to be brief. For a detailed description of the four basic auction types see Cassady (1967) or Coppinger, Smith and Titus (1980).

4. All are derived in Cox, Roberson and Smith (1982). See also Milgrom and Weber (1982).

5. See also Smith (1967) and Belovicz (1979).

6. That is, provide the individuals with more than a one-shot survey. Let them answer a survey, report the tentative results of that survey back to them, let them adjust their answers, report the new tentative results, and so forth until an unannounced stopping time. At this stopping time allow the final results to take effect.

7. Loeb (1977) considers the general comparability problems associated with relating private good auction mechanisms and public good auction mechanisms.

8. Schoemaker (1982) concludes: "As a descriptive model seeking insight into how decisions are made, expected utility theory fails on three counts. First, people do not structure problems as holistically and comprehensively as expected utility theory suggests. Second, they do not process information, especially probabilities, according to the expected utility rule. Finally, expected utility theory, as an "as if" model, poorly predicts choice behavior in laboratory situations. Hence, it is doubtful that expected utility theory should or could serve as a general descriptive model." (p. 552)

9. This function is generally a step function. The assumption that individual 1 has a lower Y than individual 2 and so forth is only a simplifying assumption to keep the mathematics simple.

10. If individual i maximizes $U_i(Y_i + m_i, 1)$ then he will select an infinite value for m_i. Only a preference for fairness or equity not modelled in this problem would cause m_i to be bounded.

5

Imputing Actual Behavior from Choices made under Hypothetical Circumstances

THE ISSUES

In our earlier (chapter 1 and 2) overview of concerns/criticisms regarding the accuracy, or interpretative meaningfulness, of value measures derived with the CVM, prominent among those were concerns for biases resulting from the hypothetical nature of the CVM's contingent "market" and the CVM payment. Thus, the potential for biases was suggested to result from the fact that the market valuation context, as well as the commodity itself in some cases, will generally be unfamiliar to survey participants; related to the "unfamiliarity" argument, biases are suggested to be exacerbated by the short time allowed for the valuation process in the CVM relative to the "weeks or months" [1] spent by individuals in gathering information—researching their preferences—for other, real-life analogous situations. Finally, but related to the above, our earlier overview made reference to research results from cognitive psychologists which suggested the use by individuals of heuristic devices in forming judgements in uncertain situations. These concerns share a common theme, *viz.*, a focus on the issue as to how individuals form judgments and values under conditions of uncertainty, or on the question: to what extent can actual behavior be imputed from choices made in hypothetical, uncertain, circumstances?

At the outset it must be re-emphasized that cause-effect statements concerning biases attributable to the hypothetical nature of the CVM have been poorly defined in the literature; in the main, they may be regarded as thoughtful, intuitive, *a priori* arguments or assertions as to why values derived from the CVM might be biased. Thus, a logically consistent method for organizing and discussing "hypothetical bias" was not received by the authors. Rather, the authors' initial task was that of attempting to sort through the myriad arguments relating to the substance of hypothetical bias, the time-unfamiliarity issue, as they appear in the CVM literature and the psychology literature concerned with decision-making under conditions of uncertainty, for two purposes: first to set these posited sources for bias in the form of testable hypotheses which relate *directly* to CVM measures; secondly, to bring together existing evidence which might be relevant for assessing these hypotheses.

These efforts resulted in the following organization for discussions of biases related to hypothetical settings and the CVM. We first consider the "incentives for accuracy" form of the hypothetical bias proposition as it (we argue) relates to hypothetical payment. Bias-related propositions concerning time, preference research and "unfamiliarity" are assessed in the section entitled Hypothetical Biases Related to Time. Related to this section's topic, propositions concerning inaccuracies attributable to distorted perceptions of commodities "traded" in the CVM are considered in the section entitled Perceptions, Framing and The CVM. In the section entitled, Attitudes vs. Intended Behavior we address the proposition that, with hypothetical goods and payments, CVM values may reflect attitudes as opposed to intended behavior. Our discussions conclude with Concluding Remarks wherein, first, the authors suggest rubrics for issues related to arguments concerning the hypothetical nature of the CVM which might lend clarity and precision to further assessments of these issues and, secondly, results and conclusions from sections B-E are summarized.

Before initiating our analysis, the reader must recognize that results from any one study which has inferential relevance for propositions considered in one section (e.g., time/information issues) may also be directly relevant for propositions discussed in other sections (e.g., perceptions and framing of information in Perceptions, Framing and The CVM). As implied above, all of this is to acknowledge that many, if not most, of the propositions concerning the extent to which actual behavior can be imputed from choices made under hypothetical circumstances are not distinguishable as separate, independent issues. In treating them separately, the authors do not suggest that they should be distinguishable issues. The partitioning of issues into seperate sections is intended to serve, however imperfectly, the expositional goals of precision and clarity.

HYPOTHETICAL PAYMENT: AN INCENTIVE FOR ACCURACY

As noted above in I.C., as well as by Randall et al. (1983), the "hypothetical bias" notion as it appears in the CVM literature is poorly defined. Too often, the issue is simply described contextually as, for example, "the hypothetical character of the CVM market precludes the derivation of values (which reliably reflect preferences)." (Burness et al. 1983 p. 675) In statements of this form, the question is begged as to *why* the hypothetical market might preclude accurate or reliable responses. On the other hand, one sees in Freeman (1979a) as well as in Feenberg and Mills (1980) a proposition for biases attributable to the hypothetical nature of the CVM which is suggestive of testable hypotheses. Thus, Freeman argues that "In the real world, an individual who takes an action inconsistent with his basic preferences, perhaps by mistake, incurs a cost or a loss of utility. In the (CVM)... there is no cost to being wrong, and therefore, no incentive to undertake the mental effort to be accurate." (Freeman 1979b, p. 916)

In its most general form, the incentives argument may be re-stated as follows. Let V be an individual's stated valuation for a given commodity X; then the hypothesis consonant with the incentives argument is:

$$V(\text{with incentives}) = V(\text{without incentives}) \qquad (1)$$

As will be argued in chapter 6, there may be many ways for providing incentives for accurate valuations depending on, among other things, one's criteria for accuracy. In the literature, however, one finds concern with this question limited to one, very specific form of (1) in which the lack of actual payment of 'offered' WTP measures explains the lack of incentives. Effectively then, actual payment = incentives, hypothetical payment = no (without) incentives, and (1) can be rewritten as:

$$H_0\text{: V(actual payment)} = \text{V(hypothetical payment)} \qquad (2)$$

We now inquire as to existing evidence relevant for the form of hypothesis (1) given by (2). The literature abounds with evidence that suggests that (2) be rejected: actual vs. hypothetical payment does result in different choices. Bohm's (1972) seminal experimental work with the CVM, wherein willingness-to-pay values for public television were derived from actual and hypothetical payments, produced results contrary to hypothesis (2)—actual payments were significantly different from hypothetical payments. From this, Bohm concludes that his results are "compatible with the general view that, when no payments . . . are involved, people respond in an 'irresponsible' fashion . . . this result may be seen as still another reason to doubt the usefulness of responses to hypothetical questions."[2] Bohm's findings are supported by results from Bishop and Heberlein's (1979) study of willingness-to-pay/accept for early season goose hunting permits. In comparing "substantial" differences in willingness-to-accept estimates for hunting permits involving actual ($63.00) and hypothetical ($101.00) payments, Bishop and Heberlein conclude "The stimulus of real dollars . . . is simply more powerful than hypothetical dollars . . . In plain words, 'money talks' and real money 'speaks louder' than hypothetical money." (pp. 928-29) As is discussed later in chapter 6, we note here that Bishop and Heberlein's conclusions in this regard are challenged in a recent paper by Carson and Mitchell (1984a). Using alternative (vis-à-vis Bishop and Heberlein) assumptions regarding upper limits for integration and for identifying non-parti-cipants, Carson and Mitchell demonstrate, using Bishop and Heberlein data, the lack of significant difference between hypothetical and "actual" payments. (p. 8) Results from two other sets of studies are relevant for hypothesis (2). First, Coursey et al. (1983b) conducted experiments wherein hypothetical and actual willingness-to-accept (WTA) and willingness-to-pay (WTP) measures were related to a subject's tasting of a bitter substance: sucrose octa- acetate. They find a significant difference between WTA and WTP measures when hypo-thetical, as opposed to actual, payment is involved, a finding explained by the authors as resulting "mainly from lack of a market-like environment." (p. 15) Secondly, results from tests of actual vs. hypothetical payment on decision strategies reported in the psychology literature[3] consistently conclude that actual payment makes a difference. Typical of these reported results is Slovic's (1969) conclusion: "It is clear that decision strategies . . . differed depending on whether the gains and losses . . . were real or hypothetical . . . results indicate the importance of committing (subjects) to the consequences of their actions." (p. 437)

In contrast to the above, the authors find little if any evidence that would support hypothesis (2). While not directly related to this hypothesis, we find one study which suggests V(hypothetical payment) has predictive value for V(actual payment) in Kogan and Wallach's (1964) conclusion: "It is evident, then, that what an individual does in a hypothetical decision context has some predictive value for a gambling type of task in which decisions represent a firm commitment in a subsequent playoff." (p. 39) Other than this, the authors find but two other studies, the results from which might be inferred as weakly supporting hypothesis (2). These are studies wherein values derived from the CVM are compared with corresponding values derived from the hedonic price method (HPM). These two studies, by Brookshire et al. (1982) and Cummings et al. (1982) are described in some detail below in chapter 6; thus, in what follows we simply point to the potential relevance of results from these studies to the issue at hand. Such potential relevance must be based on two important assumptions. First, one must accept values derived via the HPM as a measure of actual payment for a commodity—problems in doing so are detailed below. Secondly, one must accept the argument that individual biases and differences, of the type alluded to above, are immaterial for measures drawn from aggregate behavior—i.e., at higher levels of aggregation, individual biases will generally wash out.[4] In this regard, one must note the challenges to this argument by Kleindorfer and Kunreuther (1983) as well as by others.[5] Given these assumptions, comparisons of HPM and CVM (involving hypothetical payments) values may be relevant for assessing (2).[6] Defining Vh and Vc as values derived from the HPM and the CVM, respectively, Brookshire et al. (1982) axiomatically develop the hypothesis $V_h > V_c$; statistical analysis of their data result in their failure to reject this hypothesis. Thus, while not a direct proof of (2), their results can be taken as a demonstration of an appropriate relationship between V(actual payment) and V(hypothetical payment): as measured, respectively, by Vh and Vc, when V(actual payment) should be greater than V(hypothetical payment), this relationship is shown to obtain. Cummings et al. (1982) test the hypothesis given in (2), *viz.*, that Vh = Vc; as in Brookshire et al. (1982), their analysis results in failure to reject the hypothesis.

Comparisons aside, the quality of empirical measures of value from the HPM *per se* are far from a level where they might be regarded as accurate, in some sense, estimates for market values attributable to public goods. Thus, results from these comparative studies must be viewed as having questionable weight relative to earlier-described studies in terms of an assessment of (2). *Ceteris paribus*, one would then tentatively conclude that compelling reasons exist for expecting biases in hypothetical valuations of the sort obtained in the CVM, relative to individual values that would obtain under conditions where expressed valuations must, in fact, be paid. The weight and implications of this tentative conclusion are discussed below.

HYPOTHETICAL BIASES RELATED TO TIME

Consider the following statements of concern about the CVM as expressed by, first, Feenberg and Mills (1980) and, second, Bishop and Heberlein (1979).

Figuring out what an improvement in water quality of a nearby lake would be worth to you is extremely complex. If it were announced that the lake has been partially cleaned up, you might try it a couple of times, compare it with other lakes, ask friends, and read accounts of the results in the press and elsewhere. Gradually, you would decide the most appropriate modification of your recreational behavior. [p. 60]

When people buy things in a market, they may go through weeks or months of considering the alternatives. The process will often involve consultations with friends and may also involve professionals such as lawyers or bankers. It may also entail shopping around for the best deal on the product in question. And, for the majority of items in the consumer's budget, there is a whole history of past experience in the market to base the decision on. All this is markedly different than spending an hour or two at most with a mail survey or a personal interviewer attempting to discern how one might behave in a market for a commodity for which one has never actually paid more than a nominal fee. [p. 927]

These intuitive statements of concern as to the hypothetical nature of the CVM are, in their cited form, obviously not in forms immediately amenable to hypothesis testing. One sees in these statements, however, the strands of an argument which may be stated as a testable hypothesis. At the risk of over-interpretation, the above-cited concerns may be compressed into the argument that individuals *require time* in order to obtain and mentally "process" relevant information before informed, "accurate" judgements can be formed; note here that we beg the question as to whether accurate measures can be obtained with hypothetical payment, regardless of time and information used in the preference research process. If $V(t_0)$ is the expressed value for the CVM commodity X during the typical, short-lived interview used in the CVM, $V(t_1)$ the value expressed at some later, post-initial interview time, the above arguments suggest rejection of the null hypothesis:

$$H_o: V(t_0) = V(t_1) \qquad (3)$$

Variations in (3) could involve obtaining a sequence of values over time wherein endogenous (to the CVM) or exogenous information is made available to or obtained by subjects; if $I_1, I_2, \ldots$ represents increasing amounts of information, such variations would alter (3) as:

$$H_o: V(t_0, I_1) = V(t_1, I_2), \qquad (3')$$

$$t_0 < t_1, I_1 < I_2.$$

Cursory inspection of (3) and (3') suggests a number of potentially difficult problems in efforts to test them. As an example, across individuals, how does one control for differences in exogeneously-obtained information? Given that "more" information has qualitative as well as quantitative implications, how does one structure the I's? Most importantly, absent is some notion as to a "true" value (hypothesis 2) and/or any appeal to reasons why V might converge to some number as t and I become increasingly large: i.e., there is no logical, conclusive way to end the experiment. Surely alternative, better ways exist to draw hypotheses that capture the essence of the "preference research" problems implicit to the earlier-cited concerns. At a minimum, however, (3) and (3') may serve the purpose of providing a focal point for our inquiry as to the existence of evidence that relates, in one way or another, to the preference research issue.

One finds little evidence in the CVM literature that relates directly to (3) or (3'). Research results do exist, however, that have inferential relevance for these hypothesis. Burness et al. (1983) essentially focus on $V(t_0, I_1)$ in (3') and introduce three techniques designed, in their words, to break "the hypothetical barrier in CVM analysis." (p. 681) These techniques are (a) prefacing willingness-to-pay (WTP) questions with questions regarding the individual's current budget expenditures across six broad budget categories—after offering a CVM value, individuals are then asked where (from which budget category) they will obtain money required to "pay" the offered value; (b) after (and before) obtaining a WTP for a specific commodity (an EPA regulation on hazardous waste disposal), other public goods are described to the subject after which the subject may revise his/her WTP measure; (c) use of the Randall "bidding game" procedure wherein, after elicitation of an initial WTP "offer", repeated questions of the form "would you pay $1.00 more" are asked until the subject indicates: no more (a maximum WTP). Burness et al. find no significant effects on WTP measures resulting from the explicit use of a budget constraint (technique a), a finding which is also reported in Schulze et al. (1983a). The introduction of other public goods (OPG) produces mixed results. The introduction of OPG consistently lowered the offered WTP. In some cases, downward revisions are statistically significant, but in other cases they are not.[7] Even in cases where lack of statistical significance between initial and OPG-revised bids were found, such results were weakened by large standard deviations and consistent observations of absolute differences in bids of 50% or more. (p. 150) Finally, as in Schulze et al. (1983a) and Desvousges et al. (1983) Burness and his co-authors find that technique (c)—use of the bidding process—significantly affects the WTP measure.

Research results typified by those described above are suggested as relevant for assessments of at least two issues. First, they demonstrate that CVM measures are not random numbers: they vary systematically with income, substitute/complementary goods and demographic characteristics as *a priori* axioms would dictate.[8] Secondly, and of central importance for our discussions, the results are offered as evidence that CVM values are individual valuations that reflect a process whereby the subject, in offering a value, has clarified his/her objectives [9], which is to say that the CVM value *is a preference-researched bid.*[10] That techniques (a)-(c) demonstrate a preference researched value is argued to follow from the fact that results from (a) suggest that subjects have considered income – CVM commodity trade-offs implied by their offered valuation; results from (b) may imply that offered bids reflect the subjects' consideration of trade-offs between the CV commodity and other public goods; and results from (c) demonstrate that one can, in the CVM, induce subjects to clarify their objectives—research their preferences—via the repetitive-question, bidding process.

Obviously, these results have limited, but interesting, implications for (3) and (3'). Formally, techniques (a)-(c) may be seen as affecting the information term, I, in (3'), where "more" information is provided by the interviewer (technique b) or by an induced, introspective process in the case of techniques (a) and (c). Thus, these data may be seen as relevant for a special case of (3') given as follows.

$$V(t_o, I_1) = V(t_o, I_2). \qquad (3'')$$

When I reflects introspective adjustments to the explicit budget constraint (a), reported evidence suggests a failure to reject (3''). When I reflects information derived from (a) and (c), however it appears that (3'') is rejected.

Setting aside estimation problems relevant for tests related to (a)-(c)[11] two observations can be made as to how this set of research results relate to assessments of time-related dimensions of the hypothetical bias proposition. First, no objective basis exists for concluding that information effects from (a)-(c) ultimately result in a "true" or accurate measure of value. Secondly, the most that one could attribute to the above-cited results is that *at* t_0 (during the interview), values offered by subjects reflect thoughtful consideration of implied trade-offs—some degree of preference research. But even if this were the case, such evidence would fall well short of speaking to the issue underlying (3′) as it is set out by Bishop and Heberlein (1979), Freeman and others, *viz.*, that *time* per se is required for a meaningfully complete preference research process: values (even with the adjusted information set, I_2) obtained at t_0, $V(t_0,I_1)$, will differ from values obtained at a later period, $V(t_0,I_2)$. This may not always be the case, as is argued by Crocker (1984). In cases where the WTP is an addition to an access fee recently, and actually, paid "much of the environmental and preference information that the respondent had to process in order to arrive at his WTP had therefore already been used by him in his decision to pay the original access fee." (p. 5)

One finds in the literature an abundance of research dealing with learning and "information processing" capacities of individuals which relates only indirectly to the hypothesis of interest here, but which warrents brief mention. Thus, Kunreuther (1976) and others[12] suggest that, within the context of high loss-low probability events, serious questions exist as to people's ability to meaningfully absorb—mentally process—information. Limited information processing capacity—causing people to oversimplify problems—lies at the heart of Simon's (1955) "bounded rationality" thesis and the "anchoring" phenomena observed by, among many others, Miller (1956), Ronan (1973) and by Simon and Newell (1971). An understanding of the way in which information is processed by individuals is seen by Schoemaker (1982) as critical to efforts to predict choice phenomena—an understanding which is far from complete at the present time.

Brief mention of two additional sets of research results concerning information processing is warranted due to their relevance for future efforts to test hypothesis (3) and (3′). In making decisions under conditions of uncertainty, there exists considerable evidence[13] that heuristic devices are used by individuals in forming judgements, prominent among which is the "representativeness heuristic". This heuristic implies extraordinary reliance on current information irregardless of the quality of such information; prior information is given little weight. With the requisite time differentials in tests of hypotheses related to (3′), the representativeness heuristic suggests the potential for severe problems in controlling/measuring the substance of information changes, I_1 to I_2, and effects of such changes, over the interval t_0 to t_1.

Secondly, a number of experimental studies [14] suggest that, under conditions of uncertainty, individuals may partition, or isolate, decision contexts in curious ways. For example, Tversky and Kahneman (1981) have shown that individuals tend to regard the loss of a $20 theater ticket as more relevant than the loss of $20 in cash, a phenomenon suggesting that individuals mentally partition—isolate— groups of events/actions; i.e., individuals seemingly think in terms of 'mental accounts'. If indeed individuals do consider actions/events/commodities in this isolated, partitioned, mental account context[15] we know virtually nothing as to how such partitions are formed—how a mental account is defined. Thus, as examples, one might ask: are mental accounts defined hedonistically (pleasure, pain, aesthetics, etc.), or perhaps functionally (transportation, work, health, etc.)? To the extent that these partitioning contexts are real, potentially serious problems could arise in efforts to test (3′) until more is known as to how individuals structure partitions/accounts for obvious reasons: one would be unsure as to the types of information best given to subjects as relevant for approximate real-life information-gathering/processing processes in the t_0 -t_1 interval.

From the above we must conclude that little evidence exists that would support or negate hypotheses such as (3) and (3′) related to the time-dimensions of the hypothetical bias proposition: the issue remains as an open question. We defer to section entitled Concluding Remarks a discussion as to the implications of this void in data for our assessment of the state of the arts for the CVM.

PERCEPTIONS, FRAMING AND THE CVM

There is still another potential dimension of hypothetical bias which relates to the hypothetical *commodity* "traded" as a part of the CVM. The relevant line of argument in this regard proceeds as follows. Given that, e.g., environmental changes offered as commodities in many applications of the CVM are hypothetical or, more strongly, imaginary (the subject cannot see or touch the commodity nor, in many cases, can he/she draw on past experience for comparisons of consumption-levels of the commodity), CVM measures of value may not be regarded as "accurate" for two, related reasons: different values offered by different subjects may reflect different *perceptions* of the hypothetical commodity rather than, as is supposed in the CVM, different preferences; secondly, judgements/values by subjects are dependent on how the commodity is described (how questions are "framed") and different, in a *non-substantive* sense, descriptions of the commodity will yield different statements of WTP (value). Concern with this potential source of hypothetical bias is seen, for example, in Schulze, d'Arge and Brookshire's (1981c) concern with the need "to establish a precise contingent market—the 'good' (commodity) must be well-defined."[16] Issues related to perceptions and framing are discussed in the following sub-sections.

Perceptions

In terms of the "perceptions" issue one finds in the literature hypotheses concerning how people perceive risky events. It is not clear, however, that the issue is limited in relevance to questions of risk. Consider, as an example, the CVM commodity: for a particular river, a change in water quality from boatable to fishable levels. One can only speculate as to the mental image such a hypothetical change might elicit in the mind of any particular subject: an image of "murky" vs. "clear" water, or an image of a person sitting in a boat, unused fishing rod in hand vs. the angler fighting a hooked trout on a pristine stream? Surely, this image—this *perception* of the CVM commodity (or more precisely, of the *attributes* of the commodity)—would be relevant for any preference-revealing value offered by a subject. All else equal, the attribution of "accuracy" to CVM values would then seemingly require a compelling demonstration of at least four relationships: perceptions of hypothetical environmental changes (or changes in availability of any other public good) are in some sense consonant with *real* effects that would attend the posited environmental change; as something of a corollary to the preceeding issue, subject i's perception of the CVM commodity is in some sense consonant with subject j's perception of the commodity—all subjects are valuing the *same* commodity; related to the topic of the section entitled Hypothetical Biases Related to Time, perceived effects (benefits/costs) of the hypothetical commodity are invariant over time (the absence of "impulse" perceptions); and the independence of perceptions from the quality and quantity of information given to subjects. Thus, as a guide for the discussions that follow, the issues described above are, respectively, described by the following hypotheses.

$$H_0: C(p) = C(a) \tag{4}$$
$$H_0: C(p_i) = C(p_j) \tag{5}$$
$$H_0: C(t_0) = C(t_1) \tag{6}$$
$$H_0: C(p/I_1) = C(p/I_2) \tag{7}$$

where: C = the environmental 'change' used as the CVM commodity.

p, a = perceived and actual, substance of the environmental change, respectively.

t_0, t_1 = the time of the CVM interview and some later time, respectively.

I_1, I_2 = distinct information bundles.

Consider first, the hypothesis given in (4) which, essentially, poses the question: are individual perceptions of the substance of a posited environmental change consonant with—roughly the same as—the substance of effects that would actually attend the change? As an aside, we note that since such "substance" is described to individuals as a part of the CVM, in our discussion of (4) the perceptive reader may be troubled by the persistently obvious interdependence between the four hypothesis (4)-(7) and, particularly, between (4) and (7); these interdependencies will be given explicit treatment in later discussions. In terms of the limited question posed by (4), however, two sets of issues are of primary interest. The first set concerns the term $C(a)$: the *actual* substance/effect of a given environmental change. In some cases it may be technically possible to precisely define (estimate) effects that would attend a posited environmental change; as examples: changes in BOD levels in a river; resulting fish populations (by species) and, perhaps, expected catch-rates; changes in TSP or ozone concentrations and changes in visibility. In many other cases, however, the functional relationship between environmental change and the actual effects of such change are not known.[17] As but a few examples, we know little about household soiling and/or materials damages effects associated with TSP levels[18]; little is understood regarding health effects from air pollution[19] and we cannot specify risk effects of alternative policies related to the regulation of hazardous waste disposal.[20] In these latter instances, the CVM practitioner has no practical anchor for accuracy. He/she must then rely upon individual perceptions of environmental change-related effects, which then introduces issues related to hypothesis (4), which are discussed below.

In the above described cases where $C(a)$ *can* be defined, we find in some (but not in others) studies[21] extensive efforts by the authors to describe the CVM commodity (via photographs, posters, etc.) in ways (seemingly) designed to bring individual perceptions of the commodity, $C(p)$, in consonance with actual effects that would attend the posited environmental change (our $C(a)$ in (4)). We do not find, however, evidence that the authors attempted to test the effectiveness of their efforts in this regard, i.e., the authors do not address hypotheses of the sort typified by (4). Rather, the consonance of $C(a)$ with $C(p)$ is simply asserted, as in the following (relevant editorial questions in parentheses): "The (water quality) ladder's major attribute is that it easily establishes (in the minds of individuals?) linkages between recreation activities and water qualities... it directly introduces the relationship between (the individual's perceptions of?) activities and (the individual's perceptions of?)

different water quality levels." (Desvousges et al. 1983, pp. 4-11) "Bids were solicited for the same *well-defined* public good, visability at the Grand Canyon National Park. Specification of this good—implicitly, $C(a)$ vis-à-vis $C(p)$—*was assured* (emphasis added) by presenting all respondents with the same set of photographs of known visibility levels." (Schulze et al. 1983a, p. 2-2)

In terms of the second major set of issues relevant for assessment of hypothesis (4), assume that $C(a)$ is known and that it can be "adequately" described. We now inquire as to results from experimental/empirical research which directly relate to (4). We find such evidence only in the literature concerning decision-making under conditions of risk and uncertainty. In this regard, Slovic and Tversky (1974) report results from a study wherein subjects were confronted with various paradoxes; after making their choices—reflecting $C(p)$—they were given an authoritative argument *against* their choice—a representation of $C(a)$. Most subjects did *not* change their particular choices. Implications of findings such as this are summarized by Slovic et al. (1980) as follows: "A great deal of research indicates that, once formed, people's beliefs change very slowly, and are extraordinarily persistent in the face of contrary evidence . . . New evidence appears reliable and informative if it is consistent with one's initial belief, whereas contrary evidence is dismissed as unreliable, erroneous or unrepresentative." (p. 189) Thus, *given* an accurate description of $C(a)$ to individuals interviewed in the CVM, substantial evidence suggests, in terms of risky/uncertain events, the rejection of (4); an effort to adopt economic models to reflect such behavior, described as "cognitive dissonance", can be seen in the work by Akerlof and Dickens (1982). We do not find such evidence related to non-risky events; to the extent that the risky-event evidence can be generalized, however, rejection of (4) implies that variations across individuals of CVM values *may* reflect differences in perceptions of the hypothesized commodity. Finally, we note the relevance for the issue as to how individuals perceive $C(a)$ of the literature that suggests that individuals have a "threshhold" of sensitivity.[22] Thus, individuals may be insensitive to CVM commodities that represent 'moderate' environmental changes, and react (in a valuation sense) only to changes involving extremes, for example, eutrophication vs. pristine lake conditions. The result of such behavior is often reflected in *increasing* marginal value functions. Crocker and Forster 1984. "Threshhold" phenomena are seen, for example, in the works of Crocker (1984), Daubert and Young (1981) as well as in Loehman et al. (1979).

Referring now to hypothesis (5), a recurring theme in the discussions above—all subjects perceive the same commodity—was that with or (arguably) without the standard $C(a)$, variations in perceptions across individuals may severely weaken the meaningfulness of CVM measures inasmuch as individual values would be attributable to *different commodities*. In instances where $C(a)$ cannot be estimated, as noted above, the CVM practitioner may be tempted to rely on individual perceptions of the commodity, in which case comparable perceptions of the commodity by all subjects—hypothesis (5)—becomes particularly important. We then inquire as to the nature of available evidence related to hypothesis (5).

Indirect evidence related to (5) is found in the above-cited works by Slovic and others. For example, Slovic et al. (1980) find systematic differences in the perceptions of a given activity between groups of laypeople, groups of experts and between experts and laypeople. (p. 211) We find in one CVM application, however, information which *directly* relates to (5). Cummings et al. (1981) used the CVM to estimate benefits attributable to reduced household soiling which was, in turn, attributable to reductions in TSP concentrations. The researchers were unable to specify a relationship between lower TSP concentrations and reductions in household soiling (C(a) was unknown).[23] Therefore, following a *qualitative* explanation to subjects of the TSP-household soiling relationship, WTP measures were obtained for alternative percentage reductions in TSP concentrations, leaving to individuals the (perceptive) task of translating reductions in TSP concentrations into reductions in household soiling. Prior to the WTP questions, subjects stated the number of hours/week that they spent in household cleaning activities (W). Following the WTP question, subjects were asked how they expected W to be affected by the posited change in TSP concentrations; i.e., for the posited environmental change to which their WTP applied, they were asked their perception of the work savings (WS) that would attend the environmental change. Implicitly, for each individual i in the Cummings et al. (1981) survey, WS(i) may be viewed as a measure of C(p) in (5). WTP measures were regressed against the WS variable and the WS variable was found to be statistically significant—WTP measures offered by individuals varied systematically with individual perceptions of WS: individuals had significantly different perceptions $(C(p_i) \neq C(p_j)$ in (5)) and valued differently perceived WS's differently. Thus, with C(a) known, and particularly with C(a) unknown, available evidence suggests significant differences in individual perceptions of uncertain and, perhaps, unfamiliar commodities.

Hypotheses (6) and (7) involve, in large part, issues discussed above in section C. Therefore, aside from two observations of particular interest to the perception questions at issue here, time-information problems will not be belabored in this section. We should comment, first, on the (perhaps inextricable) interdependencies between (7) and (4) (and, to a lesser extent, (6) and between (7) and (5). Obviously, the provision and 'processing' of information—the substance of hypothesis (7)—is of central importance to empirical tests focused on (4) and/or (5). For example, C(a) is established by giving the subject information. In this regard, questions related to (7) include: what kind and how much information? A second, but related observation concerns the substance of information—"substance" as opposed to how questions are asked (framed), an issue to be discussed below. Referring to "information bias," Randall et al. (1983) consider the argument that "variations in the materials describing contingent markets may influence (WTP responses)." (p. 641) In this regard, they contend that CVM demonstrations that WTP values vary with information/materials may *not* be evidence of any kind of bias. Rather, if alternative materials/information given to subjects are relevant to the choice problem, "information that changes the structure of the market *should* (arguably) change the circumstantial choices made therein." (p. 641) It is not clear exactly what Randall et al. have in mind in referring to information that "changes the structure of the market"; but materials/information describing the CVM commodity is seemingly included. This statement then invites the following interpretation which is relevant for (3') as well as (7'): information that affects—changes—an individual's perceptions of the commodity *should*[24] change the individual's valuation of that commodity. In examining the implications of this interpretation of Randall et al.'s argument, it is understood that this is not necessarily *their* interpretation; while several interpretations are possible, the one which best fits the context of their arguments is examined below in our discussions of framing issues. This interpretation, however "strawman" in nature it might be vis-à-vis Randall et al.'s intended interpretation, is useful, in addressing a potential source for confusion in assessments of hypothetical bias.

If one ties perception to preferences and tastes, the line of logic: "different information *implies* different perceptions, preferences and tastes *implies* different valuations" has clear appeal in its consistency with utility theory. An important distinction arises, however, in using the market analogy to argue that this logic suggests "no bias" in CVM measures. In the market, at any instant in time, market valuations cut across, in some average sense, individuals with heterogeneous information states reflecting, among other things, different experiences/histories with the commodity and differing levels of effort (across differing time-spans) in acquiring/processing information; "new" information can then be expected to affect valuations much more slowly and, as suggested in the following, to have small *relative* effects. In the CVM, however, in the many applications wherein individuals are basically unfamiliar with the environmental commodity, particularly as it is viewed in a market context, the initial—at the interview—set of information is the *same* for all individuals and, plausibly, the variance of individual past experience/history is very small relative to market goods. Thus, changes in information, and particularly changes in time available to process information, can be expected to have valuation impacts not at all analogous to the market. In the case of the CVM, market-like heterogeneity in terms of individual preferences, tastes, experiences, etc., as would be reflected in market prices, can be expected only after considerable variation of I in $(3')$ and (7) as well as with variation in t_1—time with which to process—as each individual chooses—the information.

Framing

The second major set of issues relevant for assessments of potential biases brought about by the fact that the CVM commodity is a hypothetical commodity concerns the argument that values may be affected by the way in which the market context and/or WTP questions are framed—how they are described to the individual. Formally, if D1 and D2 are different, but 'true' or accurate, descriptions *of the same commodity* and V is the CVM value offered for the commodity, then the hypothesis of interest here is given by

$$V(D1) = V(D2) \qquad (8)$$

It is understood, of course, that perceptions affected by D1 and D2 underlie the valuations V. In following descriptions of research results relevant for an assessment of hypothesis (8), we consider this issue as it relates to two, obviously related, settings: first, D1 and D2 reflect alternative decision (market) contexts and, secondly, D1 and D2 are alternative ways of framing the WTP question within the same decision/market context.

Framing Decision (market) Contexts

A large number of studies have been conducted concerning the effects of context—words used in describing decision alternatives—on choices/decision-making (Schoemaker 1982). The focus of a large part of these studies is the extent to which individual behavior, under conditions of uncertainty, is consistent with predictions drawn from expected utility theory. In this specific regard (comparisons with expected utility theory), we simply note Arrow's (1982) conclusion concerning the case being made "for the proposition that an important class of intertemporal markets shows systematic deviations from individual rational behavior." (p. 8) Our present interests are in results from that part of the "decision-making under uncertainty" literature that relates directly to hypothesis (8). Two examples can serve to typify the general nature of experimental results relevant for this issue.

First, Tversky and Kahneman (1981) conduct an experiment wherein subjects are asked to consider two programs, programs A and B, which are designed to mitigate the effects of an outbreak of an unusual Asian disease which is expected to kill 600 people. The consequences of adopting A or B are described in two, effect-equivalent ways:

> A : exactly 200 people will be saved.
> B : 1/3 probability of saving all 600 people,
>   2/3 probability that none of the 600 are saved.
> A': 400 people will die.
> B': 1/3 probability no one will die,
>   2/3 probability all 600 people will die.

For (158) subjects given alternatives A,B, 76% chose program A. For similar subjects (169) given alternatives A',B', 87% chose alternative B'. Thus, individual choices between alternatives were, seemingly, substantively affected by framing the *same* alternatives with the context of lives saved as opposed to the "dying" context.

Similarly, a second study by McNeil et al. (1982) involved comparisons between two therapies for treating certain forms of cancer: surgery and radiotherapy. Different groups of individuals, including a group of physicians, were given one of two sets of information:

(1)   probability of survival with surgery (for 1 and 5 years)
(2)   probability of survival with radiotherapy (for 1 and 5 years)
(1')   probability of dying within 1 and 5 years with surgery
(2')   probability of dying within 1 and 5 years with radiotherapy

Probabilities in 1 (2) were one minus the probability in 1' (2'). 86% of the group of physicians given alternatives 1-2 preferred surgery (alternative 1); only 50% of the physicians given alternatives 1'-2' preferred surgery, however. As in our first example, choices are seen to be affected by differences in dying-survival contexts within which alternatives are framed.

Demonstrations of framing effects on individual choices are not limited to stark contexts involving life or death; such effects are demonstrated for choices involved in gambling and in the purchase of insurance against monetary hazards.[24] We do not, however, find demonstrations of this type of framing phenomena applied to decision settings wherein some sort of risk *per se* is not the central issue. Thus, the extent to which the above-reported results imply a *general* rejection of (8) is simply not clear. We return to this issue at the end of this subsection.

In addition to the above, one finds in the CVM literature results which relate in an interesting way to the framing hypothesis given in (8). In chapter 3's discussion of potential biases related to time and 'preference research' issues, results from one set of CVM experiments were offered as relevant for assessing the extent to which WTP measures derived in the CVM were, in some sense, preference-researched values or, at a minimum, indicative of the non-randomness of CV measures (see, particularly, above sections). This experiment set involved comparisons of CVM measures when the commodity is valued alone with those obtained when the *same* commodity is valued within a context where other public goods are discussed.[25] As discussed earlier (above sections), results from these experiments were only weakly relevant in speaking to hypothesis (3′) wherein *time* in the preference research process was of central importance. These experiments, as well as their results vis-à-vis the preference research hypothesis (3′), can be seen as relevant to our present discussions inasmuch as they demonstrated that values for a commodity, when the commodity was framed/described in isolation—D1 in (8)—*differed* from values *for the same commodity* when the commodity was framed/described within a context that included other public and/or private) commodities—D2 in (8). With this context as a means for testing hypothesis (8), the finding V(D1) = V(D2) is reported for an air quality commodity by Schulze et al. (1983), for a "hazardous waste regulation" commodity by Burness et al. (1983) and for a public facilities (park system) commodity by Majid et al. (1983).

Recall now the earlier-cited assertion in Randall et al. (1983) (in the balance of this argument, simply "Randall") that "information (read: framing) that changes the structure of the market *should* (arguably) change the circumstantial choices made therein." (p. 641) While "framing" in the sense of word/probability substitutions (e.g., probability of death vs. probability of survival) is not easily viewed as a change in the structure of the market, one might, and Randall seemingly does[26] view contextual changes of the "other goods" stripe as effectual changes in the market structure; if this view is defensible, above-described results do *not* directly imply framing-related biases in reported CVM measures: V(D1) "should" be different from V(D2). In terms of decision-making under uncertainty, received theory[27] assumes that all possible choices, states of the world and consequences (vis-à-vis states of the world) of actions are certain and known by individuals.[28] A simple application of this assumption, an extension of the more general assumption of rationality basic to economic theory, would lead us to reject the above interpretation[29] of Randall's "arguable" proposition. Thus, since individuals *know*—are perfectly aware of—the dimensions of *all* "other public goods" (the contextual frame D2) then, *ceteris paribus*, individual choices regarding one specific public good should be unaffected by whether or not (redundant) information regarding other public goods is made available; the reported findings V(D1) ≠ V(D2) must then be "explained" on grounds *other than* changes in market structure—framing bias may be one such ground.

However, there are at least two reasons for questioning the position outlined above and, by implication, for imputing some weight to Randall's argument. First, for decisions involving uncertainty—and decisions elicited in the CVM surely involve uncertainty—the rationality assumption in general, and the assumption of certain, *comprehensive* knowledge of choices, states and consequences in particular, are widely questioned as to their empirical validity, Schoemaker 1982. Indeed, as discussed above, the mental *capacity* of individuals to "process" but a very limited amount of information is suggested by results from a number of empirical studies. As an example, where C and S refer to choices and states, respectively:

> As far as C is concerned, it does not require much ingenuity to think of decision problems in which the essence of the problem is that one does not know what options are available. As far as S is concerned, it is easy to think of examples in which one cannot list all possibilities that may occur (And, of course, knowledge of S implies that no one is ever surprised: is this the case in real life?).[30]

Secondly, appealing to the "familiarity" arguments discussed above, and *accepting* the assumption that individuals are reasonably cognizant of choices in their consumption set, one might argue that the CVM involves, in most applications, what is essentially the introduction of a "new" commodity to the individual's consumption set. Given that the commodity is hypothetical, and recalling earlier discussions of perceptions, new information/materials may alter the "shape" (perceptions) of the new commodity, giving rise to what would indeed by a meaningful "change" in the commodity (*a la* Randall, a change in the structure of the market). In must be noted, however, that this argument may suggest, among other things, that the CVM may produce a decision "climate" rich in its potential for confusion.

To briefly summarize, while a strong case is found for the argument that the framing (wording) of decision contexts can affect individual choices in some settings—settings wherein some form of risk is of primary importance—the implications of this argument for hypothesis (8) as it relates to an assessment of the CVM are not clear. For applications of the CVM to environmental commodities, analogies to the "death-survival" examples are not immediately obvious. Possible analogies *might* be: increased visibilty vs. reduced haze; increased water quality vs. reduced pollution; but these analogies are imperfect at best. While results that might suggest rejection of (8) are weak, research results that might suggest acceptance of (8) are weaker still. Such "evidence" *per se* is non-existent. All that we have are arguments with questionable appeal as to why CVM-study results that suggest *rejection* of (8) might be interpreted differently. Thus, we can say little more than that the case for or against the potential for biases emanating from the framing of market contexts remains as an open empirical question.

Framing the WTP Question

In preceding discussions, our focus on market "structure" or context was, more precisely perhaps, a focus on the framing of the CVM commodity. In the death/survival examples, alternative "choices" are analogous to the alternative "commodities" in the CVM. In those experiments, however, there is nothing analogous, in terms of the framing problem[31] to the hypothetical WTP question posed in the CVM. Thus, while the WTP question—the CVM's counterpart to a market price—is obviously a part of market structure *per se* it is treated separately here inasmuch as evidence available for assessing the framing bias hypothesis (8) as it applies to the hypothetical WTP question is distinct from that relevant for assessing (8) vis-à-vis the hypothetical commodity.

We have made repeated references to the confusion that one encounters in the CVM literature arising, in large part, from imprecise rubrics for sources of potential biases; see, particularly, our earlier (chapter 2) discussion of the many "faces" of the hypothetical bias proposition. In chapter 3, reference was made to concern in CVM studies with biases emanating from (a) the payment vehicle, (b) starting points, and (c) preference research (as addressed via the explicit use of "budget constraints."[32] Given that (a)–(c) directly relate to the question as to how WTP measures are affected by the manner/context in which the WTP question is framed, it may be convenient to view these sources of bias within the rubric of framing bias; convenience aside, results from CVM experiments regarding (a)–(c) are of obvious relevance for our assessment of (8) as it relates to the WTP question.

Given the extensive discussions of CVM studies and experimental results related to (a)–(c) in chapter 3, our present purposes are adequately served by a brief review of those results Schulze 1981, Rowe and Chestnut 1983; regarding (3), we simply note in passing the *potential* relevance of the "unfamiliar commodity" and Randall's "materially-changed market structure" arguments, and the resulting conundrum, for evidence derived from this set of experiments. There have been a number of CVM experiments, which focused on issues (a)–(c). While it is no surprise that unanimity does not exist as to the interpretations of results from these experiments, the following generalizations appear (to the authors) to be reasonable. Referring to (a), tests for "vehicle bias" have focused on the sensitivity of WTP measures to descriptions (framing) of the method of payment: common examples of payment methods used in these studies are higher tax payments, higher utility bills and higher prices for goods and services purchased. Four out of five studies[33] found significant effects on WTP measures attributable to the way in which WTP questions were framed vis-à-vis the payment mechanism; obviously, such evidence suggests rejection of (8). Referring to (b), there appears to be general consensus that WTP questions framed within the context of a "starting point"—an initial value; e.g., "would you be willing to pay $10.00?"—results in biased measures. Since about 1980, CVM researchers have, therefore, followed the lead of Mitchell and Carson (1981) in using "payment cards"—the individual is given a chart on which is written many different values (e.g., from $.50 to $50.00 in increments of $.50) and is asked something liked "referring to this chart, what is the maximum amount that you would be willing to pay?" While demonstrative of the fact that the "starting points" result in framing-type biases, the issue *per se* may now moot given that "starting points" are seemingly no longer used in applications of the CVM. Finally, referring to (c), it would seem that WTP measures are unaffected by whether or not the WTP question is framed within a context where the individual's budget (income, present allocation of income across experditure categories, and expenditure category(s) to be reduced for 'payment' of the offered WTP) is explicitly considered by the individual in offering his/her WTP. One *caveat* is relevant in this regard, however: there exists one demonstration that the manner in which budget information is presented (framed) may affect the WTP response. (Schulze et al. 1983a)

By way of a summary, there is a good deal of evidence that suggests the potential for biases in CVM measures resulting from the framing—description—of commodities and payment mechanisms as well as from distorted perceptions of commodities (as described to individuals). As noted earlier, it may be possible to develop means for including perception issues in economic models from which testable hypotheses are derived;

examples in this regard are seen in the works of Akerlof and Dickens (1982) as well as in Coursey et al. (1983b). On the other hand, framing issues present a different problem. As noted by Schoemaker (1982), objective assessment of this potential is made difficult by the fact that "problem representation is inherently a subjective matter, (therefore) it is subject to only limited normative evaluation. Indeed, there exists no general normative theory as to how problems should be defined, or how language and context should be encoded." (p. 556) Notwithstanding the lack of a normative theory to guide assessments of framing-type biases, general guidelines for framing questions *do* exist, as will be discussed below in the next section. We defer to the section entitled Concluding Remarks, a discussion of the implications of these issues for our state of the arts assessment of the CVM.

ATTITUDES VS. INTENDED BEHAVIOR

Given the hypothetical, "artificial" (Bishop et al. 1983) structure of the CVM, Bishop and Heberlein (1979) have suggested that measures derived by the CVM may reflect individual *attitudes* vis-à-vis (e.g.) an environmental commodity as opposed to intended behavior (a meaningful intention to actually pay the stated WTP). Their proposition, which draws on works by Schuman and Johnson (1976), focuses attention on questions related to the causal chain—attitudes *imply* intended behavior. Thus, at issue are the questions: are attitudes indicative (good predictors) of intended behavior; is intended behavior indicative (a good predictor) of actual behavior?

In one's reading of the attitude-intended behavior controversy as it appears in the psychology literature,[34] one might be tempted to argue that the power of responses to attitudinal questions for predicting intended behavior is of no, or questionable, relevance for the CVM inasmuch as questions posed in the CVM are (or should be) well-framed questions about intended behavior *per se*: questions about attitudes are not asked in the CVM, *ergo*, attitude-behavior issues are not relevant, Q.E.D. This line of argument is implicit to Randall et al.'s (1983) rejection of the relevance of the attitude–behavior issue (also see Rowe and Chestnut 1982). After reviewing the Schuman–Johnson and Ajzen–Fishbein papers, the authors find compelling Randall et al.'s argument as to the questionable relevance of the attitude–behavior issue for the CVM, particularly in light of the comforting assurances by Ajzen and Fishbein that the potential for attitude-related biases can be mitigated by questionnaire designs wherein close consonance is established between actual and hypothetical situations via describing intended behavior in terms of *specific* actions, contexts, targets and time frames. Ajzen and Fishbein 1977, pp. 888–9. Thus, it would seem, the hypothetical question posed to restauranteurs in LaPiere's (1934) seminal work concerning attitudes and behavior "Will you accept members of the Chinese race as guests in your establishment?" elicits an attitude; intended behavior is elicited by posing—framing—the question as, e.g., "Will you receive and serve Chinese guests, Messrs. Lin and Chow (here is their photograph), at table number 12 tomorrow afternoon at 1:15 p.m.?"

The notion that attitudinal questions elicit attitudinal responses and questions as to intended behavior elicit behavioral responses, *regardless* of whether the behavior at issue is hypothetical, may be seen as consistent with results from empirical studies concerning the "preference reversal" phenomenon.[35] When asked (relatively) attitudinal questions regarding preference between bets, subjects made choices inconsistent with predictions for expected utility (EU) theory. When then asked what they would pay to participate in a bet, subjects reversed their decision (reversal of preference), and made choices consistent with EU theory; such reversals were found to occur when payment was real *or* hypothetical (also, see Schoemaker 1982, pp. 553–554). Thus, behavior-based questions elicited ". . . the 'right' answer" (Randall et al. 1983, p. 638) while attitudinal questions did not. An obvious *caveat* applies to this conclusion. The standard for a "right answer" in this context is behavior deduced from EU theory and, as discussed above, the relevance of EU theory in predicting real world decisions is widely challenged.

Thus, in response to Bishop and Heberlein's suggestion that the CVM may elicit attitudinal responses as opposed to willingness-to-pay in the sense of intended behavior, the following observations are relevant. First, purely attitudinal questions may perform poorly as indications of intended behavior. Secondly, some evidence, albeit challengeable evidence, exists which supports the argument that questions *about* intended behavior may yield accurate predictions of behavior. Third, criteria exist (Ajzen and Fishbein) for mitigating attitudinal biases in responses to questions concerning intended behavior; we note, however, the lack of definitive evidence that adherence to Ajzen and Fishbein's criteria will necessarily eliminate attitudinal biases (we also note the lack of guidelines for judging what "adherence" might mean).

We wish to close this section by providing some context for the Ajzen and Fishbein (A–F) criteria for mitigating attitudinal biases. This context is provided via an example of a CVM study wherein A–F criteria were applied in the questionnaire design process. Consider the context of the WTP question used in Desvousges, Smith, and McGivney's (1983) (DSM) earlier described study of water quality (also in this regard, see the study by Crocker, 1984). Following A–F's criteria for specific context, targets, actions and time frames, prior to posing WTP questions, DSM ask individuals earlier, specific instances when the individual has visited specific places along the Mohangahela River for recreational purposes: "your actual use" of recreational areas in the River is established in the individual's mind. The structure of their questions as to *intended behavior* is as follows: (Appendix D, pp. D-7 to D-13)

specific context: "keeping in mind 'your actual use' of recreational areas along the Monongahela River."
Specific action/time frame: "what is the most that you would be willing to pay *each year* (time frame)."
specific action: "pay in higher taxes and prices for products that companies sell."
specific target: "to raise the water quality level in the Monongahela River from x to y."

In the above, it is interesting to note that the device used by DSM to enhance the specificity of actions—higher prices and taxes—introduces the potential for framing biases of the "payment vehicle" type discussed above in V.D.2, a potential seemingly viewed as a blessing by DSM, e.g., "This payment vehicle was selected because it corresponds with how people actually pay for water quality (do subjects know this?), connotes no implicit starting point, and produces a vehicle that will *bias the response downward* (emphasis added), if in any direction, because of public attitudes towards increased taxes and higher prices." (p. 4–16) In conclusion, we note in passing that in DSM's comparisons of CVM values with values derived from the TCM (discussed below in Chapter 6) we will see that above-cited anticipation of underestimations in CVM measures attributable to framing biases are apparently forgotten in their value-comparison analyses.

In this chapter an effort has been made to organize, discuss and assess the many potential sources for bias in CVM measures that derive, in one way or another, from the hypothetical nature of the CVM's commodity, market and "payment". In cases where a set of intuitive arguments lend themselves to more precise representation as one or more statements of hypotheses, general hypotheses are offered as a tool for providing focus to an assessment of the arguments. Major sets of biases related to the hypothetical nature of the CVM and, when appropriate, null hypotheses related to them which were developed in this chapter; these null hypotheses are summarized as follows. In what follows, HB, hypothetical bias, is understood to conote the proposition: "Hypothetical bias (in the CVM measure) may result from the fact that:"

HB.1   *Payment in the CVM is hypothetical.*
V(actual payment) = V(hypothetical payment).

HB.2   *The CVM Commodity is hypothetical;*
HB.2(a)   This is to say that preference research for the unfamiliar, hypothetical commodity takes time.

$V(t_0) = V(t_1)$, and/or

HB.2(b)   This is to say that preference research for the unfamiliar, hypothetical commodity requires information and time to process the information.

$V(t_0, I_1) = V(t_1, I_2)$, and/or

HB.2(c)   This is to say that:

(i)   individual perceptions of the CV commodity will not be consonant with the 'actual' commodity offered, $C(p) = C(a)$, and/or
(ii) given a description of the hypothetical commodity, different individuals will perceive and, therefore, value, different commodities. $C(p_i) = C(p_j)$, and/or
(iii) commodity perceptions, and therefore values, will change with the passage of time and/or the accumulation of information,

HB.3   *Payment and the Commodity are hypothetical.*
HB.3(a)   Therefore, WTP measures will be affected by the context within which the commodity and payment is described, or framed.

$V(D1) = V(D2)$ and/or

HB.3(b) Therefore, the CVM will elicit responses reflecting attitudes rather than intended behavior, and attitudes do not perform well as indicators of intended behavior.

Subsumed in this structure for assessing potential biases in CVM measures attributable to the hypothetical nature of the CVM are sources for bias described in earlier works under the rubrics "vehicle bias," "starting point bias," "information bias" and "hypothetical bias."

Based on our assessments and discussions of research results drawn from the literature as they relate to HB.1–HB.3, three general observations seem apparent in terms of implied tentative conclusions regarding the state of the arts of the CVM; common to all three observations must be the understanding that, as reflected in CVM experiments conducted to date, researchers have only recently begun to address several empirical questions that must be viewed as fundamental to any demonstration which purports to establish, in a compelling way, that the CVM *can* be designed in such a way that meaningful values are derived. First, we observe that the framing questions underlying HB.3 imply the need to rationalize and apply to questionnaire design, criteria (perhaps) of the sort set out by Ajzen and Fishbein for eliciting values which (all else equal) reflect behavioral intentions. Obviously, this will be no mean task; this is particularly true for efforts to rationalize criteria in the sense of establishing standards by which the investigator can empirically test the extent to which the CVM design approximates "actual conditions." Other related fundamental questions which remain unanswered by experimental research are those related to time and (perhaps inextricably) information—HB.2(a), (b), (c.iii). Given, in many applications of the CVM, the lack of congruence between people's experiences and the hypothetical commodity, as well as the hypothetical market context within which the commodity is to be valued by them, one cannot easily dismiss the intuitive appeal of the ("familiarity") argument that information processing, which involves the introspective process of examining—researching—one's preferences, will take different forms—and, therefore, yield different value responses—over different time frames. While certainly challenging, these framing and time/information issues do not, in the authors' minds, pose impossible questions; i.e., implied questions are amenable to statements in the form of testable hypotheses. At this point at least, the relevance of these issues for one's assessment of the the CVM is an indication of ignorance—unanswered questions—as opposed to a definitive indication of unresolvable weaknesses in the CVM.

Secondly, experimental applications of the CVM to date have yet to address in a compelling way the question as to the extent to which individual perceptions of the hypothetical commodity—the item which they are asked to value—are in any sense consonant with the actual commodity offered in the CVM; in this regard, we note occasional confusion in CVM studies as to the "commodity" relevant to the valuation decision[36] and the relevance of framing issues for efforts to empirically address the perceptions issue. At a minimum, this question appears to be amenable to empirical inquiry. Such is *not* the case in instances where actual effects of (e.g.) an environmental change cannot be specified. In such cases, one cannot define a standard against which to assess commodity perceptions by individuals. Therefore, we must conclude that use of the CVM for deriving individual values for such commodities will be an empty exercise given that one cannot distinguish between value differences (among individuals) attributable to different tastes/preferences and those attributable to *different commodities*.

Thirdly and finally, there is reasonably compelling evidence that suggests the possibility of resolving most, if not all, of the above-mentioned issues (as they relate to a large class, but not all, of environmental commodities) by thoughtful design of the CVM—considerable heuristic inquiry remains, of course, for identifying and verifying "appropriate" designs which mitigate or eliminate above-described sources for bias. There remains an issue the substance of which is not related to questions of design, however, *viz.*, the large body of evidence that supports the proposition that choices involving actual payments are substantively and significantly different from choices involving hypothetical payments.[37] Given the relevance of the results from our review of advances made in Experimental Economics (chapter 4) for an assessment of the implications of this issue, we defer further discussions to chapter 6 wherein results from *all* chapters are integrated to the end of offering tentative conclusions as to the state of the arts of the CVM.

NOTES

1. Bishop and Heberlein 1979, p. 927.
2. Bohm 1972, p. 125. Interestingly, when individuals asked hypothetical questions and were then asked for *actual* payment, only 18 out of 54 changed their responses, an outcome interpreted by Bohm as reflecting people's reluctance to "imply a confession that they had lied in the first round." p. 126
3. As examples, T. Feather 1959 and P. Slovic and S.C. Lichtenstein 1968.
4. See, e.g., G.J. Stigler and G.S.. Becker 1977.
5. As examples, see T.C. Schelling 1978; and J.W. Pratt, D. Wise and R. Zeckhauser 1979.
6. Such an approach is seen in expressed efforts "to determine if people will *actually* pay (as measured by a HPM measure) what they will pay (a hypothetical payment measured by the CVM)," in Schulze et al. 1981c, p. 167.
7. See Burness et al. 1983, pp. 680:682 and Schulze et al. July, 1983c, pp. 148-150.
8. Randall et al. 1983, p. 639.
9. *Id*, p. 646.
10. This is an argument made in Schulze et al. July, 1983c, chapter 1; and Burness et al. 1983.
11. See Schulze et al. July, 1983c, section 1.F and Desvousges et al. 1983, Chapter 8.
12. See also Kunreuther with Ralph Ginsberg et al. and Louis Miller 1978. As another example of related results, see L. Robertson 1974.
13. As an example, see D. Kahneman and A. Tversky 1972; A. Tversky and D. Kahneman 1974; S. Lichtenstein and B. Fischhoff 1978; and B. Fischhoff 1980.
14. Kahneman and Tversky 1979, Tversky and Kahneman 1981, and P. Schoemaker 1980.
15. See section 1.C in Schulze et al. 1983c, for a discussion of experimental results suggestive of the mental account notion.
16. See also *ad passim* in Schulze et al. July, 1983a, p. 170; see also an earlier draft dated April, 1981.
17. See, for example, T.D. Crocker and R.G. Cummings 1984. There is yet another functional relationship of potential importance, *viz.,* "the physical production and transformation linkages between public policies and (environmental/recreational) values," S.S. Batie and L. Shabman 1979.
18. R.G. Cummings, H.S. Burness and R.D. Norton 1981.
19. See, e.g., S. Gerking and W.D. Schulze 1981.
20. See Schulze et al. July, 1983.
21. Particularly see Desvousges et al. 1983, and Schulze et al. (July, 1983c, (the Grand Canyon experiment).

22. As examples, see N. Georgescu-Roegen 1958. N.E. Devletoglou, Feb., 1971 and R.D. Luce 1956.

23. We find a second CVM study involving unknown C(a) and reliance on C(p) in Burness et al. 1983, (also reported in Schulze et al. July, 1983). Unfortunately, the authors of this study did not examine the implications of varying C(p)'s on derived WTP.

24. As examples, see P.J.H. Schoemaker, and H.C. Kunreuther 1979, pp. 603-18; J.C. Hershey and P.J.H. Schoemaker, 1980; R.S. Gregory 1982; and R. Thaler 1980.

25. See previously cited works by Schulze et al. July, 1983, and Burness et al. 1983. See also I. Majid, J.A. Sinden and A. Randall 1983.

26. The context for the citation given above is "variations in the materials describing the contingent market."; *Ibid*.

27. See J.D. Hey 1983, and more generally, G. Stigler 1950.

28. "The (only) way that uncertainty enters into the choice problem is when the choice must be made *before* it is known which . . . (post-choice state of the world) . . . will prevail." Hey 1983, p. 131.

29. An interpretation admittedly imputed to Randall's statement by the authors in their best efforts to understand the point argued in the statement.

30. Schoemaker (1982, pp. 545-547); see also K.E. Boulding 1975, p. 84.

31. We note, however, the potential relevance of earlier discussions of hypothetical v. actual payment for the framing of WTP questions.

32. See also the use of "budget constraint" arguments in assessing the time-preference research hypothesis (3') given above.

33. Two of the three studies reviewed in Schulze et al. 1981c, and studies by J.T. Daubert and R.A. Young 1982, and D.A. Greenley, R.G. Walsh and R.A. Young 1981.

34. In example, Schuman and Johnson 1976; and I. Ajzen and M. Fishbein 1977.

35. Grether and Plott 1979, this consistency is noted by Randall et al. 1983. See also Pommerehne, Schneider and Zweifel 1982; and Reilly 1982.

36. For example, Burness et al. 1983, offer an EPA regulation on hazardous waste disposal as a commodity when, it would seem, individuals are valuing their perceptions of changes in risk.

6
Comparison Studies: What is Accuracy?

INTRODUCTION

Thus far, we have examined results from studies involving experiments with the CVM, as well as from the psychology literature and studies from experimental economics, to the end of inquiring as to the extent to which potential sources for biases identified in chapter 2 have been addressed in works accomlished to date. At this point, the litany of potential sources of bias in CVM measures, along with pro-con arguments relevant for eah source presented above, may seem overwhelming; after reading these chapters, the reader may consider the case made for the psychologists' concern with problems associated with "limited capacity for information processing." In any case, one sees in these discussions the fundamental issue which must be faced if we are to meet the challenge of an objective assessment of the CVM; this issue is described by the question: against what criteria is the accuracy of the CVM to be evaluated? It would be inaccurate to say that scholars working with the CVM have ignored the issue of assessment criteria; it *would* be accurate to describe a large part of the efforts to address the issue as imprecise and intuitive. In looking to the CVM literature, the bulk of empirical evidence offered in these regards is seemingly limited to observations concerning the substance of CVM measures of the sort: "this" evidence suggests that it's good, "this" evidence suggests that it's bad. The inability to weight evidence had invited resource to "counting" types of assessments as a means for establishing accuracy in CVM measures. As examples in this regard, "(CVM studies) have generated a 'solid core' of value information which performs well." Randall et al. 1983, p. 640 "More verification of (CVM)... results through repeated application and comparison with actual behavior... is necessary." Rowe and Chestnut 1983, p. 409 "There is no objective, *a priori* manner by which the accuracy of survey measures can be proven (or... disproven...); if successful, however, repeated experiments ... (may redefine) ... economist' reservations ... (about the CVM)." (Schulze et al. 1983c, p. 12)

In considering the question as to appropriate criteria against which to assess the accuracy of measures derived by the CVM, two issues are of primary importance. First, it is useful to recall the rationale for our interest in the method. As discussed in detail in chapter 2, benefit-cost analysis is used, however imperfectly, in assessing optimal levels for a public investment. At a conceptual level, applications of benefit-cost analysis may be viewed as efforts to deduce market outcomes (vis-à-vis the level of public investment) that would obtain *if* such investments were made under market conditions. Given benefits (prices) and costs determined by market institutions, public investments would be provided at levels at which marginal benefits equal marginal costs.

Of course, for most pure public goods—particularly environmental goods—market institutions do not exist. The CVM is then used as a substitute for the "missing" market; it is used to simulate the market in the sense of eliciting revelations of preferences (a willingness to pay) analogous to those which would have resulted under market conditions. Like the market institution, the CVM must then be viewed as an "institution". Thus, the general criterion against which to assess the CVM becomes clear: the extent to which the CVM *institution*, and preference revelations drawn therein aproximates the market institution and values derived therein.

The second issue of primary importance for our discussions concerns the notion of "accuracy" *per se*; i.e., what *is* (wht do we mean by) "accuracy"? Notwithstanding the many *potential* sources of bias in CVM measures identified and discussed in earlier chapters, we must ultimately address the question: how accurate are values obtained from CVM studies? Are these values as accurate as values obtained from other traditional approachs such as the travel cost method (TCM) or the hedonic price method (HPM? Obviously, *if* both the CVM and, for example, the HPM give the same value for the same commodity under the same circumstances and *if* this can be shown to be true when repeated for many environmental commodities, and, if the HPM is viewed as providing accurate measures of value, then this may provide strong evidence vis-à-vis the accuracy of CVM measures. Unfortunately, as we argue below, all of the comparison studies undertaken to date have failed to carefully assess the accuracy either of the CVM used or the accuracy of the HPM (or TCM) used for comparison. This lack of uniform approach for evaluating accuracy across the many individual comparison studies has led to confusion and inconsistency in interpreting the available evidence.

In efforts to address these issues, our discussions proceed as follows. In the next sections we review results from the various studies which compare values derived from the CVM with values derived from alternative methods—primarily the TCM and the HPM. In reviewing these studies, the implications of any study's results vis-à-vis the accuracy issue is considered within the limited context of statistical comparisons or, more often, less formal comparisons offered by the study's authors. We then consider results from comparison studies within a broader context for "accuracy"; as a part of these latter discussions, we consider alternative, related, scientific definitions for the accuracy of measured values. In the section entitled What is Accuracy?, we examine the implications of scientific notions of accuracy, as they are used in weighting the results from comparative studies, for means by which the CVM might be assessed in state-of-the-arts terms. Concluding remarks are offered in the last section.

VALUE COMPARISONS: THE CVM AND THE TCM

Six major studies have been completed wherein primary attention is given to the comparison of non-market values for environmental commodities derived via the CVM with those derived from the travel cost method (TCM). These are from the studies reported by Knetsch and Davis; Bishop and Heberlein;

Desvousges, Smith, and McGivney; Thayer; Seller, Stoll, and Chavas; and Fisher.

Knetsch and Davis

The earliest study comparing value estimates obtained from the CVM with estimates derived from other procedures is reported by Knetsch and Davis (1965). The authors compared three methods of measuring the benefits of recreation in the woods of northern Maine. Using data obtained from an earlier survey by Davis (1963a), they compare willingness-to-pay estimates resulting from an application of the CVM to values related to individuals' "willingness to drive" and to values derived from the TCM.

CVM interviews were conducted in the Pittson Farm area (in northwestern Maine) of 185 hunters, fishers and campers using the area. The respondents were asked if their decision to use the site would change if the cost of doing so increased. Costs were then systematically increased until the respondent switched from "inclusion in" to "exclusion from" the activity. For respondents who thought the original amount excessive, costs were decreased until they switched from "exclusion from" to "inclusion in" the recreation activity. The final amount was used as their maximum willingness-to-pay to participate in recreation activities at the Pittson Farm area. The mean willingness-to-pay was 41.71 per household per day; obtained values ranged from zero to $16.66.

A measure of willingness-to-pay was then estimated by a multiple regression analysis of data derived via the CVM which demonstrated that nearly sixty percent of the variance in bid values could be explained by differences in household incomes, degree of familiarity with the site (Note: perceptions of the "commodity"?) and the average length of each visit. By administering a questionnaire to users stopped at a traffic checking station, estimates of income, length of stay and degree of site familiarity for the user population were obtained. With these two pieces of information, a demand schedule and total recreation benefits were estimated. The demand schedule was derived from ordering the user population by calculated willingness-to-pay, and the benefits were computed from the area under the demand schedule from the highest price to the price considered. Their estimate of maximum benefits (when "price" is zero) to the 10,333 household days of recreation translates to a WTP of $1.71 per household per day.

Knetsch and Davis then develop two additional estimates of willingness-to-pay. The first estimate is based on "willingness to drive" (WTD), a method earlier proposed by Ullman and Volk (1961). Individuals, the *same* individuals interviewed for the CVM, were asked how much further (in miles, beyond the Pittson area) the individual would drive to avail himself/herself of recreation facilities like those in the Pittson area if they were no longer to have access to the Pittson area. The authors assert that "willingness-to-pay was found to increase about five cents per mile as a function of willingness-to-drive additional miles." (Knetsch and Davis 1965, p. 137) A development of this finding is not given in the paper. Using this 5 cents/mile, WTD data are used to estimate benefits attributable to the Pittson recreation area; estimated maximum benefits, the area under the derived demand curve at a zero "price", were $64,000, which compares with $72,000 derived via the CVM.

The second alternative (to the CVM) value derived by Knetsch and Davis was estimated with the TCM. Visitation rates of visitors from groups of counties were plotted against travel distance. The resulting 'visitor days as a function of distance travelled' relationship was then converted into a 'visitor days as a function of costs' via costing distance at 5 cents per mile *for one-way distance*; travel costs for 1,327 respondents (out of a total population of 6,678) for whom Pittson was not the primary destination of their trip were arbitrarily weighted at .5. These TCM procedures yielded an estimate of maximum benefits, as defined above, in the amount of $70,000.

Knetsch and Davis acknowledge the crudeness of approximations derived in their WTD and TCM estimates, a topic which we will not consider here (see Mendelsohn and Brown 1983); of interest here are Knetsch and Davis's value comparisons. Knetsch and Davis do not subject their CVM, WTD, and TCM benefit estimates to statistical analysis in comparing them. Rather, their discussions in these regards focus simply on the demonstrated "closeness" of their results; i.e., upon casual inspection, $72,000 (benefits based on the CVM), $64,000 (benefits based on the WTD method) and $70,000 (benefits based on the TCM) are "close". Given the sharp divergence and disparities in assumptions underlying the three measures, the 12% maximum difference between the measures is indeed remarkable. Little basis exists, however, for interpreting this "closeness" beyond, perhaps, the authors' above-cited observation that such closeness may indicate some promise of the methods as a means for estimating benefits for recreation.

Bishop and Heberlein

The primary purpose of the paper by Bishop and Heberlein (1979) (hereafter, B–H) was to point out the biases that may result from the use of *indirect* and direct measures of values for non-market goods, specifically the TCM and CVM. After discussing several potential sources of bias with the techniques, they undertake an experiment designed to see how serious these biases actually might be.

B–H conducted three surveys of hunters who had received free early season goose hunting permits in 1978. Hunters were divided into three groups. The first sample of 237 received a cash offer in the mail for their permits. The checks ranged from $1 to $200, and the respondents were requested to return either the check or the permits. The second sample of 353 persons received a questionnaire by mail designed to elicit either their hypothetical willingness-to-sell their permit or their hypothetical willingness-to-pay for their permit. The third sample of 300 received a questionnaire designed to elicit factual information necessary to estimate a travel cost demand curve. The authors report a response rate of at least 80% for the three surveys, and report that the results of a comparison of differences in socioeconomic and other characteristics found the three samples to be relatively homogeneous.

Results reported for the B-H study are given in table 6.1. The actual cash offers resulted in a willingness-to-sell figure of $63 per permit. B-H note, however, that this figure may be conservative due to the $200 upper limit on offers; regression results indicated that 10% to 12% of those surveyed would have sold at a higher amount.

The hypothetical willingness-to-sell figure was quite a bit larger: $101 per permit. Here too, the maximum offer of $200 created some difficulty.

Table 6.1   Summary of Results (in 1978$)

Sample group	Total consumer surplus	Surplus per permit
1. Actual cash offers	$ 880,000	$ 63
2. Hypothetical offers		
Willingness to sell	1,411,000	101
Willingness to pay	293,000	21
3. Travel cost estimates		
Model 1 (time value = 0)	159,000	11
Model 2 (time value = 1/4 median income rate)	387,000	28
Model 3 (time value = 1/2 median income rate)	636,000	45

Source: Bishop and Heberlein (1979), p. 929.

Regression results indicated that 35% of the hunters in this group would have (hypothetically) "sold" if the offer were over $200. As a result, B-H assert that "had the models been truncated at a higher figure the difference between willingness-to-sell measured using actual money and measured using hypothetical dollars would have been even more pronounced." (Bishop and Heberlein 1979, p. 924) Their second comparison was between actual willingness-to-sell, hypothetical willingness-to-sell and hypothetical willingness-to-pay. Using the former as a measure of consumer surplus, (CS), they note, citing Willig (1976), that WTS ≥ CS ≥ WTP. However, B-H argue that "for the range of values we are discussing here ($1–$200) . . . willingness-to-pay, and willingness-to-accept-compensation should be quite close together." (p. 929) This however, was not the result obtained by B-H. B-H report a WTP figure of $21 per permit, far below the $63 estimate of consumer surplus. Estimates of WTS and WTP, derived via the CVM, are then compared by B-H with three estimates of travel-costs, differing only in the valuation of time spent traveling. Following Cesario's (1976) suggestion that time be valued at between 1/4 and 1/2 the wage rate, B-H set up three different travel-cost models. The first does not include a value for time; the second model values time at 1/4 of median income and the third at 1/2 of median income.

As table 6.1 demonstrates, even when the time spent traveling is valued at 1/2 of median income, the travel cost estimate of $45 is substantively (29%) below the CVM estimate of $101; both TCM and CVM values differ substantively from the "actual" cash offer ($63). Because of the divergence between the various measures tested, B-H assert that "the results summarized here must be interpreted as supporting the hypothesis that the sources of bias listed above do have significant impacts on (CVM) and (TCM) values for recreation and other extra-market goods." (p. 929)

As in the Knetsch and Davis study, B-H's comparisons of CVM measures with non-hypothetical (actual cash offer) measures and TCM measures is qualitative in nature; their *a priori* expectations for comparisons are that the measures "should be quite close together" (p. 929) and data comparisons are analyzed in terms of percentage differences: "the (TCM) estimate averages only $45.00, 29% below the (actual cash offer) benchmark figure of $63.00." (p. 929) We may then conclude little more than that, while Knetsch and Davis report CVM and TCM measures which are "close", B-H report CVM and TCM measures which are *not* "close".

Desvousges, Smith and McGivney

The study by Desvousges, Smith and McGivney (1983) (hereafter, DSM) is of particular interest for our discussions of comparative values for several reasons. It is a recent study and the authors attempt to deal with many of the measurement/comparison problems encountered in earlier studies. Most importantly, the authors attempt to go beyond qualitative comparisons of CVM and TCM values in forming and testing hypotheses concerning the relationships between such values.

DSM make pairwise comparisons of the results from three different techniques for estimating benefits attributable to water quality improvements. The authors compare user values obtained from both the TCM and CVM, and option prices obtained from both the CVM and contingent ranking approaches. The commodities at issue in this study are water quality changes in the Monongahela River in Pennsylvania. Three different types of water quality changes were considered. The first was a *decline* in water quality resulting in a complete loss of recreational activity in the River. The second and third were *increases* in water quality from boatable to fishable and boatable to swimmable levels, respectively.

The authors surveyed 303 households in a five county region in Southwestern Pennsylvania, near the Monongahela River. Personal interviews were conducted from November through December 1981. As a part of the CVM, respondents had described to them the hypothetical market, the commodity to be valued and the payment vehicle (higher taxes and prices). Respondents were then asked their valuation of the commodity. A water quality ladder was used to help the respondent establish a linkage between an index of water quality and an associated recreation activity. The respondents were divided into four approximately equal sub-groupings. One group was given a payment card with values ranging from $0 to $775 in $25 increments, and were asked to pick any amount on the card, any amount in between the values listed, or any other amount. A second group was asked their valuation directly, without the use of a payment card or suggested starting point. The third and fourth groups were given a "starting point", i.e., they were asked if they would be willing to pay $25 or $125, respectively. After their yes or no response, a bidding process was used until a maximum bid was obtained. Each group of respondents was asked their willingness-to-pay for three water quality changes: to avoid a decrease in water quality to the point where the river could not be used; to raise the water quality level from boating to fishing quality; and to raise the level from boating to swimming quality. Those who gave a positive response to the boatable-fishable increment were asked their additional WTP to go from fishable to swimmable. Only those who gave a zero bid for the boatable-fishable increment were asked the boatable-swimmable question directly. For others, it was derived by adding boat-fish bids to fish-swim bids. After the final value for each of the changes was

Table 6.2 Comparison of Benefit Estimates for Water Quality Improvements (in 1981$)

Methodology	ΔWQ = Loss of use			ΔWQ = Boatable to fishable			ΔWQ = Boatable to swimmable		
	Option price	User value[a]	Option value	Option price	User value[a]	Option value	Option price	User value[a]	Option value
I. Contingent valuation[b]									
Direct question	24.55	6.57 (19.71)	17.98	17.65	7.06 (21.18)	10.59	31.20	13.61 (31.18)	20.80
Payment Card	51.00	6.20 (19.71)	44.82	29.26	9.72 (30.88)	19.54	42.87	15.92 (51.18)	26.76
Iterative bidding ($25)	28.97	2.16 (6.58)	26.81	15.95	1.38 (4.21)	14.57	25.09	3.12 (10.53)	21.64
Iterative bidding ($125)	57.40	12.08 (36.25)	45.31	36.88	6.77 (20.31)	30.10	60.20	13.43 (48.75)	43.96
II. Contingent ranking[c]									
Ordered logit	—	—	—	60.03	—	—	108.06	—	—
Ordered normal	—	—	—	62.12	—	—	111.81	—	—
III. Generalized travel cost[d]	—	82.65	—	—	7.01	—	—	14.71	—

[a] The numbers in parentheses below the estimated user values report average values for users only. Since nonusers have a zero user value, the combined mean understates user values.
[b] These estimates are for the combined sample, including users and nonusers. It excludes protest bids and outliers detected using the Belsley, Kuh, and Welsch regression diagnostics.
[c] These estimates are for the sample of respondents with usable ranks and reported family income. Estimates evaluated at the intermediate payment level.
[d] These estimates are for survey respondents using Monongahela sites and have been converted to 1981 dollars using the consumer price index.
Source: Desvousges, Smith and McGivney (1983), pp. 8–13.

obtained, the respondents were asked how much of this value was attributable to their actual use of the river, a "user value", and how much was attributable to their desire to maintain options for future uses, i.e., their "option value".

Finally, the survey respondents were asked to undertake a contingent ranking of options. They were shown four cards, on each of which was a water quality ladder with an annual payment amount of either $5, $50, $100, or $175 paired to no recreation, boatable, fishable, or swimmable recreation water quality levels, respectively. Respondents were asked to rank the combinations from most to least preferred. An ordered logit and an ordered normal procedure (see Rae 1983) were used to estimate willingness-to-pay from the contingent ranking results.

DSM also used a generalized travel cost model to estimate recreation benefits. The model was developed from data drawn from 43 water-based recreation areas surveyed in the 1977 National Outdoor Recreation survey. The TCM data provided information on time spent at a given site, number of visits to the site, travel time to the site, and respondents' annual income. To measure travel cost, the distance to a given site was obtained from a Rand McNally Road Atlas. The marginal cost of driving to the site was assumed to be $0.08 per mile. Thus, travel costs were derived by multiplying the length of the trip (round trip miles) by mileage costs at $.08 per mile. Since hourly wages were not available in their data set, DSM used a semi-log hedonic wage model to estimate hourly wages for each individual in the sample. The mean estimated wage rate of $5.44 per hour was used as the opportunity cost of travel time, and onsite time. Of course, this method differs from the approach used by Bishop and Heberlein (1979) who, as noted above, valued travel time (only) from zero to 1/2 the wage rate.

The results of DSM's estimations of contingent valuation, contingent ranking and travel cost measures of water quality values are shown in table 6.2 for each of the proposed water quality changes. Referring to table 6.2, for increases in water quality from boatable to swimmable levels, the option prices obtained by the CVM range from about $25 to $60, depending on the valuation format used. Similarly, user values range from about $10.50 to $51.00 (users only, see footnote a). The Contingent Ranking Method (CRM) is used for estimating option prices only. Depending upon the statistical estimation technique used, the option price for the third category of water quality change was either $108 (ordered logit method) or $112 (ordered normal method). Similarly, the travel cost method yields but one value, the user value, which is about $15.00 for improvements from boatable to swimmable water quality.

Our interest is in DSM's analysis concerning value comparisons. In this regard, DSM compare the CVM with the TCM, and the CVM with the CRM. These comparisons involved two tests: a simple comparison of sample means, and a statistical comparison of individual values. In terms of CVM-TCM comparisons, the first test, a simple (i.e., non-statistical) comparison of means tested the hypothesis that the CVM bid would be less than the TC measure for water quality improvements, with the difference being slight, about 5%. Thus, they test H_o: CVM = .95TC. For water quality improvements, CVM is greater than TC, except for the $25 format, where CVM .95TC. (See Table 6.2). In the case of a loss in water quality, CVM is less than TC, as expected, but *much less* than .95TC; the TC estimate is more than two times *larger* than the CVM measure. The authors argue that this large disparity was likely the result of failure to consider the effect of substitute sites as an argument in the demand function for a particular site, resulting in an overestimation of the TC measure of ordinary consumer surplus for loss in water quality. In spite of this, the authors express some surprise at the difference in magnitudes and directions of differences between TC and CVM estimates.

But these were not statistical tests. Furthermore, the relevant comparison, they argue, is against *individual* benefit measures. To make these comparisons, they regress the CVM measure of user value on the TC measure, using dummy variables for three of the bid elicitation methods. In this respect, they test three hypotheses. If, as theory predicts, the CVM measure is only slighty smaller then the TC estimate, then the intercept of the OLS equation should not be different from zero. Equally important, if the two methods result in comparable values, then the coefficient on the TC measure should not be different from unity. If the valuation method used in the CVM survey has no influence on the resulting bid, then the coefficients on these variables should not be different from zero.

The results of these tests are shown in table 6.3. As in their "simple" tests, the relationship between CVM and TCM values differs in the quality-loss case from that in the quality-improvement cases. In the case of a *loss* in water quality, their test results seem somewhat ambiguous. The test fails to reject the hypothesis of zero intercept, suggesting that the CVM and TC measures are similar. But the test for unitary slope (see footnote b in table 6.3) rejects the hypothesis, suggesting that, given the magnitude of the coefficient on TC, CVM measures are much less than TC measures of user values. The reason for the disparity, they argue, seems to lie in the overstated TC estimates (mentioned above). "Based on the association between estimates across individuals, there is support for the conclusion that the travel cost model overstates the benefits associated with avoiding the loss of the area." (Desvousges, Smith, and McGivney 1983, p. 8–17) Thus the statistical test results seem to support the conclusion of the "simple" test.

In both cases involving water quality *improvements* their test results are clearer. Both the null hypothesis of zero intercept and unitary slope (see footnote b, in table 6.3), are rejected at the 10% level. Since both tests agree, the results strongly indicate no association between the TC and CVM estimates. The authors, however, caution against so strong an interpretation of the results, because "the generalized TC model does not permit the effect of the intercept to be distinguished from at least one of the questioning formats. In the models reported in table 6.3, the intercept reflects the effects of the iterative bidding format with a $125 starting point." (p. 8–17) They also note that "there is some (ambiguous) evidence to support the conclusion that contingent valuation method may overstate willingness-to-pay for water quality improvements." (p. 8-17) DMS's conclusions do not effectively speak to the ambiguities that arise from the stark differences in CVM-TCM relationships seen in the quality-loss and quality-improvement contexts. These differences invite speculation as to the relevance of "threshhold" effects (Crocker 1984) for their analysis, particularly in light of the positive relationship between CVM and TCM measures in the quality-loss case and *negative* relationships between the two measures indicated in the quality-improvements cases.

In terms of comparing CVM measures with those derived via the Contingent Ranking (CR) method, both methods undertake to measure compensating surplus, thus the null hypothesis tested is that CVM = CR. As table 6.2 reveals, however, the CR approach results in values that seem consistently higher than

Table 6.3   A Comparison of Contingent Valuation and Generalized Travel Cost Benefit Estimates

Independent variable	ΔWQ = Loss of area		ΔWQ = Boatable to fishable		ΔWQ = Boatable to swimmable	
	Model	Test[a]	Model	Test[a]	Model	Test[a]
Independent variable						
Intercept	21.862 (1.371)	—	33.985 (1.900)	—	59.574 (2.017)	—
Travel cost benefit estimate	.328 (1.169)	-4.357	-3.670 (-1.204)	-1.712	-2.713 (-1.141)	-1.793
Qualitative variables						
Payment care	-32.640 (-2.551)	—	51.757 (2.639)	—	77.010 (2.359)	—
Direct question	-14.602 (-2.549)	—	12.957 (-0.595)	—	21.001 (-0.693)	—
Iterative bid ($25)	-31.817 (-2.549)	—	-11.244 (-0.595)	—	-21.819 (-0.693)	—
R^2	.099		.120		.107	
n	93		93		93	
F	2.42 (0.05)[b]		3.00 (0.02)[b]		2.62 (0.04)[b]	

[a] This column reports the r-ratio for the hypothesis that the coefficient for the travel cost variable was 1.55. The contingent valuation experiments were conducted in 1981. Using the consumer price index to adjust the travel cost benefit estimates to 1981 collars would require multiplying each estimate by 1.55. Since the estimated regression coefficients (and standard errors) will correspondingly adjust to reflect this scale change, a test of the null hypothesis that the coefficient of travel cost was equal to unity is equivalent to a test that is equal to 1.55 when the travel cost benefit estimates are measured in 1977 dollars and user values estimates (the dependent variable) are in 1981 dollars.

[b] This number in parentheses below the reported F-statistic is the level of significance for rejection of the null hypothesis of no association between the dependent and independent variables.

Note: The numbers in parentheses below the estimated coefficients are t ratios for the null hypothesis of no association.

Source: Desvousges, Smith and McGivney (1983), pp. 8–16.

CVM values for water quality improvements. To test the statistical significance of these differences, DSM regress the CVM measure of option price on the CR measure, again using dummy variables for three of the bid elicitation modes, for *improvements* in water quality—CR measures were not obtained for the water quality-loss case. Since the CR value depends upon the payment level suggested by the cards presented to the respondent, regressions were run for each of three different payment levels; $50, $100, and $175. The results are shown in table 6.4. As noted above, two econometric estimating techniques were used, ordered logit and ordered normal. The three statistical hypotheses for these regressions are the same as noted above. In this case, however, neither the hypothesis of zero intercept nor of unitary slope (Test Column) can be rejected at the 90% level. This results in the failure to reject the hypothesis that CVM = CR: thus, the contingent valuation and ranking techniques move in the same direction across individuals, with the CR estimates not significantly different from the CVM estimates. The authors warn, however, that despite the fact that both methods attempt to measure option price, since the *same* survey asked for CVM and CR estimates, the strong relationship between them may simply reflect the respondent's efforts to appear consistent.

In summary, DSM's value comparisons between the CVM and TCM and between the CVM and CRM yield interesting, but somewhat ambiguous results. The authors find CVM measures to overstate WTP for *improvements* in water quality as compared to values measured by the TCM. Curiously, however, they argue that these differences "are not substantial and fall within the range of variation of the contingent valuation estimates across the question formats." (p. 8-2l) In spite of the ambiguity of the test results, the authors argue that, for *losses* in water quality, the CVM measure is found to be roughly consonant with the TC measure. The authors do find unambiguous close agreement between the CVM and CR measures of WTP.

Seller, Stoll and Chavas

One of the more recent study comparing travel cost and contingent survey methods is by Seller, Stoll and Chavas (1983) (hereafter, SSC). The authors compare a regional TCM with two forms of the CVM: an open-ended questionnaire format (similar to DSM's direct question approach) and a close-ended format (multiple starting points). Since the authors assert that the reference level of utility is nonparticipation in the activity, an equivalent measure of willingness-to- pay is derived.

The interviews were conducted with past and present users of one of four lakes in Eastern Texas: Lakes Conroe, Livingston, Somerville, and Houston. The authors used a mail questionnaire to gather the travel cost and contingent valuation data. The questionnaires were mailed to 2000 registered boat owners in the 23-county area surrounding the four lakes, identified as the major origin of most users.

The TCM involved estimating a system of demand equations,

$$V_{ij} = \alpha_j + \sum_{k=1}^{4} \beta_{jk} C_{ik} + \delta_j Y_i + \gamma_j Z_i = \epsilon_{ij} \quad (1)$$

Table 6.4   A Comparison of Contingent Valuation and Contingent Ranking Benefit Estimates

| | ΔWQ = Boatable to fishable | | | | | |
| | Payment = $50 | | Payment = $100 | | Payment = $175 | |
Independent variable	Model	Test	Model	Test	Model	Test
ORDERED LOCIT						
Intercept	−20.141	—	−23.647	—	−23.927	—
	(−1.095)		(−1.223)		(−1.227)	
Δ Payment	1.209	0.741	1.315	1.016	1.330	1.048
	(4.279)		(4.237)		(4.214)	
Qualitative variables						
Payment card[a]	−22.486	—	−22.070	—	−21.960	—
	(−2.424)		(−2.380)		(−2.367)	
Direct question	−35.267	—	−34.595	—	−34.425	—
	(−3.751)		(−3.683)		(−3.665)	
Iterative bidding	−38.045	—	−37.562	—	−37.446	—
($25)	(−4.067)		(−4.015)		(−4.001)	
R^2	.165		.164		.163	
n	184		184		184	
F	8.87		8.77		8.72	
	(0.0001)		(0.0001)		(0.0001)	
ORDERED NORMAL						
Intercept	−13.467	—	−15.565	—	−15.832	—
	(−0.839)		(−0.940)		(−0.951)	
Δ Payment	1.073	0.309	1.140	0.554	1.151	0.592
	(4 .554)		(4.528)		(4.516	
Qualitative variables						
Payment card	−22.642	—	−22.357	—	−22.286	—
	(−2.457)		(−2.426)		(−2.418)	
Direct question	−34.934	—	−34.458	—	−34.344	—
	(−3.745)		(−3.696)		(−3.683)	
Iterative bidding	−37.541	—	−37.196	—	−37.116	—
($25)	(−4.014)		(−4.004)		(−3.994)	
R^2	.176		.175		.174	
n	184[b]		184[b]		184[b]	
F	9.53		9.47		9.43	
	(0.0001)[b]		(0.0001)		(0.0001)	

[a] These estimates are for the combined sample, including users and nonusers. It excludes protest bids and outliers detected using the Kuh-Welsch regression diagnostics.
[b] These estimates are for the sample of respondents with usable ranks and reported family income.
Source: Desvousges, Smith and McGivney (1983), pp. 8–19.

ΔWQ = Boatable to swimmable

Payment = $50		Payment = $100		Payment = $175	
Model	Test	Model	Test	Model	Test
−25.661	—	−30.734	—	−31.032	—
(−0.795)		(−0.905)		(−0.906)	
1.081	0.293	1.170	0.561	1.183	0.594
(3.925)		(3.867)		(3.841)	
−46.842	—	−46.145	—	−45.961	—
(−2.877)		(−2.834)		(−2.822)	
−55.3427	—	−54.215	—	−53.935	—
(−3.353)		(−3.288)		(−3.270)	
−68.611	—	−67.817	—	−67.626	—
(−4.178)		(−4.128)		(−4.115)	
.153		.151		.150	
184		184		184	
8.06		7.94		7.88	
(0.0001)		(0.0001)		(0.0001)	
−15.153	—	−18.212	—	−18.559	—
−0.537)		(−0.626)		(−0.634)	
.962	−0.165	1.018	0.073	1.028	0.113
(4.182)		(4.146)		4.131)	
−47.108	—	−46.630	—	−46.510	—
(−2.910)		(−2.880)		(−2.872)	
−54.808	—	−54.020	—	−53.832	—
(−3.345)		(−3.298)		(−3.286)	
−67.808	—	−67.242	—	−67.112	—
(−4.156)		(−4.120)		(−4.111)	
.162		.160		.160	
184[b]		184[b]		184[b]	
8.63		8.54		8.51	
(0.0001)		(0.0001)		(0.0001)	

where
V_{ij} = the number of visits to the jth site (j = 1...4) by the ith household,
C_{ik} = costs incurred by household i while at and traveling to site k (k = 1...4).
Y_i = income of household i
Z_i = demographic variables,
$\alpha_j, \beta_j, \delta_j, \gamma_j$ = parameters to be estimated, and
$_{ij}$ = error term.

Costs were measured as gasoline expenses only, with the value of travel time set at zero, using the equation

$C_{ik} = (2d_{ik}/mpg_i \times 1.10) + E_{ik} + (gas_{ik} \times 1.10) + fees_{ik}$ 'U where
d_{ik} = one-way distance for household i traveling to site k,
mpg_i = average miles per gallon on household i's vehicle,
1.10 = average cost of gasoline (1980 dollars per gallon),
E_{ik} = other variable costs incurred by household i traveling to site k,
gas_{ik} = number of gallons of gasoline used by the pleasure boat,
$fees_{ik}$ = user and/or entrance fees.
Specifying *a priori* a linear system of equations, benefits from each site were measured using the TCM as

$$M = \int_{C_j}^{C_j} V(C_j \dots)\, dC_j, \tag{2}$$

where
M = Marshallian consumer surplus
dCD_jU = change in travel costs, with C_j the vertical intercept on V.

Of the 2000 questionnaires mailed out, 731 were used to gather travel cost data. The four demand curves generated from the data using equation 1, holding Y and Z constant, are shown in table 6.5. The authors do not report standard errors or t-statistics associated with the coefficients. The average (Marshallian) consumer surplus associated with each site was calculated as the area under V above the current expenditure level at the mean number of visits for each lake. The results are shown in column 3 of table 6.5. As is apparent by the results, willingness-to-pay for recreation at the Lake Livingston greatly exceeds that for the other three areas combined.

Table 6.5   Results of the TCM

Area	Demand equation[a]	Average consumer surplus
Lake Conroe	$V_1 = 14.46 - 0.23C_1$	$32.06
Lake Livingston	$V_2 = 10.04 - 0.12C_2$	$102.09
Lake Somerville	$V_3 = 8.63 - 0.13C_3$	$24.42
Lake Houston	$V_4 = 3.28 - 0.04C_4$	$13.07

[a] V_j = number of visits at site j (j = 1...4), and C_j = cost of visiting site j.

The CVM used two different bid elicitation approaches. One was an "open-ended" approach wherein the respondent specifies the initial value of the bid, a direct question approach similar to that used by Desvousges, Smith, and McGivney. The other was a "close-ended" approach wherein the respondent is given an "estimate" of the cost and asked to respond "yes" or "no" to the willingness to pay question.

Respondents to both forms of the survey were asked their willingness-to- pay an annual fee for a boat ramp permit. Two questions were asked in the open-ended format:

(1) How high could costs go to keep you using this site just as often?
(2) How high could costs go if you were restricted to using this site half as often?

Answers to these questions were used as two points on a Bradford-type bid curve for each individual. The bid curve is specified as

WTP = F(Q,Y)
where
WTP = the Hicksian equivalent measure of willingness to pay,
Q = the number of visits to the site (annually), and
Y = the respondents' income.

Of the 2000 questionnaires sent out, 275 using the open-ended format were used. The bid curve was estimated from this data using three different functional forms: linear, linear with a squared term in Q, and double logarithmic. The authors differentiated the log form of the bid curve to find the inverse Hicksian demand curve. Since the reference level of utility is nonparticipation in the recreation activity, the area under the Hicksian demand curve at the mean number of visits is the equivalent measure of consumer surplus. The demand curves and surplus measures are shown in table 6.6.

Table 6.6   Results of the Open-Ended CVM

Area[a]	Demand equations	Surplus	
		Gross	Net[b]
Lake Conroe	$dWTP/dV = 1.79V^{-.75}$	$9.06	-$8.65
Lake Livingston	$dWTP/dV = 1.52V^{-.80}$	$8.87	$1.09
Lake Houston	$dWTP/dV = 1.22V^{-.70}$	$3.81	-$2.28

[a] The results of the demand relationship for Lake Somerville were considered by the authors to be unreliable because the demand curve was not downward sloping and lay in the fourth quadrant. Hence no results for Sommerville were reported.
[b] Net surplus values were obtained by subtracting average launch fee expenditures from gross surplus.

Reflecting on the negative values for the surplus measures at Lakes Conroe and Houston, the authors conclude:

The negative values ... seem to indicate that people reported they were willing to pay less for an annual ramp permit than they already paid in total launch fees over the year on a per visit basis. (p. 23)

They argue that the negative and low results indicate that the open-ended questionnaire technique may be unrealiable.

For the close-ended format, respondents were asked to respond "yes" or "no" to the following question:

> If the annual boat ramp permit cost $X in 1980, would you have purchased the permit so that you could have continued to use the lake throughout the year? [p. 15]

Ten values for $X were used, ranging from $5 to $300. The authors use a binary response model (because the answers are binary—yes or no) to analyze the results. Assuming a logistical cummulative distribution function, a logit procedure (using maximum likelihood estimation) was used to estimate the probability that the respondent will answer "no" to a given value of X.

Varying the number of annual visits rom 1 to 30, a Brandford-type curve was derived from each of the lakes. Of the surveys mailed out using the close-ended format, 211 were used. Differentiating the bid curves produced a Hicksian demand curve for each lake. Finally, the area under each demand curve at the mean number of visists to each lake is the gross measure of willingness-to-pay. The results are shown in table 6.7.

Table 6.7   Results of the Close-Ended CVM

Area[a]	Gross surplus	Net surplus[b]
Lake Conroe	$53.94	$39.38
Lake Livingston	$42.40	$35.21
Lake Houston	$36.34	$31.81

[a] The results from Lake Somerville fail to produce negatively sloped demand curves, hence were considered unreliable.
[b] Net surplus values were obtained by subtracting average launch fees from gross surplus.

The authors compare the results of the TCM with both CVM formats, with two *caveats* in mind. First, the TCM produces a Marshallian measure of consumer surplus, while the CVM produces a Hicksian measure of equivalent variation. However, since the authors report a small income effect they note that the difference should be small. Second, they note that the TCM produces results for boating only. Thus, they assert that this may cause a small divergence in the two measures. The hypothesis tested in the comparison is that the CVM value will exceed the TCM value: CVM > TCM (Although they state the difference to be small, the authors do not specify how small, only "comparable").

Confidence intervals are establishd at the 95% level to test for similarity in the bids. The results of the tests are reported in table 6.8. For the open-ended questions, the null hypothesis of "comparable" means was rejected at each of the sites. As is clear in Table 6.8, the open-ended questions consistently produce smaller (in some cases negative) estimates of average consumer surplus. For the close-ended questions the null hypothesis is not rejected, the mean bids derived from the TCM and CVM are statistically equal.

Table 6.8   Logit Analysis of the Close-Ended Form of the Contingent Valuation Method

Lake	Estimated Coefficients (t Statistics)			$\rho 2^a$	N	Percent of correct forecasts
	Intercept (1nα)	Suggested price	Number of visits			
Conroe	-6.13^b	1.79^b	$-.16$	.39	70	87
	(-2.88)	(3.53)	$(-.47)$			
Livingston	-3.06^c	1.37^b	$-.67^c$	.39	74	85
	(-1.86)	(2.92)	(-1.75)			
Somerville	-4.78^b	1.26^b	$.88$	.40	47	87
	(-2.48)	(2.92)	(1.54)			
Houston	-2.32	$.99$	$-.47$	.31	15	80
	$(-.88)$	(1.75)	$(-.84)$			

[a] ρ^2 = goodness-of-fit (analogous to R^2).
[b] Significant at the .01 level of confidence.
[c] Significant at the .05 level of confidence.

In summary, one comment is in order. SSC attempt to determine the accuracy of the reported bids by relying on respondents' assessment of the accuracy of their stated bid. Survey participants were asked if they felt their stated willingness-to-pay to be "quite accurate," "accurate in a ball park kind of way," or "there is no way I could come up with accurate answers." They report that the majority (63.4%) of the respondents to the close-ended questions felt their bids were "quite accurate," while the (41%) of the respondents to the open-ended questionnaire felt they could only give "ball park" accurate responses. In addition, they report that the portion of "inaccurate" responses was higher for the open-ended format (24.8%) than for the close-ended format (9.2%). However, it seems fair to say that one can not, in fact, conclude that the close-ended question format produces results which are more reliable than alternative formats. In addition, a one-shot response to a single yes-no question gives much less information than someone's open-ended direct response; e.g., even if a response of $75 is fairly inaccurate, it probably tells us more than if the respondent said "yes" to the question "would you be willing to pay $10?" Slovic, et al. (1980) as well as Kahneman and Tversky (1974) report that individuals are *consistently* observed to overstate the degree to which their responses to questions involving some uncertainty are accurate. (See chapter 5 for a discussion of this issue.)

Thayer

Thayer's (1981) study involves the comparison of values derived via the CVM with values derived from a variant of the TCM, as the TCM is generally structured. Thayer compares CVM values with values derived from a 'site substitution' method (SSM) which, as will be shown, is reminiscent of Knetsch & Davis' "willingness to drive" method.

Thayer's concern is in comparing CVM values with values from the SSM as well as in testing methods for dealing with starting point, hypothetical and information biases—biases which are discussed above in chapter 3. Thayer conducted a survey in the Jemez Mountains of northern New Mexico. Recreators in the area were asked their willingness to pay an entrance fee to prevent the development of a geothermal power plant in the Jemez Mountains. They were also queried as to contingent site substitution plans should the plant ultimately be constructed.

Respondents were shown photographs of geothermal developments in other wilderness sites, and a map of the area where the Jemez plant would be built. In addition, the increased noise level and odors associated with geothermal power plants were described in detail. A bidding procedure was then initiated, following closely the methods used in Randall et al. (1974).

Thayer attempted to control for starting point bias by separating the respondents into two groups. For the first group, bids began at $1 and were increased in whole dollar increments until the respondent would pay no more, whereupon the amount was decreased in quarter dollar decrements until a 'no more' response was given. For the second group, the bidding process was reversed, bids began at $10, were decreased in dollar amounts, then increased in quarter amounts. A comparison of the mean bids from the first group with the second group showed the bids to be not significantly different at the 10% level.

The final test was for hypothetical bias. It was in this regard that Thayer compared results from the CVM with those from the SSM. His hypothesis was that cost of traveling to a substitute recreational area represented a minimum loss in consumer's welfare from development in the Jemez. Thus, site substitution costs should represent at least the minimum they would be willing to pay to prevent development of the geothermal power plant. If the site substitution measures are similar to derived CVM values, he argues, then CVM values are not influenced by the hypothetical nature of CVM.

Due to data limitations, Thayer was unable to perform a comparison-of-means test. Thus, as in most earlier studies, his value comparisons are qualitative in nature. Thayer observes that the range of values for additional SS travel costs—from $1.85 to $2.59—brackets the mean willingness-to-pay estimate from the CVM of $2.54 per household per day. (See table 6.9)

Table 6.9   Bidding Game and Site Substitution Results (in 1976$)

	Bidding game	Site substitution	
Group Bid	Bid	@$0.04–$0.20	@$0.05–$0.07
Daytrippers	2.56 (2.86)	1.28–6.39	1.60–2.23
Campers	2.48 (1.54)	2.01–10.05	2.51–3.52
Population	2.54 (2.53)	1.48–7.40	1.85–2.59

Note: Standard deviations are in parentheses.
Source: Thayer (1981), p. 43 (1980$).

Based on this observation, Thayer draws two conclusions. First, that "the site substitution method, used as a cross check against bidding game (CVM) results, indicates that the survey approach gives reasonable estimates of consumer's welfare loss" Thayer 1981, p. 43 and, still more strongly, that "These results indicate that the (CVM) . . . can provide *accurate* (emphasis added) estimates of . . . 127 welfare losses associated with environmental degradation." (p. 44) Secondly, and still more strongly, Thayer suggests his results "dispel the argument that inaccurate responses are introduced by the hypothetical nature of the (CVM)." (p. 43)

Fisher

Fishers' (1984) paper differs from earlier-reviewed works in that his TCM-CVM comparisons are based on primary research conducted by other researchers. His TCM values are taken from Miller and Hays' (1984) study of consumer surplus values associated with freshwater "fishing days" in five states. CVM values are taken from a study by Loomis (1983) wherein mean estimates of willingness-to-pay (per day) for trout fishing in eleven Western States are estimated. TCM-CVM comparisons can then be made for two states—Arizona and Idaho—included in each of the two studies, if we assume that values for "trout fishing" will not differ significantly from values attributable to the more general activity "freshwater fishing".

Relevant values reported by Fisher (1984, pp. 28 and 30) are as follows:

State	(Intra State Mean)	Trout Fishing Days
Arizona	$35.00	$19.54
Idaho	27.00	12.93

Drawing on, and agreeing with, arguments by Brookshire et al. (1982), Fisher argues that CVM values may usefully approximate TCM values notwithstanding "large" differences such as those seen above: "in comparing the estimates of Loomis with those of Miller and Hay . . . the TCM and CVM day values are definitely close enough to each other that either—or both—can serve as a valuable guide to resource managers." (p. 29) Related to the "order of magnitude" issue that will be discussed later in this Chapter, Fisher suggests that "if . . . information is accurate to within a factor of say, two or three, it is probably much better in most cases than no information at all." (p. 26)

VALUE COMPARISONS: THE CVM AND THE HPM

The second set of value comparison studies to be considered focuses on comparisons of values derived by the CVM with those derived from the Hedonic Price Method (hereafter, HPM). The HPM, introduced by Rosen (1974), involves, in operational terms, the identification of "attributes" associated with a market commodity and the decomposition of the commodity's market price into values attributable to each of the commodity's attributes. In applications of the HPM, the commodity's market price is generally regressed against attributes in efforts to assign values to attributes. Applications of the HPM have been prominent in the literature concerning the value of safety (e.g., Thaler and Rosen 1975).

There have been three completed studies wherein values for a public good were estimated via the CVM and the HPM. These are the studies by Brookshire, Thayer Schulze, and d'Arge; by Cummings, Schulze, Gerking and Brookshire; and by Brookshire, Thayer, Tschirhart and Schulze.

Brookshire et al.

In the recent study by Brookshire, Thayer, Schulze, and d'Arge (1982) (hereafter BTSd), the public good to be valued via the CVM and HPM was air quality in the Los Angeles metropolitan area. The authors' objective was to use this study "to validate the survey approach by direct comparison to a hedonic property value study." (p. 165) BTSd develop a theoretical argument for the existence of a rent gradient, which is a mapping onto pollution-commodity space of the differences in housing costs associated with air pollution. They show that the rent differential (dR) can be compared to willingness-to-pay (WTP), and in fact, should serve as an upper bound for WTP values. They also assert that because of the response of the people of California to pollution problems in general, WTP should exceed zero. From this argument, the authors develop and test two hypotheses. The first is that the average WTP for an improvement in air quality over a given community must not be greater than the average rent differential across that community, i.e., $dR > WTP$. Second, that average WTP must be strictly positive, i.e., $WTP > 0$.

In order to test these hypotheses, BTSd collected data on air pollution in several communities in Los Angeles. They divided the region into three areas, identifying communities as having poor, fair, or good air quality. A number of independent variables were used to characterize the hedonic rent gradient equation, but they may be characterized by four groups: housing structure variables, neighborhood variables, accessibility variables, and air pollution variables. Due to collinearity between the air pollution measures, two separate log-linear equations were generated, one using nitrogen dioxide (NO) as one of the explanatory variables, and the other using total suspended particulates (TSP).

It should be made clear that the rent gradient—the change (differential) in property values attributable to changes (differential) in air quality—is the measure to be estimated with the HPM. Thus, BSTd wish to regress housing values against the four groups of variables described above which include air pollution variables; the object, of course, is to identify that part of property value differentials which may be attributed to the site-specific property attribute: air quality. Necessary data for estimating rent gradients were obtained from records concerning 634 home sales during the period January 1977 to March 1978 for nine communities. After estimating the rent gradient, the authors then calculated the rent differential (dR) for each house in each census tract. The average rent differentials are shown in column 2 of table 6.10 for the hedonic equation using NO as the pollution variable. The results show monthly rent differentials ranging from $15.44 to $73.78 for air quality improvement from poor to fair, with a sample mean of $45.92. For improvement from fair to good air quality, rent differentials range from $33.17 to $128.46, with a sample mean of $59.09.

For the CVM application, personal interviews of a random sample of 290 households were conducted during March, 1978. In three of the communities,

Table 6.10 Tests of Hypotheses from the BTS d Study

Community	Property Value Results[a]		Survey Results		Tests of Hypothesis	
	$\overline{\Delta R}$ (standard deviation)	Number of observations	$\overline{W}$ (standard deviation)	Number of observations	t-Statistics $\mu_{\overline{W}} > 0$[b]	t-Statistics $\mu_{\overline{\Delta R}} > \mu_{\overline{W}}$
(1)	(2)	(3)	(4)	(5)	(6)	(7)
Poor–Fair						
El Monte	15.44 (2.88)	22	11.10 (13.13)	20	3.78	1.51
Montebello	30.62 (7.26)	49	11.42 (15.15)	19	3.28	7.07
LaCanada	73.78 (48.25)	51	22.06 (33.24)	17	2.74	4.10
Sample population	45.92 (36.69)	122	14.54 (21.93)	56	4.96	5.54
Fair–Good						
Canoga Park	33.17 (3.88)	22	16.08 (15.46)	34	6.07	5.07
Huntington Beach	47.26 (10.66)	44	24.34 (25.46)	38	5.92	5.47
Irvine	48.22 (8.90)	196	22.37 (19.13)	27	6.08	5.08
Culver City	54.44 (16.09)	64	28.18 (34.17)	30	5.42	11.85
Encino	128.46 (51.95)	45	16.51 (13.38)	37	7.51	12.75
Newport Beach	77.02 (41.25)	22	5.55 (6.83)	20	3.63	7.65
Sample population	59.09 (34.28)	393	20.31 (23.0)	186	12.02	14.00

[a] Rent differentials for the hedonic housing equation in which log (NO_2) is the relevant pollution variable are presented here.

[b] The hypotheses to be tested were H_0: $\mu_{\overline{W}} = 0$; H_1: $\mu_{\overline{W}} > 0$. All test statistics indicate rejection of the null hypothesis at the 1 percent significance level.

[c] The hypotheses to be tested were H_0: $\mu_{\overline{\Delta R}} > \mu_{\overline{W}}$; H_1: $\mu_{\overline{\Delta R}} < \mu_{\overline{W}}$. All test statistics indicate that the null hypothesis could not be rejected even at the 10 percent level.

Source: Brookshire et al. (1982), p. 175.

respondents were asked how much they would be willing to pay to improve air quality in their area from poor to fair. In six of the communities, respondents were asked how much they would be willing to pay to improve air quality from fair to good. Respondents were shown maps with isopleths of pollution levels in their area and photographs indicating the visual ranges in poor, fair and good air quality regions. BTSd report that the respondents had little trouble understanding the commodity they were considering. Results of the survey are given in column 4 of table 6.10. Average monthly willingness to pay (W) for improvement to fair air quality ranges from $11.10 to $22.06, with a sample mean of $14.54. For improvement from fair to good air quality, (W) ranges from $5.55 to $28.18, with a sample mean of $20.31.

Finally, the authors test the two hypothesis noted above. As shown in column 6 of Table 6.10, the calculated t-statistics for the null hypothesis that W = 0, indicate rejection at the 1 percent level in every community. Thus, BTSd conclude that W > 0. In column 7 of Table 6.10, reported t-statistics indicate a failure to reject the null hypothesis that dR > W, at the 10% level. Thus, the *a priori* hypothesis 0 < W < dR developed by BTSd is found to be supported by empirical evidence, a conclusion interpreted by BTSd as "providing evidence towards the validity of survey methods as a means of determining the value of public goods." (p. 176)

Cummings et al.

Cummings, Schulze, Gerking and Brookshire (1983) (hereafter CSGB) compare values derived via the CVM with HPM values reported in an earlier paper (Cummings, Schulze, and Mehr 1978) as they apply to a non-environmental public good: municipal infrastructure in western boomtowns. The authors begin with a discussion of the rationale for using the elasticity measure, (e), the elasticity of substitution of wages for municipal infrastructure. The hedonic wage equation used in the Cummings, Schulze, and Mehr (1978) paper is then reviewed. The hedonic elasticity measure (e) was based on 209 observations from 26 towns in the Rocky Mountain region. The regression equation resulting from the pooled cross-sectional and time-series was:

$$\ln W = 8.43 + 0.183 \ln D - 0.035 \ln k \quad (0.022) \quad (0.017)$$
where
    W = the wage level
    D = the distance from a community to the nearest SMSA
    k = the level of a per capita municipal infrastructure
    Standard deviations are shown in parenthesis. Thus, the coefficient on lnk is the measure of the elasticity of substitution of wages for infrastructure:
    $e_1 = -0.035$.[3]

For the CVM application, a total of 486 residents of Farmington and Grants, New Mexico, and Sheridan, Wyoming[4], were interviewed. The respondents were first informed of the current level of municipal infrastructure in their area, and the monetary value of the capital facilities. The respondents were then asked how they would reallocate the services provided by their city. Given this reallocation of capital, each respondent was then asked his or her willingness-to-pay for a 10% increase in the city's capital stock, to be allocated in the manner preferred by the respondent. A bidding game was then played until the

Table 6.11   Elasticity Measures

Hedonic study		Survey					
		Grants		Farmington		Sheridan	
e_1	n	e_2	n	e_2	n	e_2	n
−0.035	209	0.037	115	0.040	278	0.042	93
(0.017)		(0.031)		(0.058)		(0.078)	

Note: Numbers in parentheses are standard deviations; n = sample size.
Source: Cummings et al. (1983), pp. 4-6.

respondent's maximum WTP was reached. This WTP value, denoted dW, along with an individual's current annual salary (W), was used to calculate:

$$e_{2h} = \frac{\partial W/W}{\%\Delta k} , h + 1, z \ldots, 486,$$

where $\%\Delta k$ is the 10% increase in capital stock. Finally, an average elasticity measure (e_2) was calculated for the individuals in each sample. The results are shown in table 6.11.

Following a procedure suggested by Scheffe (1970) for comparing a regression coefficient to a sample mean, the authors find the calculated t-statistics to be 0.057, 0.083, and 0.088 for Grants, Farmington, and Sheridan respectively. Against a null hypothesis of equality between e_1 and e_2 (for each of the three towns), the authors report that such low values indicate that one fails to reject the null hypothesis $e_1 = e_2$ at any level of significance. Thus, they conclude that no statistically significant difference between the two measures exits. From this, the authors offer two conclusions. First, their results support the results reported in Brookshire, Schulze, Thayer, and d'Arge (1982) in demonstrating "that both hedonic and survey approaches yield comparable estimates for the value of selected public goods." (Cummings et al. 1983, p. 12) Second, the authors suggest that:

> While interesting, these results do not 'prove' the accuracy of survey measures for public good values; . . . survey and hedonic values may be biased vis-à-vis 'true' social values for public goods. There is simply no objective, a priori manner by which the accuracy of survey measures can be 'proven' (or, thus far, disproven ...); if successful, however, repeated experiments of the type reported above may go far in redefining some of the economists' reservations concerning the use of survey methods for valuing public goods. [p. 12]

Brookshire et al. (1984)

In a recent study by Brookshire, Thayer, Tschirhart and Schulze (hereafter BTTS) an expected utility model of self insurance that incorporates a hedonic price function is presented and applied to low-probability, high-loss earthquake hazards. While the central focus of the paper is the establishment of a hedonic price gradient for earthquake safety in the Los Angeles and San Francisco areas and a test of the expected utility model, a CVM study was also conducted in Los Angeles which provides a basis for a comparison of results. The public good of value essentially stems from the Alquist-Priolo Special Studies Zones Act passed by the California legislature in 1972 and amended in 1974, 1975, and 1976. Special Studies Zones are designated areas of relatively elevated earthquake risk as indicated by geologic studies that have identified surface rupture since the Holocene period (approximately 11,000 years ago). Existence of faults, through these geologic studies, may be directly observable through the distortion of physical features such as fences, streets, etc., as well inferred from geomorphic shapes. The total number of SSZ's designated in California as of January 1979 was 251. Of interest is the potential for the Alquist-Priolo Special Studies Zones Act to create a market for avoidance of earthquake risk where no such market existed prior to the passage of the Act. Two elements of the legislation's potential lead to the existence of such a market. First, when an SSZ is designated, property owners are notified thus alerting them to an elevation in risk relative to surrounding areas. Second, the process of selling property located in an SSZ requires notification of prospective buyers that in fact the property is located in an area subject to relatively greater earthquake risk.

The impact of the Alquist-Priolo Act through the disclosure requirements form the basis of a testable hypothesis via the HPM. The null hypothesis is that consumers respond to the awareness of hazards associated with SSZ's as illustrated in sales price differentials for homes in and out of an SSZ. The alternative hypothesis being that they do not.

The procedure, data sources and variable structures utilized in estimating the rent gradient for the HPM are those followed in the air pollution study described earlier. (Brookshire et al. 1982) Specific to the earthquake safety attribute, a dummy variable which takes on the value 1 for homes in an SSZ and zero otherwise is used in the hedonic equation. Separate equations using housing data for 1972, a period before the Alquist-Priolo Act was passed, and data for 1978, a period after the Act was passed, were estimated. The dummy variable was insignificant in the 1972 equation and significant and of a negative sign in the 1978 equation, indicating that a significant safety variable was in fact a result of the successful enhancement of consumers' awareness of earthquake risk.

In the CVM study, homeowners in and out of SSZ's were asked willingness-to-pay (WTP) and willingness-to-accept (WTA) questions related to the potential transfer of homeownership. Homeowners located in SSZ's were asked how much more they would pay to purchase the same home outside of an SSZ. Homeowners located outside SSZ's were asked how much less expensive their houses would have to be for them to be willing to relocate in an SSZ.

Utilizing a non-linear specification of the HPM, Los Angeles County results indicate that if all other variables in the specification (e.g., housing attributes, etc.) are assigned their mean values, then living outside of an SSZ causes an increase in home value of approximately $4,650 over an identical home located in an SSZ. The CVM results—the amount that subjects would be willing to pay to purchase the same house outside of an SSZ—indicates that only 26% of the subjects would be willing to pay some positive amount to move outside of the SSZ. An average of all CVM responses, including zero bids, was $5,920 which is close to the average sale price differential of $4,650. Homeowners outside an SSZ, when asked how much less expensive their house would have to be to move, responded on average with a value of $28,250.

The results indicate that the WTP measure stemming from the CVM study are quite similar to the HPM. However, the asymmetry between WTA and the WTP is quite striking. The WTP versus WTA dilemma aside, the results suggest a consistent comparison of the HPM and CVM results as applied to earthquake risks.

WHAT IS ACCURACY?

Before interpreting the results from comparison studies reviewed above, several comments are in order. Notwithstanding the "closeness" of comparative values observed by Knetsch and Davis, the above demonstrated notion that CVM-TCM value comparisons generally raise more questions than they resolve, in terms of contributing to assessments of the CVM, should not be surprising. This follows from the myriad of problems with the TCM *per se* as a method for estimating values for non-market goods. These problems include (according to Mendelsohn and Brown 1983; McConnell and Bockstael 1983, 1984; and Hueth and Strong 1984) value-allocation assumptions related to multi-purpose "visits"; dependence of costs on assumptions concerning fixed/variable direct travel costs, costs (benefits?) of time spent in travel and on-site; and problems involved in obtaining values which are appropriately "marginal" vis-à-vis the site/activity in question. The latter, "marginal" issue may be best treated by Thayer's site substitution approach (Knetsch and Davis "willingness to drive" approach). These problems result in the dispelling of what was once regarded as the TCM's greatest potential strength: appealing to the notion that visitor values must equal or exceed travel costs (otherwise, the visit would not be made, see Knetsch and Davis 1965, pp. 138-140), the TCM must establish a *lower bound* on "true" values. While, conceptually, this may be true for simple out-of-pocket travel costs, results from empirical efforts to measure total travel costs seemingly belie this posited "strength" of the TCM. As demonstrated above, the relationship between TCM values and values derived from the CVM (or any other method) depends, simply, on what is assumed. Thus, Knetsch and Davis find TCM ($70,000) ≃ CVM ($72,000) assuming *one-way* travel costs valued at 5 cents/-mile; the value of time is not addressed. Bishop and Heberlein find TCM ($28.00-plus) > CVM ($21.00) with time valued at one-quarter or more of wage rates. Desvousges, Smith and McGivney (not surprisingly, perhaps, in light of the above), find the TCM value in excess of CVM for deteriorations in water quality and, more remarkably, TCM values *less than* CVM values for water quality improvements with time valued at full, estimated market rates. Finally, Thayer, abstracting from 'time' issues, finds TCM ($1.28-6.39) less or greater than CVM ($2.48-2.56), depending on one's estimates for out-of-pocket travel costs.

All else equal, the HPM might be expected to result in value estimates which more closely approximate market values, thereby offering an appealing standard against which CVM values might be compared. Notwithstanding estimation problems in implementing the HPM—problems which weaken the "presumption of validity" often accorded methods based on "real" transactions (Randall et al. 1983, p. 636)—some bases exist for viewing HPM measures, competently estimated, as minimally providing "qualitative, order of magni-tude", estimates of value. The adjectives "qualitative, order of magnitude" may describe casual observations as to wage/quality of life trade-offs implied for example, by migrations of workers to Alaska during the construction of the Alaskan pipe-line: some part (hedonic price) of the high reported wages required to attract workers for that project was surely attributable (broadly defined) to environmental amenities. More formally, the results of Ridkers' (1967) seminal work provide compelling empirical evidence of income-environmental trade-offs accepted by individuals: income reductions (hedonic prices) *are* accepted (paid) by individuals for quality of life amenities, including environmental amenities.

Estimation problems abound in efforts to implement the HPM—to name but two: persistent collinearity between "important" variables and extraordinarily low explanatory power in regression equations. (Brookshire et al. 1984) One can only speculate as to the position of estimated HPM values in the range of deviations around a "true" value for any non-market commodity. In this light, the authors reject as inordinately, and unsupportedly, strong Brookshire et al.'s (1982) interpretation of results from their comparisons of HPM and CVM values as providing evidence related to the *validity* (presumably, "accuracy" vis-à-vis "true" values) of the CVM as a means for valuing public goods.

One cannot deny, however, the provocativeness of value comparison results reviewed in the above section. Given the *differing* methodological weaknesses which we understand *a priori* to be peculiar to each method, the compatability of HPM and CVM measures demonstrated in the four experiments reported in these works is remarkable—admittedly, it may also be puzzling. Of course, this observation is reminiscent of Randall et al.'s (1983) comment: "Given the relatively weak incentives for careful decision-making in contingent markets . . . the relatively strong performance of (the CVM) is perhaps surprising." (Randall et al. 1983, p. 641)

While interesting, surprising, provocative or remarkable, the issue remains as to what one might *conclude* from the above-reported HPM-CVM value comparisons. Of course, conclusions in this regard require some standard as to accuracy. Thus, our purpose in this section is to reconsider the comparison studies discussed above within a context wherein we first attempt to assess in broad terms the accuracy of each technique. We follow the traditional definition of scientific accuracy which results in statements such as "the measurement is accurate to within ± x percent of the measured value". Such a definition of accuracy is essential because estimates of accuracy which economists have implicitly employed, such as the standard error of a regression coefficient in a hedonic equation, do not reflect the many possible sources of inaccuracy such as improper choice of functional form, simultaneous equation bias, or inappropriate assumptions on the distribution of the disturbance term, etc. The only way to incorporate a broader estimate of the total possible range of error is to catalogue the documented range of deviation in measured values for a particular technique. For example, Leamer, in an article aptly entitled "Let's Take the Con Out of Econometrics" (1983), argues that the only way to assess the true accuracy of econometric estimates is to perform sensitivity analysis over such factors as choice of functional form. Summing up demonstrated possible sources of error as a percent of estimated values then allows determination of an economic equivalent of "reference accuracy".

Reference accuracy is defined as the "limit that errors will not exceed when the device is used under reference operating conditions." (Van Nostrand 1970, p. 18) Thus, in scientific applications the "device" is a measuring instrument such as a scale used for obtaining weight, whereas in economics the "device" would be an estimation method such as the CVM, TCM, or HPM. "Reference operating conditions" (ROCs), in scientific applications refer to limits on the relevant circumstances under which the measurement is taken such as temperature, atmospheric pressure, etc. In economic applications such as the CVM, limits also exist. For example, in using the CVM, to maintain the hypothetical nature of the survey and avoid strategic bias, the technique possibly should not be employed for current political issues where individuals perceive their answers will influence immediate outcomes. (Rowe and Chestnut 1983)

We will further specify reference operating conditions for the CVM below, but note that, based on discussions given above in chapters 3 and 4, the technique must use willingness-to-pay as opposed to willingness-to-accept measures of value and should not be applied to commodities with which people have little or no experience in making prior choices or which involve a high degree of uncertainty.

A second aspect of scientific accuracy, significant digits, should be noted since it is often a point of irritation when non-economists, especially natural scientists, examine benefit estimates produced by economists. An example will make the point clear. An economist might report that the average bid in an application of the CVM was $11.41. the natural scientist will respond that reporting the result in this way is inappropriate since four significant digits are used, which does not reflect the accuracy of the measurement method. In this regard, the standard deviation reported with the average bid is not relevant for assessing accuracy, since a large value can result solely from different individuals having different values (tastes) for the same public good and since a highly biased average bid may have a small standard deviation. Four alternative ways of reporting the example average bid used above and the *implied* accuracy of each are as follows:

Number of Significant Digits	Average Bid	Implied Accuracy
4	$11.41	±$ .005
3	$11.4	±$ .05
2	$11	±$ .50
1	$1 × 10^1$	±$5.00

Note that the implied accuracy is one half of the value of the last reported digit. (Kreyszig 1979, p. 758) Economic value estimates are almost always reported as though they have at least three significant digits. We will argue below that they, in fact, have a level of accuracy which implies no more than one significant digit, i.e., an accuracy no better than about +50 percent of the measured value.

A third view of the accuracy of scientific measurements relates to the "order of magnitude" of the estimate. For example, a scientist may argue that the amount of CO gas dissolved in the earth's oceans (an important quantity in estimating the likelihood that burning fossil fuels will alter the earth's climate through the greenhouse effect) is only known to within one order of magnitude. What this would imply for estimating the accuracy of economic measures is shown on the vertical scale in figure 6.1, which is logarithmic in that each unit of distance on the scale, moving from bottom to top, implies a tenfold increase in magnitude. Based on discussions given above, a willingness-to-pay bid of $10 obtained using

Figure 6.1
Order of Magnitude Estimates

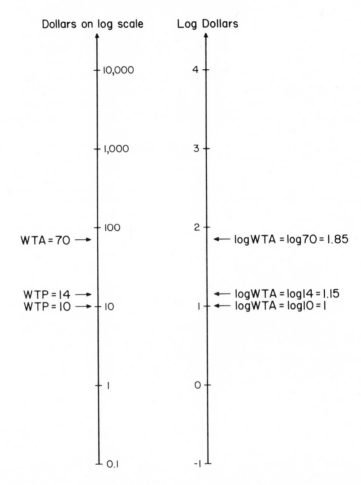

the CVM payment card might be raised by 40% to $14 by applying iterative bidding. A corresponding willingness-to-accept bid may be as much as five times greater than the WTP measure, or $70.00. The arrows in figure 6.1 illustrate these example bids along the logarithmic scale. Note how the $10 and $14 bids are relatively close, "of the same order of magnitude", while the $70 bid is close to the $100 level on this scale, an order of magnitude larger than the previous two bids. Thus, one might argue that the iterative and non-iterative willingness-to-pay bids are "close," of the same order of magnitude, while hypothetical willingness-to-pay and hypothetical willingness-to-accept measures are not "close" and may differ by about one order of magnitude. Physical scientists and health scientists often argue that "order of magnitude" estimates are the best that can be made for complex environmental processes which may be relevant for many benefit-cost studies. As a result, economists may be in a *relatively* comfortable position if they can avoid errors as large as one order of magnitude such as implied by the difference between hypothetical willingness-to-pay and willingness-to-accept measures of value.

The range of possible error for the CVM derived from selected sources of bias is seen in Rowe et al. (1980b). Rowe et al. state that in examining the effects of starting point, vehicle, information, and strategic bias, as reported in several studies reviewed by them, only strategic bias did *not* seem to have a significant affect on bids. They conclude that the sum of starting point, vehicle and information bias can be as large as 40 percent of the estimated value. One additional source of bias is relevant. Schulze et al. (1981b) show that use of a payment card to record bids, results in bids as much as 40 percent lower than obtained with the use of iterative bidding. Even though, based on the experimental evidence of chapter 4, we reject outright hypothetical willingness-to-accept measures of value, the sum of the demonstrated possible biases is about 64 percent. In other words, an upper bound bid of $10 could be reduced to $6.00 by the sum of the effects of starting point, vehicle and information bias and further reduced to $3.60 by choice of a payment card for collecting bids. Averaging $10.00 and $3.60 gives an example midpoint bid of $6.80. If we report this bid, $6.80 as having an accuracy of ± 50 percent, the implied range would be $10.20 to $3.40, very close to the range implied by known potential biases in the CVM. Thus, one might tentatively conclude that, given the current state of the arts, the CVM is not likely to be *more* accurate than ± 50 percent of the measured value.

How accurate are the HPM and the TCM? Unfortunately, detailed estimates of the possible sources for and magnitudes of errors associated with these techniques are not available. Even though HPM and TCM (indirect market) techniques are regarded by some as yielding accurate, market-analogous values, a large number of theoretical and econometric issues are relevant to their use in estimating values for public goods. For example, a possible identification problem which may arise in the use of indirect market methods for value estimation has been analyzed by Brown and Rosen (1982). As noted above, a special problem exists with respect to assumptions made concerning the value of time spent in travel when willingness-to-pay estimates are derived using the TCM (see for example, Cesario 1976; Mendelsohn and Brown 1983). All of these problems suggest that estimating willingness-to-pay values for environmental commodities via indirect market methods may well involve sources for errors that exceed, in substance and number, those relevant for estimates of ordinary demand equations for market goods. However, we can show that even estimation of ordinary demand equations is subject to surprisingly large errors. Since no systematic study has been done of the possible errors in indirect market methods, we will assume that the errors in these methods are at least as large as those which can be shown to exist for estimates of market demand.

Coursey and Nyquist (1983) apply a number of estimation techniques which allow for alternative assumptions about residual distributions of errors (including least squares, least absolute errors, Huber, Cauchy, exponential power and student's t) in estimating demand equations for six market commodities in three different countries. Thus, 18 separate demand equations were estimated using six different procedures. Strong evidence was found that the assumption of normality on the disturbance term was generally violated and that the use of robust alternatives to "normality" assumptions was appropriate. Further, estimates of the intercept, income elasticity and own-price elasticities in each case were highly sensitive to choice of estimation technique. Changes in estimated intercepts from the use of different techniques varied from 5 to 747 percent and exceeded 50 percent in 8 of the 18 demand equations. Changes in estimated income elasticities across techniques varied from 3 to 851 percent and exceeded 50 percent in 5 of the 18 demand equations. Finally, changes in estimated price elasticities ranged from 14 to 183 percent across techniques with a change greater than 50 percent in 12 of the 18 demand equations.

A few calculations will show that even if initial price and quantity are equal, variations in estimated price elasticity like those commonly found in the Coursey and Nyquist study will result in variations in estimated willingness-to-pay which are greater than ± 50 percent. For example, for the United States, the estimated price elasticity of demand for clothing varies from about -.05 to -1. For a 20 percent increase in quantity, the ratio of upper to lower bound estimates of willingness-to-pay is then about 3.2 assuming that the price elasticities are constant. A 3 to 1 ratio is, of course, consistent with an error range of ± 50 percent. It would be most useful if we had information as to the sensitivity of measures estimated by indirect market methods to the use of alternative functional forms and alternative included variables as well as the relevance of simultaneous equation bias and alternative assumptions on the disturbance term. However the potentially large errors in estimating the parameters of ordinary demand equations, discussed above, would seem to suggest that the accuracy of values estimated with indirect market methods is likely to be no better than ± 50 percent.

If errors in the CVM and the two indirect market methods, HPM and TCM, are likely to limit accuracy to *no better* than ± 50 percent of measured values, what are the implications of the comparison studies? If, for example, the measured value for a particular commodity using the CVM IS $10.00 and the same commodity, under the same circumstances is valued at $28.00 using the TCM, are the two measures different? Many of the authors of the comparison studies would argue that these measures are not only different but, that since the TCM is based on actual as opposed to hypothetical behavior, it must be the correct value. In contrast, one might argue that, based on the analysis of accuracy presented above, these two example values are not distinguishably different since the CVM value has a range of at least $5–$15 and the TCM value has a range of at least $14–$42 and these two ranges overlap.

Table 6.12 presents a summary of results from the comparison studies reviewed earlier in this chapter. Some of these studies offer a range of values for the valuation methods employed based on calculated variances, standard errors, etc.; however, in none of the studies does one find considerations relevant for the "reference accuracy" of measures associated with their estimation techniques. The most striking aspect of data in table 6.12 is that of the 15 comparisons given for the 7 studies, none of the comparison studies show a significant difference between values drawn from alternative techniques using our criterion for accuracy. In other words, if reference accuracy is expressed in terms of ± 50 percent, ranges for reference accuracy for the CVM and indirect market methods overlap in 13 of the 15 cases (excluded are Desvousges, et al. 1983 and Brookshire et al. 1982). This finding of a lack of a significant difference between CVM and indirect market values extends to Brookshire et al.'s case (a)

Table 6.12 Summary of Results from Comparison Studies

	CVM Results		Indirect Market Study	
Study	Commodity	Value[a]	Method	Value[a]
Knetsch and Davis (1966)	Recreation days	$1.71 per household/day	TCM	$1.66 per household/day
Bishop and Heberlein (1979)	Hunting permits	$21.00 per permit	TCM value of time=0 value of time=¼ median income value of time=½ median income	$11.00 $28.00 $45.00
Desvousges, Smith and McGivney (1983)	Water quality improvements: a) loss of use b) boatable to fishable c) boatable to swimmable	User values:[b] average (across question format)[b] $21.41 $12.26 $29.64	TCM	User values: $82.65 $ 7.01 $14.71
Seller, Stoll and Chavas (1984)	Boat permit to: Lake Conroe Lake Livingston Lake Houston	Close-ended consumer surplus: $39.38 $35.21 $13.01	TCM	Consumer surplus: $32.06 $102.09 $13.81
Thayer (1981)	Recreation site	Population value per household per day: $2.54	Site substitution	Population value per household per day: $2.04
Brookshire, et al. (1982)ₐ	Air quality improvements: a) poor to fair b) fair to good	Monthly value[c] $14.54 $20.31	HPM (property values)	Monthly value: $45.92 $59.09
Cummings, et al. (1983)	Municipal infrastructure in: a) Grants, N.M. b) Farmington, N.M. c) Sheridan, WY.	Elasticity of substitution of wages for infrastructure −0.037 −0.040 −0.042	HPM (wages)	Elasticity of substitution of wages for infrastructure; 29 municipalities: −0.035
Brookshire, et al. (1985)	Natural hazards (earthquakes) information	$47 per month	HPM (property values	$37 per month

[a] Mean values among respondents.
[b] Values apply to post-iteration bids for users of the recreation sites.
[c] Values for sample population.

if reference accuracy is stated in terms of ± 52%, and to Desvousges et al.'s case (a) when reference accuracy is expressed in terms of ± 60%. Thus, in the 50-60% range—surely a palatable range given the +50% range of error attributed to estimates of ordinary demand relationships—CVM values are consistently "accurate" estimations for values derived with indirect market methods.

The reader may easily draw an incorrect conclusion at this point. This result does not establish the accuracy of CVM measures for *any* particular commodity. Rather, it simply appears that values derived from the CVM fall within the range of "reference accuracy" (given the admittedly large error bounds developed above) for those commodities where indirect market measures can be obtained. *Assuming* that, within the range of +50%, value estimates derived from indirect market methods include "true" valuations by individuals, these results suggest that CVM values may yield "accurate" estimates of value in cases where individuals have had some opportunity to make actual previous choices over that commodity in a market framework. These studies do not demonstrate that people are capable of providing market like values using the CVM for commodities which are *not* already being traded in existing markets, at least to a limited or indirect degree. In this latter regard, examples include such "commodities" as existence and option values for preserving an environmental asset over which people have no experience in making prior choices. We will examine this argument in greater detail below.

IMPLICATIONS FOR ASSESSMENTS OF THE CVM

If, as suggested above, the CVM is indeed "accurate" vis-à-vis estimates for individual values derived from indirect market methods, we must then inquire as to the general implications of this observation for one's assessment of the CVM. In this regard, we are left with the necessity of defining conditions—"reference operating conditions" (ROC)—relevant for estimation methods which may be expected to yield value measures which satisfy the criterion of reference accuracy. To this end, we begin by considering ROC's implied by the institution underlying indirect market methods: the market.

In our society "the market" consists of many amorphous "markets" which differ in such things as degrees of organization and the necessity for negotiation. Thus, as observed by Knight (1951, p. 68):

> In economics... the "market" means the whole area, often indefinitely defined, within which buyers and sellers of a commodity come together and fix a common price... The wheat market is practically the world... the market for... brick from a small factory may not extend beyond a few miles.

As further examples in these regards, the market for groceries is relatively well organized and exchange involves little if any negotiation. Towards another end of the spectrum, the market for used furniture is less well organized and exchange can, in some settings (e.g., the flea market), involve considerable negotiation.

Also of importance for our consideration is the fact that economic deductions drawn from "the market" are complicated by the fact that commodities traded in a market are often heterogeneous. Thus, Knight asks: "is wheat in Paris the same commodity as wheat in Chicago? . . . is a physically equivalent . . . can of peas with a label which is a guarantee of quality, effectively the same commodity as if it had an unknown name?" (p. 69) In terms of the efficacy of the market vis-à-vis fixing "a common price", these complexities are substantively increased when dissimilar commodities are *jointly* offered. An example might be a house; to paraphrase Knight, are two physically equivalent (floor space, rooms, paint, appliances, etc.) houses, one located in (e.g.) neighborhood A and one in neighborhood B, the same commodities? Most often, the answer is "no" inasmuch as other neighbor-related "commodities" are offered in joint supply with the house: crime rates, quality of schools, proximity to beaches, theaters, etc., and, possibly, environmental (air) quality. Each of these commodities, in most cases valued and desirable in their own right, are obtained only in the housing "package". Since one cannot, in choosing a house, pick the crime rate from one neighborhood, the school system of another and air quality from still another, the implicit market valuation of these commodities—"attributes" of the house in a given neighborhood—will be imperfect measures of "true" values associated with these attributes.

Whatever the characteristic of any given market, one of the most important characteristics of the set of interrelations involving the process of competing bids and offers which we call "the market" is its capacity to "generate high quality information at low cost." (Heyne 1983, p. 125) Thus, "the conspicuous cause for discrepancy between the most important single cause of exceptions to (market laws) . . . is found in the condition: people do not know the facts." (Knight 1951, p. 69) The better organized the market, the better that people will "know the facts." In these regards, prices provide valuable information and "the more such prices there are, the more clearly and precisely they are stated and the more widely they are known, the greater will be the range of opportunities available to people." (Heyne 1983, p. 125)

Thus, key "reference operating conditions" (ROCs) relevant for the market institution include; first, the process of competing bids and offers which generates experience—familiarity—with that process; secondly, and implied by the preceeding, the generation of information via repeated trials whereby again, experience and familiarity with commodities and exchange are derived; and thirdly, incentives for an individual's acquiring and "processing" information imposed by his/her limited income juxtaposed with a more or less strong desire to maximize consumption/savings opportunities (maximizing behavior).

The importance of the ROCs described above is made manifest in experimental economics wherein efforts are made to simulate these conditions in an experimental setting. In Smith's (1982) recent experiments with auction mechanisms for public goods the following rules (institution) are imposed: (1) subjects offer bids within a well-defined information context which allows subjects to calculate their net (monetary) gains; (2) repetitive trials are required, which, along with a veto mechanism, provide experience and familiarity—the opportunity to *learn* maximizing strategies; (3) rules for group equilibrium are defined (in this case, unanimous agreement). (Smith 1982, p. 927) Aside from Smith's work, results from experimental economics in general make clear the importance of market-like incentive structures and the trial-feedback-learning process in *any* effort to form incentive compatible institutions and/or, more importantly, to elicit true, market-like preference revelation. As noted in Smith's work, the importance of repetitive trials—a sequence of trials whereby the individual "learns" optimal strategies appropriate for the new institution—is further reflected in Coppinger et al.'s (1980) observation: "(one may) question whether any meaningful one-shot observation can (therefore) be made on processes characterized by a dominant strategy equilibrium." Moreover, we know from our discussions in chapters 4 and 5 that efforts to simulate the market institution require that elicitation modes focus on WTP (as opposed to WTA) measures and that there be little uncertainty associated with outcomes of bidding processes.

From the above, we may deduce the following ROC's relevant for the CVM.

1. Subjects must understand, be familiar with, the commodity to be valued.
2. Subjects must have had (or be allowed to obtain) prior valuation and choice experience with respect to consumption levels of the commodity.
3. There must be little uncertainty.
4. WTP, not WTA, measures are elicited.

ROCs 1 and 2 derive directly from the market institution (which provides high quality information at low cost). Moreover, in terms of ROC 1, results from psychological research (chapter 5, above) point to distortions in decision processes (framing biases, etc.) that arise when individuals are unfamiliar with decision contexts; regarding ROC 2, results from experimental economics emphasize the importance of iterative trials which serve to provide subjects with valuation and choice experience—subjects must "learn" maximizing strategies; ROC 3 derives directly from research in psychology and experimental economics: under conditions of uncertainty, valuation decisions may be subject to distortions resulting from the use of a wide range of heuristic devices. Finally, as discussed above in chapters 3 and 4, WTA measures are generally found to be highly distorted vis-à-vis "true" valuations as a possible result, psychologists would argue, of cognitive dissonance.

The relevance of the above-described ROC's lies in our expectation that, if the CVM institution satisfies them, we would expect the resulting measure of value to approximate market-analogous values within a range of error defined by "background" sources of error, suggested at the present time to be no less than ± 50 percent. If ROC's are not satisfied, the range of reference accuracy increases, reflecting the errors associated with the excluded ROC.

A major state-of-the-arts problem is that we know little about the errors associated with the Reference Operating Conditions (table 6.13). Received research results suggest that if WTA measures are used rather than WTP measures, the WTA measure may be 3 or more times larger than WTP. In terms of ROC's 1-3, however, we lack the data that would allow us to quantify reference accuracy. As noted above, results from psychological and experimental economics research tell us only in qualitative terms that distortions —errors—will result when these ROC's are unsatisfied.

In table 6.14, data are given concerning the extent to which ROC's were generally satisfied in selected applications of the CVM; these applications are described in considerable detail above and in chapter 3. Thus, in Brookshire et al.'s (1982) study of air quality in Los Angeles, subjects were clearly familiar with the commodity, "smog"; with average turn-over of housing in the L.A. area of 3 years, subjects *generally* can be assumed to be knowledgeable of the air quality attribute related to housing and housing cost (advertisements for

Table 6.13   Reference Operating Conditions and Implied Reference Accuracy

Reference operating condition	Implied reference accuracy if ROC not satisfied
1. Familarity with commodity	unknown
2. Valuation/choice experience	unknown
3. Little uncertainty	unknown
4. WTP measure	at least 300%

housing in the L.A. newspaper will many times *include* a description of air quality), in which case subjects had some degree of experience in valuing choices with respect to "consumption levels" of the commodity (improved air quality). Also, uncertainty played a negligible role in Brookshire et al.'s CVM application wherein WTP measures were elicited. Analogous arguments apply to the study of municipal infrastructure by Cummings et al. (1982).

To generalize these observations, we can identify eight studies which, to differing degrees, essentially satisfy the above described ROC's: those given in table 6.12. In each of these studies, indirect market measures of value (using either the TCM or the HPM) were derived in addition to value measures derived by the CVM. As indicated above, using ± 50 percent for reference accuracy, *in each of the eight cases we would fail to reject the hypothesis that the CVM measures and the indirect market measures are the same.* If one accepts Hedonic (or Travel Cost) measures as including, within a ± 50 percent range for reference accuracy, values which reflect market- analogous revelations of preferences, then one's acceptance of the accuracy of CVM values for applications wherein the ROC's are satisfied turns on the question: do the fifteen comparisons given in these eight studies constitute the preponderance of evidence required in science to establish "facts"?

Table 6.14   ROC Satisfied in Selected Applications of the CVM

<table>
<tr><th></th><th colspan="4">CVM EXPERIMENT</th></tr>
<tr><th>Reference operating condition</th><th>Brookshire, et al. (air quality, Los Angeles)</th><th>Cummings, et al. (Municipal Infrastructure in boomtowns)</th><th>Schulze, et al. (Visibility in Grand Canyon)</th><th>Burness, et al. (toxic wastes)</th></tr>
<tr><td>1. Familiarity with commodity</td><td>Yes</td><td>Yes</td><td>No</td><td>No</td></tr>
<tr><td>2. Valuation/choice experience</td><td>Yes</td><td>Yes</td><td>No</td><td>No</td></tr>
<tr><td>3. Little uncertainty</td><td>Yes</td><td>Yes</td><td>Yes(?)</td><td>No</td></tr>
<tr><td>4. WTP measure</td><td>Yes</td><td>Yes</td><td>Yes</td><td>Yes</td></tr>
</table>

Finally, we must ask: what of the CVM studies which do *not* satisfy one or more of the ROCs—particularly ROCs 1-3 about which we know little in terms of reference accuracy (e.g., referring to table 6.14, the study designed to derive existence and option values for visibility in the Grand Canyon by Schulze et al. (1983b) and Burness et al.'s (1983) toxic waste study). In such cases we can say no more than that there exists no positive evidence that would support the accuracy of such measures vis-à-vis market or market-related values. It must be said, however, that *negative* evidence in this regard does exist. Order of magnitude differences between initial valuations and valuations derived after prior experience (from iterative trials) with choice mechanisms are suggested by research in experimental economics. Research in psychology has firmly established the distortions in choices which attend decision environments characterized by uncertainty and unfamiliar learning/decision contexts. In short, we can neither confirm nor deny the accuracy of CVM values derived in applications which do not satisfy the ROCs; given the *present state of the arts*, however, available evidence suggests that such measures may be seriously distorted.

FINAL REMARKS

The six chapters of part I of this book have focused on three major issues relevant for the CVM. First, an effort was made to provide the reader with some flavor for how and why interest in the CVM was initiated as well as the rationale for and nature of early experimental efforts to develop the method; these were the topics addressed in chapters 1 and 2. Secondly, the authors surveyed the literature to the end of identifying claims for sources of bias in value measures derived with the CVM, after which the authors drew on research results reported in the economics and psychology literature in efforts to assess the potential nature and importance of these biases; our efforts to assess the strengths and weaknesses claimed for the CVM were the substance of chapters 3 through 5. Third, and finally, in this chapter—chapter 6—the authors have attempted to focus the results of earlier analyses on the question of central interest in this book: how might one assess the accuracy of measures derived with the CVM, and what are the implications of such an inquiry for the state of the arts of the CVM as a means for valuing non-market, public goods?

Before summarizing results from the authors' considerations of this state of the arts question, the reader is reminded of the ultimate end sought in this work, *viz*, a broad, profession-wide evaluation of the CVM. Something akin to this broad assessment of the CVM is sought in the Conference described in chapter 1 at which the state of the arts question is to be considered by several scholars involved in one way or another with the CVM as well as by a Review Panel consisting of outstanding scholars in the economics and psychology professions. Thus, the authors offer no "conclusions" *per se* at this time. We have suggested a framework for assessing the accuracy of CVM measures which will hopefully be found as provocative in the Conference's *collective* considerations of the CVM. The following summary of the authors' arguments are offered within this context. The response to this assessment framework by Conference participants will be described in Part II, and efforts to draw final conclusions as to the state of the arts of the CVM will be given in chapter 13.

Our approach to assessing the state of the arts of the CVM is couched in terms of instruments and scientific measuring systems wherein "accuracy" is defined as follows: "conformity of an indicated value to an accepted standard value, or true value ... accuracy should be assumed to mean reference accuracy." (Van Nostrand 1970, p. 17) Reference accuracy, expressed in terms of a range or span around the measured variable (measure $\pm$ X%), defines the limits that errors will not exceed when a measure is obtained under Reference Operating Condition. Since our accepted standard, or true values, are market values, the ROCs for the CVM suggested by the authors are drawn from what we know of the market institution, as well as what has been learned in analyzing market-like behavior in experimental economics and in psychology-related research. These suggested ROCs are:

1. Subjects—participants in the CVM—must understand, (be familiar with) the commodity to be valued.
2. Subjects must have had (or be allowed to obtain) prior valuation and choice experience with respect to consumption levels of the commodity.
3. There must be little uncertainty.
4. WTP, not WTA, measures are elicited.

Ideally, experimental research would have defined limits on errors associated with applications of the CVM which fail to satisfy any one of the ROCs. This is not the case, however. In the present state of the arts, such limits (very large limits) are known only in terms of ROC 4: WTA measures may approximate market values only in a range of some $\pm$ 300%— plus!

In considering indirect market values—values estimated by the TCM and HPM—we assert that reference accuracy for these measures can be expected to be *no better* than that for estimates of parameters of ordinary demand functions (which arise from assumptions on residual distributions), which is the measured value plus-or-minus 50%. State of the arts information allows one to go beyond simply deducing ROCs for the CVM and, essentially, *asserting* that CVM applications which satisfy the ROCs will yield reference-accurate measures. Eight studies have been identified (table 6.12 above) which derive CVM values as well as values from indirect market methods and which satisfy the ROCs for the CVM. In each case, one fails to reject the hypothesis that the CVM measure is the same (in reference accuracy terms) as the indirect market measure. Thus, if one accepts the reference accuracy of $\pm$50% as including "true" market values, one has six tests which consistently infer that Reference Accuracy measures derived from the CVM are "valid". Whether or not these six cases constitute the preponderance of evidence required in the scientific method to establish "facts" is, of course, a matter of judgement.

One may find little comfort in these observations in terms of the general promise of the CVM as a means for estimating "accurate" values attributable to broad categories of public/environmental goods. This follows from the fact that, given the present state of the arts, a limited number of environmental "commodities" are amenable to CVM applications, where the ROCs are satisfied. For such applictions, where the ROCs are not satisfied, the present state of the arts does not allow us to conclude that accurate or inaccurate measures will result. It must be said, however, that while positive evidence vis-à-vis the accuracy of CVM measures derived under these circumstances does not exist, considerable negative inferential evidence does exist in this regard.

In closing, the authors recognize that while an assessment framework based on reference accuracy and the Reference Operating Conditions may in form parallel objective frameworks for assessing accuracy in other sciences, it may fall well short of "objectivity" vis-à-vis assessments of the CVM. This follows from the obvious fact that while the ROCs per se may be objectively deduced from market institutions, their application to assessments of a CVM study may generally be subjective. For example, one may ask: what degree of "familiarity" with a commodity is required to satisfy ROC 1; how much value/choice experience (or how many repetitive trials) is (are) required to satisfy ROC 2; and how much is "little uncertainty" (ROC 3)? In response to these questions, our knowledge of markets, lessons drawn from experimental economics and psychological research tell us little more than that, in moving from pure public goods to common market goods, we can expect something of a continuum in meeting ROCs as exemplified in figure 6.2. Thus, moving from an "existence value" to a hamburger, we expect individuals to be increasingly familiar with the "commodity" and to have had greater market-related experiences; along this continuum, uncertainties as to outcomes of transactions and the potential for problems related to cognition are reduced.

In efforts to deal with these issues, the state of the arts is one wherein we can simply say that evidence exists which supports the proposition that

Figure 6.2: ROCs and Market, Non-Market Commodities

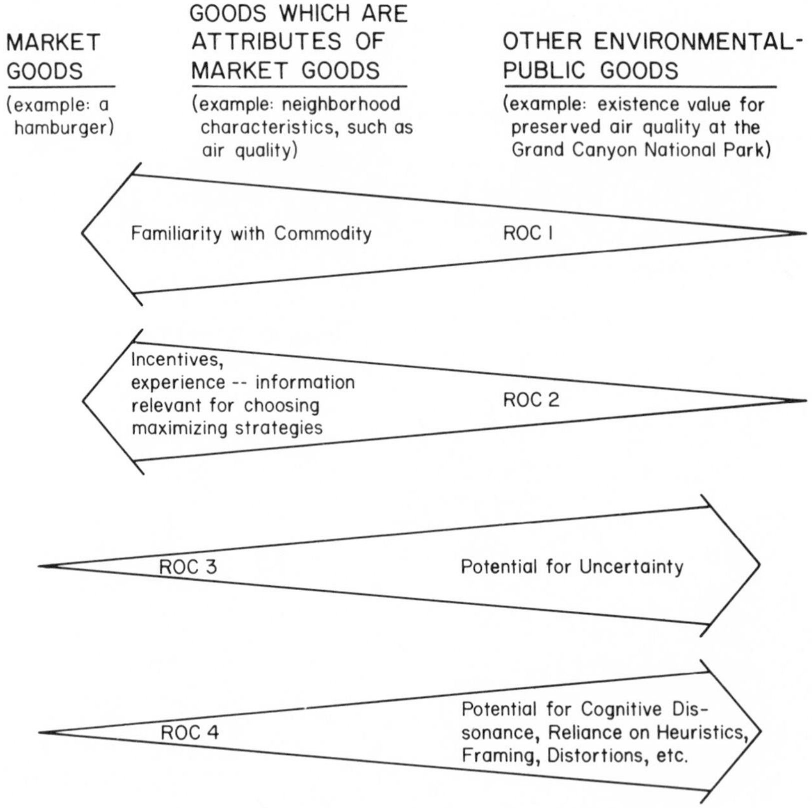

MARKET GOODS	GOODS WHICH ARE ATTRIBUTES OF MARKET GOODS	OTHER ENVIRONMENTAL- PUBLIC GOODS
(example: a hamburger)	(example: neighborhood characteristics, such as air quality)	(example: existence value for preserved air quality at the Grand Canyon National Park)

Familiarity with Commodity   ROC I

Incentives, experience -- information relevant for choosing maximizing strategies   ROC 2

ROC 3   Potential for Uncertainty

ROC 4   Potential for Cognitive Dissonance, Reliance on Heuristics, Framing, Distortions, etc.

indirect market experience with a commodity may serve to satisfy the ROCs: when the environmental good is a distinct attribute of a market-related good (water quality in a time/travel cost recreation trip or air quality as an attribute of housing locations/costs), experience/familiarity with the market good *seemingly* spills over to the individual's ability to value the attribute. Thus, while not totally answering the "what degree" and "how much" questions regarding the satisfaction of ROCs, comparison studies *may* suggest classes of environmental/- public goods which may be taken *a priori* as those which would satisfy the ROCs for the Contingent Valuation Method.

NOTES

1. While Rosen may be credited with the initial, rigorous theoretical development of the HPM, the HPM per se was used in earlier studies, most prominently in Ridker 1967.

2. Researchers at the University of Wyoming have developed data amenable to CVM and HPM analysis related to ozone concentrations in Southern California; drafts of final comparative results are unavailable at the time of this writing, however.

3. Although the authors do not discuss the robustness of these results, performing simple two-tailed tests on the coefficient on lnk—where the null hypothesis is that it is not significantly different from zero—the null hypothesis is rejected at the 5% level. Thus e is negative and significantly different from zero.

4. These towns were included in 26 towns from which data were used in the HPM study.

Part II

The Assessment Conference and Conclusions: The State of the Arts of the CVM

7
The Assessment Conference: Overview

On July 2, 1984, a conference "Valuing Environmental Goods: A State of the Arts Assessment of the Contingent Valuation Method" was held at the Hyatt Palo Alto Hotel in Palo Alto, California; some eighty professional researchers with interests in the public goods valuation issue attended the conference. Most conference participants received part I, of this book (chapters 1–6), or an Executive Summary of part I, several weeks prior to the conference.

The conference format was as follows. During the morning session, papers were presented by Professors Richard Bishop (University of Wisconsin), A. Myrick Freeman (Bowdoin College), Alan Randall (University of Kentucky) and V. Kerry Smith (Vanderbilt University). Papers presented by these four scholars are given below in chapters 8–11. Generally, these authors address two major issues in their papers: their critical review of this book's part I (chapters 1–6), and their individual assessment of the state of the arts of the CVM. The afternoon session was devoted to comments offered by a Review Panel. Members of the Review Panel were: Kenneth Arrow (Stanford University), Daniel Kahneman (University of British Columbia), Sherwin Rosen (University of Chicago) and Vernon Smith (University of Arizona). Based on their pre-conference reading of this book's part I and the four papers presented in the morning session, comments by the review panel were focused on each panel member's assessment of the strengths and weaknesses of the CVM as a means of estimating social benefits attributable to environmental (and public) goods. Comments by the review panel are given below in chapter 12.

Thus the following five chapters review the results from the assessment conference and provide the reader with diverse views concerning first, the authors' analysis of the CVM given in part I and, second, the strengths, weaknesses and promise of the CVM. Conference results presented in these five chapters serve to set the stage for the ultimate task of this book: the offering of *conclusions* concerning the state of the arts of the CVM. The development of such conclusions is the topic of chapter 13 given below.

8

The Possibility of Satisfactory Benefit Estimation with Contingent Markets

Alan Randall

Department of Economics

University of Kentucky

Skepticism about the contingent valuation method (CVM) has always focused on value data quality. It has long been clear that, if the value data can be trusted, these data (unlike the data used in weak complementarity and hedonic price theory approaches) can be directly interpreted as estimates of welfare change consistent with accepted economic theory. (Bradford 1970; Randall et al. 1974a; and Brookshire et al. 1980) However, CVM data are self-reported by participants in interaction with a researcher or his/her representatives. This gives rise to obvious concern that various self-reporting biases, and other biases inadvertently introduced by the research design and/or the interaction between researcher and participant, may be endemic to CVM.

On the other hand, a quite considerable body of empirical evidence can be broadly interpreted as supportive of CVM. True, unexpected and perplexing results occur from time to time. Nevertheless, the broad thrust of the empirical evidence is to corroborate CVM findings. This was my perception prior to reading the Cummings et al. "State of the Art" document, (hereinafter referred to as CBS) and that document tends to reinforce my prior perception.

My experience with the contingent valuation method was gained in the course of research sponsored by the U.S. Environmental Protection Agency, the U.S. Fish and Wildlife Service, Resources for the Future, Inc., and New Mexico Agricultural Experiment Station. The viewpoint expressed in this paper has been influenced by more than a decade of interaction with many of my colleagues in environmental economics. My close working relationship for the last several years with John P. Hoehn has provided countless opportunities to develop and refine the argument.

The Cummings et al. document also reinforces another of my prior perceptions: that the research approach toward investigating data quality in CVM has been skewed toward the empirical. In some cases, empirical experiments have been designed to address data quality issues. In others, data quality issues have been addressed ad hoc, as apparently anomalous results have seemed to require ex post interpretation. The net result has been the accumulation of a detailed taxonomy of "biases in CVM". One problem with this approach has been a tendency to promulgate empirical laws on the basis of a few small-sample data sets. Another has been a rather widespread failure to critically scrutinize the notion of "bias" itself, to specify what conditions are sufficient for an unexpected result to be correctly interpreted as attributable to bias inherent in the data collection method.

Resolution of controversies about data quality in CVM seems sure to require a formal theory of the behavior of participants in CV exercises. John Hoehn and I (manuscript) have recently developed the rudiments of one such theory. In this paper, I will outline the intuition behind this theory and suggest its usefulness in (1) predicting the direction of any deviations of CVM-reported benefit values from optimally formulated values, (2) explaining certain empirical results previously thought anomalous, and (3) identifying procedures to improve the accuracy of CVM and render the direction of the remaining inaccuracy more predictable. I hope the following discourse will achieve two objectives: to illuminate the data quality issues in ways that empirical evidence alone cannot do; and to demonstrate, by methodological example and through its results, that CVM is a progressive research program in the sense of Lakatos (1970).

A THEORY OF CVM-PARTICIPANT BEHAVIOR

Many of the purported biases in contingent valuation seem to be rather simple concerns that can be avoided or minimized through careful attention to research design, sampling, and administration of the experiment or survey. Two concerns that are genuinely interesting are: (1) individuals may behave strategically, misreporting their "true" valuations in order to benefit themselves by influencing the outcome of policy research; and (2) individuals may treat the whole exercise as inconsequential, and thus devote little effort to the introspection that is necessary to discover what one's "true" valuation really is. Hoehn and I (manuscript) address these two concerns, assuming a rational, self-seeking respondent and using simple economic-theoretic models to predict her behavior in a CVM setting.

Value Formation

First, assume the individual—an experimental subject or survey respondent—believes the results of the valuation exercise will influence policy. It is not essential to believe that it will be decisive; influential is enough.[1] Assume also that the individual perceives that she is a member of a sample of citizens participating in the exercise. Does she "take it seriously?" It is reasonable to assume she will take it at least as seriously as voting in elections or participating in a political poll (where, again, her influence is magnified because she is a member of a sample chosen to represent a larger population). Since policy choices are more focused and more precisely specified in CVM than in elections and political polls, it is possible that participants may feel that CVM offers them an unusually favorable opportunity to influence policy choice.

Now, assume that formulating ("figuring out") her WTP/WTA for specified changes in Q (or, even more difficult, specifying her total value curve) is not so simple a task that it can be accomplished instantaneously and costlessly. The choices offered in the contingent market will seldom be familiar and routine, even with the best research design. There will be a positive relationship between the effort she invests in value formulation and the precision of the value at which she arrives. If the value formulation task is very difficult and/or the individual limits the effort she invests therein, she may solve the value formulation problem incompletely or imprecisely.

This places in perspective the difference between contingent markets and "real" markets. First, the goods offered in contingent markets are not always familiar, and individuals may not associate these particular goods with trading possibilities. Nevertheless, unfamiliar goods are often introduced in "real" markets and, especially, in market experiments. So, this distinction between "real" and contingent markets is, if anything, a matter of degree. Second, the penalty for a wrong decision may be substantial in "real" markets: your money is gone and you are left with some purchase that has disappointed you. There is, however, a penalty for a wrong decision in a contingent market: one's opportunity to influence policy is wasted or misused and one's chances of facing a less-preferred policy environment are accordingly increased. Again, the distinction between "real" and contingent markets is, if anything, a matter of degree. Sub-optimal individual decision making can be expected in both kinds of market, but may be more prevalent in contingent markets.

If value formulation is imperfect in contingent markets, the formulated values would include some error. Can we identify the direction of that error? It turns out that if valuation is performed in the Hicksian compensating framework (i.e., WTP for increments in Q and WTA for decrements), imperfect value formulation would lead to understatement of WTP and overstatement of WTA.

The intuitive explanation of this result is as follows. In order to formulate her WTP, the participant must first solve the problem: minimize expenditure subject to utility constrained at the initial level. Imperfect solution of that problem can have only one kind of outcome, the identification of some expenditure larger than the minimum. This overestimation of minimum expenditure must lead the participant to underestimate her compensating surplus, WTP. Thus, any error in formulating WTP in a compensating framework would lead to its understatement. [2] This line Of reasoning further suggests that WTP is nondecreasing in the time (and by extension, other resources) allocated to solving the value formulation problem.

To summarize, incomplete value formulation in a Hicksian compensating context tends to understate WTP (and overstate WTA); and the magnitude of the error is nonincreasing as more effort is invested in the value formulation process.

Value Reporting

Now, assume the individual is not above strategic behavior, which we define as reporting something other than one's formulated value in order to influence policy in one's favor. Some participants would reject this kind of behavior on moral grounds, while others would recognize that strategic behavior is itself resource-consuming and decide not to use resources that way. Nevertheless, it is surely prudent to consider what kind of effect those who choose to attempt a strategic response might have on reported contingent valuation results.

To identify optimal strategies for participants, we must first specify the incentives that they face. For simplicity, assume that $U = U(Q,Y)$, where Q is a nonmarketed amenity and Y is a numeraire consisting of "all other goods." Assume the individual gains positive utility from both Q and Y. In other words, she likes Q and does not like taxes or payments that would reduce her disposable income for purchasing other goods. The key issue, then, is how her participation in the exercise is likely to influence (1) the chances that a policy to increase Q will be implemented and (2) her disposable income, if the policy is enacted. One can model a variety of alternative contingent markets to examine how their structure affects these things. Here we outline some of these models for WTP; the arguments are analogous for WTA, where the effects are usually similar but of opposite sign.

We can dispose quickly of two rather obvious cases.

a) The agency will provide the increment in Q without regard to the outcome of the benefit cost analysis. The researcher will collect stated WTP from each participant at the end of the exercise. However, Q is nonexclusive and participants will enjoy the increment in Q regardless of their reported (and paid) WTP. Strategizing respondents would report zero or very low values for WTP.

b) The agency will provide the increment in Q if and only if the estimated benefits for the affected population exceed the costs. The researcher never collects the stated WTP, and nor does anyone else. The participant is forever immune from bearing any of the costs. Strategizing respondents would state high values for WTP in order to increase the probability of implementing the policy.

These cases can immediately be dismissed, since they are quite false representations of the policy environment. Case (a) is of some interest in experimental economics, as the case most likely to elicit free-rider behavior. However, it is not common policy practice to implement proposals independently of benefits and costs, and to finance them through contributions determined by self-reported WTP. Case (b) has some appeal on the surface, since in BCA practice the researcher seldom collects WTP. However, a deeper analysis suggests that participants realize that if the exercise is to affect policy they will eventually pay—usually through some combination of user fees, higher taxes, and higher prices—for increments in Q. The assumption that the participant is forever immune from contributing toward the costs of policy is untenable.

Cases (a) and (b) share an interesting characteristic: they deviate from the policy choice model in that the respondent is not attempting simultaneously to influence Q and Y. In case (a), Q is given and the respondent has only to maximize Y. In case (b), Y is not at issue and a Q-loving respondent has only to maximize the probability that Q is provided.

More relevant models of the incentives influencing behavior in contingent markets include the following cases:

c) The proposal is implemented if the estimated benefits exceed the costs, and citizens pay in proportion to stated WTP. In this case the respondent influences her payment in the event of policy implementation and the probability of implementation. She faces uncertainty about project costs and about the aggregate reported benefits.

d) The proposal is implemented if the estimated benefits exceed the costs, and citizens pay their share of the costs, as determined by some pre-specified rule. In this case the respondent influences the probability that policy is implemented and payment exacted. She faces uncertainty about project costs (and thus the size of individual cost shares) and about reported aggregate benefits.

e) The proposal is implemented if a plurality of citizens approves it, given information on the individual payment to be exacted. Since the expression of approval is conditional on a stated level of payment, the level of payment can be varied and the question of approval reiterated. The respondent is uncertain about how others will "vote", which provides incentive for participation. Uncertainty about the true level of policy costs is neither essential nor damaging to the incentive properties of this decision rule.

In each case the participant who likes Q but dislikes bearing additional expenses must devise a strategy designed to increase the expectation that the policy is implemented but, *ceteris paribus*, reduce the expected cost she will bear.

Optimal reporting strategies for cases (c) through (e) are:

c) Report WTP equal to or less than one's formulated WTP. Optimal reporting strategy is related to sample size. Generally it is best to report WTP approaching one's formulated WTP, if one believes the sample is small. With very large samples the tendency toward free-riding is stronger if the CV exercise is treated as a one-shot game; if it is treated as one play in a repeated game with an indefinite end-period, the cooperative strategy of truthful reporting may emerge.

d) If one suspects one's formulated WTP is quite different from that of other citizens, exaggerate the difference so as to shift the sample mean reported WTP nearer to one's own formulated WTP. If one expects one's WTP is a little higher than the mean, report a value still higher; likewise, if one's WTP is likely to be lower than the mean, report a value still lower. Again, if the CV exercise is treated as one play in a repeated game, truth-telling may be prevalent.

e) No strategy is individually preferred to truth-telling. If the stated individual cost is lower than one's formulated WTP, it is optimal to report approval; if one's WTP is lower than the stated cost, it is individually optimal to report disapproval.

What effect would these individually optimal strategies have on estimated benefits of increasing the level of Q? In case (c) there may be a tendency to underestimate benefits. In case (d) the variance of individual WTP may be increased, widening the confidence interval around estimated benefits. If reported WTP is limited to a minimum of zero but has no upper limit, mean reported WTP might be biased upward. However, there are statistical methods for dealing with this problem. If these methods are used, total estimated benefits would be unaffected by reporting strategies.

In case (e) there is no reporting bias. Note that in this case the results are expressed in terms of "number of participants expressing approval/disapproval of the proposal given a per capita cost of $." These results are not immediately interpreted as WTP. All we know is that those who approve have formulated a WTP greater than the stated cost, while those who disapprove have formulated a WTP less than the cost. Nevertheless, all is not lost for the benefit cost analyst. If (1) the sample is subdivided and different subsamples respond to different stated costs and (2) the data are analyzed with appropriate statistical tools (e.g., logit analysis), valid benefit estimates can be obtained. An alternative approach is to repeat the "approve/disapprove" question with the same participant, stating different levels of individual cost. In that way te researcher could iteratively approach the participant's indifference point, while retaining the desired anti-strategic properties of the "majority vote" format.

Implications

This conceptual analysis of the participant's likely behavior in a contingent valuation exercise, in formulating and reporting her responses, has several implications; and these implications appear to have been corroborated in empirical applications.

First, while the incentives for careful decision making and truthful reporting of valuations are perhaps not as strong as in private goods markets, they are by no means absent in contingent valuation exercises. This suggests that carefully designed contingent valuation studies will collect a substantial body of serviceable value data. Economists have long recognized that private goods markets do not require, for their efficient functioning, that all participants make near-optimal decisions. Price-making at the margin is disproportionately influenced by arbitrageurs, and the mistake-prone are eliminated from the market. Public goods markets ("real" or contingent) do not have these characteristics. Thus a minority of "dubious" value observations tends to persist in these markets. The earlier intuition of Randall et al. (1981) that empirical analysts focus on identifying the "solid core" of reliable observations, seems sound in light of these considerations. CVM results, whether in the form of aggregate benefit estimates or tests for "bias", should not be overly influenced by a relatively few eccentric observations.

Second, for a fairly wide range of contingent market designs, we can be confident that any biases introduced in formulating and/or reporting WTP will have the effect of understating it. This applies to contingent markets based on Hicksian compensating measures of value, and assumes use of appropriate statistical analyses. Following Hoehn and Randall (manuscript), we can define a *satisfactory benefit cost estimator* as one that correctly identifies all proposals that would not generate a potential Pareto-improvement (PPI) while correctly identifying at least a subset of those that would bring about PPIs. It follows that any BC estimator that reliably reports WTP (i.e., benefit) estimates no greater than their "true" values and WTA (i.e., costs) no less than their "true" values is satisfactory.[3] Thus, we can identify a considerable class of CVM formats that are satisfactory BC estimators.

Third, contingent valuation formats come in considerable variety, and their performance characteristics will differ in ways that are, to some extent, predictable. Thus, the quality of contingent value data can be improved with careful attention to contingent market design. Use of Hicksian compensating value measures and referendum formats, as in case (e), are obvious ways to minimize bias in estimated benefits while ensuring that any remaining bias is toward understatement. Since strategic misstatement can be minimized or eliminated in this way, the commonly expressed fear—that routine use of CVM to guide actual policy decisions would lead to rampant "strategic bias"—seems misdirected. On the contrary, it seems desirable to emphasize the connection between CVM and policy decisions, to enhance the incentives for careful value formulations.

Fourth—since we have concluded that (a) a class of formats can be identified in which any inaccuracy would tend to understate WTP and overstate WTA and (b) the divergence between WTP and WTA is nonincreaseing with value formulation inputs; and Coursey et al. (1983b) (manuscript) have provided empirical evidence entirely consistent with our theoretical conclusions—I see no great merit in the Cummings et al. recommendation that the profession abandon attempts to measure WTA with CVM.[4]

Finally, the identification of a class of satisfactory benefit estimators that use CVM data is not an invitation to complacency. Our definition of satisfactory BC indicators permits adverse evaluations of some proposals that would generate PPIs. Obviously, it would be desirable to continue refining our understanding of CVM to identify approaches to reduce the frequency of this kind of misevaluation.

INFORMATION BIAS AND POLICY EVALUATION

In 1983 I wrote (with John Hoehn and David Brookshire) some cryptic comments about what has been called "information bias," arguing that such bias may be an illusion. We wrote: "information that changes the structure of the market should (arguably) change the circumstantial choices made therein." This argument piqued the curiosity of Cummings et al., who devoted several pages to wondering what we could have meant. The economic-theoretic analyses that I have discussed above provide a sound basis for further explicating our argument.

Stripped to its barest essentials a contingent market offers a public policy for approval or disapproval. From the respondent's perspective any such policy is a pairing of commodities delivered and payments exacted. Thus, the rational respondent bases her contingent market decision on (1) the value to her of the commodity or amenity offered, (2) the rule by which the agency decides whether or not to provide the commodity, and (3) the rule that determines the payment exacted from the respondent. Note that all three are relevant to policy evaluation and a change in any one of them could chnge CVM results. However, only item (1) directly enters the standard economic model for valuing nonrival goods. In this vein, the concept of incentive-compatibility addresses the issue: do (2) and (3) encourage reporting of (1) inconsistent with the standard economic model of value?

The empirical evidence that Cronin and Herzeg (1982), and Rowe et al. (1983), *inter alia*, have marshalled to support charges of "information bias" shows that changes in (1), (2) and/or (3) tend sometimes to change reported WTP. We emphasize that contingent policy evaluations should be expected to change as these things change. A policy evaluation tool with results invariant to important changes in these conditions would surely be misleading and uninformative. Exit "information bias".

Nevertheless, for economic valuation of nonrival goods, the issues of incentive compatibility and the satisfactoriness of PPI indicators remain. As Hoehn and I have shown, careful analysis of the CVM structure with respect to (2) and (3) serves to identify structures that generate satisfactory data for nonrival goods valuation.

Note that markets can be viewed as a special case of a more general class of resource allocation mechanisms or policy choice mechanisms, all based on individual utility maximization within the constraints imposed by fully specified public decision rules (item 2, above) and individual payment rules (item 3). It seems logical to expect that satisfactory contingent valuation designs could be constructed for any member of this class of mechanisms. Especially when the commodities to be evaluated are both nonrival and nonexclusive, contingent valuation formats may fruitfully be designed consistent with the more general class of policy choice mechanisms. again, the policy choice referendum format is clearly admissable (and is a member of the same class of resource allocation mechanisms that includes traditional contingent markets).

CONCLUDING COMMENTS

The economic-theoretic approach has been fruitful in clarifying the incentives facing a CVM respondent. A class of satisfactory BC estimators has been identified. Some empirical results once thought anomalous—including but not limited to those pertaining to so-called "information bias" and the divergence between WTP and WTA—are now seen as rational and predictable responses to the costs and opportunities inherent in contingent markets. Some simple principles have emerged that will be useful in improving CVM by reducing the extent of benefit understatement associated with compensating WTP and the prevalence of results that seem anomalous.

But perhaps most important, our work leads us to be conscious that contingent markets are not devoid of incentives for reasoned decision making therein. Further, there exists a class of contingent valuation mechanisms that are immune to strategic manipulation. Together, these findings place CVM in a new perspective.

Simplistic dismissals of CVM—"it is utterly devoid of incentives for reasoned decision making," and "it is riddled with opportunities for strategic behavior"—must themselves be dismissed. Arguments that practitioners must consciously downplay any association between CVM results and policy outcomes, in order to contain "strategic bias", must be rejected. On the contrary, policy relevance would appear to enhance the incentives for careful value formulation. A dilemma commonly claimed to bedevil CVM—"increased policy relevance causes strategic bias, while decreased policy relevance causes hypothetical bias"—simply does not exist, if one uses CVM mechanisms selected from the class of satisfactory BC indicators.

The defense of CVM no longer rests on empirical case study evidence that seems to fly in the face of reason. We have shown that theoretical analysis of the incentives inherent in CVM offers some support for the method, as well as some suggestions for its improvement.

NOTES

1. Some economists tend instinctively to question whether citizens would rationally behave as though they could expect to have any influence on policy. Their skepticism is apparently based on the standard free-rider model, itself a result of single-period analysis of voluntary provision of pure public goods. However, recent theoretical models of repeated games with uncertain ending periods have demonstrated that free-riding is not always individually optimal. It may be rational to cooperate in maintaining the institutions of social stability.

Empirical evidence from elections indicates that many people participate and that, within the limits implied by the electoral system, they pursue their self-interest therein. Savers, investors and those who favor limits to redistribution tend to vote for Republican and/or "conservative" candidates. Debtors, low-wage earners and welfare recipients tend to vote for Democratic and/or "liberal" candidates. The "misery index", which rises with unemployment and inflation, remains the best predictor of election results: high levels of this index bode ill for incumbents.

One need merely appeal to casual observation to confirm the considerable investment of time and effort expended by ordinary individuals in gathering and processing political and policy-related information and attempting to influence policy via individual and voluntary group activities.

2. If equivalent measures of value are sought, the results of formulation error are not so clear. There are two problems to solve: (a) the "with policy", or subsequent utility level must be found by maximizing utility given the subsequent opportunity set, and (b) expenditure must be minimized subject to utility constrained at the subsequent level. Formulation error at stage (a) would understate subsequent utility and thus expenditure, while error at stage (b) would overstate expenditure. The final outcome is ambiguous when equivalent measures of value are used.

3. Thus, the now commonplace empirical finding—that CVM tends to generate larger differences between WTP and WTA than Willig (1976) and Randall and Stoll (1980) would predict—is in no way inconsistent with the satisfactoriness of CVM in the compensating mode.

4. This is a clear departure from my previous position on this issue. (Brookshire et al. 1980)

9

Does Contingent Valuation Work?

Richard C. Bishop

Department of Agricultural Economics

University of Wisconsin

and

Thomas A. Heberlein

Department of Rural Sociology

University of Wisconsin

Two tasks have been assigned to us: First, we have been asked to critique part I of this volume, the part prepared by Cummings, Brookshire and Schulze. Following the precedent they establish, we will refer to part I as CBS. Second, we are to give our own assessment "of the promise, strengths, and weaknesses of CVM."

To accomplish these assignments we must begin with some background material that will help to justify our views. As CBS point out, our team at Wisconsin is investigating the validity of CVM by comparing contingent values for hunting permits with values from actual cash transactions. Our experiment involving goose hunting permits has been described by CBS, but a brief discussion will help clarify some additional points. More importantly, we will introduce some preliminary results from a new experiment involving deer hunting permits. Results here are germane to a number of questons raised by CBS as well as to our own views about the accuracy of CVM.

Drawing on these experimental results, the second section will comment on CBS. Let it be said at the outset that we find much to commend in their work. It is certainly timely to systematically assess what has been learned and to chart a course for the future. Their stubborn insistence on clearly stating and testing hypotheses is laudable. It is also high time that researchers explicitly recognize the potential pitfalls of using market data in TCM and HPM. Surely CVM will work better in some contexts than others. Hopefully, a systematic, empirically verified, set of conditions for successful application of CVM will be developed.

On these and many other issues, we heartily support CBS in their efforts to evaluate what has been learned during 20 years of research on CVM. However, we find much that is questionable in the specifics of CBS's presentation. They are not very definite when drawing conclusions concerning bias. Their endorsement of iterative bidding is not well founded empirically. They need to recognize the potential usefulness of field experiments as powerful complements to laboratory experiments. These and other points will be raised and clarified in the section entitled Implications For CBS.

In our own assessment of CVM—to be presented in that section—we will attempt to answer the question posed in our title: Does contingent valuation work? Obviously, to state the issue in this way is an oversimplification. There is not a categorical answer. Rather, the question is really: How well does CVM work?

Our position on CVM is interesting in light of where we started. In 1978, when we first began our own research on CVM, we were among the most cynical. It would not have surprised us to learn that CVM produces totally meaningless results. In the coming pages we will argue that, while CVM is inaccurate even under the best of circumstances, it is still capable of producing policy-relevant values when competently applied in suitable situations.

EXPERIMENTAL RESULTS

Goose Study Design

Since this study has already been published (Bishop and Heberlein 1979; Bishop et al. 1983) and summarized by CBS, we will be brief, but some clarification is desirable. Our three samples of hunters had been issued permits to take one Canada goose in the Horicon Zone, an area of 24,600 acres in east central Wisconsin where geese concentrate each fall. These permits applied only to the period between October 1 and October 15, 1978, and a hunter was allowed only one Horicon Zone Permit for the entire 1978 hunting season. The permits were free. A total of almost 14,000 permits was issued.

The first sample (237 hunters) received actual cash offers by mail to forego their 1978 Horicon hunting opportunities. Dollar amounts were assigned at random between $1 and $200. The second sample consisted of 353 people who were involved in a mail survey in which the principal CVM question was worded identically to the actual cash offers, except that the hypothetical nature of the proposed transaction was emphasized. Other CVM questions including WTP questions were also included. The third sample (300 hunters) was surveyed after the goose hunt and the results used to estimate a TCM model. All samples were surveyed for specific attitudes regarding goose hunting and general socioeconomic characteristics. In all cases response rates exceeded 80 percent.

Goose Study Analysis

The responses to the actual cash offers were either yes or no. These dichotomous responses were analyzed in a logit model of the form

$$\pi = (1 + e\ Y\ ) - 1$$

where π is the probability that a hunter will accept an offer, Y is a vector of explanatory variables, and e is a vector of coefficients. Some results from the maximum likelihood estimation of this model for the actual cash offers and parallel contingent market are given in table 9.1. The explanatory variable, ln Dollars, is simply the natural logarithm of the dollar offer amount. Model 2 includes a second explanatory variable Commitment, which is a four item attitude scale expressing the level of commitment each hunter had to goose hunting with larger values expressing greater commitment. Both explanatory variables have the expected signs. i.e., larger dollar amounts would be expected to increase the probability of selling while increased commitment would be expected to reduce the probability of selling. Chi-squared tests comparing actual cash equations with respective CVM equations showed statistically significant differences at the .05 level for both models.

Examining the coefficients in Model 1 indicated that increasing the dollar amount had a much stronger effect for the actual cash offers than for the hypothetical offers. Thus, when the expected value of a permit was calculated, it was $63 for actual cash offers and $101 for the hypothetical ones. To obtain these values we truncated the model at $200, the largest amount for which we had data. The medians, defined as the dollar amounts where the probability of acceptance was 0.5, were $29 and $80 for the cash and hypothetical markets, respectively. A parallel willingness-to-pay question was asked where respondents were requested to assume that they had not received a permit and asked whether they would pay a specified amount, again set randomly between $1 and $200. The expected value here was $21. The median was $5.

Table 9.1 **Regression Analysis of Simulated and Contingent Markets for Willingness-to-Sell Goose Hunting Permits**

Explanatory variables	Model 1		Model 2	
	Simulated	Contingent	Simulated	Contingent
Constant	3.99[a]	3.24[a]	1.72	−.58
	(.66)	(.54)	(.98)	(.81)
In dollars	−1.18[a]	−.74[a]	−1.16[a]	−.84[a]
	(.18)	(.13)	(.18)	(.14)
Commitment			.21[a]	.40[a]
			(.07)	(.07)
Number	189	306	189	306

[a] Indicates coefficient significantly different than zero at .01 level.
Note: Standard errors are given in parentheses.

To set the record straight, it needs to be stated that Bishop and Heberlein (1979) emphasized that all results in that paper were preliminary, including the TCM values which were reported by CBS to be between $11 and $45, depending on assumed value of time. Later modifications of our TCM model, which we believe are more in keeping with the current state of the art for travel cost work, yielded a value of $32 assuming a value of time equal to 50% of the income rate.

This is the value which we prefer to use as the TCM result for our study. See Bishop, Heberlein, Kealy et al. (1983) for further discussion.

Goose Study Interpretation

How are such large differences in values (ranging from $21 to $101) to be explained? Setting aside for the time being the travel cost result, what about the apparent errors in CVM values for willingness-to-pay and willingness-to-accept-compensation?

Let us explicitly state that our actual cash transactions are not a perfect criterion against which to evaluate CVM results. As CBS repeatedly emphasize, we would all be quite satisfied if CVM approximated values from a real market. Our cash transactions do not fully measure up to this standard. Disequilibrium may be a factor. Respondents to our actual cash offers get only one opportunity to engage in a transaction while real markets, even for durables such as automobiles and houses, generally involve repeated transactions over long periods of time. The opportunities to gain experience, obtain information, and "research preferences" must be much more extensive in real markets. To go a step further, our cash offers may well share some of the bias problems that CBS have outlined for CVM. To take an extreme view one might even speculate, for example, about strategic bias. Suppose that individuals receive a cash offer from us as part of a single experiment and that they see some advantage in influencing final results in an upward direction. They might well refuse offers which they would accept in a real market in order to further their long run goals. We have repeatedly called attention to the fact that our cash offers do not constitute a full-blown market by referring to our approach as a *simulated market.*

Still, the simple result remains that people did not respond to hypothetical offers in the same way that they responded to cash offers. Our results clearly show that people refused hypothetical amounts that they would have accepted in actual dollars. Why? As CBS points out, we attribute this behavior to the artificiality of CVM procedures. (Bishop, Heberlein, and Kealy 1983) Look at table 8.1 again, this time focusing on Model 2. While ln Dollars had a stronger influence in the simulated market, commitment had a much stronger influence in the contingent market. Our interpretation is that people have never tried to value goose hunting before and do not know what they would accept when confronted with a questionnaire. To answer, they fell back on their commitment to goose hunting and related tastes and preferences more than they would have if real money was before them. Real money draws more attention than hypothetical money and helps them to "research their preferences" in a more realistic economic milieu. Thre is more incentive to consider a real offer because the losses from making an error are greater. As we have said before, money is a strong stimulus and real money is a stronger stimulus than hypothetical money. This argument clearly parallels CBS's treatment of bias due to hypothetical payment.

Like most researchers, we have not been able to resist the temptation to reach beyond our empirical results and speculate about their broader implications. Suppose we are correct that hypothetical bias in the form just described is the central problem in CVM. In which direction does the bias lie? Clearly the results presented here indicate that CVM willingness-to-accept-compensation will be an overestimate. To move to the willingness- to-pay side is more tenuous because we had no actual cash transactions involving payment for permits. Nevertheless, we argued (Bishop, Heberlein and Kealy 1983) that people respond to the artificiality of CVM by giving conservative responses. They refuse hypothetical offers unless they are certain they really would accept. If this same conservatism is exercised on the willingness-to-pay side, people will indicate refusal to pay unless they are relatively certain that they really would pay. This would make CVM willingness-to-pay an underestimate. This appears to be consistent with the empirical evidence we have. First, attempts to work income into various logit and travel cost equations consistently produced coefficients that were small and insignificant. This absence of an income effect appears to imply that willingness-to-pay real dollars should be $63 as well, except for the possible influences of disequilibrium mentioned above. Second, we did have a measure of actual willingness-to-pay in the TCM estimate of $32. By comparison, our CVM value using the hypothetical offer to sell permits to hunters at fixed prices was $21. The CVM survey also included an open-ended question asking the respondent to write in maximum WTP. Here, the mean was $11. (Bishop, Heberlein and Kealy 1983, p. 627) This was our viewpoint when we initiated the deer hunting study. Empirical research can hold surprises, as we shall see momentarily. First, however, CBS makes rather prominent mention of the unpublished criticisms of our goose study analysis by Carson and Mitchell (1984). Let us digress, therefore, to address their concerns.

Carson and Mitchell (hereafter CM) claim that two groups of hunters included in our analysis should be eliminated because their responses are invalid, or as CM put it, they were not genuinely participating in the studies. They show that when these "nonparticipants" are eliminated from the analysis, the estimated values provided by the CVM and the simulated market are statistically the same. We disagree with the assumptions underlying their analysis, and argue that our original estimates are correct.

First, in the cash market only, CM eliminate the 15 hunters who neither cashed the check nor returned it, refusing the offer. We classified these hunters as refusals to sell, while CM claim they are nonparticipants. Since each hunter had already received his/her permit, and since the permit would not be invalidated unless they cashed the check, it is highly likely that most of these "nonparticipants" simply took the easy way of refusing, that is, destroying the check. Further, Hanemann's (1983) analysis found no effects of a nonresponse dummy variable on the estimated cumulative density function for acceptance.

The second group of "nonparticipants" eliminated from CM's analysis are a proportion of those who refused to sell at amounts above a particular truncation point. They specify the appropriate point as that "beyond which no further sustained (statistically) significant increase in the acceptance rate occurs." Therefore, they eliminated from the cash market analysis those respondents who refused to sell at $75, $100, $150 and $200 (i.e., ten percent of the total) and from the hypothetical market analysis those who refuse to sell at $50 and above (over 50 percent of respondents!). They suggest that these respondents are not genuinely participating in the study, but are "protesting" the study or the idea of selling goose permits in an open market by refusing to sell at a price well above their true permit value.

On the face of it, we find it implausible that many hunters would forego $75, $100, $150, or $200 for the privilege of expressing such an opinion unless the goose permit itself were very close to the amount offered (and refused). The fact that the refusal rate levels off between $50 and $200 simply indicates that most of the people who did not sell for $75 would not sell for $100 to $200 either. These hunters are those who place a high value on opportunities to hunt at Horicon, and it would take perhaps much more than $200 to buy their permits. CM's analysis assumes that this minority group of high-value hunters does not exist, and/or that their values shuld not be included in an estimate of "public" values. Had we been able to offer larger amounts, $500, $1000 and so on, we might have found the point at which the last of these high-value hunters would give up the permit, but it would certainly be greater than $200, and our estimate of $63 is therefore a conservative one (as noted by Hanneman).

Detailed analyses of several attitudinal variables provide further support for our hypothesis and refute CM's hypothesis of "protest." Attitudes toward valuation research and attitudes toward paying for hunting privileges were not related to WTA when the dollar amount of the offer was contolled. Further, hunting commitment did have a direct effect on refusal to sell, controlling for dollar amount, in both the simulated and cash markets.

In sum, we disagree with CBS's statement that "Carson and Mitchell demonstrate, using Bishop and Heberlein data, the lack of significant difference between hypothetical and 'actual' payments"; (p. 108) however, we will await the publication of Carson and Mitchell's comment to make a more comprehensive response.

Deer Study Design

Our reasons for developing a second simulated market experiment extended far beyond mere replication of the goose study results. The goose study did not include simulated market evidence on willingness-to-pay, yet researchers have been more interested in willingness-to-pay measures than in measures of willingness-to-accept. Our valuation mechanism in the goose study (take-it-or-leave-it offers) was rather unorthodox. Most past CVM studies have used bidding games or open-ended valuation questions. As CBS point out, many researchers prefer bidding games because they feel that the bidding process encourages more carefully reasoned consideration of respondents' maximum values. With respect to the goose study, one has to wonder how bidding would have affected both the simulated market and CVM results. In a broader perspective, we also wanted to determine whether the large differences between WTP and WTA, documented consistently in CVM studies, carry over to treatments involving actual cash transactions.

To address these issues, we conducted a study of the value of deer hunting at Sandhill Wildlife Demonstration Area in Wood County, Wisconsin. This is a 12-square mile wildlife research area with a deer-proof fence around the perimeter. Recent research on deer has emphasized management for trophy bucks. In order to maintain the deer population within habitat limits and satisfy multiple-use goals for the area, a deer hunt has been permitted over the past several years. During the past three years, hunters were allowed to take one deer of either sex using their regular Wisconsin deer hunting license. In addition to that license, each Sandhill hunter had to be the winner of a lottery. For the 1983 hunt, which took place on November 12, 150 permits were issued for 6000 applications.

For purposes of the experiment, the 150 successful applicants (i.e., lottery winners) were divided into two groups of equal size. The first group was told that we intended to purchase four Sandhill permits from those who bid the lowest amounts in a sealed-bid auction. Each successful bidder would be paid his/her bid and would not be able to hunt at Sandhill in 1983. The other group of 75 successful applicants received contingent valuation surveys with parallel wording.

A random sample of 600 individuals was drawn from the pool of unsuccessful applicants. Half of these individuals were involved in actual auctions to buy a total of four Sandhill hunting permits issued by the state for research purposes. The other half were involved in comparably worded contingent valuation auctions. Four different auction systems were used. One-fourth of the participants were given the opportunity to simply submit a sealed bid. Their initial bid was the bid that was entered into the auction. A second auction which we will term Bidding Game 1, involved an initial sealed bid. However, these individuals were later contacted by telephone and allowed to raise or lower their bids in a bidding game format. The third auction mechanism involved an initial contact by mail which included a fixed initial bid chosen at random between $1 and $500. Respondents could respond positively or negatively to this initial bid and it served as the starting point for bidding games conducted during later telephone interviews. This will be designated as Bidding Game 2. The fourth auction mechanism involved sealed bids. However, in this case respondents were assured that if their bid was of the four highest bids, they would not be required to pay their full bid, but a lesser amount equal to the fifth highest bid across all the auctions. Thus, this treatment was like the Vickrey auction discussed by CBS, except that it was a "fifth price" auction rather than a second price auction. The economic incentives are the same as in the Vickrey format, with expected utility theory indicating that hunters would bid their full compensating surplus in such a situation. All study subjects were surveyed by mail after the bidding was completed and all were paid $5 for timely participation, including return of the questionnaire.

Preliminary Results

A total of 689.3 hunters (91%) participated fully in the auction. Actual cash bids to accept compensation ranged from $25 to $1,000,000. The $1,000,000 bid was interpreted as a response of "not for sale" and deleted from the analysis that follows. The next highest bid was $20,000. Accepted bids were $25, $62, and two bids of $72. Hypothetical bids to accept compensation ranged from $0 to $20,001. WTP cash bids to buy a permit ranged from $0 to $200, with accepted bids being $200, $177, $152, and $150. Only the $152 bid came from the Fifth Price Auction and this person actually paid $142.

Considerable further analysis remains to be done on the results of this experiment. Bid functions have not been estimated, for example, so we can not yet say whether commitment to hunting, income, and other variables played a systematic role in determining bids. Our TCM work is only now getting underway. Still, the preliminary results do suggest some tentative conclusions.

Table 9.2 shows means and other statistics for the willingness-to-accept-compensation side of the experiment. The mean cash offer of $1,184 was not significantly different from the CVM mean bid of $833. The estimated standard deviation of the bids was quite large.

Table 9.2   Willingness to Accept Compensation for Sandhill Deer Hunting Permits

	Mean	Median	Mode	Standard Deviation	N
Cash offers[a]	1184[b]	550	1000	2475	70
Hypothetical offers	833[b]	102	100	2755	70

[a] $1,000,000 cash bid excluded as an outlier.
[b] Indicates that mean of cash offers and mean of hypothetical offers not statistically significant at the .05 level.

For willingness-to-pay, our preliminary results are given in table 9.3. Cash offers averaged between $19 and $25 in the different auction formats and the null hypothesis that these means were equal could not be rejected at the .10 level. Mean hypothetical bids varied between $31 and $44 and there were also no significant differences among the auction formats. Comparisons of cash and hypothetical bids within auction formats shows that the hypothetical bids are significantly different at the .10 level in three out of the four cases. In all four cases the mean hypothetical bids were *larger*.

Next consider the effects of bidding. The format designated as Bidding Game 2 in table 9.3 most closely parallels the traditional CVM bidding game. Respondents here, it will be recalled, answered yes or no by mail to a starting bid. Then, bidding by telephone followed using the starting bid at the outset. Table 9.3 reorts the mean final bids, which are amazingly close to those from the other treatments. The telephone bidding process did not produce significantly higher or lower results than the Sealed Bid Auction, the Fifth-Price Auction, or Bidding Game 1. This was true whether the comparison was across hypothetical or cash auctions.

In Bidding Game 1, the respondents were asked to submit sealed bids by mail. If they read the "fine print" carefully, they would have seen that the possibility of later changing the bid was kept open, but this possibility was not emphasized in order to get valid sealed bids, yet make the contracts for cash offers legally binding. No mention was made of later telephone bidding or any other mechanism for changing the bids. The initial bids averaged $14 and $25 for the cash and hypothetical groups respectively. Telephone bidding caused 42% of the cash bids to increase. The final bids averaged across the entire subsample increased by $5 to reach the $19 final bid reported in Table 3. For the hypothetical sample, the mean final bid was $43, an increase of $18. Of the 62 people we were able to recontact, 52% increased their bids. Comparing the mean increases showed that people tended to increase their bids more in the contingent auction than in the actual cash auction, with the difference being significant at the .01 level.

By way of summary, preliminary results from the deer experiment seem to point to four conclusions:
1. The large differences between WTP and WTA compensation so often observed in CVM studies carry over to transactions involving real money and real recreational opportunities. In our contingent auctions, WTP averaged $40

Table 9.3 Willingness to Pay for Sandhill Deer Hunting Permits.

Auction format	Mean($)	Median($)	Mode($)	Standard deviation($)	Number of observations
Sealed bids					
Cash	$24	$15	$ 5	$35	68
Hypothetical	32	11	10	64	71
Bidding game 1[a]					
Cash	19[b]	10	5	23	65
Hypothetical	43	21	0	58	62
Bidding game2[c]					
Cash	24	15	0	30	68
Hypothetical	43	20	0	69	69
Fifth price					
Cash	25[b]	20	10	30	69
Hypothetical	42	21	10	70	70

[a] Respondents set initial bids.
[c] Indicates hypothesis that mean cash bid equaled mean hypothetical bid for these auction formats was rejected at the .10 level.
[c] Initial bids chosen at random.

across all auction formats combined, while WTA averaged $833. When real money and real permits were involved the difference was slightly larger at $23 versus $1,184. This latter result is consistent with findings of Knetsch and Sinden (1984). Large differences between WTP and WTA are not simply a phenomenon of CVM.

2. WTP was significantly higher in the contingent auctions than in the cash markets. We suspected a tendency to bid higher in the cash auction measure of WTA, but the difference was not statistically significant in this data set. We will return to this point momentarily.

3. Bidding did not seem to make much difference. People in Bidding Game 1 did tend to raise their offer amounts and the tendency was stronger for the hypothetical bids. Those tendencies, however, did not produce changes that were large relative to variations in mean bids due to intersample differences. Bidding Game 2, which closely parallels traditional bidding games used in CVM studies, produced results nearly identical to other auction formats.

4. As one might expect, based on the literature on experimental auctions cited by CBS, the Fifth-Price Auction did not produce the significantly larger bids that theory would lead one to expect. Vickrey auctions seem to be of questionable value in CVM studies, a point that we will discuss further in our evaluation of CBS in the section below.

Deer Study Interpretation and Plan for Further Research

These results contradict what we expected based on the goose study. As noted above, we expected CVM estimates of WTA to be much larger than cash experiment estimates. If anything, the WTA results tend in the opposite direction and the difference is not statistically significant. While our evidence was not as strong, we thought that a good case existed for arguing that CVM estimates of WTP tend to be underestimates of true WTP. The deer study had hypothetical WTP offers significantly higher than comparable results based on cash offers. How are these differences to be explained?

Of course, a larger number of hypotheses could be stated to try to explain these differences. As our analysis continues, and particularly as we estimate bid functions, additional possible explanations may become apparent. At this writing, our best guess is that a large part of the difference between the goose study and deer study results are attributable to the added uncertainty present in the deer study.

The goose study respondents made their decisions under relative certainty. If they accepted our fixed, predetermined offer they received the amount of money offered. If they rejected the offer, they maintained the opportunity to hunt a goose.

The problem for our deer hunters was more complicated. The effect of bidding on the cash position and hunting opportunities of any given respondent depended on how much she or he bid and *the bids of all other auction participants*. The bidding behavior of others, particularly given the absence of any information from past auctions, must have been very uncertain. As CBS point out in some detail, people do not seem to react to uncertainty in ways that are consistent with what utility theory would lead us to expect. Theory would lead us to expect very similar behavior in simulated markets involving fixed take-it-or-leave-it offers and simulated markets involving various bidding frameworks, particularly the Fifth-Price Auction. However, respondents have reacted to the added uncertainty inherent in bidding against others in ways that led to very different results. We suspect that people tended to adopt a "heuristic" which led them to behave very conservatively in response to the uncertainty about other's bids.

Consider the cash auction where we offered to buy four permits from the lowest bidders. Participants in this auction had won the lottery with odds of 0.025:1 (150 winners out of 6,000 applicants). They were then asked to state the minimum amounts they would accept. People may have figured that by stating a high bid they increased the risk of losing the auction, but then they could always go hunting. If a high bid was stated, but other bids were even higher, the bidder would lose the hunting opportunity but receive a relatively large amount of money. Making a relatively low bid improved the chances of winning, but winning the auction would entail loss of the hunting opportunity and the monetary gain would be small. We suspect that this sort of logic tended to lead our study participants to state relatively large bids in the cash auction to estimate WTA, bids in excess of their true compensating surplus. The same rationale could have been active in the CVM treatment, but naturally would have been less powerful because study subjects knew that they could go hunting regardless of how they responded.

On the WTP side, this same conservatism would work in reverse. Consider the point of view of a hunter drawn to participate in the cash auction. If he or she bid a relatively low amount, then the result would probably be loss of the auction, but there was some chance that others would bid even lower amounts, thus making the person in question a winner. In this way, our auction provided a small chance of a real bargain for those who bid relatively small amounts.

Certainly bidding higher would improve the chances of winning, but more of the potential compensating surplus will be lost due to the higher cash payment required. People may have had a tendency to bid toward the lower side of their compensating surplus. We hoped that the Fifth-Price Auction would reduce this tendency, but apparently uncertainty was the overriding consideration. In the CVM auctions, hunters knew that they would not have the opportunity to hunt regardless of their answers and tended to react by bidding higher than they would have in the cash auction.

This scenario, though plausible, is only speculative at this stage. More definite conclusions must await further research. The 1983 Sandhill study involved only four permits because of legal constraints that are no longer binding. For the 1984 hunt, we can deal in any number of permits so long as the requisite number of hunters to meet biological objectives is present. This will make it possible to construct a 1984 study like the goose study. Simulated market participants on both the WTP and the WTA sides will receive opportunities to buy and sell, respectively, permits at predetermined prices. This will make uncertainty about other bids irrelevant. Our guess is that CVM WTP will tend to increase slightly and that CVM WTA compensation may fall a bit. More importantly, we hypothesize that this new format will have a large upward effect on simulated market WTP and a large downward effect on simulated market WTA. Using SM to symbolize "simulated market" our hypothesis is that:

$$\text{CVM WTP} < \text{SM WTP} > \text{SM WTA} < \text{CVM WTA}.$$

However, we expect large differences between SM WTP and SM WTA to remain.

Having thus stated what we have learned about CVM from our own research let us return to CBS for some implications.

IMPLICATIONS FOR CBS

CBS have provided a great deal of food for thought in the first part of this book. Much is said to which we can readily agree. Rather than dwell on these points of agreement, we will focus in on areas where we disagree or at least think more should be said. The evaluation of CBS will be organized around a series of rhetorical questions in the hope of focusing attention on major issues.

Is Contingent Valuation Biased?

CBS make many good points in this regard, but even after reading them carefully, we are not quite sure where they stand on the question of bias.

What is meant by bias here? CBS suggest that "market prices are appropriate measures of the 'benefits' (social welfare) of concern in cost-benefit assessments and, therefore, represent a standard for accuracy, or 'appropriateness.' against which CVM measures are to be compared". While we will raise some questions later regarding specific interpretations of this statement in the context of WTA, the basic principle is clear: CVM values are accurate to the extent that they approximate values that would be obtained in a well-functioning market.

This is why we believe that our experimental results are powerful. Although—as noted above—our simulated markets for hunting permits lack some of the characteristics of real markets, they should provide considerable information about how comparisons with real markets would come out. Furthermore, the comparisons are being conducted under rather ideal conditions. Hunting permits are not a public good, since the excludability condition for private goods is not fulfilled. Furthermore, the commodities—goose hunting or deer hunting opportunities—are well-known to the study subjects. Vehicle bias should not be a problem, since both the hypothetical and cash transactions employed the same vehicles. All study subjects, whether in the real or hypothetical markets, had the same information. The only difference in the treatments was that part of the transactions involved hypothetical payments and recreational opportunities and part invovled real payments. Clearly, if contingent valuation is capable of giving unbiased estimates of real values, it should have done so here.

The results, however, indicate bias. People were more willing to sell their goose hunting permits for real dollars than they indicated they would be in the contingent market. Preliminary results from the deer study indicate that in an auction framework, CVM will overestimate willingness-to-pay. On the WTA side of the deer hunting auction, bids varied too widely to say for sure, but it appears that CVM may have erred slightly on the low side.

How would this bias be classified within the system described by CBS? Hypothetical bias related to the lack of real transactions appears to be the problem. As we have said before, money is a powerful stimulus and real money is more powerful than hypothetical money. In fairness to CBS, they seem to be very explicit in recognizing this point. For example, citing us and other studies, they point out that, "actual vs. hypothetical payment does result in different choices" (emphasis in original). However, somehow this does not seem to be a major point in their overall argument. In an earlier section of part I, they refer to hypothetical bias as "one of the most important unresolved issues for any assessment of the efficacy of CVM." They mention our result, but quickly point out that Carson and Mitchell cast doubt on the conclusions. Similar, though less specific, questions are raised about Bohm's findings and those of Slovic and others. With the added evidence from the deer study—to which, admittedly, CBS did not have access, since it is as yet unpublished—we think the evidence for bias related to hypothetical payment is rather convincing.

Furthermore, this source of bias lies at the crux of the matter. CVM's dominant characteristic is the hypothetical character of the transactions. Starting point bias, information bias, vehicle bias, and biases relating to perceptions and framing may well arise in circumstances that are less ideal than ours. However, even if these problems are solved to a satisfactory approximation, bias due to hypothetical payment will still be a threat. Stated differently, no matter how closely the "Reference Operating Conditions" (ROC) proposed by CBS in chapter 6 are met, hypothetical bias will remain. In fact, it is hard to imagine any real world setting where the ROCs would be more closely met than in our experiments, except that we measured only WTA in the simulated market for goose hunting permits. Hypothetical bias deserves more explicit recognition by CBS outside of chapter 5.

Do CBS Deal Adequately With Accuracy Issues?

To ask "What Is Accuracy?" in the context of nonmarket evaluation is long overdue. Thus, CBS have produced much that is thought-provoking and we hope that they and others will pursue this topic with diligence. However, we have some serious reservations about the specifics of their accuracy assessment. It may be necessary to accept accuracy no better than ± 50 percent in estimates from CVM, TCM, HPM, and market data, but CBS's arguments for such a limit are hardly convincing.

CBS claim that, "The range of possible error for the CVM derived solely from potential biases is easy to establish." They then cite Rowe et al. (1980b) as showing that the sum of starting point, vehicle and information bias can be as large as 40 percent. They also cite Schulze et al. (1983a) as showing that payment cards may produce results as much as 40 percent lower than iterative bidding. Applying these percentages leads CBS to conclude that "CVM is not likely to be *more* accurate than ± 50 percent of the measured value" (emphasis in original).

Surely such a wide range of error need not be accepted. Rowe et al. are not using the term "bias" in its strict sense of deviations from the "true" value. Instead, they showed that varying starting point, vehicle, and information can cause final bids to vary greatly. CBS argue (and we add our support below) that experimental techniques should be very helpful in reducing such variation by indicating which CVM techniques come closest to approximating true values. Surely many of the sources of error found by Rowe et al. can be reduced or eliminated through experimental studies. As for the results of iterative bidding found in Schulze et al. (1983a), either iterative bidding helps bring people closer to their true values or it does not. Experimentation should be able to produce strong evidence one way or the other. Thus, the studies cited by CBS are not indicative of the magnitude of errors that are inevitably present in CVM and that must be accepted in setting error bounds.

Similar problems may exist in CBS's assessment of the errors in value estimates from market information. Unfortunately, the paper they draw on Coursey and Nyquist 1983 is unpublished and therefore unavailable to us. We were unable to follow the argument as described by CBS.

Thus, we would question whether CBS' assessment of bounds for CVM estimates and market demand analyses are meaningful. This is not to say that the bounds are necessarily less than or greater than 50 percent. More research is needed to implement the specifics of CBS's sound overall ideas about accuracy.

Furthermore, an important concept is missing from CBS's exposition on scientific accuracy. This is the concept of "calibration". When a new method of scientific measurement is developed it is often necessary to calibrate it against old methods. It may prove feasible through experimental studies to calibrate CVM methods that can then be used in the field to arrive at more accurate values. Thus, establishing error bounds on existing CVM techniques is a worthwhile goal, but reducing those bounds through calibration should be the long-run goal.

Does Iterative Bidding Improve Accuracy?

CBS give a rather strong endorsement to iterative bidding. They repeatedly emphasize that this procedure emulates "market-like" processes, helping respondents to "research their preferences". Also, the experimental literature is cited to show that in auctions people may require several rounds of bidding before they learn their optimal strategies. Iterative bidding allegedly provides a substitute for this learning process.

Considerable evidence can be mustered to the contrary. The evidence is not strong enough to reach categorical conclusions yet, but there are substantial indications that iterative bidding biases CVM results.

CBS review a great many studies that have attempted to test for starting point bias in traditional bidding games. Some found an upward bias, while several others did not. We would submit that all of these studies provided relatively weak evidence because they involved only two, or at most three, starting bids. Furthermore, sometimes the range of starting bids was too small to pick up starting point bias.

To further examine the question, members of our research team have recently analyzed data from three studies employing bidding games. These include a CVM study of the value of scenic beauty along the Lower Wisconsin River (see also Boyle and Bishop 1984); the deer hunting permit study, Bidding Game 2 as reported above, and a study of the value of sport diving around offshore petroleum structures. (Thompson and Roberts 1983) In the first two studies starting bids were randomized across a range of values that were deemed *ex ante* to be plausible. In the Thompson and Roberts study, six alternative starting bids were used ranging from $20 to $400 for a year of diving.

To test for starting point bias, we hypothesized a linear relationship of the following form:

$$BF = a + b\ BS + e$$

where BF is the final bid, BS is the starting bid, a and b are constants and e is a random disturbance term. The equation was estimated for four different sources of data: (1) the Wisconsin river contingent valuation results; (2) the deer study results from contingent bidding; (3) the deer study results from cash bidding, and (4) the Thompson and Roberts study. The results are reported in Boyle, Bishop and Walsh. The estimate of b was positive and significantly different from zero at the 0.01 level for all three CVM data sets. The estimate for b was negative and *not* significantly different from zero at the 0.10 level for the cash bidding for deer permits. We would interpret this as evidence for the hypothesis that the starting bid has a significant positive influence on final bids in contingent markets. Furthermore, this phenomenon does not seem to be present once real money becomes involved.

By way of a *caveat*, we should say that these results are new. Discussions are already underway with Alan Randall about their validity. Randall would argue that perhaps our range of starting bids included some that were too far removed from most people's final bids. He suspects that when the bidding process starts at such high levels people tend to become tired of and bored with the bidding process. They then terminate the bidding by accepting bids which are higher than their true values simply to be done with the process. This may or may not be a problem in our approach. Further analysis and perhaps additional research will be needed to test this and possibly other concerns. In the meantime, we are taking a rather dim view of traditional bidding games.

The solution proposed by CBS is to let the respondents state their initial bids, perhaps with the aid of a payment card. Whether payment cards introduce a starting point bias of their own remains an issue for future research. The alternative is simply to let the respondent state an opening bid without the prompting of a payment card. This is like our Bidding Game 1. There, it will be recalled, respondents often did increase their bids both in the contingent and cash auctions. However, the increase in the mean bid was statistically significantly larger for the contingent auction. Stated differently, the process of iterative bidding in the contingent auction caused people to bid money that they would not bid if the money was real. One study is obviously not definitive, but our evidence is contrary to the argument by CBS and others that bidding helps people research their preferences. We would think that it tends to encourage them to exaggerate their willingness-to-pay.

As a final note, the reader may wonder why all this is necessary, since final mean bids from Bidding Games 1 and 2 in the deer study were not significantly different than the results of the other mechanisms. Assuming that this result is replicated in later studies, it does raise additional questions about the efficacy of bidding games. Bidding rules out mail surveys and thus forces the use of more costly telephone and personal interviews. The ultimate conclusion may be that iterative bidding is not worth the trouble and expense.

Are Experimental Approaches the Key to Assessing and Improving CVM?

We agree that experimental approaches have great promise here. The experiment by Coursey, Schulze and Hovis (1983) (hereafter CSH), described in detail by CBS, is among the most interesting work done on CVM since its inception and illustrates well the potential usefulness of laboratory experiments. We hope that it will soon be one of many such studies. In this, we are in agreement with CBS.

Nevertheless, one has to wonder whether CBS are a bit one-sided in their emphasis on the virtues of laboratory experiments. Field experiments have a long established role in many disciplines, yet CBS repeatedly imply that anything done outside the laboratory is second-rate science. In fact, our work does not warrant mention in their chapter on experimental economics, presumably because it was done entirely outside the laboratory. This is a very unfortunate precedent to set in this new area of economic research because it may divert attention from promising field experiments.

Perhaps research in acid rain biology will illustrate the need for combining laboratory and field experiments. Despite dozens of laboratory studies on the effects of acidity on aquatic organisms, many questions remain about what happens in natural ecosystems when pH is lowered from an external source. Such natural habitats can only be simulated to a limited extent and lab results are suspect because aquariums remain relatively artificial. Under a project supported by USEPA, Wisconsin scientists are constructing a plastic curtain to divide a lake in the northern part of the state. One side of the lake is to be acidified while the other will serve as a control. Biological effects will then be monitored to see which laboratory results are applicable under field conditions.

Does a similar problem exist for laboratory work on CVM? The virtue of the laboratory, as CBS emphasize, is a high degree of control. What they fail to bring out is that such control is gained by creating conditions that are highly simplified and highly artificial. A fish in the laboratory is still a fish, but the aquarium is not a wild habitat. Likewise, a human being in an economic laboratory experiment is an economic actor, but the laboratory situation is simplified and artificial. The result is that without field research there will always be questions about the applicability of results to the real world.

Consider again the CSH study. Again, our purpose is not to detract from their potentially very valuable contribution. Also, let us explicitly state that all we have for documentation is CBS' summary. We have not yet been able to acquire the papers that CBS cite. Nevertheless, CSH will help illustrate the limitations of laboratory experiments.

Suppose that a study of the economic losses due to air pollution in an eastern city is being planned. How much help would the CSH results provide? Could one generalize from bad tasting liquids to reduced visibility? The "commodity" in the CSH experiment was quite simple, while air pollution is complex, involving visibility, physical discomfort to eyes and the respiratory system, damage to public and private assets, and long-run health effects. Is behavior involving simple environmental "bads" in the laboratory necessarily indicative of behavior involving complex environmental bads in the real world? CBS do not describe the socioeconomic characteristics of the subjects in the CSH experiment, but presumably they would not be typical of a cross section of the population of the city in the air pollution study. Can we generalize from the laboratory subjects to the population in the applied study? The artificiality of the laboratory is also present in the way money enters in. Presumably—although again CBS are unclear—the CSH subjects were given some money to start with, at least those on the WTP side. Is it known what effects this had and whether people would behave differently in spending money out of their regular incomes?

Two points follow. First, in setting the agenda for future research, field experiments should go hand in hand with laboratory experiments. Second, all research results should be interpreted with care and laboratory results are no exception. Consider, for example, the use of CSH results to further discredit contingent WTA.

Should Willingness to Accept Be abandoned in CVM Applications?

WTA has been a continual embarrassment to practitioners of CVM. Persistent, large differences between WTP and WTA have seemed at odds with theory and WTA values often seemed, in the eyes of the economic researchers at least, to be unrealistically large. Many studies have not even bothered to estimate WTA. Now CBS would use the results of the CSH experiment to drive a final nail in the coffin. Such a burial seems premature.

The deer-hunting study indicates that large differences between contingent WTA and contingent WTP are at least somewhat indicative of how people would behave if real money was involved. Further evidence is provided by CSH. There, the large differences persisted through at least four iterations of the actual cash auctions. Only after some unspecified—at least by CBS—number of trials did WTA collapse.

Objections to drawing general conclusions from this result come quickly to mind. Surely the arguments of the preceding section regarding differences between laboratory and real world conditions caution against automatically assuming that WTA will collapse under all conditions where CVM is applied. Furthermore, it should be noted that the CSH result was unexpected and somewhat mysterious. Assume that theory is correct in predicting that, for any individual, WTA and WTP will be equal, once equilibrium is achieved, except for the income effect. Assume also that CBS are correct in arguing that large observed differences between WTP and WTA during initial iterations of simulated markets and in CVM studies, reflect only the need of respondents to learn more about the market and their optimal strategy. Wouldn't learning be equally necessary for WTP? Wouldn't one expect *a priori* to see WTP and WTA converge in the middle, rather than convergence being solely the result of the collapse of WTA to roughly one-fourth of its mean value in early iterations?

Questions therefore arise about whether the CSH results reflect some basic economic principle with broad ramifications for all CVM studies or whether they only reflect something about the laboratory environment created by CSH. One can imagine, for example, high bidders seeing their low bidding competitors repeatedly drinking the SOA and making $10 or so. As the time in the lab comes to an end, such high bidders might reason that if they are going to make any money from the experiment they must underbid the competitor before the experiment ends. CBS do not provide enough information to even begin to judge whether such an "end-point bias" was operative. For example, did WTA taper off over several trials or collapse suddenly toward the end? How many trials on average were required? Were the lower values of WTA stable over several iterations after collapse or were they a transitory phenomenon? The CSH experiment is brimming with titillating possibilities for further research, but unless the papers are a great deal more persuasive than CBS—it is hardly grounds for deciding to do away with WTA in all contingent valuation studies everywhere.

In fact, one might argue that recent research is grounds for *more* WTA research. From a theoretical standpoint, WTA is no more and no less to be preferred as a welfare measure than WTP. So long as one could appeal to Willig (1976) and Randall and Stoll (1980) to say that the two measures were equal except for a probably small income effect, their joint existence was not a great concern. However, CSH and both of our experiments show that, at least during initial iterations, the differences are likely to be large, even though real money is involved. This phenomenon may have important ramifications for welfare measurement.

Use our deer permits as an example. Assume for the sake of argument that the cash auction WTP and WTA values of $23 and $1,184 respectively, are "true" first-iteration values and that the problems of uncertainty alluded to in our discussion of the study do not exist. If the collapse of WTA, which CSH results lead us to expect, turns out to be a general principle, we would expect the WTA for deer permits to approach $23 eventually. However, for the 1983 hunt, the study subjects told us that, on average, it would take $1,184 to compensate them. If the 1983 hunt had been cancelled and it was somehow determined WTA was the appropriate welfare measure, surely the average loss would be $1,184 per permit, and not $23. Admittedly, if it were impossible to measure WTA, then that would make it impractical to use it as a welfare measure regardless of its theoretical niceties. However, in both of our experiments and in CSH, CVM worked about as well or perhaps better in estimating first-iteration WTA as in measuring WTP. Only in the long run is it necessary to worry about whether CVM is grossly overestimating WTA. In the short run, CVM estimates of WTA may well be relevant to policy and as capable of measurement as WTP.

Will the Application of Vickrey Auctions Improve the Accuracy of CVM?

Among the many themes developed by CBS, the advocacy of Vickrey or second-price auctions as a method to be employed in CVM studies stands out as a dramatic departure from past thinking. Have CBS discovered a valuable new tool? We would rather think they have introduced a red herring.

The theoretical reason for needing a Vickrey format in actual sealed-bid auctions is quite clear and convincing. The quote from Vickrey himself given by CBS makes the point well. Consider a situation where two men, A and B, are bidding for a single unit of a good. Assume that there is no collusion and that a first-price, sealed-bid auction is to be conducted. Suppose that CS(o) would be A's compensating surplus from consuming the good *if* he could get it for free. Let PA be his bid and PB be B's bid. Looking at the problem from A's point of view, he will not bid more than CS(o) since this would imply a welfare loss is he wins the auction. Thus, PA < CS(o) must hold. Setting PA equal to CS(o) is not a particularly desirable strategy either. If A wins (i.e., PA = CS(o) > PB) then A will have to pay his full potential compensating surplus and be no better off. On the other hand, if PA is set sufficiently low that CS(o) > PA > PB then A can realize some net consumer surplus equal to CS(o) minus PA and be beter off for entering the auction. On the other hand, if the outcomeis CS(o) > PB > PA then A will lose out and wish he had bid more. This is what A must balance in setting PA. He will tend to bid less than CS(o) to increase the gap between CS(o) and PA but he will also try to bid enough so that PA > PB. The exact bid will depend on his probability density function on PB. Still, the end result is a tendency to bid less than CS(o).

A Vickrey auction simplifies the problem greatly. The optimal strategy will be to set PA = CS(o). If A wins (i.e., PA > PB), he pays only PB and realizes a net gain of CS(o) minus PB. If A loses, PB > CS(o) so that A is no worse off. Thus, in a Vickrey auction, there is indeed an incentive to bid one's full WTP.

Note, however, that this is very different from what is done in a traditional CVM study. The hypothetical market in such studies does not ordinarily place subjects in a situation of bidding against each other for a limited number of units of the amenity in question. Rather, the problem is simplified to one of determining at what price one would drop out of the market. In a way, this is more like an English auction where various participants drop out as they reach their respective maximum WTP's. In an English auction, as CBS point out, all people except the winner have an incentive to express bids up to their maxima. Thus, previous CVM studies have not failed to elicit maximum WTP simply by neglecting to have participants assume that they would actually pay the next lowest bid.

Of course, one could try to argue that it would be preferable in future CVM studies to have people assume they are bidding against others in a second-price auction for a limited supply of the environmental amenity in question. This would be theoretically as acceptable as the traditional approach, but not theoretically superior. Furthermore, the theoretical argument that people will reveal full WTP in a second-price auction depends critically on the assumption of expected utility maximization. It would hardly seem desirable to introduce uncertainty about what others will bid into CVM studies, given people's well-documented tendencies to behave in counter-theoretical ways under uncertainty. Also, since people are not familiar with second-price auctions, much more care would need to be exercised in designing survey instruments and even then there is risk of confusion. And, as CBS point out, several iterations may be required before respondents learn how to capitalize on the second-price format. It is not clear to us how one would structure the survey to provide a hypothetical situation conducive to learning what one would learn by actually winning and losing such auctions. Merely playing an iterative bidding game for a few minutes with an interviewer would not be much of a substitute for such experiences and could introduce additional problems. Repeated visits with reports of hypothetical auction results as proposed by CBS sounds fine in theory but would be expensive, might cause respondent exhaustion, and would increase nonresponse problems as people became difficult to recontact. Without some way to encourage learning, the deer study indicates that a Vickrey format will not produce results significantly different from traditional results. Thus, the Vickrey framework would introduce additional uncertainty, respondent confusion, expense and complications into CVM applications with gains that are dubious.

Similar questions could be raised about the other departure from traditional CVM techniques suggested by CBS, the "tatonnement process". Here, bidding and voting in successive iterations would occur until unanimity about payment and pollution allocation is achieved. Such tatonnement processes would allegedly "out perform" more traditional procedures. To sustain this argument, however, at least two assumptions must hold. In traditional CVM applications to commodities with true public good characteristics (e.g., visibility), normal procedures in essence ask respondents to pretend that the commodity is a private good. Thus, for the procedures advocated by CBS to be necessary, it must first be assumed that study subjects are unable or unwilling to imagine the commodity as a private good. This assumption seems doubtful given the lack of evidence of free riding described by CBS. Even if the first assumption does hold, one would also have to assume that going through a *hypothetical* Grove-Ledyard procedure would cause respondents to reveal their true preferences and values. If, contrary to present evidence, they are already free riding, why should they change in a hypothetical situation? The alternative of increased cost, increased confusion, and lower response rates seems a more likely result of attempting such procedures.

Is Attitude-Behavior Research Relevant to CVM Research?

Beginning with our first publication on the goose study, Bishop and Heberlein 1979 we have attempted to introduce economists to the research by social psychologists on attitudes and behavior. We argued that CVM expressions of WTP and WTA are, in psychological terms, "attitudes", while actually buying and selling things is "behavior". In questioning whether contingent values are accurate, economists are, in a sense, asking whether attitudes (expressions of WTP) correspond to behavior (how people would behave if a real market was created). A major result from the attitude-behavior literature was introduced. In general, the relationship between measured attitudes and actual behavior varies greatly and in many cases is quite low. In the current context, this serves as a warning against assuming automatically that people actually will pay or accept what they say in a survey they will pay or accept.

We certainly underestimated the barriers to interdisciplinary communication. Our proposal that economists consider the attitudes-behavior literature has met with indifference or hostility. CBS are no exception. Nevertheless, we continue to believe that this material is relevant and that economists are the losers for ignoring it. Allow us to attempt to make our case clearer.

An attitude is a mental state relating to some object. That is, a person has an attitude about something. The object may be very general as in the case of environmental attitudes or very specific as in one's attitudes about one's spouse [Heberlein, 1981]. Attitudes generally have three related components. The "cognitive" component refers to dispassionate facts and beliefs. For example, a person might say that the water in Lake X is clean. Second is the "affective" component. Affects have to do with the evaluative and emotional aspects of attitudes. A person might say "I like swimming in clean lakes." The third component is "behavioral intentions". Continuing the example, a statement of behavioral intent might be, "I plan to swim in Lake X this summer." For the most part, responses to contingent valuation questions are, to the social psychologist, statements of behavioral intention. In a WTP question, people are saying that if a market existed for the amenity in question, their intention would be to pay certain stated amounts. No actual behavior has taken place, but people have expressed an intention to behave in a certain way.

As in any discipline, social psychologists adapt the terminology to their own needs. In the present case, Ajzen and Fishbein (1977), as cited by CBS, use the term attitude more narrowly to refer to the affective component only and apply the term behavioral intention separately. Terms do not really matter here, so long as confusion is avoided. The ideas are the same. Our terminology is more consistent with the bulk of the literature and we will continue to use the term attitude in the broader, more all- encompassing sense.

The left-hand side of figure 9.1 illustrates the linkages between the three components of attitudes. In everyday language, when we "think about" something, the three components interact. For example, liking clean lakes (an affective component) may, over time, encourage us to gather information about which lakes are clean, building the cognitive component. The arrows run both ways. For example, leraning that Lake X is suffering from declining pH due to acid rain (a cognitive component), I might decide that I only like clean lakes that are also unaffected by acid rain. My behavioral intentions toward Lake X may change as a result.

Social psychologists draw a very basic distinction between attitudes and behavior. This is depicted by the vertical double line in figure 9.1. To observe that Lake X is clean or to state that one likes swimming is not the same as actually going swimming. Even stating plans to go swimming is not the same as actually doing so. Only when one actually gets in the water is the link between attitudes toward Lake X and behavior with respect to Lake X completed. Behavior is something that can be observed in the real world. Attitudes are not directly observable, but must be inferred, usually from survey responses.

These relationships were clear in the goose study. Recall how commitment came into the equations for both the hypothetical and cash offers. Commitment expressed how the subjects felt about goose hunting. An element of behavior intention may also have been present in committment. The cognitive component included new knowledge in the form of a real or hypothetical offer from the University. Both commitment and the amount of the offer interacted to influence the economic behavioral intention (yes, I would sell or no, I would not). However, the cognitive component was different in the two treatments. In one case, the respondents knew the offer was real while in the other they knew it was hypothetical. Thus, there was a divergence between the behavioral intentions expressed in the contingent market and behavior in the simulated market. Most probably didn't purposely mislead us, but the different cognitive components lead to a different set of interactions as they thought about the offers. Commitment tended to have more influence for hypothetical offers;

Figure 9.1
Schematic of Attitude-Behavior Relationships

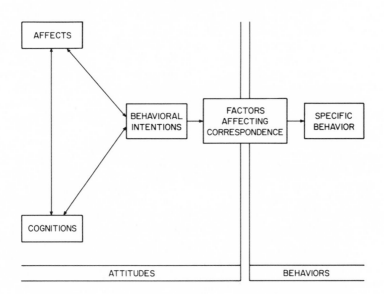

dollar amounts had more influence for cash offers; and the result was a substantial difference between behavioral intentions and behavior.

That attitudes do not always predict behavior should not be surprising. Focusing attention on the box near the center of figure 9.1, many factors affect attitude-behavior correspondence besides attitudes. An interesting example can be drawn from the CSH experiment. Consider those who at the outset said that they would require almost $10 on average to taste SOA, based on a verbal description. However, in part II they tasted the stuff without being paid anything (at the margin) to do so. Here is a simple case where attitude ("I'd have to be paid $10 to taste the stuff.") and behavior (tasting free) did not correspond. Obviously, there was an additional factor at work. They had signed up for and were presumably being paid to participate in an experiment and behaved as they did because tasting SOA was part of the experiment.

As noted already, one of our goals in introducing all this was to warn economists that attitudes, including behavioral intentions, are not necessarily the same as behavior. A second reason for linking economics and social psychology is becoming increasingly clear. The attitudes-behavior work is a rich source of both theoretical and empirical insights of direct relevance to CVM studies. Let us attempt to further support this assertion.

We will illustrate application of attitude-behavior concepts by referring to our own current research on acid rain. (Bishop and Heberlein 1984) Reductions of 50 percent in sulphur emissions from power plants east of the Mississippi may cost as much as $5 billion per year. This raises questions about the magnitude of associated benefits. In the aquatics area, economists can estimate the value of fishing losses in areas such as the Adirondack Mountains. In fact, such studies are in progress. Both economists and noneconomists are asking whether such *use* values alone will fully capture the economic losses associated with acid rain. Thus, our own work is focusing on the "non-use" or "intrinsic" values.

The terminology of intrinsic values has not been agreed upon by all resource economists. In our thinking, intrinsic values fall into two broad categories, option value and existence values. Option value is too complex to be dealt with in any detail here. It must suffice to say that option value is a premium, positive or negative, associated with uncertainty about future use of the resource. (Bishop 1982, Graham 1981, Smith 1983, Freeman 1984) Existence values, on the other hand, have to do with values that people would still hold even if use were constrained to zero. The concept can be traced back to Krutilla's (1967) landmark article on conservation economics. Other conceptual work appears in Krutilla and Fisher (1975), Mitchell and Carson (1981), Randall and Stoll (1983), and Desvousges, Smith and McGivney (1983).

Elsewhere (Bishop and Heberlein 1984) we have argued that existence benefits for reductions in acid deposition rates could be positive for several reasons, including: (1) bequest motives; (2) benevolence toward relatives and friends; (3) sympathy for people and animals affected by environmental damages; and (4) feelings of responsibility for environmental damages caused, for example, by use of electricity generated by coal-fired power plants.

Existence benefits from reduced sulphur emissions could, of course, be estimated using CVM. Even if small on a per household basis, such benefits, when added up over millions of households, could be quite large. In fact, we suspect that, given the widespread concern about acid rain and the relatively limited extent of documented current and probable, near-term future damages, existence benefits estimated using CVM will dwarf use benefits. The direction that the economic scales tip could well depend, at least over the next decade or two, on whether the existence benefits have credibility. Thus, economic conclusions about a major national policy issue may depend on whether CVM estimates of existence values are accepted as valid or not.

Empirical assessment of the validity of contingent existence values will not be easy. Field experiments like those involving hunting permits do not appear promising. Laboratory research might be feasible, but experimental designs are not obvious to us. This is where the attitude-behavior research could prove useful.

The question is a relatively straight-forward one of attitude-behavior relationship. Would people expressing the behavioral intention of paying a certain amount for reduced acid emissions actually pay that amount if a market for existence were created? There is a large body of research on the conditions favorable to attitude-behavior correspondence.

As CBS recognize, the strength of the attitude-behavior relationship can be assessed by looking at the specificity of the behavioral intention measure. Drawing on Fishbein and Ajzen (1975), behavioral intentions are stronger predictors of behavior the more specific they are about targets, actions, context, and timing. Target specificity has to do with how definite survey and interview questions are about the actual target of behavior. For example, one would expect a question about existence value of fish in a certain Adirondack region to be more highly correlated with behavior in a real existence market than very general questions about vaguely defined acid-rain damages. In the present context, action and content specificity have to do with stating whether payments will be higher monthly utility bills, taxes, prices or other modes of payment, rather than asking vague questions about "WTP". Timing is important because attitudes change. The shorter the time between attitude statement and actual behavior the better is the relationship between the two. Thus, one would expect contingent valuation questions to predict better, other things being equal, the more specific they are about timing of hypothetical payments and the shorter are the time horizons designed into the contingent valuation mechanisms. *Ex ante*, the researcher can and should take these factors into account in designing studies. Indeed, the better practitioners of contingent valuation are already doing so. The point here is that after the contingent valuation mechanism has been designed and applied, one can be more confident about validity, the more successful one was in designing specificity into the mechanism.

Going beyond contingent valuation mechanism design, other data can be gathered during the survey process to evaluate the possible extent of attitude-behavior relationship. By definition, expressions of WTP for the existence of reduced acid deposition rates involves altruistic behavioral intentions toward the environment. Previous research, dealing with environmental altruism with respect to littering, early use of lead-free gasoline, and energy conservation (Heberlein 1975) has isolated two factors that are particularly important in activating actual behavior consistent with such altruistic behavioral intentions. These are awareness of consequences (AC) and acceptance of personal responsibility (AR). AC has to do with cognitive understanding of ecological effects and particularly awareness of effects on other people. AR refers to how strongly people believe that they are personally to blame for environmental degradation. People with low AR may place blame on other people, corporations or the government. People with high AC and AR have a stronger tendency to carry altruistic behavioral intentions toward the environment into actual altruistic acts, while people with low values for either or both tend to have low correlation between attitude and behavior.

The concepts of AC and AR match well with economic intuition that valid existence values must be related to bequest, benevolence, sympathy, and/or other motives discussed previously. For example, a person who expresses a high existence value for acid rain reductions based on bequest motives is implying (1) awareness that acid rain damages will affect future generations and (2) that he or she is personally responsible for reducing these effects.

Thus, a clear direction for acid rain research emerges. It is important not only to measure people's contingent existence values, but also the major reasons why they may be expressing those values. Cognitive attitudes about acid deposition and its consequence should be measured. Attitudes toward future generations and the stewardship role of the present generation should be examined. Knowledge about and sympathies toward relatives and friends who might be affected by acid rain may also be important. Questions relating to actual altruistic behavior toward the environment and other "causes" (e.g., recycling cans and bottles, membership and level of activeness in environmental organizations and charitable contributions expressing sympathy for people and animals) should be included in the survey instrument. If bid equations show significant positive relationships between CVM existence values and these variables, this would support the hypothesis tha the prerequisites for carrying altruistic behavioral intentions into action are present. If no relationship exists, doubts would arise about the prospects for strong attitude-behavior relationship. The validity and, hence, policy relevance of the economic values would then be more questionable.

CBS are very pessimistic about general prospects for accurately measuring existence values using CVM. Our own remarks should not be interpreted as indicating that we are taking lightly the concerns they express. It is particularly disturbing that there is so much scientific uncertainty about the nature and extent of acid rain damages. The presence of this uncertainty must surely be incorporated into the valuation process. Preference reversal and other observations from experiments involving uncertainty are cause for concern. Still, if conditions for high attitude-behavior correspondence are fulfilled, some grounds would exist for arguing that legitimate economic values are being established at least to a rough approximation.

Hopefully, the acid rain example illustrates that the attitude-behavior literature is of value to CVM researchers. In fact, CBS can find substantial empirical support for many of their conclusions in that literature. For example, their first two ROC's (familiarity with the product and prior experience) appear to be quite consistent with social psychological research results.

OUR ASSESSMENT OF CVM

Tony Scott (1965, p. 37) once remarked, "Ask a hypothetical question and you get a hypothetical answer." We came to CVM research with the same cynicism. To some degree, our research has added empirical support to Scott's assertion. Hypothetical bias does appear to be an inherent weakness of CVM.

Still, we have been surprised at how well CVM does work. In the goose study, the dollar amount in take-it-or-leave-it WTP and WTA offers was consistently the most powerful variable in predicting response, always coming into the logit equations with the expected sign and with significance at the .01 level. Most of our respondents certainly understood what was being asked of them and there was a tendency to respond in the same way they would in a real market, albeit in an imperfect way. Similar conclusions seem to follow from the deer study. On the WTA side, the hypothesis that hypothetical and cash offer means were equal could not be rejected at the .10 level. The CVM mean for WTP was significantly higher, but was certainly not outrageous. Deer management decisions in Wisconsin would probably not be greatly different if based on the CVM estimate of $40 per permit rather than the cash auction mean of $23.

Thus, while CVM appears to be biased even under the best of circumstances, the degree of bias does not appear to be sufficiently high to rule out use of the results in public decision-making. While asking a hypothetical question does elicit a somewhat hypothetical answer, it is also true that if a well-constructed question is asked, people try to give honest answers. This, in our judgement, makes CVM promising.

To fully capitalize on this potential will require a new commitment to methodological research. Past research in this area has not been as conducive to real methodological progress as it might have been for two reasons. First, it was probably necessary for CVM to go through a prescientific stage. Most of the history of CVM brings to mind children with a chemistry set pouring chemicals at random into a test tube to see what will happen. (Perhaps the most recent installment is to "stir in" a Vickrey auction.) Second, there has been very little truly basic research on CVM. Most of the research has had to justify its existence by claiming to address real-world problems. Methodological research had to be done as an add-on to these applied studies. It is little wonder that after 20 years, we are still debating such basic issues as whether iterative bidding improves accuracy.

CVM has shown itself sufficiently promising to warrant a major basic research effort. CBS are quite correct in suggesting that experimental techniques are the key, particularly if they will admit the importance of field as well as laboratory studies. Their hard-headed insistence on stating testable hypotheses may help us get beyond the "chemistry set" approach. The ultimate goal ought to be to go beyond error bounds and counting significant digits to actually overcoming hypothetical bias through calibration.

Agencies such as EPA that have a large interest in developing CVM techniques need to recognize that such basic reseach probably will not be feasible in the context of the policy issues of the day. To address such policy issues more effectively, funds need to be set aside for studies in settings that are more ideal for methodological research. Such research may have to deal with commodities such as SOA and hunting permits before we can do a better job on acid rain in the Northeast and air pollution in Los Angeles.

To pause and examine the state of the art after 20 years and millions of dollars worth of research is worthwhile. A great deal has been learned about CVM, but so much is unknown even now. We do know that CVM is the most promising technique for applying an economic yardstick to many of the nation's seemingly most valuable environmental and resource commodities. Enough positive evidence has accumulated to warrant a major investment in full development of the contingent valuation method.

NOTES

Research on this essay was supported by the College of Agricultural and Life Sciences, University of Wisconsin–Madison; Resources For The Future, Inc.; the Graduate School of the University of Wisconsin–Madison; and the Electric Power Research Institute. The Sandhill deer permit valuation study was done with the help of the Bureau of Research and the staff of the Sandhill Wildlife Demonstration Area, Wisconsin Department of Natural Resources. Glen Anderson, Kevin Boyle, and Michael Welsh made many helpful comments on an earlier draft. All errors are the sole responsibility of the authors.

10

On Assessing the State of the Arts of the Contingent Valuation Method of Valuing Environmental Changes

A. Myrick Freeman III

Department of Economics

Bowdoin College

INTRODUCTION

The subtitle of the report we are discussing is "A State Of The Arts Assessment". This is a felicitous choice of words, I think, because the impression I got from reading the Assessment is that the design and implementation of a CVM survey is still more of an art than a science. Although we have learned a lot about the problems involved, we must still rely to a large extent on the good judgement of the researcher in dealing with such problems as incentives to strategic behavior, starting point bias, the best way to describe the commodity being valued, the choice of a payment vehicle, and so forth. Also, as is the case with the arts, the criteria for evaluating CVM research are not well defined. Judgements concerning the usefulness of the technique and the validity of individual CVM surveys appear to be to a large extent subjective. Different people reach quite different conclusions about the merits of the technique as a whole and individual studies.

This assessment is valuable, at least in part, in that it attempts to move beyond subjective and impressionistic judgements and to place the evaluation of the CVM technique on an objective, scientific foundation. It does this by focusing attention on the question of the accuracy of CVM measures of value, by formulating hypotheses about factors that might influence the accuracy of CVM responses and by reviewing the evidence about these hypotheses that can be gleaned from the accumulated body of CVM data.

In what follows, I, too, will focus on the question of accuracy. I will first discuss the forms for evaluating the CVM, one of which is accuracy. I will then discuss the two forms of inaccuracy in CVM measures, bias and random error. I will then discuss the authors' concluding assessment and provide some conclusions of my own. I will also provide some specific comments on points where I take issue with the authors' analysis. My assignment was to provide two assessments: one of the authors' report and one of the CVM itself. I have chosen not to organize my response along these lines. Rather in what follows, my ideas concerning the CVM are intertwined with my comments on the authors' assessment.

Before turning to a detailed discussion of the Assessment, I want to point out what I think is a serious limitation in the scope of the Assessment. The authors (hereafter referred to as CBS) restrict their discussion to those contingent choice methods designed to elicit *directly* a monetary valuation of the environmental good. There are at least four types of what I would call contingent choice mechanisms which have in common the objective of eliciting information which can be used to determine a monetary value by posing to individuals hypothetical or contingent questions of the form "What would you do if . . .?" or "How much would you pay if?" The first type, which is analyzed in this Assessment, asks for information on the monetary value that the individual attaches to a specified change in the quantity or availability of the environmental good. The second type, which is more relevant for the analysis of private goods demand, asks the individual to indicate the quantity she would wish to purchase at a specified price.

The third type is the contingent ranking method. With this technique individuals are given a set of cards, each card depicting a different set of conditions with respect to the use of the environmental good, including differences in the level of provision of the environmental good itself and perhaps different prices or admission fees for use of the resource. Individuals are asked to place their cards in order of preference. Marginal rates of substitution and monetary values can be inferred from these rankings. Examples of contingent ranking studies include Desvousges, Smith, and McGivney (1983) and Rae (1981).

Finally, individuals might be asked how they would alter activity patterns such as rates of visitation to different recreation sites in response to changes in the level of provision of an environmental good at one site. In some circumstances it may be possible to infer monetary values from reported changes in activity levels. Examples of this technique include the willingness to drive model of Knetsch and Davis (1965) and the site substitution model of Thayer (1981).[1]

A comprehensive assessment of contingent choice methods would include a consideration of whether any of these techniques has any advantages over the CVM in terms of ease of implementation, reduction in the various forms of possible bias, or accuracy of the inferred valuations. For example, appropriate strategies may be more difficult to discern in the case of contingent ranking or site substitution models, thus reducing the likelihood of strategic bias. And both of the latter models appear to avoid starting point problems. But since they ask "What if . . ." questions, they may be subject to what has conventionally been termed hypothetical bias. At least it seems to me that these are important questions to take up in a comprehensive and full assessment of contingent valuation methods.

CRITERIA

Any assessment of a technique for eliciting a valuation must be carried out in terms of one or more agreed upon criteria or standards. CBS are aware of this as their discussion of the need for standards for proving or disproving hypotheses (pp. 9-10) indicates. But I would have thought that CBS would devote more attention to the criteria to be employed in this assessment at the beginning of the paper. It is not until chapter 6 that we find an explicit statement of the criterion they propose to employ in the following assessment. There they say:

> Thus, the general criterion against which to assess the CVM becomes becomes clear: the extent to which the CVM institution, and preference revelations drawn therein, is comparable with the market institution and preference revelations drawn therein.

Unfortunately, I find this statement somewhat confusing. It is not clear which is thought to be more important, the comparison of the institutions or the revealed preferences and valuations. And the statement does not distinguish between individual and aggregate responses. I want to offer an alternative statement of what I think the principal criterion for an assessment should be. I agree that the principal criterion should be the accuracy of the resulting measure of value. By accuracy I mean the degree of correspondence between an individual's stated value (or his revealed value in the forms of contingent choice methods) and his true value. It is imporant to make it explicit that individuals' responses are at issue so as to distinguish between problems in eliciting accurate values on the one hand and sampling from a population and aggregating across individuals on the other. Sampling and aggregation problems are not at the heart of the controversy over CVM. Finally, the nature of the CVM instrument should not be part of the criterion. The CVM institution itself is of direct significance only to the extent that it facilitates the revelation of true or accurate values.

I want to spend a little more time to consider just what I mean by the "true value". According to the standard definition of a compensating measure of value, the true value is that sum of money which the individual would give up (or accept) to restore himself to his original utility level given an increase (or decrease) in the quantity of the environmental good.[2] In other words, the true value is the income/environmental good trade-off which maintains the individual on his original indifference curve. It is conventional to assume that individuals have well defined preference orderings and that they know the shape of their indifference curves. Thus, if we observe an individual to accept a trade-off between income and some other good, we believe that he has revealed something about his preference ordering and the shape of his indifference curves. But the inference that revealed trade-offs reflect true valuings or preferences is correct only if individuals do in fact have full knowledge of their preference orderings.

Suppose that due to a change in relative prices or income or the introduction of a new good, an individual has an opportunity to choose from among a set of consumption bundles that are unfamiliar to her, that is, which she has had no prior experience with. It seems plausible that she might experiment with several different consumption bundles before settling into a new equilibrium position. This experimentation can be viewed as an effort to explore an unfamiliar part of her preference ordering. We can only accept revealed preferences as reflecting true preferences after this exploration has been completed. Therefore I want to define the true value of the environmental good as that substitution between income and the environmental good which we would observe after repeated trials or opportunities for the individual to alter her consumption position.

The reason that we have confidence that individuals reveal true preferences in their market behavior is that they have many opportunities to modify their choices in light of what they learn about their preferences and the characteristics of goods. Similarly many economists, myself included, have expressed confidence in measures of the value of environmental goods derived from hedonic price models and travel cost models because they reflect choices made by individuals who have an opportunity to learn from their experiences and modify their choices accordingly.

A measure of an individual's value of a change in the provision of an environmental good is accurate to the extent that the measured value corresponds to the true value as defined above. Inaccuracies or errors in the measured values produced by a given technique or instrument can have two components. The first is a random component or random error reflecting some structural problem or fault in the technique. In the next section, I consider sources of bias or systematic error in CVM measures. In the following section, I discuss possible random errors in the CVM technique. But before turning to these discussions, I want to mention two additional criteria that may be relevant in the choice of a technique for estimating values for environmental policy making.

One criterion is how much information does the technique provide on the individual's preferences or valuation for the environmental good. Ideally, we would like to recover the individual's inverse demand function for the environmental good so that measures of value for the individual can be calculated for a wide range of changes in the quantity of the environmental good under a wide variety of conditions. An individual's response to a single willingness-to-pay question is an estimate of the integral of the compensated inverse demand function over the range given by the postulated change in the environmental good. But this does not provide enough information to make reliable estimates of the individual's value for larger or smaller changes in the environmental good. The single response can also be interpreted as one point on a Bradford bid curve. (Bradford 1970) The responses to additional questions postulating different changes in the environmental good yield additional points on the Bradford bid curve. If sufficient information can be obtained to estimate the bid curve, then the income compensated inverse demand curve can be recovered by differentiation.

The other criterion is cost. Some people have suggested that contingent valuation experiments are easy to set up and provide an inexpensive source of valuation data (e.g., Randall, Hoehn, and Tolley; forthcoming). From my own observation of the design and implementation of the Vanderbilt survey of the benefits of hazardous waste regulations, I am not convinced that CVM surveys are either easy or cheap. It seems likely that the cost of a survey is an increasing function of its accuracy. Accuracy is likely to be a function of both sample size and the effort devoted to reducing sources of bias and measurement error in the design of the survey instrument. We need to know more about the cost and accuracy of CVM instruments as well as the cost and accuracy of alternative measurement techniques where they are available before we can advise analysts concerning the selection of measurement techniques in particular circumstances.

BIAS

In this section I will discuss strategic biases, starting point bias, information bias, and vehicle bias. Since I lean toward the view that the hypothetical nature of the

CVM instrument is more likely to lead to random measurement error than to bias, I defer my discussion of hypothetical bias to the section entitled Vehicle Bias.

Strategic Bias

The first source of bias to consider is that resulting from conscious attempts by individuals to influence either their payment obligation or the level of the provision of the environmental good through their stated valuations. One form of strategic bias arises from the efforts of respondents to "free ride", that is, to reduce their repayment obligation by stating low values. Others involve efforts to influence the level of provision of the environmental good by stating artificially high or artificially low values. It is important to note that the opportunity for strategic behavior arises only when the valuation questions are asked in a setting in which it at least appears that the actual outcome will be affected by individuals' responses, that is, in other than the purely hypothetical or contingent market setting.

My own view is that strategic behavior should not be a significant problem in carefully designed CVM instruments. This judgement is based on three considerations. The first is the absence of strong evidence for free rider behavior in experiments designed to test the free rider hypothesis. (Smith 1979a; Marwell and Ames 1981) The second is the fact that most CVM instruments do not offer obvious opportunities or incentives for attempting to manipulate the outcome. And finally, visual inspection of the distributions of bids does not suggest strongly biased responses, although this is admittedly a weak test.

Designing CVM instruments to avoid serious strategic bias may involve an element of art or at least judgement on the part of the analyst. The art involves providing a realistic description of the environmental good to be valued and policy scenario while making it clear that real world policy decisions are unlikely to be directly affected by the values revealed by the survey. There may be some situations which invite inflated responses from some groups, in which case CVM surveys would not be likely to provide reliable data. For example, suppose there was a widely publicized proposal to dam and flood the Grand Canyon. A CVM survey of visitors to the Canyon asking their willingness to pay to preserve the Canyon would offer people an opportunity to register their disapproval of the proposal. Thus CVM surveys may be less reliable when they deal with highly politically charged policy questions.

There is a problem which is somewhat related to strategic behavior about which I cannot be sanguine. That is the significant number of refusers and protest zero bidders that are often found in CVM studies. The person who refuses to state a monetary value on the grounds that it is unethical to do so or that he has an inherent right to the environmental good must be dropped from the sample when mean bids are calculated. If a person bids zero on the grounds that he has an inherent right to the good, the bid is not an indicator of his true valuation. Thus an effort should be made to distinguish protest zeros from true zeros so that the former can be dropped from the sample, too. It seems plausible that at least some refusers and protest zero bidders are using a noneconomic means of expressing high economic values. If this is so, then there is a kind of self selection bias at work resulting in a downward bias in estimated sample mean bids. On the other hand Carson and Mitchell (1984a) suggest that many nonrespondents are poor and have low levels of education. If their true values are relatively low, then the mean of remaining responses is an upwardly biased measure of the true mean value.

This analysis suggests three considerations in the design of CVM instruments and the reporting of results. First, efforts should be made to word the CVM question so as to minimize the numbers of protest zeros and refusers. Pretesting of survey instruments should help to detect those aspects of questions which stimulate protest behavior. Second, all zero bidders should be queried so as to identify protest zeros; and protest zeros should be dropped from the valuation sample.[3] And third, the proportion of the original sample which is dropped because of refusal or protest zero bids and the characteristics of other nonrespondents should be reported as an indicator of the possible bias in responses due to self selection.

Starting Point Bias

There is ample evidence that starting point bias can be present when a starting bid is announced by the interviewer and the offer price is adjusted upward or downward until the respondent agrees on the stated value. Also there is evidence that when the respondent is asked to name a value for willingness to pay, he can be induced to adjust this upward by a series of iterative questions. There are a couple of ways in which the starting point problems might be dealt with effectively.

First, consider the starting point bias problem in its simple form. If the mental mechanisms which lead to starting point bias are such that the bias is a function of the absolute value of the distance between the starting point and the individual's true value, and if the upper and lower starting points are equidistant from the true sample mean value, then the two biases can be made to cancel out. With the sample equally divided between low and high starting points, the best estimate of the true value is the mean of all responses.

Another possible approach is to derive an iteration procedure from the "bracket and halving" procedure used to adjust naval gunfire to strike a target. The procedure would be to announce a starting point chosen at random for each respondent within the range of likely values. This offer would be adjusted in the appropriate direction by a large enough step so as to bracket the individual's likely true value. Successive adjustments would involve halving the interval between the two preceding offers as appropriate until the individual agreed on the stated value. This procedure is designed to close as rapidly as possible on the true value, thus reducing the likelihood of a boredom effect. Also choosing the initial bid at random avoids the indicative effects of nonrandom starting points. Thus, even if each individual's response has a systematic error related to his starting point, these errors can be made random across individuals so that aggregate values are unbiased.

Information Bias

Two kinds of information bias have been discussed in the literature. One refers to the effect of providing information on values and costs (for example, the cost of providing the environmental good, the costs and/or values of other kinds of public goods, or bids offered by other respondents). If this kind of information is provided, it would appear to lead to bias through a kind of indicative effect akin to that leading to starting point bias. For this reason it seems that this kind of information should not be provided to respondents.

The second type of information bias is said to result from changes in the information provided to individuals about the environmental good itself. Evidence that individuals' bids can be changed in systematic ways by changes in the description of the environmental good should be taken as favorable to the CVM. This evidence indicates that people use the information provided to form a perception of the environmental good and base their valuation responses on their perception. I think that two conclusions can be drawn about the design of a CVM instrument and the interpretation of its results. First, it is important to provide a clear and meaningful description of the environmental good of concern. Here, too, the art of CVM instrument design is important. Second, statements about the results of CVM measures should take the following form: "The value of the environmental good *as described in the CVM instrument* is $X." This qualifying phrase makes it clear that what is being valued in the CVM exercise is the environmental good described to the individual. The relevance of the CVM results for valuing the outcome of a real world environmental policy depends upon the degree of correspondence between the environmental good described to individuals and the proposed real world environmental change.

Vehicle Bias

Vehicle bias refers to systematic differences in responses depending upon the postulated means of collecting payments from individuals. Some studies find systematic differences between payment vehicles while others do not. Interpretation of those studies which do find differences is hampered by our inability to state which payment vehicle, if any, provides "true" values and which payment vehicles lead to bias. Here again, the artful instrument designer may be able to learn from an examination of earlier studies how to specify payment vehicles so as to minimize vehicle bias. One approach to learning about vehicle bias might be to ask attitude questions about various payment vehicles in an effort to identify those which do not invoke negative attitudes in given circumstances.

Summary

I have argued that the problems of strategic bias and starting point bias can probably be minimized by the careful design of the survey instrument. Information bias that results from a divergence between the true environmental good and the description provided to respondents probably should not be termed a "bias". It is the description that is biased, not the valuation of what is described. Vehicle bias and self-selection bias resulting from protest zeros and refusers are more troublesome. The likely presence of vehicle bias can be identified if two different vehicles are tested in the same instrument. But we lack an objective means of determining which, if any, of the vehicles indicates the true value and therefore the direction of bias is unknown. It seems likely that self selection will bias willingness to pay values downward and that this bias will be stronger the larger the proportion of refusers and protest zeros in the original sample. But this is a conjecture. In the absence of an independent way of estimating individuals' true values, this conjecture cannot be tested.

In this section I will discuss what I in my book (Freeman 1979a, pp. 97-99) called the problem of accuracy as distinct from bias (I now regret that choice of terminology) and what others have called hypothetical bias (which may or may not be bias, but results from the hypothetical nature of the CVM instrument). In my earlier treatment of the problem I argued that the accuracy of a revealed value (that is, the degree of correspondence between the revealed value and the true value) depended on the time and mental energy devoted to the decision process. Since time and mental energy are costly, increasing accuracy comes only at increasing cost to the individual. The benefit of accuracy is the avoidance of foregone utility due to nonoptimal choices. I argued that in the hypothetical settings of the CVM. since individuals did not have to live with the consequences of their choices, the incentives to make accurate responses were weak. Although I was not explicit on this point, I believed that those errors would be random with zero mean.

I now believe that there is another element to the individual choice problem in a hypothetical setting which can lead to potentially large random errors in individuals' reported values over and above those associated with the absence of incentives or time. This element has to do with individual's familiarity with the environmental good and their experience with changes in its level of provision. Note that these two terms, "familiarity" and "experience" are used by CBS in defining the reference operating conditions for the CVM. (p. 199) Their treatment of this set of questions in Chapter 6 has helped clarify my thinking on this issue.

It is conventional to assume that individuals have well defined preference orderings over all goods, including public goods and environmental goods. We assume that these preference orderings can be represented by utility functions of the form $U = U(X,Q)$ where X is a vector of private goods and Q is the level of an environmental good. It is conventional to assume that individuals have accurate knowledge of their preference orderings over the full range of bundles in their choice sets. My key assumption is that individuals have better or more accurate knowledge of their preference orderings in the neighborhood of those consumption bundles they have actually experienced. If shifts of the budget constraint induce an individual to move into an unfamiliar region of his preference ordering, he is likely to make mistakes in his initial choices of consumption bundles, that is, initial choices will not be accurate reflections of the true underlying preferences. Only after the individual has had a chance to learn about or gain experience with this region of his preference ordering and correct any initial mistakes in choices can we infer true values from revealed choices. This is what I had in mind above in defining a true value as one reflected in repeated choices and implying the absence of regret.

Now suppose that the level of the environmental good has been at Q^* throughout an individual's life. It is reasonable to believe that the individual knows his marginal rates of substitution between Q and other goods in the region of Q^*. But for levels of Q substantially different from Q^*, the individual may have only a vague idea of his marginal rates of substitution between Q and other goods. This means that given a substantial change in Q, the individual's initial adjustments in the quantities of private goods purchased may be different from the consumption bundles finally settled upon after gaining experience with the new level of Q. I hypothesize that the difference between the initially revealed preferences and the final or true revealed preferences will be random and will be on average larger, the larger is the change in Q.

A corollary of this hypothesis is that CVM responses to questions about small changes in Q in the neighborhood of Q^* will be more accurate than CVM responses to questions about large changes in Q, especially if the individual has had no prior experience with the alternative postulated level of Q. Also, it seems to me, these errors should be random with zero mean, but more on this point below.

CBS must have had a model of choice and learning of this sort in mind when they produced their reference operating conditions 1 and 2. In this sense my analysis is consistent with theirs. However they did not explicitly adopt this framework in their chapter 5 "Imputing Actual Behavior from Choices Made Under Hypothetical Circumstances." In this chapter CBS make a valuable contribution in that they attempt to deduce testable hypotheses about the relationships between hypothetical values and true values from various arguments that have appeared in the literature, and to subject these hypotheses to empirical tests based on existing CVM data. However I think that CBS are not entirely successful in this effort. But this is at least in part because the arguments that they are evaluating have not been well formulated, and in part because of the difficulty in finding operational measures of some of the theoretical constructs.

For example, CBS quote me on the implications of the absence of incentives to accuracy, and then formulate the null hypothesis: values revealed when incentives to accuracy are present will be equal to values revealed with no incentives to accuracy. In my formulaton, the incentive to accuracy was the avoidance of the foregone utility associated with nonoptimal choice. But they equate incentive with a requirement to make the offered payment, so that the null hypothesis becomes: values revealed with no requirement for payment will be equal to values revealed when payment is required. This is clearly a different hypothesis. And evidence brought forth to test this hypothesis probably has more to say about the likelihood of strategic bias than it does about measurement errors due to the hypothetical nature of the instrument.

Similarly in the next section CBS quotes two sets of authors on the role of time in gathering information and learning about preferences. They then formulate the null hypothesis: the value expressed with little time for learning will be equal to the value expressed after the passage of time. But clearly what matters is not the passage of time alone, but whether that time is used to gather information about and experience with the new level of th environmental good. And the data reviewed by CBS do not shed much light on this question.

If the arguments offered here about unfamiliarity and learning are accepted, then it follows that any individual's response to a CVM question about a large change in the environmental good from the existing familiar level will include a potentially large random error component. But if these "hypothetical" errors are truly random with zero mean, then they will tend to cancel out over large samples. Thus with adequate sample size, sample mean responses may not be seriously inaccurate measures of the true mean values of the population.

Some authors have argued that there may be a systematic component to the kind of hypothetical error I have been discussing here. For example, Bishop, Heberlein, and Kealy (1983) argued:

One resulting hypothesis worth future investigation is that people respond as they do to contingent markets because of uncertainty (presumably concerning their preferences). This may lead them to state answers which imply conservatively high requirements for compensation, amounts at which they are relatively certain they really would sell. They would even recognize the possbility that they might sell at lower amounts, but still give conse rvative answers in order to "play it safe." (p. 629)

Randall, Hoehn, and Brookshire (1983, p. 643) reach similar conclusions on the basis of more formal analysis. The required compensation for the loss of an environmental good is that sum which enables the individual to remain at the initial utility level after the loss. That sum is found by solving the expenditure minimization problem for the initial utility level. If because of ignorance the individual does not find the expenditure minimizing solution, he will ask for higher compensation, thus overstating the willingness to accept compensation. A similar argument yields the conclusion that the stated willingness to pay for an increase in the environmental good will be less than the true value of willingness to pay. The argument is based on the assumption that individuals know their preferences well enough to identify alternative consumption bundles which yield the same initial level of utility but make mistakes in determining which of these bundles minimizes expenditure. But if individuals also lack accurate information on their preferences, they can make mistakes in attaching utility levels to different consumption bundles. Thus they may base willingness-to-pay responses on consumption bundles which turn out to yield either more than or less than the initial level of utility and thus state willingnesses to pay that are either less than or more than the true value. The Bishop, Heberlein, Kealy and Randall, Hoehn, Brookshire arguments are based on a more limited kind of ignorance. Ignorance that extends to the specific characteristics of one's preference orderings implies random rather than systematic errors in stated values.

ASSESSMENT

Chapter 6 is perhaps the most interesting chapter of the report in that it is here that the authors confront the question of accuracy head on and discuss comparisons of CVM values with values derived from other methods. In this section I will offer some comments on their assessment and provide my own assessment of the CVM.

In reviewing the evidence from comparative studies, CBS make it clear that these comparisons are at best suggestive because of inaccuracies inherent in the TCM and HPM. Any quantitative estimate of the accuracy of the CVM requires that we know the true value being measured. Yet the HPM and TCM have errors that may be large, are not well understood, and are arguably of the same order of magnitude as those associated with the CVM. Their discussion of this point is a refreshing, perhaps chilling, reminder of the limitations of our empirical models.[4]

CBS conclude that if certain reference operating conditions are satisfied, the range of error associated with a CVM estimate of value is likely to be plus or minus 50 percent. This statement has a very ad hoc quality. I have some criticisms of the reasoning offered by CBS as to how they reached this estimate of accuracy. And I am not sure how it is meant to be interpreted. They do not distinguish between bias and random error in measurement. However their later discussions appear to focus on biases. As I have argued above, not all of the kinds of bias they mention need to be present in a well-designed CVM study. Nor do all types of bias necesarily operate in the same direction and therefore decrease accuracy. Two biases of equal magnitude but opposite sign can offset each other resulting in an accurate measurement.

CBS appear to be making a statement about the accuracy of the aggregate value derived from a CVM study. Yet most of their argument deals with possible errors in individuals' bids. There is no discussion of the relationship between errors in individuals' bids (systematic or random) and errors in the aggregate value, or of the influence of sample size and aggregation technique on errors in the aggregate value. The effect of random error in the measurement of individual values on the aggregate measure obviously depends upon sample size among other things.

Any quantitative assessment of the accuracy of the CVM must begin with the description of the CVM instrument to which it applies. The assessment should have two components. The first is a consideration of the likelihood of bias from each of the sources of bias discussed above and if possible an estimate of the likely magnitude and direction of each possible bias. The second is a consideration of the description of the environmental change being valued and of the respondents' familiarity with the environmental good and experience with changes in the environmental good over this range. If the CVM instrument is carefully designed to minimize the likelihood of various kinds of bias, and if the familiarity and experience criteria are satisfied (as for example in the Los Angeles air pollution study of Brookshire, et al. 1982), then I would not be surprised if we could argue for accuracies substantially better than plus or minus 50 percent in the aggregate. However, even if biases are minimized but the instrument calls for individuals to consider positions outside the range of experience and familiarity (as for example in the case of existence or preservation values for unique environmental resources), then one cannot be so sure about the likely accuracy. This is because what is involved is the larger but, we hope, random error in individual responses perhaps being offset by large sample size.

To close this section, I would like to offer a somewhat more formal framework for the consideration of the question of accuracy. Let B^* denote an individual's true bid or willingness to pay for an increase in the provision of the environmental good. Let B be the individual's response to a CVM question and assume that B is a random variable with a mean B'. The question of bias comes down to whether B' is greater than, equal to, or less than B^*. The random component of measurement error is $e = B - B'$, which has a zero mean. The analysis of the accuracy of the CVM response must focus on the magnitude of $B' - B^*$ and on the variance of e.

Consider the case of starting point bias. Assume for the moment that there are no other sources of bias and that for the individual e is identically equal to zero. Suppose that a set of identical individuals were asked CVM questions using one of the two approaches I suggested above for mitigating starting point bias in the aggregate mean bids.[5] Although I haven't given the matter much thought, it seems possible to argue that the expected value of the mean bid is equal to B^*. In other words, starting point bias in individual bids may be treated in such a way as to result in only random measurement error in the aggregate. It may be possible to develop similar arguments for the other sources of bias in individuals' responses.

Let us now assume that all bias problems have been successfully dealt with in the design of the CVM so that $B' = B^*$ for all of the identical individuals. Asking the CVM question of a sample of the population of identical individuals yields an estimate of B^*. And of course, the accuracy of this estimate increases with the size of the sample. Very large variances in the error term in individual responses can be compensated for if the sample is large enough. It may be that the so-called problem of hypothetical bias is not that serious, at least if the error in hypothetical settings is really random.[6]

TWO MISCELLANEOUS COMMENTS

My first comment has to do with CBS's suggestion that the frequently observed large differences between willingness-to-accept-compensation questions and willingness-to-pay questions may be due to cognitive dissonance. CBS do not spell out their line of reasoning on this point, and I am not able to provide a convincing explanation based on what I understand about cognitive dissonance. If CBS have such an explanation in mind, it would contribute to our understanding of this puzzling empirical phenomenon if they were to make it explicit. Note that it is not sufficient for the theory to predict willingness to accept being greater than willingness to pay. We already have such a theory based on income effects. To be helpful, the theory should predict potentially large differences.

My second comment concerns the inferences that CBS draw from experiments with the second price auction for the design of CVM instruments. They say:

> Individuals must be placed in an 'all or nothing' situation in the questionnaire where no strategic holding back can help them. . . . Secondly, an iterative option framework is suggested. Because of the reported demand revelation 'learning period' associated with the second price auction, individuals also should be placed in a survey situation which provides them with tentative information about allocations before results are finalized. (p. 90)

And in footnote 6 they go on to say:

> That is, provide the individuals with more than a one-shot survey. Let them answer a survey, report the tentative results of that survey back to them, let them adjust their answers, report the new tentative results, and so forth until an unannounced stopping time. At the stopping time allow the final results to take effect. (p. 102-A)

I have two comments concerning this suggestion. First, the second price auction provides a rule for determining the price of the actual transaction. Its purpose is to eliminate the incentives for strategic behavior on the part of bidders. But in a CVM survey, there is no actual transaction and, we hope, no incentive for strategic behavior. Thus no purpose is served by presenting survey respondents with a second price rule. In fact, this further complicates the survey instrument and may lead to confusion on the part of respondents.

My second comment concerns their proposal to report back information on the aggregate bids and carry out further iterations. This procedure proved useful in experimental settings where the end result was an actual transaction. CBS argue that this procedure helped participants to learn about the incentive compatibility features of the second price auction where actual transactions are to take place. But the iteration procedure probably does not help individuals to learn more about an unfamiliar region of their preference ordering. Thus the iterative procedure does not seem likely to contribute to a reduction in the random measurement error associated with the hypothetical nature of the CVM survey.

CONCLUSIONS

I will conclude by offering some summary comments about the Assessment offered by CBS and then offering my own assessment. On the positive side, I think this Assessment makes a substantial contribution in the following respects: (1) its emphasis on the question of accuracy of responses; (2) the effort to base the Assessment on the formulation and testing of hypotheses concerning such things as biases and sources of error; (3) the introduction of the notions of familiarity with the environmental good and experience with changes in its quantity as important conditions for extracting accurate measures of value.

On the other hand, the CVM technique for eliciting monetary values from respondents represents only one member of a family of contingent choice techniques. It would have been useful to consider the extent to which all of the members of this family suffer from similar problems due to their hypothetical nature as well as to consider the relative strength and weaknesses of these different approaches to estimating values. Second, the Assessment should have incorporated a more precise definition of reference accuracy and an analysis of the separate roles of bias and random error in determining the degree of accuracy of any specific contingent choice technique. Finally, it would have been helpful to integrate the concepts of familiarity and experience into their discussion of hypothetical responses and their efforts to test hypotheses in chapter 5.

My comments on the CVM itself are somewhat encouraging in one respect. That is, at least some of the bias problems appear to be manageable; and if measurement errors due to the hypothetical nature of the instrument are random and not too large, then larger sample size is a potential means of coping with them. However, there is a negative side of this assessment. On the basis of the familiarity and experience arguments, it appears that the CVM is likely to work best for those kinds of problems where we need it least; that is, where respondents' experience with changes in the level of the environmental good have left a record of trade-offs, substitutions, and so forth, which can be the basis of econometric estimates of value. But for those problems for which we need something like the CVM most, that is, where individuals have little or no experience with different levels of the environmental good, CVM appears to be least reliable.

NOTES

1. Thayer's comparison of values obtained by the CVM and site substitution models is a comparison between techniques which belong to the same family of contingent choice or hypothetical valuation approaches. Thus the comparison should not be construed as a test for hypothetical bias.

2. The equivalent measure of value can be defined in a similar manner. Some CVM studies have sought to obtain equivalent measures in the form of willingness to pay to avoid the loss of an environmental good. See, for example, Brookshire, Ives, and Schulze (1976) and Desvousges, Smith, and Mcgivney (1983).

3. Alternatively Carson and Mitchell (1984, p. 16) suggest using one of the available techniques for imputing missing willingness-to-pay values on the basis of the remaining sample data.

4. Not all estimates of the benefits of environmental improvements are subject to inaccuracies of this magnitude. For example, if an improvement in air quality in a small region leads to an increase in the output of an agricultural commodity without significant input or crop substitution effects or impact on market price, then the observed increase in output can be combined with a presumably accurately measured market price to yield a reasonably accurate measure of the benefits of increased output. The problems of estimation arise when there are significant price effects and behavioral responses which must be modeled and quantified to produce defensible benefit estimates.

5. That is, either dividing the group equally and employing an appropriately set low starting point with one group, etc., or using the "bracket and half" technique with randomly chosen starting points.

6. For example suppose that we interpret CBS's estimate of a plus or minus 50 percent error to refer to the individual response error and (assuming that e is normally distributed) to mean that the interval of B^* plus or minus two standard deviations is $.5B^* - 1.5B^*$. Alternatively the probability is approximately .95 that B will be in this interval. A sample of 16 identical individuals is sufficient to reduce the error of the sample mean as an estimate of B^* to plus or minus 12-1/2 percent. Similarly, if the error in the individual responses is plus or minus 100 percent, a sample of 100 individuals yields an error of plus or minus 10 percent.

11

To Keep or Toss the Contingent Valuation Method

V. Kerry Smith

Centennial Professor of Economics

Vanderbilt University

INTRODUCTION

In concluding his essay on the rhetoric of economics, McCloskey (1983) dicussed the role of surveys under a subheading "Better Science", presumably intended as an admonition to the economics profession. He observed that:

> Economists are so impressed by the confusions that might possibly result from questionnaires that they abandon them entirely, in favor of the confusions resulting from external observation. They are unthinkingly committed to the notion that only the externally observable behavior of economic actors is admissible evidence in arguments concerning economics. [p. 514]

He continued this discussion, questioning such views by acknowledging that:

> Foolish inquiries into motives and foolish use of human informants will produce nonsense. But this is also true of foolish use of the evidence more commonly admitted into the economist's study. [p. 514]

Of course, these comments should not be interpreted as an endorsement for the contingent valuation method. Rather they represent a call for a more open attitude in judging the sources of information used in evaluating (or implementing) economic models. At the same time, however, they do present a reasonably accurate summary of the attitudes of a majority of economists. While there has been somewhat more acceptance of the potential usefulness of survey information associated with individuals' or firms' attitudes or plans, these are always regarded as less desirable sources of information relative to "hard" statistical data or the predictions of econometric models based on those data.[1]

Unfortunately, environmental economics encounters a wide range of resource allocation decisions wherein we would not expect, because of the nature of the resources themselves, the market interactions of economic agents to reveal information which would assist with these decisions. Many, if not most, environmental resources exchange outside markets; they exhibit some of the features of public goods; and they are not easily measured or translated into a quantitative scale. For example, good air quality implies an absence of air pollutants. Thus, we might consider measuring it by using this relationship and records on the ambient concentrations of pollutants. However, these technical measures do not necessarily translate readily into either the household's perceived air quality or the features of pollution which impair health or the aesthetic dimensions of the environment.[2] As a result of all these limitations, the empirical practice of environmental economics has come increasingly to rely on the use of direct interviews to obtain information on individuals' valuations of environmental resources.

Increased interest in and requirements for measures of the benefits associated with changes in one or more aspects of environmental resources have focused attention on the use of the direct interview or contingent valuation method as a basis for deriving such estimates. The objective of this paper is to use the recent comprehensive review and evaluation of the contingent valuation method by Cummings, Brookshire, and Schulze as the basis for an independent appraisal of the method and, with it, a commentary on these authors' judgments.

Cummings et al. have provided a thorough review of the conceptual and empirical issues associated with contingent valuation methods (CVM). Their study has integrated a large and diverse set of CVM studies and attempted to extract from them a summary of what this work has determined concerning the performance and viability of the contingent valuation method. One interpretation of the authors' bottom line (or reference operating conditions) would suggest that: *CVM can be expected to perform best for commodities where we would be least likely to want to use it.* That is, respondents should be familiar with the commodity, have choice experience assocated with its consumption, and be relatively certain about the conditions of availability posed in any CVM valuation question. In these circumstances there are often other methods for estimating individuals' valuatons of environmental amenities (see Freeman, 1979a). Indeed, it is the presence of these other methods for such cases that has provided the opportunity to perform comparative analyses of the benefit estimates derived using CVM in relation to another indirect method (i.e., one based on the observable actions of households). These comparative analyses have, in turn, led to the definition of the Cummings et al. reference operating conditions. When we relax one or more of the reference operating conditions, the authors suggest that the performance of CVM cannot be easily judged. This conclusion is not surprising because there does not exist a basis for a comparative analysis of estimates from different methods in these cases.

Rather than cover the same groundwork developed in the Cummings et al. analysis, we will approach the evaluation of CVM from a somewhat different perspective. Assume that the objective of CVM research is the estimation of individuals' valuation of changes in specific environmental amenities (so that each type is consistently reflected in these valuations). Given this goal, it should be acknowledged at the outset that we will never *know* how well CVM or any other method performs in estimating their "true" valuations. Consequently, to evaluate these methods we have two choices. We can formulate a model that describes the consumer's decision process, including the valuation of the relevant amenities, examine within the context of that model how CVM's responses would be made, and compare the model's prediction of those responses with the model's true valuations. Alternatively, we can attempt to devise an experimental setting that would mimic the essential elements present in a real-world CVM application (tailored to the limits of the experimental setting), collect data on responses, and evaluate CVM in comparison with what was expected from the experimental design.

Both approaches require assumptions to use their respective findings in evaluating CVM in a real-world context. For the first it is a matter of the correspondence between the model of consumer behavior and its representation of individuals' responses to CVM in comparison to reality. Not all maintained hypotheses can be tested in the absence of knowledge of individuals' true valuations. In the second, a similar issue arises in the authenticity of the experiments' description of the actual decision process. Experiments necessarily require simplifications (as do models). Relating the findings from each approach to the performance of what is evaluated in the real world involves gauging the importance of these simplifications. In short, professional judgment plays a significant role in either of these exercises. As a consequence it seems reasonable to begin an evaluation of CVM with an inquiry into the realization of these judgements in the appraisal of other economic data bases. That is, in what follows, we consider a selected set of surveys, involving both households and firms, and examine the attributes of some of the questions posed in these surveys. Based on this partial review, it appears that in many cases our objective data are based on questions that require judgements, responses that may be subject to strategic biases, and valuation responses under hypothetical circumstances. Indeed, they are subject to many of the problems discussed as if they were exclusively associated with CVM data. Moreover, some of these "offenders" (i.e., cases where the effects of these sources of bias may be important) involve the data that have been used in several of the indirect approaches to benefit estimation. Following this review, the section entitled Tasks Requested of Survey Respondents, discusses in more detail the attributes of the questions that are asked and how these characteristics appear to affect our willingness to accept individuals' (or firm's) responses as objective data. While there are a number of considerations associated with what Medoff and Abraham (1979) describes as "having contact with units of observation" (see note #1), the most important stumbling block to the CVM approach appears to be the combination of a hypothetical question and changes in the resources that are outside the range of an individual's experience. Consequently, the section entitled The Problems with Hypothetical Questions discusses the implications of the arguments against using responses to hypothetical situations as indicative of consumer's valuation should these situations in fact be realized.

The last section considers what this perspective on CVM implies for the use of its results and for further research. An appendix clarifies some inaccuracies (in the authors's opinion) in the CBS summary of the research.

NON-CVM DATA: HOW OBJECTIVE ARE THEY?

Table ll.1 summarizes a sample of data sets that are used in a variety of economic models. While many have a direct relation to empirical studies in environmental economics, they are not exclusively so. In each case, one of the the uses of the data, the name of the survey, a variable observed, the questions used to derive it, and a judgemental evaluation of the response are reported.

There are several aspects of the table which are relevant to an evaluation of CVM. First, and perhaps most interesting, responses to hypothetical questions play a prominent role in two of these cases. The hedonic property value model, usually regarded as the most promising indirect, market-based alternative to CVM has often been based on data from either the Annual Housing Survey or the Census of Population.[3] Both data sources report, for owner-occupied units, the owners' appraisal of their selling prices *if they were to sell their homes*, not the market prices. Thus, hedonic models based on these data reflect the owners' perception of the prices they would realize and not necessarily the equilibrium locus as hypothesized. These individuals are being asked a hypothetical quesiton and it should clearly be recognized as such. Of course, it may be reasonable to assume that the respondents form their perceptions of the relevant market price based on past sales in their neighborhoods. Nonetheless, this is not necessarily a good proxy for actual price. It will depend on the number of homes selling in their neighborhood, as well as on each individual's ability to translate these sale prices into a corresponding estimate of the price of his (or her) home. There does not appear to have been a comparison for specific cities of the results that would have been derived using the survey or the census in comparison to the use of the actual sales and their implied hedonic price function. Therefore, it is difficult to judge the implications of the use of these hypothetical data.

Another example with hypothetical responses playing a tangible role in the development of "hard" or objective data arises in one of the constituents of the CPI. In January 1983 the CPI changed its treatment of the components of the cost of shelter. Under the old method, this cost was measured based on changes in the cost of five items—home purchase, contracted mortgage interest rates, property taxes, property insurance, and maintenance and repair. The new approach attempts to measure the change in the cost of obtaining, in the rental market, housing services equivalent to the rental home. These are measured with actual rents. However, the weights used to reflect their contribution are based on a question in the 1972–73 Consumer Expenditure Survey asking households for how much they *think* their home would rent.[4] This is a hypothetical question which may well be more difficult for households than to gauge the selling price for a home, especially since their knowledge of the relevant rental market may be quite limited.

Secondly, there are incentives for strategic responses even in the questions reporting so-called "hard" data. One of the more controversial of these concerns the reporting of employment status for young men.[5] Discrepancies in the implied unemployment rates based on the Current Population survey (CPS) and the National Longitudinal Survey (NLS) of Young Men (see Freeman and Medoff 1982) have led to several studies to investigate reasons for differences in responses based on essentially the same questions. It should also be noted, as the entry in table 11.1 for the CPS indicates, these questions impose additional requirements on respondents by calling for an interpretation of "looking for" work and an appraisal of an individual's future intentions. Both issues are reported by proxy respondents for youths with the CPS survey and by the youths themselves with the NLS. Freeman and Medoff (1982) report some evidence that the differences in responses used to infer unemployment rates may be biased at least partially because the proxy respondent's self esteem (in the CPS) was affected by the answers given.

The responses by firms to questions on pollution abatement costs also provide a case where strategic responses would seem likely to be a factor in interpreting the quality of these data. To date, however, there appears to be increasing use of these data without appreciable concern for these biases.[6]

A third area involves requests for "sensitive" information. These requests have long been recognized to offer the potential for biased responses. Questions involving income and wage information are examples. The latter has also served in indirect benefit estimates (hedonic wage models). While recent estimates of the magnitude of the differences between means of self-reported and employer-reported wage rates seem fairly large (i.e., 4.8%) and are significantly different from zero,[7] Mellow and Sider's (1983) overall results indicate that "the estimated structure of the wage determination process is essentially independent of the source of information." (p. 342)

There are further examples in table ll.1. However, these three classes of problems are sufficient to draw attention to the potential for significant limitations with many (if not all) objective data sources for economic analysis. Only artificial data (i.e., data generated from a controlled model) are perfect. This is hardly surprising and not the point.

When any data are derived from surveys we can expect they will be subject to limitations. Nonetheless, with the major surveys similar to those identified in Table ll.1, these limitations have been accepted as tolerable. Results derived from most of these data sources are routinely accepted by the relevant subset of the economics profession as plausible—not as the last word on any subject, but rather they are judged to be worthy of consideration and review, as constituents to a body of developing empirical evidence on a particular subject. In effect, they have passed an implicit standard of tolerance for the quality of data. By contrast, data from CVM experiments appear to fall below this standard in the judgement of the majority of economists. Consequently, one approach to understanding the potential limitations with the contingent valuation method is to examine the reasons for these revealed preferences of economists. That is, we must consider what attributes of CVM prevent its data from passing the professional "muster".

Before addressing this issue, however, it is important to recognize, as Mitchell and Carson have observed in their recent review of the Cummings et al. appraisal (appendix to chapter 13)—not all CVM studies have been of equal quality. Not only have the sample sizes been quite small in some cases, but quality of the questionnaires used to elicit responses to complex questions has also been diverse. This is to be expected since the development of CVM has been a learning process. Thus it should be acknowledged that past quesionnaires have introduced confusion in what was elicited and may not indicate the prospective performance of the method with appropriate attention to questionnaire design. The debate over the interpretation of Greenley, Walsh, and Young's (1981) estimates of option value (see Mitchell and Carson, forthcoming) is but one example where what was communicated to respondents is at issue since it provides the only basis for the results.

Unfortunately, the Cummings et al. review seems to treat all CVM studies *as if* they conveyed equal information on the properties of the method. Clearly, they do not. It is, of course, difficult to judge on the basis of the published summaries of such studies where these limitations might be. Since this issue has implications for future research, it will be discussed in the last section of this paper. At this point, it is important to note that the available CVM estimates

Table 11.1 Selected Sample of Sources for Non-CVM Economic Data

Objective	Name of survey	Variable(s) measured	Question	Evaluation of response
1. Benefit estimation				
Hedonic property value	Annual Housing Survey and Census of Population	Measure of the price of housing unit[a]	What is the value of this property, that is, how much *do you think* this property would sell for if it were for sale?[b]	Asks for estimate of value under hypothetical situation
Hedonic property value	Annual Housing Survey	Measure of perceived neighborhood amenities	Do you have satisfactory _____? (public transportation, schools, police protection, neighborhood shopping, outdoor recreation, hospitals and health clinics)	Asks for judgment as to satisfactory
2. Benefit estimation[c]				
Recreation participation models	Heritage Conservation and Recreation Service General Population Survey	Measure of recreation use	I am going to read you a list of outdoor recreation activities. For each activity please tell me if you have participated in this activity during the past 12 months. (30 activities considered, number of times requested or desire to)	Asks for extensive recall of detailed activities
Recreation participation models	Heritage Conservation and Recreation Service General Population Survey	Demand response	If the price of gasoline doubled within the next 6 months, would this be likely to limit or curtail the number of trips you might take by automobile for outdoor recreation activities?	Asks for hypothetical demand response
3. Benefit estimation				
Damage function	Health Information Survey	Measures of morbidity effect	Not counting the days in bed, lost from work and lost from school, were there any (other) days during the past 2 weeks that _____ cut down on because of illness or injury?[d]	Asks for recall and judgment of usual

Table 11.1 (continued)

Objective	Name of survey	Variable(s) measured	Question	Evaluation of response
4. Benefit estimation				
Hedonic wage models	Current Population Survey (and others)	Measure of wage rate	How much does ――― usually earn per week at this job before deductions? How many hours per week does ――― usually work at this job?	Asks for recall for different individuals and judgment as to usual
5. Price index measures				
CPI weights	1972–73 Consumer Expenditure Survey	Weight for owner's equivalent rent	If you were to rent out your home today, how much do you think it would rent for monthly, unfurnished, and without utilities?	Asks for judgment in hypothetical circumstance
6. Employment and unemployment measures				
Determinants of employment	Current Population Survey	Measure of unemployment	Has ――― been looking for work during the past 4 weeks? Does ――― intend to look for work of any kind in the next 12 months?	Asks for judgment "on looking for" by individual other than respondent, and of intentions in the future
7. Household production[e]	Income Dynamics Panel	Measure of value of repairs	During (year), did you (or your family) do any of your own repair work on your cars? About how much do you think you saved doing this last year? Was it about $25, $50, $100, $200 or what?	Asks for recall and judgment of market price

Objective	Name of survey	Variable(s) measured	Question	Evaluation of response
8. Cost estimates	Survey on Pollution Abatement Costs and Expenditures	Abatement cost recovered	Report your best estimate of the value of materials or energy reclaimed (costs recovered) through pollution abatement activities and either reused in production or sold by form of pollution abated. (Exclude the value of items if they would have been recovered, sold, or reused in production in the absence of any pollution control regulations.)	Asks for cost saving allocation; has strategic incentives; judgment on no-regulation case
Cost estimates	Survey on Pollution Abatement Costs and Expenditures	Annual operating costs for pollution abatement	Report the annual operating costs and expenses for pollution abatement in (year). Distribute total operating and maintenance cost in terms of percent by *form of pollution abated* (air, water, solid)	Asks for cost allocation; has strategic incentives.

[a]Applies to owner-occupied housing units. A comparable question is used to acquire rents for occupied rental units.
[b]Emphasis is added.
[c]Similar questions asked in the site-specific Federal Estate Survey along with recall of past trips to an area and number of hours of travel.
[d]Asked after similar inquiries on days in bed, lost from work, and lost from school; asked of one person for each member of the household.
[e]This is one small aspect of the panel's questionnaire which deals with nearly all aspects of a household's activities, including information on the attitudes and feelings of its members.
Sources: *Annual Housing Survey: 1980*, Current Housing Reports, H-170-80-1, February 1984, U.S. Department of Commerce, Bureau of the Census, U.S. Department of Housing and Urban Development.
Consumer Expenditure Survey: Diary Survey 1980-81, Bulletin 2173, September 1983, U.S. Department of Labor, Bureau of Labor Statistics.
1980 Census of Population and Housing, Users Guide, Part A, U.S. Department of Commerce, Bureau of the Census.
Bureau of Labor Statistics, *Handbook of Methods, Vol. II, The Consumer Price Index*, Bulletin 2134-2, U.S. Department of Labor, Bureau of Labor Statistics, April 1984.
Bureau of the Census, U.S. Department of Commerce, Current Industrial Reports, *Pollution Abatement Costs and Expenditures, 1982*, MA-200(82-1), February 1984.
Survey Research Center, *A Panel of Income Dynamics*, Vol. 1, (Institute for Social Research, University of Michigan, 1972).
Paul R. Portney and John Mullahy, *Ambient Ozone and Human Health: An Epidemiological Analysis*, Vol. II, Draft Report to Officer of Air Quality Planning and Standards, U.S. Environmental Protection Agency, September 1983 (source of questionnaire for 1979 Health Interview Survey).
Heritage Conservation and Recreation Service, U.S. Department of the Interior, *The Third Nationwide Outdoor Receration and Plan, Appendix 11*, Survey Technical Report 2, December 1979.

reflect both a learning process in the use of questionnaires (as economists discovered the survey research relevant to eliciting value information) and the inherent properties of the approach as a basis for valuation information. Separation of these two influences inevitably involves judgement. This judgement is reflected in the contrast between the Carson-Mitchell (Appendix) appraisal of the sources of error in CVM and that of Cummings et al. Nonetheless, even with these problems, there do appear to be features of what CVM asks that can be distinguished from what is elicited in the surveys that are judged "acceptable" by most economists.

TASKS REQUESTED OF SURVEY RESPONDENTS

Surveys request individuals to undertake a number of different types of response tasks. The list below attempts to classify and describe each type of task. They have been ordered according to what appears to be (based on an admittedly limited reading) the profession's perception of the likely accuracy of the responses.

(a) recall: to remember patterns of behavior over some past time period (often in detail). This task can include requests for information on the actions of the individual or of members of the household. It can extend as long as a year and require a time-sequenced report, either through an ongoing diary or an *ex post* report.

(b) *partitioning*: to assign a portion of time or expenditures to engage in certain activities or meet particular objectives. A detailed accounting of the types of recreational activities undertaken and the days spent at each is an example of this task from table figs 11.1.

(c) *judgement*: of a state: to appraise a condition based on a described set of criteria, e.g., seeking work or evaluation of health status.

(d) *truthful response on sensitive information*: to report sensitive financial or personal information that may be factual but is regarded as confidential by the individual, e.g., income or assets.

(e) *evaluation of attitudes*: to evaluate sentiments and feelings with regard to an issue or condition.

(f) *projected responses to hypothetical circumstances*: to describe actions under proposed conditions that have not occurred, e.g., what would a person do if some action took place; or to judge what he or she perceives another individual or institution would do if an action took place.

The first three tasks seem relatively uncontroversial. While there is some tendency to question aspects of information derived from these types of inquiries, with our discussion of concern over available measures of the employment status of young men as one example, these issues have not led to the dismissal of the data involved. There is a large literature in survey research on the question of sensitive information. Income questions are always at the end of a questionnaire. The income supplement to the CPS, for example, is asked of the group rotating out of the sample, not of the individuals expected to continue to be a part of the survey whose future participation and responses are valued. Nonetheless, when responses are given, they are routinely accepted for subsequent economic analysis.

For the last two categories, however, economists are at best skeptical of the merits of the information. Cummings et al. acknowledge the mistrust of attitudinal data. Both their volatile nature and the difficulty in developing standards for gauging the comparability of these responses across individuals has limited their acceptance in economics. At the same level of acceptability as attitudinal information, or perhaps below, come the tasks involving hypothetical questions. This is why CVM is faced with justifying the plausibility of its information.

However, our brief overview of some established survey data bases indicates that they also involve responses to hypothetical questions. Yet, in these cases, the concerns that economists express with CVM do not appear to have been raised. Why? The answer seems to be fundamental differences in the hypothetical tasks requested. Markets do exist for the commodities involved and it is assumed that the individual is fully aware of them. Consequently, under the most favorable interpretation, the responses that are requested could be considered as asking the individual to match his (or her) commodity with the relevant existing market and report the current price. Of course, the nature of the markets for heterogeneous commodities, such as housing, are not completely consistent with this view. Moreover, each individual's knowledge of these markets can be expected to vary; and this requested matching process will be affected by the individual's perception of his (or her) home. Nonetheless, the nature of what is asked is fundamentally different. It is not to search one's preferences, recognize financial constraints, and respond with a bid. Rather it is to report what each individual perceives *the market would yield as a price or a rent for an existing commodity*.

It appears that Cummings et al.'s reference operating conditions impose a similar requirement on CVM. That is, under their ROC, individuals must have had the ability to obtain "choice experience with respect to consumption levels of the commodity." This implies that there is some mechanism available to individuals to enable them to select the different levels of the resource involved. If there are not formal markets, then we must ask what the mechanism is. If it leads to the equivalent of an implicit market, then we must assume that choice experience is the equivalent of knowledge of the features of the implicit market. Indeed, Cummings et al. state as much in their closing arguments, observing that:

> The state of the arts is one wherein we can simply say that evidence exists which supports the proposition that *indirect* market exprience with a commodity may serve to satisfy the ROC's: when the environmental good is a distinct attribute of a market-related good (water quality in a time/travel cost recreation trip or air quality as an attribute of housing locations/costs), experience/familiarity with the market good *seemingly* spills over to the individual's ability to value the attribute. (p. 207)

Consequently, reference operating conditions amount to a requirement that we accept CVM studies only where they involve hypothetical questions comparable to those in existing surveys—asking for implicit market outcomes for hypotetical changes. This is not the same as asking an individual's bid for a commodity that is not exchanged.

Consequently, the most important limitation to the acceptance of CVM appears to be its use in eliciting an individual's response to a hypothetical situation. Responses that involve individual judgements as to the nature of market outcome (either formal or implicit) in response to a hypothetical change are not viewed with the same degree of skepticism. Therefore, to evaluate the prospects of CVM we must consider why the responses to these questions are viewed as unreliable and determine if there is existing or new research which might resolve the issues involved.

THE PROBLEMS WITH HYPOTHETICAL QUESTIONS

The principal problems with hypothetical questions concerning an individual's behavior can be summarized using three questions:

1. Will each respondent really take the decision circumstances seriously, since there are no tangible incentives to do so?
2. Is an individual capable of processing the information involved in what is often a completely new (or at least an unfamiliar) set of conditions, and responding with his or her actual valuation, even though this value would ordinarily be derived after time for consideration?
3. Does an individual's response require repeated experience to form an appraisal of the valuation of the hypothetical question?

The first and third questions are components of Feenberg and Mills' (1980) critique of the survey approach as a basic source of valuation information. While all three are identified in Cummings et al. discussion, these authors do not explore their implications for other methods for benefit estimation. That is, indirect methods which are based on households' observed behavior would also be affected by the decision frameworks implied by questions (2) and (3). All indirect approaches assume the individual has complete information on the available commodities (including those whose purchase is tied to the receipt of an environmental resource). If repeated experience is necessary to form a judgement on the features of the resource and to value it, then the role of experience must also be reflected in the models used to derive indirect measures of households' valuations of environmental resources. Of course, these questions are not independent. Repeated experience provides information that may assist in the decision process described (i.e., question (2)). None of the existing indirect benefit measures reflect this type of decision process. Thus, if this view describes behavior then all of the indirect methods will be biased in an unknown way.

Both approaches to estimating individual's valuations for nonmarketed commodities involve hypothetical conditions. To use either approach requires a judgement of the correspondence between their predictions (or responses) and actual behavior. For the indirect methods we formulate a hypothetical description of an individual's behavior in the presence of a specified characterization of what is known and what constrains decisions. This framework is then used to evaluate actual decisions *as if* they were guided by it. The direct or contingent valuation approach formulates hypothetical circumstances and asks what an individual's behavior would be. Neither escapes the *hypothetical*. Consequently, criticisms that are based on a belief that individual decision processes are too complex to be adequately determined from one-time hypothetical questions will also be relevant to the indirect methods.

Of course, what is important is by how much is each approach affected by its respective assumptions. Cummings et al. results suggest we don't know the answers for the contingent valuation method. However, it seems the same conclusion would be drawn for the indirect approaches. Few economists would contend that housing markets behave in accordance with the hedonic model— assuming that we can exactly measure an equilibrium price structure with home sales within any period. However, there does appear to be a reasonably wide consensus that, despite the errors introduced by departures from equilibrium, the estimates of the marginal willingness to pay for site attributes are usable. That is, it is tacitly assumed that these errors are not sufficiently large to invalidate the practice. In fact, there has been no appraisal of the extent to which the model's assumptions affect its performance. Judgmental evaluations of Maler (1977) and Freeman(1979b) are at opposite extremes in terms of their respective interpretations of the importance of the model's assumptions. Thus, if one accepts these criticisms of the contingent valuation method, it is unlikely that comparative analyses of CVM to indirect approaches, whether hedonic property value or travel cost, will resolve matters.

What is needed is an evaluation of the models as they have been asked to perform. For example, with the hedonic property value model we might ask:

(a) Does an equilibrium matching of buyers and sellers under real-world conditions lead to a smooth continuous price function?

(b) Is the specification for the equilibrium price function derived under the conventional fitting criteria of econometrics likely to provide accurate estimates of the marginal valuations of site attributes, such as environmental quality?

(c) Is the mechanism an individual uses to form perceptions of site characteristics (or diversity in mechanisms across individuals) important to the viability of the method?

(d) Can these marginal willingness-to-pay estimates be used to derive an individual's inverse demand for a site attribute?

The literature abounds with analytical answers to parts of these questions, but none are designed to comprehensively evaluate the methods under conditions that resemble the real world.

Equally important, we *do not have a model of how individuals will respond to CVM questions*. Hoehn and Randall (1984a) have suggested that we can identify the direction of the errors by simply considering the optimal strategies for participants within a simple model of their decision process. Their model identifies two key incentives to the character of participants' responses: judgements as to how participation is likely to influence a policy designed to increase the environmental amenity of interest; and judgements as to the level of disposable income if the policy is undertaken. Both rely on individuals acting strategically in their responses—in effect taking the process seriously. Thus, while the Hoehn-Randall framework is an interesting beginning in the modeling of individuals' response to CVM, it does not address the fundamental issue—how will individuals behave when their stake in the process is not clear? Some researchers have argued truth-telling is the simplest response. Others follow Feenberg and Mills indicating that they will be more likely to provide attitudes that will vary with whatever happens to be the most recent stimuli or information influencing these attitudes.

At this point there can be no answer to this issue until there is a model of the process itself. Moreover, there is unlikely to be a model forthcoming until those economists involved in CVM perform research on how individuals respond to these types of questions—in effect, attempt to understand what will guide individuals' responses to questions eliciting their valuations of hypothetical changes in nonmarketed resources. It should be acknowledged that economists have not had experience in this type of research.[9] Moreover, there is no assurance that it will lead to sufficient information to permit the response process to be understood and modeled. There are, however, companion research efforts that with efforts to model responses to CVM should enhance our ability to judge CVM. They include:

(a) *Evaluations of the Indirect Methods*

Comparisons of indirect and CVM estimates are largely useless unless we can bound the nature of the errors associated with the indirect estimates. Evaluation of the performance of indirect methods under something resembling real-world conditions is essential to interpreting these findings. While such an evaluation will not establish results for CVM that would be relevant to its application under conditions without an implicit market, it can help to answer whether individuals will take CVM questions seriously in the absence of clear incentives or consequences for their behavior.

(b) *Evaluate Infrequent and New Commodity Decisions*

There is no reason why the issues associated with learning about the nature of a new commodity or judging how to interpret behavioral decisions with infrequently purchased goods could not be investigated for market commodities. What type of information is acquired? What are the roles of service and maintenance patterns, price, etc.? The analysis should provide empirical information on these issues that would be relevant to the interpretation of CVM in circumstances that involve completely new resources, one-time or very infrequent decisions, etc.

(c) *Experiment with CVM Formats*

As Cummings et al. acknowledge, laboratory experiments provide an opportunity to understand some elements of the performance of CVM. They can never provide the answers to all CVM questions because they also require assumptions to transfer their findings to real-world circumstances. For questions involving the evaluation of institutional structures they can be invaluable. In understanding how individuals respond to hypothetical changes in an environmental resource, their value is more limited because the experiments require control, and with it simplification.

THE BOTTOM LINE

The objective of the Cummings et al. summary and analysis of the contingent valuation method to benefit estimation was to take stock of what has been accomplished and evaluate whether, despite most economists' skepticism concerning the method, its continued use can be justified in benefits research. In effect, can we hope for acceptance of CVM research results more generally by professional economists? These authors' conclusion recognizes that the only standard available from current research is itself an estimate of the unknown "true" value of an individual's valuation.[10] Consequently, Cummings et al. must argue that the standard used in these comparisons has some level of accuracy— i.e., it includes the true value in a plus or minus 50 percent confidence interval. With this assumption, then, the authors argue that CVM estimates derived from studies satisfying their reference operating conditions will lie within plus or minus 50 percent of the standard (i.e., the indirect estimate). Of course, there are an infinite number of ways that a CVM confidence interval could include the indirect estimate without having a comparable likelihood of including the true value.[11] Their summary is a valiant attempt to use the available information to judge CVM. Unfortunately, it does not establish a confidence interval for the CVM approach. At this stage it cannot, without acceptance as a maintained hypothesis that individuals will attempt to report their true values and therefore the variation observed across individuals (after taking account of socio-economic characteristics), can be treated as a random error due to each individual's differential understanding of the full implications of what is asked.

Indeed, there are several general statements that can be made independent of the Cummings et al. appraisal concerning CVM.

1. There has been no research designed to systematically evaluate CVM for benefit estimation. Moreover, we do not have the information available to develop a confidence interval for indirect benefit estimates applied under the conditions in which they are applied. Their assumptions are not satisfied and most economists recognize these failures. We do not know how much these violations in assumed conditions affect the performance of the estimates. The Cummings et al. reference accuracy for the indirect method is their judgement interval estimate. What is the likelihood the true value will fall in this interval? We cannot answer that question. Indeed, on an analytical basis we may never be able to do so.

However, we can use our models to gauge the sensitivity of results to the assumptions most likely to be violated. This would seem a necessary first step in evaluating the available comparative evidence. Until we know how good the indirect methods are, it will be impossible to judge the meaning of proximity of point estimates from CVM and a particular indirect approach.

2. One reason why there has been diversity among CVM researchers in their judgements as to its performance is the use they intend for the benefit estimates. In effect, one must ask how will the CVM estimates be used. We may be able to tolerate low levels of accuracy for some purposes. It appears that those evaluating CVM have quite different end users in mind. The old adage—"good enough for government work"—may well be literally relevant in some applications of CVM estimates. Not all benefit-cost analyses will require CVM estimates with the same accuracy. A wide range of estimates may still permit a yes/no decision to be made. This was Hoehn and Randalls (1983) point some time ago.

By contrast, however, tests of specific hypotheses or indeed some benefit-cost decisions may hinge on the accuracy of the estimates of individual valuation. These end users and their implied standards should be identified. CVM may prove acceptable in some cases and not others. We cannot hope to provide this type of answer if the questions fail to recognize the implications of the potential differences in the uses of CVM results for any evalation of the methodology.

3. At present the evaluation of CVM results is exceptionally difficult because of the lack of uniformity in reporting information. Broad professional acceptance of CVM results requires clear and comprehensive reporting of *all* the details of the survey. The estimates are only as good as each individual respondent's understanding of what is asked. External reviewers cannot hope to be aware of all of the details of each application. A uniform reporting system with the assurance of backup detailed information would facilitate the evaluation of the influence of questionnaire and survey design on the results.

There has been no research designed exclusively to evaluate CVM. Rather studies have been conducted to serve multiple objectives. In such a setting it is essential to have full information on these design issues in order to gauge the plausibility of the CVM estimates.

The bottom line on CVM is not what Cummings et al. suggest. In this author's judgment *we can draw no conclusion on its accuracy based on what we know from research to date*. After over a decade's expeience with CVM, this is certainly not a satisfying conclusion, especially given the volume of research resources currently involved in using it for some valuation objective. However, this judgement must also be considered in the context of what we really know about other methods for benefit measurement. There is no more reason for being confident of the estimates derived from indirect benefit methods. The degree of uncertainty over their estimates cannot be judged as any less than CVM based on the research record to date. Consequently there is no basis for rejecting CVM especially if it is tied with an effort to try to understand how individuals make decisions about infrequent or unfamiliar consumption choices. Early economists, such as Marshall, emphasized the importance of observation of behavior as a key to economic modeling. When that behavior cannot be observed, economists must find ways of understanding how individuals make their choices. The use of CVM, with full recognition of the learning which has accompanied survey research in other social sciences, appears to be the best available basis for understanding individuals' decision making in these areas. This conclusion does not endorse an exclusive reliance on CVM. Moreover, it implies that the surveys should not have an exclusive focus on deriving valuation estimates. Rather, contingent valuation experiments should be regarded *as experiments* that may permit economists to understand decision processes in areas where unfamiliar or new choices must be made. Theory may help us understand what ought to be the key elements in these decisions. It can therefore contribute in substantive ways to CVM design. Equally important, more explicit attempts to integrate what is learned from CVM experiments with conventional economic theory should be an essential dimension of future CVM research.

Thanks are due Dan Saks and Sharon Smith for some especially helpful discussions of this topic. They are, of course, not responsible for my use (or abuse) of their suggestions. This research was partially supported by the United States Environmental Protection Agency. However, the views expressed are those of the author and not of the agency.

NOTES

1. There are important exceptions. For example, Medoff and Abraham (1979) in discussing productivity performance and earnings make a general comment on empirical testing in economics, noting that:
Unlike physical scientists, economists typically are not involved in the collection of the data they use, and unlike other social scientists, economists generally avoid having contact with their units of observation. As a result, the proper data for testing numerous important beliefs that many economists hold have not been gathered and the knowledge of those who are likely to really know what is going on has been ignored. [p. 48]
Maital's (1982) recent discussion of the role for psychology in economic modeling brought the Medoff-Abraham's quote to my attention.
2. A simple analytical discussion of the implications of air quality measures for monitoring policies was recently reported by Evans (1984). However, no explicit attention was given to the importance of perceptions in affecting what the author describes as "optimal environmental metrics."
3. See, for example, Linnmann (1980), (1981), Krumm (1980), and a large number of others.

Bartik and Smith (1984) have recently reviewed the use of hedonic models to evaluate the role of urban amenities and provide further references.

4. I am grateful to Sharon P. Smith for calling this distinction in the sources of rental information for the calculation of the CPI to my attention.

5. This difference is important because Flinn and Heckman (1983) report, based on the NLS sample, that the categories "unemployed" and "out of the labor force" are behaviorally distinct labor force states. They conclude that:

Our empirical results indicate that unemployment and out of the labor force are behaviorally distinct, so that in general it is not legitimate to aggregate the two states into a single unemployment state when analyzing labor market dynamics. (p. 38)

6. Two recent examples include Crandall's (1983) recent critique of air pollution policies where he uses these cost data, along with other cost information, to judge the efficiency of current air quality standards. A second study by Pashigian (1984) uses these data to evaluate the effects of environmental regulation on plant size. Neither directly addresses the prospects for bias with the self-reported data. It should, however, be acknowledged that Crandall assembles several sources of cost data to support his arguments.

7. Mellow and Sider (1983) reported the mean difference in the log of each wage (i.e., log(employer reported)-log(employee reported)) and the variance for this difference. This conclusion is based on testing whether the population mean difference was different from zero. It yielded at ratio of 7.895.

8. It is not because of the early concerns over the prospects for strategic responses. Strategic behavior does not appear to pose problems with carefully worded questions.

9. A different judgement on the importance of environmental economists' lack of experience with the techniques of survey research that provides an explanation for Carson and Mitchell's (Appendix) evaluation of the prospects of contingent valuation methods. They suggest that the quality of CVM valuation responses is directly related to questionnaire design, concluding their recent paper on non-sampling errors in contingent valuation research by noting that:

CVM (contingent valuation) remains an important and viable method to measure the benefits of many nonmarketed goods. CVM is virtually the only method capable of measuring most non-use benefits, such as the value people place on the provision of wilderness areas even when they do not intend to designed and executive CVM summary. (p. 21)

10. It is also important to note that there is no reason to believe that the indirect methods' estimates all exhibit the same sampling distributions. The Cummings et al. comparisons of CVM and indirect results treats the travel cost model and hedonic models as equivalent in their accuracy. Each requires quite different assumptions and can be expected to exhibit rather different performance patterns.

11. Strictly speaking, their formulation of the process of developing confidence intervals is confused. Comparison of point estimates of an unknown parameter (an individual's valuation of some environmental amenity) without some information on the nature of the variation in these estimates and their sampling distributions cannot conclude anything in a formal sense.

The authors recognize this and have tried to provide what might be called a judgmental comparison. Such evaluations are inevitably controversial because they require reliance on the analyst's judgement as an alternative to an explicit model of the process leading to each method's estimate, and with it a formal derivation of the properties of each estimator.

12. Maital (1982) made a similar general point in calling for closer coordination between economics and psychology. He noted that the conventional definition of economics leaves out the "why" of the questions (in Knight's terms) that are answered by an economic system (see especially his pp. 15-170).

APPENDIX:

SOME QUIBBLES ON THE CUMMINGS, BROOKSHIRE, SCHULZE SUMMARY OF
CVM RESEARCH

Several points in the Cummings et al. summary of past research that should be clarified.

Starting Point Bias

The record on starting point bias seems more clearcut than the Cummings et al. summary appears to suggest. There does appear to be stronger evidence that starting point does matter to CVM estimates using the iterative bidding approach. Tests of the differences in mean option price bids between $25 and $125 starting points in Desvousges et al. (1983) indicated significant differences for all water quality levels. This seems to be consistent with Rowe et al. (1980b), and with Mitchell and Carson's (forthcoming) interpretation of the Greenley, Walsh and Young (1981) work. a possible explanation for earlier results where no differences were found between starting points follows from the fairly narrow range in the starting points used for these experiments.

One of the issues that remains unresolved is the relationship between all questioning formats. Here the evidence seems less clearcut than the Cummings et al. report would seem to indicate. For example, the performance attributed to the payment card approach based on recent experiments involves changes in the conditions of what was being elicited (e.g., additional bids were requested after respondents were informed their initial bids would not assure the outcome that had been described to them).

Iterative Bidding

The iterative bidding process cannot be paralleled to the learning process that accompanies repeated involvement in an auction process (as is frequently observed in laboratory experiments). Learning time varies, as the authors acknowledge, with the complexity of experimental market process. However, in all cases, market periods involve several minutes each (the time varying with the number of participants) and intervals between these periods, usually for calculations and learning. In some cases, the process can involve over an hour for each experimental trial. by contrast, an hour is often the upper maximum for survey interviews involving a large number of questions. Iterative bidding questions wuld involve a small fraction of this time and no mechanism for the individual to learn based on responses to earlier questions. Thus, the parallel to experimental findings with auction mechanisms may be tenuous.

The Desvousges, Smith, McGivney Comparative Analysis

Several aspects of the report's summary of Desvousges et al. (1983) comparative analysis are inaccurate.

1. The survey elicited option price, not option value. The interview involved explaining to each respondent the components of total valuation, requesting an option price bid and then asking how much of that response was attributable to anticipated use of the river under improved water quality conditions.

2. The travel cost model developed as part of the research did consider the opportunity cost of travel time; it did not assume a constant wage rate for all individuals; and it did evaluate the role of model specification, the treatment of on-site time, and the character of the survey data for the travel cost models.

3. Our comparative analysis was clear on the interpretation of the relationship between contingent valuation and indirect measures of the valuation of water quality. We found that CVM estimates appeared to overstate the travel cost estimates of the value of water quality improvements. This finding was

based on our statistical analysis of sixty-nine users' bids and the projected consumer surplus increments for each individual (a total of 94 observations including 16 cases where individuals went to multiple sites). Simple comparisons of the means had the travel cost estimates of consumer surplus falling within the range for the estimated user values across questioning formats. The same was not true with a deterioration in water quality. In this case (where water quality was assumed to deteriorate to a level preventing any use of the river), CVM estimates were substantially less than the travel cost estimates and significantly different (as measured using a hypothesis test of unity for a slope parameter from a regression of the CVM estimate of user value on the travel cost estimate). It was argued that because the travel cost model had to ignore the role of substitute sites, it would be likely that this model would overstate the loss in consumer surplus associated with a water quality reduction hypothesized to lead to the loss of the use of the river's sites for any recreational activities (see Desvousges et al. (1983) pp. 8–16 to 8–18). Thus, the ambiguity in the findings suggested in the Cummings et al. summary of the results is misleading (see their discussion, chapter 6, p. 163).

12
The Review Panel's Assessment

INTRODUCTION

The preceeding four chapters contain the views of economics scholars whose own research has been focused on the development of the CVM; their interests and expertise in (with) the method was reflected in our repeated references in part I to their earlier works.

As stated in chapter 1, the breadth of our assessment of the CVM is greatly enhanced by looking also to outstanding scholars whose research interests are a step removed from CVM research for their assessments of the state of the arts of the method. Thus, our review panel, consisting of Professors Arrow, Kahneman, Rosen and Smith, offer the comments given below in response to, first their pre-conference reading of part I and secondly, the conference presentations of Professors Randall, Bishop, Heberlein, Freeman and V. Kerry Smith.

COMMENTS BY PROFESSOR KENNETH ARROW

The fundamental question being raised by the CVM approach (but not confined to it) is the transferability of results from one realm of observation—observation of human behavior—into another realm.

For various welfare reasons, we agree that a certain kind of pseudo-pricing will be, if demonstrably accurate, a useful basis for deciding on certain public goods measures, environmental measures, or whatever. We have a set of observations that don't relate to that field. We want to use these other observations, in this case responses to verbal criteria—in other words a different kind of behavior—and transfer them. Now this occurs not only in the context of public goods. In fact, it occurs not only in the context of economics; psychologists are always making observations in the form of experiments as well as in the form of field observations in certain limited circumstances and extrapolating to make inferences to other circumstances. At least that is presumably the purpose of the inquiry. One is not seriously interested in the response of a few college students to waving little rewards in front of their faces. Presumably you are using questionnaires because you are learning something, let's say, about your subjects' resistance to new information; their ability to translate given conditions into certain actions, which is a little more fashionable today; or to learn about difficulties of communication, say restricted communication networks, and how they manifest themselves in certain behavior.

Unfortunately there does not seem to be any systematic methodology for transferring results of experimental, rather small scale, situations to other situations, more specifically to uncontrolled situations. Now probably this transition will never be done well anywhere. Since I misspent part of my life as a meteorologist, I am acquainted with the fact that knowing physics very well is only of mild usefulness for weather forecasting, and yet we know very well that the elementary principles which determine the weather are in fact governed by the laws of physics, and our knowledge there is far deeper than we have in psychology or economics. So it is not surprising that these transfers from one situation to another are difficult—it is very typical.

One question is, does it mean anything at all? If you ask somebody a question you will get an answer. What this had to do with how much somebody really values something is conjectural. What kind of evidence do you bring to bear on this? One source of evidence is the consistency in the answers.

Actually, we generally do feel fairly safe for the most part (and psychologists certainly do, I think with some good reasons) in transferring the *qualitative* implications of their experiments. We learn that if people have taken a strong position it is not too easy to get them to change it, even in the presence of overwhelming information. This corresponds to the observations we make in real life, say, when we deal with our students. I don't know anybody who has made the attempt to say how much teaching will we need to overcome a given amount of *a priori* information.

One curious thing which was a subject of interest in psychology for a while and seems to have a lesson for us, is the work scaling of subjective phenomena, particularly by S.S. Stevens and his students. He would, for example, play a couple of notes on the piano and then play a third note and then ask "Is this closer to note A or note B?" The first time I ran across this on a doctoral examination I kept on asking the student what the question meant. From my ordinalist viewpoint, I couldn't imagine what it could possibly mean. Finally his professor said, "Anybody but an economist would understand that."

There was reality there. To be sure, if you ask a question you get an answer. The reality was that you start again with two different reference notes. You get a scale which is a linear transformation of the original scale. That is a refutable hypothesis—at least I was being assured of the fact that it was not refuted. It tested out very very well. This meant that here was some reality. Unfortunately it isn't very clear sometimes whether that is the reality we are interested in for our purposes. I do notice that for whatever reasons that line of investigation seems not to have gone any further.

Now we do find a problem. Consider the structure of an ordinary demand curve. We have a lot of observations, let's say a cross-section comparison on prices and quantities, and we derive the demand curve. In chapter 6 of the Assessment Report, it is noted that, in deriving this demand curve, when you do something as simple as change your assumptions on the distribution of the residuals, you get wildly different elasticities. This points to the fact that, in assessing methods such as the CVM, the demand curve should not be considered as some kind of "reality" to which we should hope to aspire. As pointed out by the authors, demand curves themselves are problematic.

Consider a problem closer to the sort of things we are talking about (the CVM)—a businessman who wants to produce a new product. He wants to know what he can sell it for. Of course there are questions of his costs, but that is in essence a private type of information that he or she can dispose of. What he or she has to look at is the worth. How much will the public pay for the product? Businessmen don't know, and more than fifty percent of all the new products put on the market fail. I don't mean fifty percent of *ideas* don't succeed, I mean fifty percent of the products which have already reached the point of market introduction are failures. So it is obvious that the estimation of the demand functions by businessmen is tinged with a large degree of error.

I'm trying to put some context on this question of what the CVM may really provide, how much one can expect from it. One more word on this subject—I think this was brought up by one of the speakers—about field experiments.

By considering contingent valuation as compared with other forms of indirect measurement, we have unduly limited the number of possible ways of getting information. There are others, and indeed field experiments—though not quite parallel to these—were, at least a few years ago, a major source of economic inquiry. The income-maintenance experiments, the health insurance experiment, the housing allowance experiments, were large-scale field experiments. These studies typically involved private goods, so the results we got from them had as much significance as one could possibly place on them, and should have been (at least in principle) a great deal more reliable than the observations made from uncontrolled observations —the sort of thing you've been dealing with in CVM experiments. In fact, very interestingly, the results were not all that different from results obtained from earlier studies based on secondary data. And furthermore, rather significant ranges of error were found in those field experiments concerning private goods; for example, a considerable range of error was found in elasticity of the supply of secondary labor in the case of the income-maintenance experiment, depending on what was being controlled for, or what you were allowing to vary.

This suggests some basic research. Now that may be the last thing one wants to hear around here, given the emphasis earlier on the scarcity of research funds, but one possible line is to take a field where CVM is unnecessary. This is just the place to do the research. The reason is, of course, that this is the only way you will ever be able to calibrate your measures. Comparisons of the CVM with other methods with all the associated difficulties described in chapter 6 are extremely important. If you are finding, by two conceptually quite different methods, numbers that are the same or similar, then—while you can't be quite sure that the reality that you are reaching is the reality that you *want*—at least you are reassured that you are likely to be measuring something real. We were reassured in this way in Steven's work on scaling. He scaled by several different methods, some of which seemed totally improbable to an economist, and yet the results were consistent. So I think trying to reconstruct ordinary demand curves by survey methods as well as by field experiments seems the sort of thing that is needed to validate the CVM for that other rather large class of cases where CVM seems to be the only method that makes any sense, short of course, of sheer *a priorism* or guesswork.

There have been a lot of statements made on the matter of the "hypothetical elements" of the CVM and I would like to comment on several classes of what has been referred to as hypothetical bias. One problem is that the commodity in the CVM is hypothetical. Again, that is not as unique as it seems to be, because as indicated, every time there is a new product you have a hypothetical element in your story. There are questions. Whether the answers are guessed by the producer or by some kind of consumer inquiry is another matter. The fact is we are in a world in which there are new things, and this is not exceptional—new products are constantly introduced in the market. In many industries, where we define the word "product" rather narrowly, fifty percent of the products sold at any time are less than three years old. In these industries there is always guessing about the receptivity of the market, and the guesswork is pretty cler from the fact that they fail every now and then. That we are dealing with hypothetical commodities is not so much a drawback as a fact.

I find the hypothetical bias concerning payment more serious than that about commodities. This is the concern of those who follow the economists' tradition which criticizes hypothetical questions. Verbal answers don't hurt the way cash payments do. Some evidence suggested that there was a real difference between cash payments and hypothetical payments. But on the whole the discrepancy was not as bad as one might fear.

Any time you have an irreversible element, especially one of some significance, you are changing the world, and the situation is hypothetical. It can never be put back. Now in the case of some environmental situations there is some chance for correction in the sense that there are similar situations in diverse geographies, so one can have a feedback process. If in retrospect it turns out you wished you hadn't made some change, you needn't make it elsewhere. This is the process which prevents blind investment from being totally disastrous—that there are enough similarities to be able to make an inference from one case to another. This reminds me that I haven't seen any discussions of cross-situation comparability, which is a way to get demand curves by essentially comparing situations at different times, and/or different places. It is not clear to me whether there has been enough attention paid to this. There's too much geographic specificity in the studies reported here.

Let me continue by discussing briefly some of the other biases addressed here. Neither the empirical evidence nor the theoretical arguments convinced me that strategic bias is liable to be significant. Sherwin Rosen does raise a point: Supposing I am asked, "From now on will you use the survey data?" That is, will survey data form the basis of our judgements? Then, indeed, I suppose one might have some problems. But let's not think that far ahead. This means the whole discussions about Vickery auctions and the like, which are basically incentive-compatibility methods, are really beside the point. I don't think this has much to do with the basic issue.

Several other biases were mentioned, and I will go over them very briefly. One was the vehicle bias. I must say, I didn't have a conviction from my reading that the vehicle bias does indeed matter. There is nothing irrational about a difference in responses in this case. If I'm going to finance a change by use permits, it is significantly different from the case where I finance it by general taxation. Let me put it differently—it would be irrational if you did *not* get a difference in the responses in these two situations. It is a fact that WTP depends on who gets the "P", and on what that means. This is very reasonable in some circumstances. Now for others, it may not be. You can get the framing problem. Say you get two methods of payment where every individual in fact is paying the same amount, or at least his or her random expected payment is about the same. Then if the responses differ, you may have a real vehicle bias. But if it is merely that taxing according to one principle, like use permits, gives a different result entirely than putting a general price, for example a bonus tax, on the public at large, then I find nothing remarkable. I do not have the conviction that these two different sources have been well expressed.

We need to see more data than is usually supplied, because these distribution of willingness-to-pay were very skewed. The mean was always much higher than the median. If you have a highly skewed demand, so that few people have a high value for it, there are certainly implications for methods of financing. It certainly suggests that a method which captures the surplus by individuals, even though it may be inefficient in some technical sense, may be superior to an alterntive which tries to distribute the cost, say, in some very broad way. It seems to me that the implication of this distribution is not that there is an error of measurement. Now, it may be, but I am assuming that it is not. It is a perfectly real possibility that some people value these things much more highly than others would—visibility or the right to hunt or whatever. It does suggest that some method of benefit taxation is appropriate. There are such striking differences that averaging them out may be unfair and may have legitimate political repercussions.

Again, on the information bias topic, I found that several different strands seem to have been drawn together, some of which are not biases at all. There was a lot of reference to information about other people's preferences. Now, in some sense this is the last thing you want. If you are worried at all about strategic bias, then you do not want information about other people's preferences, because you make strategic bias easy to achieve and you may induce it by your method of response. There is another reason that you might be concerned with other people's preferences and that is second-hand information: "Now, if everybody else thinks it's a good idea, it probably is a good idea, and I know I am uninformed and other people know a good deal more about it." But that requires deliberate modelling to take that into account. It can't be done by simply adding up WTP's.

Other kinds of information seem to be proposed which are simply explaining the matter in greater detail, greater specificity. These are already connected with hypothetical bias with regard to commodities. They are simply trying to explain the commodity in greater detail. Someone who knows more about surveys than I do would be better able to evaluate just how much you can present, for example, before the difficulties in processing the information presented begin to outweigh the benefits from having more information. This is something that I assume something is known about, with the many years of survey research in this country.

How you make a survey situation realistic is something I don't know. My impression is that the evidence indicates that the more you structure a situation to be a pseudo reality the more real-like are the results you elicit. But of course that usually has some price.

Finally, addressing the question of accuracy, there is an interesting question: What, even ideally, do we mean be accuracy? What is the reference? What is the reality to which we refer? We want to compare the outcome to some truth. Well, suppose we had infinite research resources, what would we mean? I suppose we want some kind of ex-post valuation—even that, of course, is hypothetical. One trouble is that in economics, as well as in other social sciences, almost all economic reality has to do with counterfactuals. What do we mean by saying that you quote a price? Is this price the cost of the commodity, or what you would give up to buy it? This is fully of the subjunctive mood. This is not confined to economics, but economics has developed this logic. Almost everything, all the concepts of marginalism, are counterfactual statements. They are statements comparing something to what would be true if it were not so. "If you produce one unit less," or statements of that kind—"if your income was one unit higher." There is a certain impalpable air of alterntives that are not being realized in some sense. Sometimes, very occassionally, nature will supply you with that experiment, or you might deliberately induce it, but in general there is a problem of this nature, and I don't have any answer to it. I am only pointing to some fundamental questions here about what we mean.

I am not going to try to answer the question "Should we have the CVM?" I think you can see my attitude is very sympathetic; there are a lot of difficulties in CVM and there are a lot of difficulties in any kind of measurement which purports to do the same thing, for example to give values appropriate for welfare judgements. Also, in my few brushes with actual environmental analysis or health analysis, it appears to me that in the estimates produced by our technological colleagues—our medical colleagues, our engineer friends—errors on the order of one to ten are considered to be perfectly normal. On one such project on which I was associated, for example, they were asked "What is the effect of nitrogen oxides emitted by supersonic transports on the ozone content of the stratosphere?" Well, the chemists had some laboratory experimental data, but they didn't know how long the nitrogen oxide would stay in the atmosphere. They didn't know whether the same chemical effects would occur because the reaction took place in the presence of a large mix of other chemical species that might upset the situation. There were some other factors involved. Although the effect they expected was there, there were other effects due to the supersonic transports that they hadn't allowed for. These scientists were perfectly aware of the limitations of their knowledge, and there were many more problems, problems which will turn up in that or any other effort.

The question is, should we be disturbed if we think that our error is within the factor of plus or minus fifty percent, or even double that? Let's talk about ratios of 3:1 or 5:1; compared to the other sources of ignorance in most of these environmental fields or the technological ignorance, and basic science ignorance, is this something to worry about, is this one of the biggest sources of uncertainty inside the environmental assessment?

COMMENTS BY PROFESSOR DANIEL KAHNEMAN

The "State of the Arts" document (chapters 1–6) is an impressive piece of work. I was struck by the close correspondence that is sometimes observed between directly assessed market values and estimates derived from people's answers to hypothetical questions. Although psychologists commonly have greater faith in hypothetical questions than economists do, I was surprised that it was possible to do so well with the CVM method. I was also impressed with the intellectual rigor and honesty of the analysis. The critical task is to specify the conditions under which the CVM is likely to be valid and useful. Indeed the Reference Operating Conditions (ROC's) that are listed in chapter 6 define restrictions, warnings, or *caveats* on the use of this method. I would like to add a few more. It is my impression that several restrictions that were not mentioned in this volume should be considered. The purpose of my remarks is to suggest new ROC's, to ensure that the use of CVM be constrained to problems in which its results can be trusted. To emphasize the continuity of my concerns with those of the authors of the book, I shall continue their enumeration of ROC's, in adding to the four that they stated.

Reference Operating Condition # 5: The CVM should be used only for problems that have a "purchase structure."

Let me now define what I mean by a "purchase structure". I distinguish two structures of transactions: purchase and compensation. In a purchase somebody pays to obtain one of two general kinds of things. People pay for improvements, gains, goods and services that make them better off than they were; they also pay to prevent a normal and expected deterioration. It is perfectly normal for a patient who has an illness and expects to get worse to pay for a treatment that will preserve her current level of health. I describe transactions of this general kind as having a purchase structure. Transactions that have a different structure often occur in the context of environmental affairs. In what I call a "compensation structure", we start with somebody who has an endowment—for example a nice view, or clean air—which is threatened by some deliberate and optional action of other people. Giving up this part or aspect of the endowment will make the individual worse off than before. The individual is requested, and sometimes coerced, to see part of his or her endowment diminished in order to benefit someone else or society at large.

It is not always easy to determine whether a problem has a purchase structure or a compensation structure. The key diagnostic is whether the change in the individual's endowment is a normal, expected, and natural event, or an optional and therefore avoidable one, which only occurs because some economic agent or some social institution chose to follow a particular course of action. The optional and voluntary nature of the loss of endowment defines transactions that have a compensation structure. Let me illustrate the distinction by an example. Trees can be lost either to pests or to human action. Thus, a beautiful view may be ruined because a virus has attacked the trees, or because someone is logging or mining the area. What is the value of the view to the individual who is threatened by its loss? I wish to defend the controversial idea that the value of the view is not the same in these two situation. The loss of the view to the pests, which the individual might pay to prevent, creates a purchase structure. The loss of the view to someone else's voluntary action naturally creates a compensation structure. If someone makes me worse off, I expect to be compensated.

There is an obvious relation between the two structures of transactions that I have distinguished and the two methods of evaluation commonly used in CVM: willingness-to-pay (WTP) and willingness-to-accept-compensation (WTA). Standard economic theory assures as that the values assessed in the two ways should differ only by a (usually small income effect. Because it is clear that the use of WTA measures in CVM often yields obviously absurd numbers, the spirit of previous chapters is to allow using WTP measures as a substitute for WTA measures, even when the transaction that is contemplated has a compensation structure for which WTA is appropriate. I have to make it clear at the outset that I do *not* favor the use of the WTA, which I believe to be very problematic.

However, I suggest a restriction on the use of the measure that is favored by most of the authors represented in this document: "Willingness-to-pay should not be used as a measure of value in transactions that have a compensation structure." The proposed restriction is based on the idea that the value of the difference between two states depends on the cause of this difference, and on which of the two states is considered normal. Thus, the same loss of view will not have the same value if it is caused by a pest or by the intervention of a government agency. This is a psychological claim which, if accepted, has significant implications both for CVM and for public policy.

I shall try to defend this position, which may strike many of you as heretical, on the basis of theory rather than data. Specifically, I want to relate the idea to a central aspect of a theory of choice—prospect theory —that my colleague Amos Tversky and I have developed. (Kahneman and Tversky 1979, 1984; Tversky and Kahneman 1981) The theory includes an analysis of value that compares each valued outcome or attribute to a neutral or normal reference point (see figure 12.1).

Improvements or gains appear to the right of the reference point, and the value of all improvements is positive. Deteriorations and losses appear to the left, and their value is negative. The value function in the Figure is drawn crudely in two segments, with the function distinctly steeper in the domain of losses than in the domain of gains. The figure illustrates the phenomenon that we have called "loss aversion:" losses generally loom much larger than corresponding gains (Kahneman and Tversky 1984).

To give you a sense of loss aversion, try comparing the intensity of the pain of losing $50 to the pleasure of finding $50. In another context consider a simple gamble, where on the toss of a coin you stand to win or lose a certain amount, with equal probability. The caution with which people approach such gambles

Figure 12.1
A Hypothetical Value Function

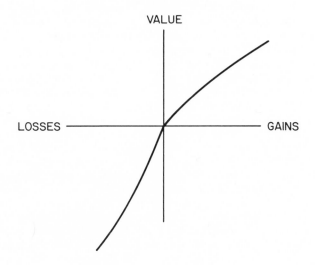

far exceeds what could be explained by a concave utility function for money. For example, when I sked my students what minimum prize would induce them to put a $10 stake on the toss of a coin, the average amount they demanded was over $25. There is no way of deriving such extreme loss aversion from any sensible notion of utility for wealth, but the observations are readily explained by assuming that a gamble on even odds only becomes acceptable when the possible gain is inflated to compensate for the much higher sensitivity to possible losses—as illustrated by the slope of the function of Figure 12.1 in the positive and in the negative domains.

To see the contribution of loss aversion to our story, consider the difference between dirty air and clear air. I argue that this difference can be legitimately evaluated in two different ways, depending on what is viewed as the normal reference point. First consider an individual who has dirty air. He lives in one of the areas of Los Angeles that are most afflicted by smog, and has now been offered the opportunity to purchase clean air, perhaps by moving somewhere else, or possibly by paying a share of a public clean-up project. In this case of a purchase structure, I propose that the difference between dirty air and clean air should be valued on the positive side of the value function.

Now consider an individual who lives in an area where the air is clean. Clean air is the normal state of affairs for this individual, but now a company wishes to move in, and to take action that will pollute the air. This case has a compensation structure. I propose that the same difference between dirty air and clean air should now be valued on the loss limb of the value function, which happens to be a great deal steeper. Thus, the value of the same difference between clean air and dirty air depends critically on *where one is coming from*. Note, however, that the present state of affairs does not always determine the relevant neutral reference point. For example, if the air is currently clean but is expected to get dirty from natural causes, as in the case of trees that still look good but are actually dying from a disease, the reference point is adjusted at least in part to the anticipated change. Gains and losses are probably relative to a state is expected for the near future, rather than to the status quo.

If loss aversion is accepted as a fact of valuation, it follows that WTP is an acceptable method only for purchase transactions. In particular, WTP should not be used as a measure of value for people who are made to lose their clear air or their trees because of the interventionl of some other agent. The fairest way to represent such cases is by recognizing that the experience is a genuine loss, and that the compensation should reflect this fact. I do not recommend using the WTA method to estimate this value, because I agree with the recommendations of the panel that this method is likely to produce useless results. My point is only that the use of WTP is likely to yield serious underestimates of the value of a good in a compensation structure.

There is a fair amount of evidence for the phenomenon of loss aversion on which the present argument rests. There have been many reports, in your own literature and in other contexts, of the so-called buying-selling discrepancy. (Gregory 1982; Kahneman and Tversky 1984; Knetsch and Sinden 1984; Thaler 1981) This discrepancy can manifest itself by a difference between buying and selling prices, or by other measurement of reluctance to trade.

Among the examples of buying-selling discrepancy discussed in the present volume, the 3:1 ratio of estimates of WTA and WTP for hunting permits appears to be very solidly documented. It indicates, in the present terms, that the value of a hunting permit is not the same if one is receiving it or giving it up. Another striking example is that of the effects on housing values of formally designating some areas of California as high in the risk of earthquakes. When people who discovered that they lived in such a region were asked how much it would be worth to them not to face the risk—that is, how much they were willing to pay to have the same quality of life in an area that is free of that risk—the value was about $5000. When people in other areas were asked what sum might induce them to move to a designated high-risk one, the estimate was $28,000. This huge discrepancy cannot be explained by self-selection. It is probably produced in part by some people who say "I won't do it, I would never willingly accept the risk!" The frequent refusal even to entertain the idea of a trade is one of the banes of the WTA method.

I repeat these examples in the present context to emphasize the idea that loss-aversion, the buying-selling discrepancy and reluctance to trade are highly robust effects that we ought to accept as such. It does not appear tenable to argue that, simply because economic theory says that there should be no difference between WTP and WTA, then there is no difference. This is one of those cases in which, when there is a conflict between observations and theory one should give the observations a chance.

The discrepancy between buying and selling is not a universal effect—it can be made to vanish experimentally, and it frequently vanishes in the real world. What are the conditions under which we may expect no discrepancy between WTP and WTA? Reversible transactions offer one obvious example in which a large discrepancy simply makes no sense. The money that is spent to buy a loaf of bread is surely not evaluated as a loss. The 2:1 ratio for the values of losses and of gains, which is suggested by observations in just acceptable gambles, is certainly not applicable to routine payments. The attitude to the downside of transactions may change for recurrent reversible exchanges, in which one becomes familiar with the experience of getting a thing and giving it up. What is given up is eventually perceived as an opportunity cost rather than as a loss, and loss aversion is then not a factor.

When a loss is imposed on an individual on a unique occasion, however, there is no reason to expect the evaluation of gains and losses to be so balanced. Can we legislate that an individual is not allowed to have a steeper value for losses than for gains, at least in unique and nonreversible transactions? I submit that it is not reasonable to legislate preferences to that extent. We must therefore pay considerable attention to the buying-selling discrepancy when it exists. When it does, and when the problem has a compensation structure, the use of WTP to measure value must, in my opinion, be avoided. Tricky issues will arise, of course, because of the complex mixture of objective and subjective considerations in the problem. How should we evaluate trees that are taken out to permit mining, but were doomed anyway by a pest? Is the individual allowed to ignore the fact (if indeed there is such a fact) that utility bills may rise significantly unless the trees are torn down? Obviously, the determination of the neutral reference point cannot always be left to the individual, but the fact remains that there are situations of genuine and legitimate loss, for which WTP measure will not provide a fair assessment.

Let me repeat in closing this topic that I have not spoken as an advocate of the WTA measure. Indeed, my aim was to raise a problem rather than offer a solution: by restricting the scope of CVM to measures of willingness-to-pay in problems that have a purchase structure, we may have restricted the application of the method quite substantially. There are surely many cases of compensation structure in which we would like to measure value, but the measure of WTA is suspect and WTP is not an acceptable substitute. The development of adequate methods of evaluation for such problems is for the future—and it will require much harder work.

ROC #6: The use of CVM should be restricted to user values, rather than to ideological values.

The thrust of this suggestion is that we should exercise great caution in measuring option values and reservation values, because the responses that are obtained in such measurements are likely to be heavily loaded with ideological content. To illustrate the notion of ideological loading, I shall quote from telephone surveys that Jack Knetsch and I have been conducting among residents of Toronto, in which they were asked WTP and WTA questions about a number of hypothetical environmental changes. The key observation is that there is a class of problems in which people's answers to preference questions seem quite insensitive to the numbers that are mentioned in these questions. Indeed, people seem to be ready with an answer before the relevant numbers are specified. Professionals who are skilled in analyses of tradeoffs know that it is not possible to give a sensible answer to the question "What is more important, health or income?" without specifying how much health and how much income is at stake. Naive responsdents have no such difficulties and they may be expected (this is a question we have not, in fact, asked) to state a clear preference for health over income. Similarly, I suppose that naive respondents will have a clear answer to the question: "What is more important to making people happy at work, the challenge of the job or the quality of the social life?" The willingness to choose among inadequately specified options suggests that the possibility of tradeoffs is neglectd. Preferences of this kind appear to reflect a hierarchy of ideological values.

It is reasonable to assume that the CVM, which is offered as a substitute for the market, is not intended to measure ideological values—but it may nonetheless be contaminated by such values. How can such contamination be detected? Common sense is a help, of course, but more formal diagnostics can also be applied. I will describe one, which I call "symbolic demand".

Consider the three demand curves of figure 12.2. Frst, imagine that the dotted line represents the proportion of customers who are willing to pay different prices for 10 pounds of apples, and that the dashed line similarly represents the demand for a pair of shoes. What can we say about the demand for a package that combines the apples and the shoes? The answer depends on the distribution of demand for apples and shoes and on the possible covariation of the two goods in the demand of individuals. The figure illustrates a special case in which the demand for both goods is about equal. If in addition the goods are independent, as apples and shoes probably are, the vertical sum of the two seperate demand curves provides a fair approximation to the demand for the package. In any event, the solid line can only represent demand for the package if the two goods are entirely redundant, so that either on its own is as good as the combination of both.

The three curves on figure 12.2 do not in fact represent demand for apples and

Figure 12.2: Expressed Willingness to Pay Tax for Cleanup
to Preserve Fishing in Muskoka, Haliburton, and All Ontario

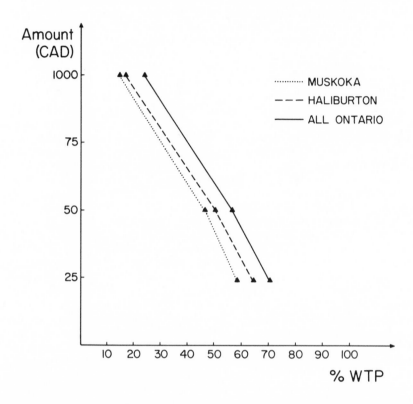

shoes. Instead, they represent answers of three groups of respondents in our telephone survey, who were asked about their willingness to pay an extra tax to maintain the fishing in some regions of Ontario. The leftmost curve represents the proportion of respondents who are willing to pay $25, $50 or $100 or more for cleaning up the lakes in the Muskoka region. The next curve to the right displays the willingness-to-pay for a similar cleanup in the Haliburton region, and the rightmost curve describes the willingness-to-pay to clean up *all* the lakes in Ontario. The demand functions for the three cleanup operations are strikingly similar.

The results indicate that people seem to be willing to pay almost as much to clean up one region or any other, and almost as much for any one region as for all Ontario together. We know from other surveys that these responses do not reflect expectations of personal enjoyment from the cleaup, since Toronto residents are willing to pay substantial amounts to clean up the lakes of British Columbia! People seem to answer such questions as if they had been asked "What do you want to do about keeping fish in our lakes?" and "How important is the issue to you?" The dollar number merely expresses the strength of the feeling that is aroused by these questions. Because the questions all elicit symbolic expressions of the same attitude, there is not much difference between the numbers that are attached to a single region and to all of Ontario. I suspect that this pattern is hardly unique, and would expect similar failures of summation of demand for other value-laden "goods," such as human lives that could be saved by social action: the hypothesis is that willingness-to-pay to save lives will be largely independent of the number of lives that are to be saved. I call this "symbolic demand" because it is true of symbols that quantity is sometimes irrelevant: a small lag can be as good a symbol as a large one. The economically incoherent pattern of demand illustrated in figure 12.2 can be a helpful diagnostic of evaluations that are dominated by ideological commitments.

The main point of these remarks is to question an assumption. As an outsider, both to economic analysis and to the use of CVM, it is natural for me to ask "What are the basic presuppositions of the work reported in the present volume?" One central cluster of presuppositions is that there exists a set of coherent preferences for goods, including non-market goods such as clean air and nice views; that these preferences would be revealed by a proper market; and that these preferences can be recovered by CVM if only the biases in CVM are eliminated. I find these to be very strong assumptions. In particular, I question the existence of a coherent preference order at the individual level, which is waiting to be revealed by market behavior. I am not sure that I have a "true" dollar value for the trees that I can see out of my window; that the market defines the perfect way of revealing the true dollar value of the trees; that the only problem of valuation is to discover that dollar value; and that it is therefore the task of methods such as CVM to achieve estimates of the market value.

An alternative way of looking at things would start from the assumption that preferences are often shaped by the eliciting procedure. This is, I think, the real significance of the starting point bias, about which so much has been said in this volume. For example, Jack Knetsch and I have tried a number of starting points in questions about the value of cleaning up lakes. We found that the proportion of respondents willing to have their taxes increased by $50 to clean up Ontario lakes varied from 18% to 64% depending on the starting point. The implication of this huge bias is that the respondents have no clear idea of how to answer the valuation question and that they consequently clutch at straws. One of the straws that is provided is the dollar amount that is mentioned in the question. Let me suggest a hypothetical reconstruction of the thinking that a respondent may do in answering a valuation question. They ask whether I would be willing to pay $25 to clean up the lake. I have no idea, really, but $25 is probably a number that divides the population about equally. What I do know about myself is that I seem to feel (more/less) strongly than many other people on environmental issues . . . I feel the government isn't doing enough . . . or there are too many environmentalist crazies blocking economic progress for the sake of fish and ducks. The initial Yes or No could well be determined in this manner and the magnitude of the anchoring bias suggests that it often is.

By the way, there is sad news for anyone who thinks that the bidding card will eliminate the problem. Several recent studies by Jack Knetsch and Robin Gregory have confirmed the highly predictable result that the bidding card is susceptible to anchoring biases. Responses obtained with a bidding card are unlikely to be free of anchoring biases, for the simple reason that the range of values on the card provides information. Indeed, the middle region of the card is a hint about what the experimenter considers a reasonable answer to the questions. There is no magic way of preventing respondents from latching onto such weak hints as they may find in a question, when they have no better way of answering it.

A specific recommendation about CVM use may be in order here. No study of CVM should be conducted without manipulation of the potential anchors or suggestive numbers in the valuation question. Furthermore, these manipulations should be powerful enough to elicit the anchoring effect in all its beauty; it is all to easy to fail to find a significant bias by using a biasing manipulation that is too weak. The use of the anchoring results depends, I suggest, on the magnitude of the bias that is observed. If the bias is small or moderate, values obtained with different anchors can be averaged to obtain an improved estimate. If the bias is large, however, a different conclusion may be in order: when the estimates are too susceptible to anchoring or to starting point bias, perhaps we should stop our analysis right there. Like the incoherent pattern of demand that was discussed earlier, extreme susceptibility to suggestive numbers may be taken as an indication that the dollar values that we hope to measure simply do not exist. Doubts about the existence of a coherent preference order are not only raised by anchoring biases, and are not restricted to non-market goods. Tversky and I have studied a wide variety of choice problems in which preferences are highly susceptible to what we call framing effects: preferences are affected by inconsequential variations in the *descriptions* of options. (Kahneman and Tversky 1982a; Tversky and Kahneman 1981) Framing effects violate a principle of invariance, which Kenneth Arrow has called "extensionality." Framing effects are probably common in studies of CVM. Any demonstration that preferences are susceptible to such effects in a particular context would raise doubts about the applicability of the method to that context.

In the early days of CVM, one of the main concerns was with the possibility that respondents may wish to disguise their true values, for strategic reasons. A more realistic concern, I submit, is that users of CVM often deal with people who simply do not have the kind of coherent preference order that the theory assumes—especially in domains for which they lack market experience. The cautious recommendation is to avoid using the method in such cases.

ROC #7: Accurate description of payment mode is essential to the CVM.

My final point echoes a remark that Kenneth Arrow made earlier, to the effect that preferences are highly sensitive to procedures as well as to outcomes. This, as Ken has pointed out, is perfectly rational. It may not have been emphasized to a sufficient degree in the teatment of CVM in the present volume. The social arrangement within which the payments in WTP are going to take place is an essential aspect of the payment method, and I put that as my last ROC.

The classic theory of public goods incorporates an idealization that one should not forget. The theory adopts the assumption that I urged you earlier to reject: that people have a specifiable demand for the good in question, and that the task in public-good demand estimation is merely to aggregate the demand of all the members of the community. The aggregate demand or the aggregate WTP is then accepted as the value of that particular public good. If you are beginning to be suspicious about this assumption, then some qualificatons are in order. In particular, it is likely that the value of a particular product of social action to an individual depends strongly on the details of how that action is performed—for example on the equity of the distribution of payments.

There is a bind here: we intend the CVM to mimic what a free market would generate. But a free market is inconceivable for many of the goods that we wish to value. The only realistic way to achieve some goods is by government intervention or by social action, and the cost of this action must be distributed, either progressively or equally, among members of the community. In such cases, it is indeed impossible to separate the value of a good from the procedure by which that good is obtained. In particular, WPT will then depend on others' payments. Note that this is a concern for equity, which is not the same as a strategic attempt by individuals to minimize their payments and maximize their benefits. What happens here is simply that if I am asked to pay $50 to preserve Ontario fish, I would like to know who else is going to pay $50. This is a legitimate concern or a person to have, but it is one that severely constrains the validity of the CVM: the value that is estimated when a particular social arrangement is assumed by the respondents may not be transferred to another.

In conclusion, there are cases in which the CVM in effect provides a market survey for a good that could indeed be marketed—the more successful applications of the CVM appear to be of this kind. However, when we deal with goods that can only be provided by the public, the survey, whether we like it or note, actually provides an estimate of the results of a referendum on a special-purpose tax, or on the fair allocation of a particular good. This view of the CVM has implications that extend even to the proper statistical analysis of survey results. My impression is that the tradition of using the *mean* of WTP derives from the idea that the quantity to be estimated is the total demand for the public good. Total demand is naturally assessed by estimating average individual demand, which is then multiplied by population size. If what we have is actually a pattern of voting on a policy question, then the *median* amount that people are willing to pay might be just the measure that we want. My suggestion is not that the median should always be used. The point that I wish to make is that the statistics that we employ must be adapted to the structure of the decision problem, and to the structure of the social mechanism by which the public good will be provided.

COMMENTS BY PROFESSOR SHERWIN ROSEN

The study is a very useful one that lays out the picture very clearly and completely. Speaking as someone who has a small stake in some of these issues and whose a priori views tend towards skepticism, the report made a convincing and positive case for the CVM.

Three little criticisms refer to some "cheap shots" that detract from the document as a whole in my opinion. One concerns a quote of Joan Robinson's in chapter 1, to the effect that there is no possibility for empirical truth in economics. That may or may not be true, but what is the virtue of raising it in this context? Besides, the quote was just naive in terms of empirical controversies in other sciences.

The second point concerns the discussion of social welfare measurement (chapter 2), where a suggestion is made that market prices don't reflect values. I fail to see the point of unqualified statements of this sort. The authors are all economists and they should take the thorough economic point of view. Let other experts take different positions. Distrust of the market often appears in environmental protection discussions and is popular in some quarters. But the proper audience to influence first is economists, and economists won't take this position. Apart from externalities there are cases where market prices don't reflect social values involving taxes and other distortions, neither of which are mentioned and could be taken into account.

The third point concerns raising very general questions about the validity of utility theory and rationality. Again I don't see any payoff for that in this context because I don't see what alterntive there is to utility theory in a cost-benefit calculation, and cost-benefit theory is all we have to go by in this business. Besides, there are tests of rationality in this context, e.g., integrability tests.

Now, on to the main points. There is little question, as I said at the beginning, that the CVM approach is a promising one and a progressing research program. Sometimes there is a flavor in the report of some Olympian battle among methods here. Yet the question is extremely well posed: how much are people willing to pay for certain things? What we are trying to achieve is a good method of answering that question; the *question* to be answered isn't controversial at all. These methods are not really mutually exclusive. I certainly don't see them that way. We shouldn't be looking for the Best Method; a universal Best Method probably doesn't exist. One method shouldn't be excluded over the other, because the best empirical research looks at the problem in alternative ways and through varieties of evidence. The more varieties of evidence we have, the more assured we will be of the correct answer. Another value of this enterprise is the value of learning how to do survey research. Economists have little skill at survey research though we certainly use much survey data generated by people in other professions which is not necessarily ideal for our purposes. I am very hopeful that some of the work here will spill over into other aspects of survey techniques in economics.

We particularly need more evidence on validity and reliability of the method. In this respect I found Chapter 6 of the report the most interesting. It is the only one that gives really hard numbers on a comparison of this approach with some others that leads to some indication of validity or reliability. On this, I think the authors sometimes use difficult theoretical arguments when the numbers speak for themselves, and no theorizing is needed.

I would like to suggest an additional approach: The use of replication studies. I don't see any evidence where a contingent market had been replicated. Such studies may be boring, but if we are doing experimental work here of this sort, I think you have to get some replication. I would like to see how the "goose study" done in Oregon compares with the one in Wisconsin, and perhaps in some other place. These repeated trials are an important way of learning how valid the method is.

I also would like to make a point on this WTP and WTA difference, since I strongly disagree with Kahneman on the interpretation of Brookshire's study on earthquakes. To my mind there is a basic confusion here between whether preferences are inconsistent—whether indifference curves exist and so on—and whether there are *differences* in preferences among subjects. People who live on the fault will answer a question differently than people who don't live on the fault. This is how I read the description of the Brookshire study. People who don't live on the fault are more worried about earthquakes and require much larger compensation to live there than the people who choose to live there. They have different preferences, and if one is labeled WTP and the other labeled WTA, you are heading into big trouble. There is a study by Glen Blomquist about the value of lake views in Chicago, where someone who lives in the high rises right on the lakeshore was asked "How much would it take to get you to move off the lakeshore?" How much would they have to be paid to give up their lake view? The response was a lot different than the amount that people who didn't have a lake view would be willing to pay to get a lake view. It is obvious that the people who didn't have a lake view self-selected themselves—they didn't care that much about it.

Another point that deserves emphasis relates to the strategic hypothetical bias argument. The point attributed to Rick Freeman in the volume is important and bears repeating. There is no strategic bias so long as the CVM is strictly hypothetical. If it is hypothetical, then the respondent knows his answer won't affect any policy, and there is no incentive to misrepresent preferences. But if it is hypothetical, there is no great incentive to go through the effort and cost of sharp calculation to elicit true preferences. This is the real conundrum in the method and underlies my initial skepticism about the CVM. It is worrisome that there are only four or five studies where one can make empirically meaningful comparisons. Now, one can argue theoretical points until doomsday, but we need some more empirical comparisons to check the validity of these methods. In this respect also, I don't view the hypothetical bias argument as so ill-defined as the authors suggest. It is an economic argument, a cost benefit question on the cost of calculation in answering a question. It seems difficult to test this. The authors want to make a formal test of the proposition; but I don't see how a true test can be devised except by comparison with some alternative method.

I found the section on accuracy (chapter 6) to be unclear. Perhaps I missed something, but the 50% number that was derived for assessing accuracy appears *ad hoc*. Precisely what scientific argument was used to arrive at that number? The 50% figure also seems to imply that people don't know their own minds. Suppose that we had a perfect CVM, as good as we could make it, and a person could calculate down to the last nickel how much a project is worth to him. Why isn't that a fairly accurate number? Why should it be valid only up to 50%?

I also would argue with some of the supporting textul material concerning this point. The results on the variation in estimates of demand elasticities, discussed in chapter 6, are not all that interesting, since not all of those studies are equally valid. For example, everybody's estimate of the demand for sugar or whatever should not be counted in calculating standard errors. Some of those studies are awful and should be thrown out of court. They are no good. Some are much better than others.

Let me give you an example. In standard demand theory some years ago, a well-known study rejected the theory of demand because the Slutsky matrix wasn't negative semi-definite, on translog specifications. People have reworked that very same data—it was aggregate time series data—using much weaker revealed preference tests rather than a translog system. Revealed preference tests never reject the theory of demand. There is not enough price variation to get true revealed preference comparisons in the actual data and all the budget sets are nested. So what apparently happened in that study is that the translog analyses imposed a lot of curvature on the data that just isn't there. That curvature was invalidly imposed as a maintained hypothesis, and it came out wrong.

Let me close with some questions that I don't feel were addressed by the study, that perhaps should be. One concerns the scope and limitation of the method. What kind of problems is the method best addressed to and used for? Where would we be most comfortable in using it? Goose hunting is one thing, but how about nuclear hazards, nuclear power radiation, promotion in the Southwest for fossil fuel generation and so on? Not only do we need clarification on where these methods might be more useful; but also whether they should be confined only to environmental issues. Perhaps they would be useful for other kinds of public goods decisions, the size of the military for example.

Another question that wasn't addressed is the cost of implementing the method relative to alternative methods. Perhaps other methods are cheaper. We need more information on this. Surveys are expensive, and we are not told how expensive these surveys are.

The third period has to do with "selectivity effects". The earthquake site case is one example of it. The on-site experiments on CVM certainly select users by their taste. Let me go back to the goose hunters—I was thinking while that was described that I would be willing to pay a few bucks to prohibit all goose hunting. I don't want to get shot when I go to view the Canada geese. More seriously, what is the relevant population for a survey in this area of research? How does this relate to such things as protest votes, refusenicks and so on, and precisely what is their role in the method?

The fourth point concerns the question of strategic bias which might arise if this technique was put on line and seriously used on a large scale. While reading the report, I had a vision of everybody hooked up via their PC's, direct on-line with EPA in Washington, making Groves-Ledyard votes one hour per day every day. If this technique gets serious and widespread use, we might well expect the results on strategic bias and so on that we are getting from current results to be invalid. At least I'd worry about extrapolation.

The fifth point is that the report, perhaps, adopts a fairly naive approach to economic policy. In fact, it is the approach I would have taken myself four or five years ago, before I'd been exposed to the work of some of my colleagues, especially Stigler and Becker. We really have to address the political economy of EPA and other kinds of regulations. This is the kind of regulation that seems to use very little economic input. There are uniform standards, very little price incentive, and a lot of other things that apparently can be rationalized only by political considerations in pressure group politics. This raises questions of how the respondents act when they answer these questions. Do they take these kinds of political considerations into account? Is that another potential form of hypothetical bias?

COMMENTS BY PROFESSOR VERNON SMITH

Kerry said that one of the disadvantages of going last is that everything has already been said. But that is not really true for an experimentalist who goes last, because we nearly always have some data that we can show. I do want to show some data a little later on that are taken from experiments based on joint work with Peter Knez and Arlington Williams. These have to do with the subject of calibration. We are studying private goods market situations, but we are also asking WTP and WTA questions.

As economists, our primary tool for solving a problem is to think about it. This leads us to slip, perhaps unconsciously, into the assumption that economic agents also solve their decision problems by thinking about them. In testing decision-theoretic propositions by interrogation methods, I think psychologists and others seem also to have assumed that the economist models the decision maker as a consciously analytical agent. This seems to be implicit in procedures that ask subjects to choose among a set of alternatives. Yet, I think the typical subject in a market experiment, based at least upon my experience, does not appear to operate in this manner. For example, some subjects "learn" over time to adopt demand-revealing dominant strategiees, but they really couldn't articulate why they do this. Some never learn; some seem to latch on to it right away, but I think they would have a lot of difficulty explaining to you why.

In more complicated experimental markets than the simple auction, subjects really learn to do quite well for themselves, and also for the theory of competitive markets, without having an understanding or even a perception of the market as a whole, which is nothing like our rigorous models of market analysis. This strongly suggests the possibility that rational behavior may not be consciously calculating. Specifically, it suggests the hypothesis that direct decision responses from individuals based upon thinking about alternatives may lead to violations of the principles of rational behavior, but what individuals actually do in the sequential replicating market context may not violate those principles. Hence, people may in some sense learn to be rational through market experience.

Now, in chapter 6 we find a report of some laboratory experiments by Coursey, Schulze and Hovis, which shows clearly that what people say about WTP and WTA is not necessarily what they do asymptotically in a repetitive market experience. I want to emphasize the importance of this hypothesis and these corroborating results for any program that will apply to the contingent valuation method, by briefly discussing some similar experimental results that involve a rather different market context than those used by Coursey et al. (1983b). Let me begin by providing some reinterpretation of WTP and WTA data as it applies to estimating the value of a particular good, such as the right to avoid tasting sucrose acetate, which is, I think, the commodity used in the Coursey et al. experiment. Or the right to hunt a goose or a deer. In discussing the difference between WTP and WTA measures, I think it is important to distinguish between differences for the same individual and differences among individuals, and I have a feeling that has been confused in the discussion. I think the former has been claimed to violate rational choice theory if there is a "large" difference between WTP and WTA, though "large" is not very well defined as I read this literature. Most of the observers seem to find that such differences are larger than they expected. But this assessment is really subjective. For example, Coursey, Schulze and Hovis note that the income effect should be small since WTP and WTA are small relative to income. Well, I think Don Coursey should remember the subject at the University of Arizona who, when she collected the $25 to $30 earned in a market experiment, commented that I had just saved her a pint of blood. Now, people who derive income from blood sales seem unlikely to satisfy the assumption that income effects will be negligible.

I think it is well to bear in mind that all these speculations here are just highlighting the fact that we really don't know. The guy says the divergence is larger than he expected based on the theory, but that requires an *interpretation* that might be incorrect. Now, differences in WTP and WTA across different individuals, even if large, should not disturb us, since that is the kind of divergence in valuation that is the basis for exchange. Large differences may simply mean that we can expect to observe low volume in market trading. The point here is that unless the distributions of WTP and WTA are disjoint, across individuals, there will be no gains from trade.

Insofar as the CVM is used to value private, non-traded goods, such as goose hunting and deer hunting permits, it seems to me that the objective is to measure market value, which can be quite different than mean WTP or mean WTA. Let me illustrate what I have in mind. I give you the standard freshman diagram, which I am going to use to lead into some of the experiments that I am going to report. In figure 12.3, the downward sloping line is a set of WTP measures that you might get by interrogation from a group of individuals and the upward sloping line is a set of WTA measures that you might get from the same group and it shouldn't surprise anyone that the mean WTP might be different than the mean WTA; or that both of these might be different from the market value (MV)—the value that maximizes the gain from exchange. In figure 12.3, area B is buyer's surplus, area S is seller's surplus, and B + S is the total surplus from competitive market exchange.

The experiments I am going to tell you about were not set up as WTP or WTA experiments. They had a quite different purpose; in fact, the study had been going on for six or seven months before it occurred to me that it might be a good vehicle for asking WTP and WTA questions. The experiments involved studying rational expectations theory in an asset trading context. In these experiemtns, twelve subject might participate in an asset trading market, and each subject is given an endowment in cash and an endowment in securities. One subject might get $9.50 in cash and no securities, another might get $5.00 in cash and one security, and so on. The securities all pay a random dividend with a distribution which is known to everyone. The understanding is that after each period of trading we will draw from this dividend distribution and everyone who holds some inventory of securities will receive that dividend, with everyone receiving the same dividend.

We have been using this vehicle for looking at rational expectations theory, as I mentioned, and we also wanted to use it to see if we could create market bubbles and crashes in the laboratory. Parenthetically, I'll mention that we began with an assumption that it might be very hard to do this. It turned out that we were quite wrong, it was very easy to do in these finite games—in a fifteen period game we had people's expectations of capital gain causing them to bid up prices in a bubble-like market, sometimes followed by crashes from the price peak as some began to wonder if they would be able to find another "fool" who would pay the high prices they had just paid. This, at least, is our interpretation of the results.

It occurred to us that a simple version of this game might be a good environment in which to look at WTP and WTA measures. Suppose everyone has gone through the instructions in one of these experiments and each knows their initial up-front cash and securities endowment. Then we can ask them the maximum they would be willing to pay for an additional unit of securities added to their inventory position; or what is the minimum they would accept to sell out of inventory. Our thought was to ask them these quesions—*hypothetical*

Figure 12.3
WTA–WTP Relationships

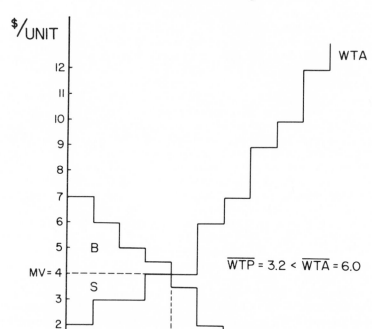

questions—and then put them in a single period of trade and see what trades occur and observe the actual trading prices. Now maybe we will get off-the-wall answers to the WTP and WTA questions, but on the other hand the resulting hypothetical market value might not be a bad predictor of trading prices. If we got the results, for instance, shown in figure 12.3, in a particular survey, those results would predict, on the basis of an interrogated supply and demand, that the mean price in the market will be around $4.

So that was one of our questions: How good a predictor is this hypothetical vehicle, even though there might be a lot of evidence of some sort of irrationality in the answers to these questions—the point being that it is possible that our theory of preferences is bad but that our theory of markets is not so bad. That is, our markets may do a pretty efficient job, given whatever preferences are, even if those preferences do not conform to our *a priori* expectations based on expected utility theory, or what have you. Another question, and this one relates to the Coursey et al. study, was that we wanted to see whether, if there were some wild choices in WTP and WTA responses, these would tend to disappear, and get more reasonable, as the subjects obtained market experience.

Figure 12.4 shows you some responses to hypothetical WTP and WTA questions that we asked nine individuals who are about to trade a simple gamble. The questions were put, and answered, prior to observing these people trade. The gamble has an expected value of about $1.25, paying $.50 with probability 1/2 and $2.00 with probability 1/2. We got some crazy answers here—referring to Panel A, figure 12.4, someone says they're willing to pay $3.00 for this gamble! For Subject 7, the WTP was $3.00 and the WTA was $4.00. Subject 2 will sell for $.50—that is, WTA was $.50—but was willing to pay $1.25 for an additional unit. You can see that some responses are all over the place. In fact, the mean willingness to pay is $1.39, the mean willingness to accept payment is $1.83, and the predicted price is $1.25, the expected value of the gamble! There is an old principle in economics that the cutting edge of the market is what the marginal sellers and buyers are going to do. It doesn't make any difference if you have some wild intramarginal WTP answers so long as they are balanced by comparable WTA answers. You may have these kinds of responses, and yet the market as a whole may not be making such an irrational prediction as to what's going to happen. Here, in fact, the prediction of these interrogations is the same as what rational expectations predictions would be—namely a price of $1.25.

After these questions were asked, the subject traded. They followed New York Stock Exchange trading rules: any buyer can make a bid, any seller can make an offer, for a single unit. If either a bid or an offer is accepted, acceptance becomes a contract. The subjects make the market—there is no auctioneer, except in the form of a rule. There are various kinds of rules governing the market, and the participants must subscribe to them, but there is no conscious intervention by any kind of super-agent; the subjects are doing all the trading. In trade, the mean price on that market was $1.30, compared with the predicted price (by both interrogated supply and demand and rational expectations), which was $1.25.

At the end of the first period of trading we reintialize everybody with the same endowments of cash and securities that they had before, and we ask them the same question again, and Panel B of figure 12.4 shows the answers they gave us. WTP and WTA are starting to tighten up, but they are predicting a higher price. The market clearing price on the basis of the hypothetical interrogations is now about $1.42. As it turned out, that wasn't too bad a predictor of what they did, since the mean price we observed in trading was $1.50—quite a bit *above* the expected value of the gamble. In fact, both the prediction by the WTP and WTA measues and the actual market were well above the expected value of the gamble. Most of these experiments were repeated five times. In this particular case I will just show you results for three periods.

Panel C of figure 12.4 gives results for the third period. The interrogation (hypothetical) procedure predicted about $1.48, and the mean we observed was $1.52, again both above the predictions of the rational expectations model.

In figure 12.5, if you look at how total surplus changes, it seems to me you see something of how much people and preferences are coming together across three trials. You can see that total surplus is falling. Most of the decline is over the second or third iteration. After this it stabilizes.

Figure 12.4: Tentative Results from University of Arizona Experiments

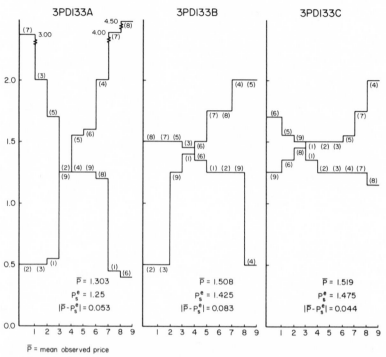

$\bar{P}$ = mean observed price

P_s^e = predicted price based on stated WTP and WTA

Hypothetical WTP and WTA are certainly not an accurate predictor of what the people do. They do poorly in predicting volume—each interrogation provides a prediction of what the volume of trade will be, and volume was nearly always higher than that. But across all replications, the hypothetical WTP/WTA measure does better than the rational expectations prediction as to what the mean observed price will be.

Now we ask the question that Coursey et al. asked, to see whether in our case, as in theirs, most of the adjustment came from the WTA side, with the WTP remaining quite stable: How does the seller surplus change relative to total surplus? Referring to figure 12.5, you can see that we do not have evidence (in terms of the surplus measure) that most of the adjustment was coming from the seller side. Actually, we haven't computed the means of WTA and WTP yet. We hadn't seen those means as particularly significant, because we were thinking in terms of private goods, of course, but we'll do that and maybe the means *are* adjusting more on the WTA side than on the WTP side.

Let me close by coming back to a point made by Ralph d'Arge. I think it was said that the real test is whether economists can come up with proposals for introducing markets in the allocation of environmental goods. As I read the CVM work, it seems to me that what you are mainly working on is proposals for some sort of a substitution for the market, a calculation substitution. I really

Figure 12.5: Change in Seller Surplus Relative to Total Surplus

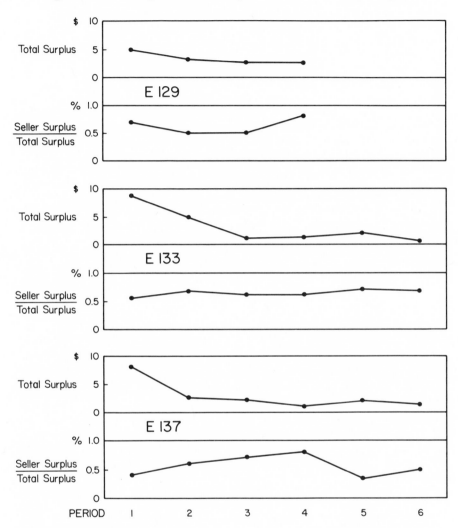

think we ought to devote a little time to thinking about whether there might be the possibility of creating markets where they don't now exist, and let the market do the calculation. In fact I have a proposal, one which involves the estimated 45,000 wild horses and asses that are in Nevada, Arizona and Utah. These have been very controversial—apparently the population is growing at the rate of about 12% a year, and of course there is heavy pressure on grasslands—the ranchers want to shoot them all and the Wild Horse Annies wants to save them all. There is an "Adopt a Donkey" program, which I understand works pretty well for the attractive ones, but the ones that are ugly, well, they just can't find anyone to adopt them.

So I have a very simple proposal: We take membership of the Sierra Club and the Friends of the Earth and other environmental organizations and also all the members of the Cattlemen's Association of Utah, Nevada and Arizona, and distribute among them at random 45,000 options to shoot a horse. Then we list these options on the Pacific Stock Exchange, and allow them to be traded in an open market. And so, if a rancher wants to shoot a horse, he has to buy one of these certificates and then shoot the horse and turn the certificate in. An environmentalist who wants to save a horse buys one of these certificates and sits on it. So the idea is you use the market to manage that stock of animals. To keep the floating stock of certificates equal to the stock of animals, the U.S. Wildlife Service would estimate the animal stock, say every five years. If the animal stock exceeded 45,000 less the number of redeemed certificates, they would just declare a certificate dividend such that the certificate stock equals the number of animals. If the animal stock was less than this figure, they would declare a negative dividend in certificates to maintain the equality. This would allow the stock of certificate claims to keep pace with the net biological change in the animal stock. Sherwin Rosen says he would be willing to pay something to keep anyone from shooting the geese—if he feels the same about these animals, all he needs to do is go out and buy all 45,000 of the certificates.

13
Summary and Conclusions

OVERVIEW

The reader has at this point been exposed to our initial assessments of the CVM (chapters 1–6) as well as to reactions regarding those assessments by a wide range of scholars, along with *their* assessments of the CVM, presented at the Assessment Conference and reviewed in chapters 7–12. We were particularly impressed with the quality of the interchange between conference participants concerning new and provocative ways of looking at where we are and where we might go in terms of the development of the CVM. In addition to the invited responses to part I of this book which are given in chapters 8–12, we received comments on the pre-conference draft of part I by Drs. R.C. Mitchell and R.T. Carson (Resources for the Future, Inc.). The points raised by Mitchell and Carson in their comments represent substantive contributions to the assessments of interest in this book; thus, with Mitchell and Carson's permission, their comments are included in an appendix to this chapter. As will become quickly apparent to the reader, the insightfulness of Mitchell and Carson's comments is reflected by our repeated references to them throughout the balance of this chapter.

Our task now is to draw together our discussions of the CVM in part I with those by Conference participants in Part II to the end of suggesting final conclusions as to the state of the arts of the CVM as a method for valuing public goods. As an aside, the reader should understand that in response to the many constructive criticisms of our assessments of the CVM offered by Conference participants, we have *not* altered the pre-conference conclusions set out in Part I—we have left the "warts" in our earlier discussions and conclusions as they were. Thus, as we develop final conclusions in this chapter, the reader is part of—can participate in—the intellectual assessment *process* wherein constructive, critical interchange between scholars is used to mold conclusions which ultimately reflect (we hope) some degree of concensus. State of the arts conclusions regarding the CVM are developed below in the following manner. In the section entitled Structural Biases in the CVM, attention is focused on the weight of structural bias in the CVM: biases which have been argued to result from such things as starting points, choice of payment vehicles, strategic behavior and information. The section entitled Hypothetical Biases in the CVM considers an issue that, in chapter 5, was presented as being of central importance for assessments of the CVM: the potential for hypothetical bias in CVM measures of value. In the section entitled The Accuracy of CVM

Measures of Value we address the question of primary importance for our state of the arts assessment of the CVM: how does one evaluate the *accuracy* of CVM measures? These discussions are brought together in the section entitled The State of the Arts of the Contingent Valuation Method wherein we consider the bottom line: What *is* the state of the arts for the CVM? The chapter concludes with the section entitled Critical Issue for Future CVM Research wherein we define critical issues for future research with the CVM.

Four structural types of bias in value measures derived with the CVM were given particular attention in earlier chapters of this book and were of particular concern at the Assessment Conference. These potential biases, discussed in turn below, are: strategic bias, starting point bias, information bias, and vehicle bias.

Strategic Bias

In general, the views of Conference participants concerning strategic bias in CVM measures parallel those developed in chapter 5. Freeman notes the absence of strong empirical evidence for free-riding behavior, which in his view suggests that individuals will not behave strategically in purely hypothetical or contingent market settings—a point of view seconded by Rosen. Professor Arrow finds neither theoretical arguments nor empirical evidence compelling in terms of strategic behavior by CVM subjects.

Both Freeman and Rosen emphasize, however, the potential dependence of the "no strategic bias" conclusion on the fact that, within hypothetical settings, subjects in the CVM study are not offered obvious opportunities to manipulate outcomes; i.e., as noted in chapter 5, the potential for strategic bias is less, the more hypothetical the valuation process in the CVM. Such dependence, if it exists, raises two related problems, however. First, and most obviously, a trade-off is suggested between strategic bias and hypothetical biases—this issue will be discussed in detail below in the section below. Second, a number of researchers are currently advocating alternative structures for the CVM wherein emphasis is placed on the subject's perception that his/her response *will influence* policy. Thus, Randall's theoretical model (chapter 8) is based on the assumption that subjects believe that the results of the valuation exercise will influence policy; within this framework, the "penalty" for a non-preference-researched response is argued to be that the subjects' opportunity to influence policy is wasted or misused. Such focus on influencing policy, as noted by Randall, is suggestive of referendum formats; indeed, Kahneman views the CVM as it stands as effectively simulating a referendum. Carson and Mitchell (appendix) look to referendum formats—political markets—as an alternative framework for the CVM and as a means for identifying "reference operating conditions" relevant for assessing the accuracy of CVM measures (appendix, part 4).

Ceteris paribus, the use of referendum-type formats as a means to investigate hypothetical bias may be questioned on the grounds that the more real is one's perception of the relevance of his/her responses in terms of influencing policy, the greater is the potential for strategic bias (see, in chapter 12, Rosen's "personal computer" analogy). It is not clear that such is the case, however. As implied by Carson and Mitchell, couching the CVM within the context of a referendum may in fact amount to the adaptation of the CVM to an institution which differs markedly from the market institution which common applications of the CVM attempt to simulate. The possibility of tying the CVM to alternative institutions (vis-à-vis the market institution) is an interesting and potentially important point and is considered in some detail below in the section entitled Critical Issues for Future CVM Research.

Starting Point Bias

In chapter 3 we noted that when the CVM valuation process is initiated by the interviewers' question: "Would you be willing to pay \$X," post-bidding valuations tended to cluster around \$X. The dependence of CVM values on the initial or "starting point" value of \$X was described as a "starting point bias". We noted empirical evidence supporting the existence of such biases—Carson and Mitchell (appendix, section 2.a) suggest still stronger evidence for such biases and argue that studies suggesting the absence of such biases may be flawed by the low power of tests used to examine hypotheses concerning starting point bias. At least two methods have been suggested for eliminating/mitigating starting point bias: the use of a payment card (c.f. chapter 3), and Freeman's naval gunfire analogy of "bracket and halving." (chapter 10)

Professor Kahneman (chapter 12) proposes quite a different context for treating and interpreting starting point bias. Kahneman suggests that the finding of starting point bias is indicative of a CVM "commodity" for which subjects are unable to answer valuation questions. For some types of commodities, lack of experience or familiarity with the commodity results in subjects' having great difficulty in putting dollar values on the commodity—subjects are not "hiding" anything from the interviewer nor are they attempting to be clever, they simply do not know how to answer the valuation question in a meaningful way. Thus, rather than adopting means to eliminate starting point biases, Kahneman seemingly views means to identify the existence of such biases as an important part of the study design: the presence of such biases indicates that subjects are too ignorant of the commodity to be able to value it meaningfully, in which case the CVM should not be applied to the commodity in question. Kahneman offers further "sad news:" use of a payment card does *not* eliminate the problem inasmuch as value ranges on the bidding card provide the potential for "entering biases" (indications of "reasonable" responses).

When starting points are used in CVM studies, we concur with Carson and Mitchell that the evidence suggesting starting point biases is indeed compelling. While, as is discussed in the section entitled Hypothetical Biases in the CVM, Kahnemans' concern that a subjects' lack of experience/familiarity with a particular environmental good may result in his/her having difficulty in placing monetary values on the good—indeed, familiarity, and/or experience is an ROC in chapter 6—received empirical evidence does not seem to support the notion that such difficulties are made manifest by starting point biases. Following Mitchell and Carson's suggestions (Appendix), higher powered tests for such biases may well result in starting point biases showing up in CVM studies involving commodities with which subjects *are* reasonably familiar—see the seven studies wherein derived CVM values are shown to compare favorably with values derived from indirect market methods (table 6.12). Thus, we would argue that starting point bias may well reflect other phenomena, e.g., the subjects' interpretation of starting points as indicative of actual costs for a proposed environmental improvement. Moreover, it would appear that payment cards can be structured so as to eliminate the potential for the "entering biases" of concern to Professor Kahneman. Thus, while an issue of concern, the authors conclude that starting point problems should be amenable to control through care in the design of the CVM payment card.

Information Bias

In chapters 3 and 5, the authors pointed to the confusion that one finds in the literature as to the substance of what is referred to as "information bias"; at the heart of this confusion is the failure on the part of many writers to distinguish between effects on CVM valuations arising from the subject's exposure to more information ("more" in quantitative and/or qualitative terms) regarding the commodity or valuation process as opposed to the subjects exposure to *different* information—"different" in the sense that two sets of information imply two different market (valuation) structures or two different commodities.

Randall (chapter 8) suggests that such confusion is eliminated as follows. Rational subjects base their contingent market decision on (a) the value of the commodity offered; (b) the rule by which the agency decides to provide or not to provide the commodity; and (c) the rule that determines the payment to be exacted from the subject. Since, according to Randall, only (a) is relevant for valuing nonrival goods, the pertinent question is: do (b) and (c) encourage accurate reporting of (a)? In this vein, Randall argues that different information which affects (b) or (c) *should* affect reported measures of willingness to pay. Such changes in information then result in effects on WTP measures that are expected *a priori*. Such effects, therefore, are not biases. In this manner, Randall rejects the notion of "information bias."

Related to Randall's point (c)—as well as to (b)—is the design question as to whether or not a subject in the CVM should be given information concerning bids by other subjects. Arrow argues that such information should *not* be given due to the potential effect of this information in eliciting strategic behavior. Moreover, Arrow views such "second hand" information as possibly leading to biases resulting from subjects' dependence on more informed judgments of others, as implied by their bids. Freeman argues that such information could lead, in effect, to a form of starting point bias. Along a slightly different line, Kahneman sees information concerning (c) as an integral part of the valuation process—any one individuals' "true" willingness to pay is inextricably related to what all other individuals are paying for the commodity in question, i.e., Kahneman implicitly rejects the economists' commonly-used assumption of independent utility functions.

However, Randall's arguments concerning (a)–(c) address only one part of the sources of information of concern in chapter 5: changes in information affecting value structures and/or commodities; his arguments do not seem to speak directly to the relationship between reported valuations and the quantity/quality of descriptive information concerning the commodity. In these regards, it would seem that in cases where systematic differences in valuations are associated with changes in the quantity or quality of information describing the CVM commodity, the implied "bias" may well be attributable to difficulties in "information processing" described in chapter 5. Arrow points to the difficulties in balancing the potential benefits of providing subjects with descriptive information with the subject's difficulties in processing that information. Freeman sees such biases as positive vis-à-vis assessments of the CVM inasmuch as they may be interpreted as indicative of subjects' approaching the valuation process in a meaningful way; i.e., subjects *use* information provided to form perceptions of the CVM commodity and base their valuation responses on that information.

Thus, in terms of information which has the effect of altering the nature of the CVM commodity, rules for providing the commodity and/or rules which determine actual payment, we would concur with Randall's judgment that one would expect such changes to alter bids, in which case a bias *per se* is not implied. On the related subject concerning a subject's exposure to bids offered by other subjects, we find the argument that such information may result in undesireable biases compelling; in this regard, we note that, while a substantive issue which perhaps warrants future inquiry, Kahneman's rejection of the assumption of independent utility functions weakens results from virtually all benefit assessment methods. Finally, in terms of biases which may result from different levels of purely descriptive information given to CVM subjects, two concluding observations appear salient. First, an integral part of pre-tests of questionnaires must be the effort to balance the subject's need for information with his/her general capacity to absorb—process—the information. Secondly, as suggested by Freeman, one must avoid interpretative generalizations of CVM results to environmental changes *other than* those specifically described in the CVM instrument.

Vehicle Bias

Conference participants, particularly Professors Arrow, Kahneman and Randall, took sharp issue with chapter 5's discussion of vehicle bias. The essence of our discussions of vehicle bias in chapter 5 is reflected in Freeman's (chapter 10) statement of the vehicle bias problem: our inability to determine which payment vehicle, if any, provides "true" (unbiased) values and which payment vehicles lead to biased values. Arrow, Kahneman and Randall argue that the search for an unbiased payment vehicle is misguided—"biases" are not implied by systematic variations in offered values and payment vehicles.

The essence of Arrow and Kahneman's argument (see Kahneman's ROC number seven in chapter 12, Comments by Professor Daniel Kahneman) is that the social arrangements by which payments are to be made—the payment vehicle—is an integral part of the CVM commodity *per se*, i.e., one cannot separate the value of the commodity from the procedures by which the commodity is provided and payment is made. Of course, this is Randall's argument (c) concerning information bias which was discussed above. In this regard, Kahneman rejects the notion that values based on one set of "social arrangements" may be transferred to a different set; Arrow sees differing preferences—and therefore values—related to purchases via use permits, general taxation and/or general price effects, as rational. Thus, Arrow suggests that WTP depends on the structure of "P."

These arguments are surely compelling and have important implications for the design of and interpretation of results from the CVM. First, following

Kahneman, reflecting the *fact* that our commodity is not a market commodity, but a commodity which can only result from social action (government intervention), the CVM's mode of payment is selected on the basis of realism—what payment vehicle would most likely be employed, in fact, if the commodity were to be provided? Secondly, paralleling Freeman's interpretative limitations related to information bias, we explicitly acknowledge, without apology, the potential dependence of obtained valuations on the adopted payment vehicle.

Conclusions

In terms of the potential structural biases in CVM values which this Section addressed, the current state of the arts in the CVM may be described as follows. First, all else equal, strategic bias does not appear to be a major problem in applications of the method. Two caveats are relevant for this conclusion, however. Interactive information concerning other subjects' values, as *might* attend efforts to bring standard CVM practices together with experimental techniques, may introduce incentives for strategic behavior. Further, efforts to reduce the potential for hypothetical bias (discussed below) in the CVM, *a la* Randall's proposed dependence on a subject's belief that his/her response will actually affect public policy, may invite strategic behavior in applications of the CVM which rely on market institutions—the implications of structuring the CVM in *alternative* institutions are discussed below in Section L.

Second, the authors submit that the use of carefully structured payment cards can effectively mitigate starting point bias in applications of the CVM involving commodities with which subjects have had some degree of market-related experience—where subjects are reasonably "familiar" with the commodity. For other commodities, Kahneman's concern with starting point bias—with or without a payment card—may be well-founded, but it is unclear to the authors how one would distinguish between anchoring-sorts of biases in these cases and biases attributable to the myriad hypothetical-related issues concerning decision-making under uncertainty, attitude/behavior and others which arise when individuals begin at the bottom of a learning curve relevant to an environmental commodity.

Thirdly, the "information bias" rubric seems to serve no useful purpose for assessments of the CVM; indeed, it may be counterproductive. In terms of the quantity/quality of descriptive information concerning the CVM commodity, it seems reasonable to expect that pre-tests of questionnaires can be used to balance information needs with information processing capacities for "appro-priate" commodities. Once again, the familiarity issue arises as does the relevance of the authors' suggested ROC's. In the case of unfamiliar goods, in the authors' minds, it appears sanguine to expect that processing capacities can be balanced with the bulk of information that might be required to elicit reasonably informed valuations from subjects.

Finally, in terms of information concerning rules pertaining to the provision of the commodity and/or to payment, we see little to distinguish these information "biases" from those considered under the rubric of "vehicle bias." In these regards, we consider the state of the arts as one wherein the notion of vehicle bias, broadly defined, is without substance. One acknowledges that such rules are an integral part of the valuation process. Values derived via the CVM are then interpreted as simply applying to the specific commodity described in the questionnaire, provided under the "social arrangement" (rules for provision and payment vehicle) described in the questionnaire. In this context, one views with equanimity the rational fact that different payment/provision institutions— social arrangements—may result in different valuations.

HYPOTHETICAL BIASES IN THE CVM

The reader will recall the many "faces" of hypothetical bias discussed in chapter 5. As one might expect after reading that chapter, the issues associated with hypothetical bias, and the implications of such biases, served as a source of interesting exchanges at the Assessment Conference. Reflecting some degree of concensus among conference participants, the major issues related to hypo-thetical bias, as they are relevant to our state of the arts assessment of the CVM, are: the preference research issue(s); the comparability of WTA and WTP measures; and the attitude v. intended behavior issue. Those issues are considered in the discussions that follow.

Preference Research Issues

Under the rubric of "preference research" developed in chapter 5, three distinct lines of argument can be discerned from the conference papers and discussions: the role of incentives for accurate valuations; the importance of a subject's familiarity/experience with the CVM commodity; and the (related) learning issue.

Incentives and Accurate Valuations.

In chapter 5, arguments by Freeman (1979a) and by Feenberg and Mills (1980) concerning the lack of incentives for "accurate" valuation responses in the CVM were distilled into a hypothesis of the form: valuations with *actual* payment equal valuations *without* actual payment (i.e. with hypothetical payment). Underlying this hypothesis was Freeman's notion that, since individuals suffer no utility loss from inaccurate responses to CVM valuation questions, they lack incentives to engage in the mental effort (and consumption of time) required to research preferences and formulate meaningful evaluations. Our review and interpretation of the literature related to the above hypothesis—primarily the works by Bohm (1972), Bishop and Heberlein (1979), Coursey et al. (1983) and Slovic (1969)—resulted in our conclusion that results from research to date belie the above stated hypothesis, i.e., substantive differences in values result when real and hypothetical payments are involved. Obviously, the implications of this conclusion would not bode well for the CVM. If hypothetical payment does not provide incentives for accurate responses in the CVM, and absent means for quantifying such biases, the viability of the method may be seriously questioned.

Mitchell and Carson (appendix) take sharp issue with our conclusion. Based on their reworking of data used by Bohm and by Bishop and Heberlein, they find that results from these works concerning actual/hypothetical payment are much weaker than those reported in the authors' original papers. In turn, however, we should note Bishop and Heberlein's critiques of Mitchell and Carson's reworking of their data, given in chapter 9. Moreover, Mitchell and Carson challenge the relevance of results from the Coursey et al. study inasmuch as the study's focus is on WTP-WTA differences, and results related to actual/hypothetical payment differences are simply inferential. Finally, referring to the literature in cognitive psychology, their discussions with Slovic suggest that, first the general literature on this topic shows equivocal findings; and second, that results from Slovic's 1969 study do not strongly support the sweeping conclusion offered by us in chapter 5.

Of course, Mitchell and Carson do not argue that hypothetical payment does *not* result in bias; rather they argue that the question remains open. Arrow seemingly agrees that the question is open. He argues (chapter 12, comments by Professor Kenneth Arrow) that in the pseudo-reality of the CVM, well-structured questionnaires which create real-like markets may well be capable of generating real-like results. Randall (chapter 8) offers a stronger argument: notwithstanding hypothetical payment, incentives for a subject to research preferences and formulate accurate valuation responses are provided by the subjects' concern with foregoing an opportunity to influence policy—we have noted above the potential conflict between this position of Randall's and the strategic bias issue noted by Arrow, Freeman, and Rosen. Perhaps still stronger in these regards are results from laboratory experiments conducted at the University of Arizona reported by Vernon Smith (chapter 12). Based on these experiments, Smith concludes that interrogated WTP/WTA values (corresponding to hypothetical payment/compensation) were found to be *better* predictors of post-trading equilibrium values for prices than *a priori* predictions from expected utility theory. Moreover, while pre-trade predictions of trading volumes were typically inaccurate, Smith notes that predicted (hypothetical) valuations were generally close (around 95%) to actual market-clearing prices.

There remain, however, the results of Bishop and Heberlein's recently completed study of Sandhill deer hunting permits (chapter 9). As in their early goose-hunting permit study, Bishop and Heberlein find significant differences between bids involving cash and hypothetical payments in all of their WTA experiments (table 9.2) and in three of the four auction formats used in their WTP experiments (table 9.3). Based on these findings, Bishop and Heberlein conclude that the evidence for bias related to hypothetical payment is rather convincing. Moreover, they argue, no matter how closely the Reference Operating Conditions are met, hypothetical bias (attributable to hypothetical payment) will remain.

Bishop and Heberlein's conclusions, as well as the results from their impressive Sandhill study, are not readily dismissed. No matter how weakened by Mitchell and Carson's analysis, there exist research results from several studies (reviewed in chapter 5) supportive of those offered by Bishop and Heberlein. But there exists a great deal of evidence which challenges the weight of Bishop and Heberlein's conclusions. In this regard, we note the above-cited observations by Mitchell and Carson and by Arrow, as well as, partcularly, the experimental results reported by Vernon Smith. Moreover, results from Chapter 6's analyses of seventeen comparison studies demonstrates remarkable (in our view) consonance between values derived with the CVM and values derived from indirect market methods—a degree of consonance which is, at worst, inconsistent with the full weight of Bishop and Heberlein's conclusions, particularly as their conclusions refer to commodities which to some extent satisfy our ROC's. Similarly, these demonstrations argue against the strong conclusion suggested *by us* in chapter 5.

In offering, then, a state of the arts conclusion concerning the incentives issue generally, and biases attributable to hypothetical payment particularly, the authors feel compelled to soften their conclusions in chapter 5 and to concur in principle with Mitchell and Carson: at worst, evidence from research to date provides equivocal results concerning the hypothetical payment issue; at best, for public goods which satisfy the ROC's, evidence from comparative and experimental studies suggests that minimal biases in CVM measures may result from hypothetical payment.

Familiarity/experience as a Prerequisite for CVM Commodities.

A second preference research issue developed in chapter 5 concerns the extent to which subjects in the CVM interview can place meaningful values on commodities with which they are unfamiliar—they have no experience in trading/valuing the commodity in question. Hypotheses related to this issue developed by the authors in chapter 5 focused on time and information requirements by subjects if they were to research preferences in a meaningful way to the end of formulating accurate valuation responses. In our search for research results relating to these hypotheses, myriad problems associated with such things as cognitive dissonance, mental accounts, information processing— more generally, bounded rationality—we were compelled to conclude that results from the received literature offered little that would support the notion that subjects, during the relatively brief period of the CVM interview, could define their preferences for a new, unfamiliar commodity in any meaningful way—thus, our use of ROCs 1 and 2 developed in chapter 6.

The familiarity issue, and our requirement for experience/familiarity with CVM commodities as a Reference Operating Condition, was the subject of considerable controversy at the Assessment Conference. Freeman (chapter 10) essentially accepted the familiarity/experience issue as being on equal footing with the hypothetical payment/incentive issue as a potential source of bias in CVM measures, and expanded the familiarity argument in the following way. In contrast to conventional theory, Freeman argues that individuals have more accurate knowledge of their preference orderings in the neighborhood of those consumption bundles *that they have actually experienced.* In instances where individuals are moved into unfamiliar regions of their preference orderings, accurate preference orderings—and therefore accurate valuations—will result *only* after the individual can learn (via trial and error experiences) about this "new" region of consumption bundles. Thus, if the CVM involves small changes around neighborhoods of experienced consumption bundles (the individual is, therefore, somewhat familiar with the commodity), valuation responses will be more accurate than for CVM studies involving changes (or new commodities) which move individuals to regions of preference orderings with which the subject has no experience.

V. Kerry Smith acknowledges the potential importance of the familiarity issue, but takes the argument along two somewhat different lines. First he argues that the relevant state of the arts is one wherein we can say little, qualitatively or quantitatively, about the implications of the familiarity problem inasmuch as we have no model of how individuals behave/respond in the CVM milieu; he notes Hoehn and Randall's (1983a) interesting beginning in this regard, to which we would add the logic suggested by Freeman (chapter 10). Secondly, and somewhat curiously, Smith argues that, in accepting the ROC's which require that subjects be familiar with the CVM commodity and its (at least) indirect market exchange, we require that the subject's choice experience is the equivalent of his/her knowledge of the features (outcomes) of the implicit market; i.e., such CVM studies elicit the subject's perception/estimation of implied market *outcomes* for hypothetical changes *rather than* the subject's personal valuation of the commodity.

V. Kerry Smith's latter point warrants a closer look. If the CVM commodity was a loaf of bread, the subject's knowledge of market outcomes (the price that bread commands in the supermarket) would surely be reflected in the subject's bid. But the familiarity requirement for *public* goods is not this strong, nor is the requirement for *indirect* market experience. In Chapter VI's example of air quality in Los Angeles, satisfaction of the familiarity ROC was argued on the grounds that subjects were (a) aware of (familiar with) air quality differences in various areas in the basin, and (b) that equivalent houses in areas with better air qualities would cost "more". Individuals may have rough ideas of how much more beach-side homes cost than the housing counterpart in Pasadena, but it would be heroic to assume their access to hedonic measures which attribute values to the myriad attributes of the beach-side house (proximity to beach, crime rates, etc., *and* air quality). Faced with the question: "Living in Pasadena, what would you pay for (beach-side) levels of air quality?", a basis for the subject's calculation of a market solution *a la* Smith is not readily apparent. Thus, while Smith's call for modeling efforts concerning individual behavior within the setting of the CVM is (and was, at the Conference) well-received, his assertion that CVM applications for commodities satisfying the familiarity ROC's imply the generation of implicit market outcomes, rather than an individual's revelation of preferences, is not (to the authors' minds) convincing.

Kahneman argues that the requirement of familiarity does not go far enough in terms of imposing limits on applications of the CVM which may lead to *a priori* expectations of reasonably accurate responses. In chapter 6, the authors, in describing the implications of the ROC's, noted that the ROC's precluded the derivaton of value estimates for unfamiliar, and uncertain, commodities, such as those related to option, preservation and bequeathment values. Kahneman suggests the use of a distinct ROC which precludes the application of the CVM for deriving *any* value with ideological content—i.e., only *user* values should be the subject of CVM applications. In support of his argument, Kahneman draws on the notion of "symbolic (or incoherent) demand". Symbolic demand reflects an individual's hierarchy of values which, Kahneman argues, must inject itself into any economic or political context. Manifestations of symbolic demand— manifestations of ideological "loading"—are seen in subject's inability to differentiate between values attributable to related, but nonsubstitute goods; e.g., a subject's inability to differentiate, in value terms, between improved air quality in area A, areas A and B, and air quality throughout the United States (this particular example of symbolic demand is found in Schulze et al. 1983b, chapter 1). Thus, to the extent that familiarity and uncertainty ROCs do not eliminate all possible applications of the CVM to commodities with ideological content, we are asked to expand the ROCs to preclude such applications.

The Learning Issue

While inextricably related to the familiarity question discussed above, questions concerning "learning" are sufficiently distinct to warrant their separate treatment. At issue in these regards is the efficacy of various methods and techniques in assisting subjects in the CVM to first, more effectively research their preferences; and/or secondly, to more completely understand the nature of the contingent market and incentive-compatible behavior appropriate for that market. Methods/techniques of concern in these regards are: the iterative bidding process; the use of repetitive valuation trials; and more generally, the transferability of techniques used in laboratory experiments to applications of the CVM.

A recurring theme through chapters 3–6 is the authors' view that the iterative bidding process must be used in CVM applications if meaningful measures of subjects' *maximum* willingness to pay are to be derived. This admittedly strong view was based primarily on three arguments developed in those chapters. First, the heuristic argument (chapters 3 and 4) that, at the outset, subjects may not fully appreciate the "all or nothing" character of the contingent market and that the bidding process "prods" the individual to more completely research his/her preferences vis-à-vis the contingent commodity; as in any auction, demands on the subject's judgment as to the extent to which he/she really wants the commodity, increase as the stated price increases. Secondly, results from experimental economics demonstrate that subjects require time and repetitive valuation trials before they begin to fully appreciate the nature and implications of the valuation process. Third, and finally, the considerable empirical evidence which demonstrates significant differences between initial, one-shot values and final values derived with the bidding process.

While acknowledging that initial, one-shot, bids may underestimate a subject's maximum willingness to pay, Mitchell and Carson (appendix) reject the notion that the iterative bidding process solves the problem; in so doing, they challenge each of the three arguments used by us in developing our contrary conclusion. The heuristic "prodding" argument is turned 180 degrees to suggest that the bidding procedure may in fact "bully" subjects into bidding more, given their awkward social position of having to say "no" to the interviewer's inferred request for a higher bid. While agreeing that CVM scenarios should include iterative elements which permit learning, Mitchell and Carson argue that the iterative trials of experimental economics are unnecessary to accomplish this end, and moreover, do not make the case for using the iterative bidding process. The necessary use of iterative trials in experimental economics, they argue, may well be related to the nonintuitive, second-price auction institution. In terms of one's understanding of the WTP format, they point to the data presented in table 4.1 of chapter 4 which shows (for WTP trials) minor differences in bids across the repetitive trials. Finally, the interpretative weight of our empirical evidence demonstrating differences between initial and post-bidding values is implicitly challenged by Mitchell and Carson by the question: "To what does one attribute the observed differences: downward bias (as we argue) or a 'bullying' effect?"

Bishop and Heberlein (chapter 9) also criticize the "categorical conclusion" regarding the need for iterative bidding suggested by us in earlier chapters. Like Mitchell and Carson, they point to the weak statistical tests in demonstrations of bid differences with and without iterative bidding processes and report results of their analysis of three bidding game studies wherein starting and iterated bids are positively correlated with hypothetical payment, but *not* correlated with actual cash payments. Referring to results from their Sandhill study, Bishop and Heberlein suggest that iteratve bidding encourages subjects to exaggerate their willingness to pay; one should note, however, that only one iteration was used in their study. Finally, noting that iterative bidding precludes the use of mail surveys in application of the CVM, they suggest as an "ultimate conclusion" that the iterative bidding process may simply not be worth the trouble and expense.

In chapters 4 and 6, the authors devoted considerable attention to developments in experimental economics and the potential promise of laboratory methods/techniques used by experimental economists for structuring and testing questionnaires to be used in CVM field interviews; particular stress is given to the use of "Vickery Auctions" and tatonnement processes—basic methods used in experimental economics—as means by which more accurate responses might be obtained with the CVM.

Our enthusiasm for lessons learned from experimental economics, vis-à-vis their meaningful transferability to the CVM, was not totally shared by Conference participants. Bishop and Heberlein criticized our stress on the need to conduct laboratory experiments while ignoring the contributions of field experiments—a position supported by Arrow. In chiding the authors' "one-sided" emphasis on the virtues of laboratory experiments they point to the highly simplified and artificial settings of *all* laboratory experiments, and question the transferability of such results to real-world situations—a criticism echoed by Mitchell and Carson as well as by V. Kerry Smith.

The emphasis given to Vickrey auctions and the tatonnement process in chapter 4 was found particularly disconcerting by a number of Conference participants. In terms of the Vickrey auction—a "discovery" viewed by Bishop and Heberlein as a red herring—Mitchell and Carson (appendix) as well as Bishop and Heberlein (chapter 9) acknowledge the effectiveness of the method in assessing institutional structures for private goods involving *actual* exchanges (see also, V.K. Smith, chapter 11), but fail to see how the method is to be used for hypothetical markets for public goods wherein exchange is impossible; in this regard, these authors argue that our reliance on the Coursey et al. (1983) experiment, involving the private good SOA, does not support our general conclusions. Given the nonintuitive format of the Vickrey auction, and (as we report in chapter 6) the repetitive trials required for subjects to learn incentive-compatible behavior implied by the format, both Bishop-Heberlein and Mitchell-Carson question how such repetitive trials are to be implemented wthin the CVM framework (see, also, Freemans' remarks in chapter 10). Iterative bidding, these authors maintain, does not substitute for the repetitive exchange trials of the Vickrey auction format. Similarly, in terms of our suggested use of tatonnement processes as a part of the CVM, Bishop-Heberlein assert that, for hypothetical *public* goods of interest for the CVM, Groves-Ledyard proedures for implementing such processes may not cause respondents to reveal true preferences and may result simply in increased costs, increased confusion and lower response rates. In this regard, reliance on tatonnement processes for the large groups of subjects generally included in CVM studies "boggles" the minds of Mitchell and Carson.

While we accept the "Red Herring" comment of Bishop and Heberlein in the spirit of intellectual mischief in which it was intended, we do feel that the role of experimental economics in contingent valuation research has been misunderstood, most likely due to a failure in our exposition in chapter 4. Rather than serving as guidance for the structure of hypothetical survey questions for the CVM, the demand revealing mechanisms developed by public choice theorists and experimental economists show how to obtain value estimates which are close to "true values" in laboratory situations. It turns out that even in the laboratory, it is fairly difficult to obtain "true" demand revealing values. First, one must use an incentive structure such as a Vickrey auction for private goods. However, this *not* sufficient. In addition, individuals must be given a number of repetitive learning trials to understand the auction mechanism and learn that demand revelation is their best strategy. Only by using *both*, a demand revealing mechanism and by allowing sufficient learning experience to accrue via repetitive trials, do about 70% of the subjects actually reveal demand in laboratory settings. Thus, based on their observations, the Bishop and Heberlein study (described in chapter 9) which actually attempted to repurchase hunting permits likely did not reveal demand for hunting permits since no opportunity for repetitive learning trials was given to participants and subjects most certainly had no prior experience selling their hunting permits. It then follows that experimental economics sheds little light on Bishop and Heberlein's hypothetical values, but suggests their "true value" obtained from actual behavior may have been biased for reasons other than those acknowledged by them. The primary lesson from experimental economics is, therefore, concern methods by which values may be obtained which are demand revealing as a basis of comparison for alternative, hypothetical measures of value.

These discussions conclude our capsulization of the controversies surrounding the preference research issues: issues concerning the need for incentives for accurate valuations, the subject's need for familiarity/experience with CVM commodities, and the efficacy of iterative bidding and methods/techniques drawn from exprimental economics for assisting subjects in their preference research processes. As to the implications of these discussions for the state of the arts of the CVM, conclusions in this regard are but deferred until we have considered other issues related to hypothetical bias. Thus, the authors' conclusion concerning issues related to preference research are given below.

The Comparability of WTP and WTA Measures

In chapter 6, the authors submit as a Reference Operating Condition for assessing the accuracy of CVM values, the requirement: "WTP, not WTA, measures are elicited." The rationale for the authors' imposition of this ROC was based on two related lines of argument. In chapter 3 we note that in spite of theoretical arguments (which relate to *private* goods) that WTA should equal WTP, empirical studies (table 3.2) consistently demonstrate wide divergences between WTA and WTP measures; generally, estimated WTA measures are orders of magnitude greater than estimated WTP measures (table 3.2). In chapter 5 we argue that such observed disparities between WTA and WTP may be attributed to cognitive dissonance, which, in the context of chapter 4's discussions, is reflected (via the Davis et al. experiment) by subjects' failure to recognize dominant strategies in a Vickrey auction, i.e., in some cases, iterative trials, whereby subjects learn that full demand revelation is their dominant

THE ASSESSMENT CONFERENCE AND CONCLUSIONS

strategy, results in the convergence of WTA to WTP measures. Such convergence was found to generally obtain (in the Coursey et al. (1983b) experiment) under nonhypothetical circumstances, but *not* under hypothetical circumstances, an anomaly attributable to the lack of a market-like environment in the hypothetical experiments. In retrospect, we note the implications of this finding for earlier-discussed criticisms of our enthusiasm for the use of Vickery auctions in the hypothetical setting of the CVM. We also note the consistency of laboratory results with Randall et al.'s (1983) argument (also, see Randall's arguments in chapter 8) that WTP underestimates "true" values while WTA overestimates such values.

A considerable amount of interesting and constructive criticism of our WTA/WTP arguments and conclusions was offered by Conference participants. First, various participants questioned our attribution of WTA-WTP differences in *hypothetical* settings to "cognitive dissonance" and our implied reliance on results from iterative trials in *one* experiment (the Coursey et al. (1983b) experiment) as a means for eliminating cognitive dissonance. Thus, Bishop and Heberlein question the lack of symmetry of learning effects from iterative trials on WTP and WTA measures in the Coursey et al. experiment: iterative trials affect WTA measures but, seemingly, *not* the WTP measures. Moreover, Freeman (chapter 10) questions our attribution of WTA-WTP differences to "cognitive dissonance" and the link between cognitive dissonance and our learning-via-iterative-trials arguments. In this regard, congitive dissonance refers to the beliefs of a subject (on which preferences are based) which are persistent over time and in the face of contrary "facts," and which are changed by subjects via their selection of information sources which are consistent with "desired" beliefs. Ackerlof and Dickens 1982, p. 307 Thus, all else equal, the cognitive dissonance argument would lead us to expect little if any changes in bids with additional information. (Arrow 1982) In these terms, a subject's lack of *understanding* of a Vickrey auction (or any other valuation institution) may be viewed as distinct from an individual's value-related beliefs which are subject to cognitive dissonance. Our "evidence" from experimental economics, with reference to iterated trials, then suggests the subject's need to learn *a "new" institution*, but does not necessarily establish cognitive dissonance as an explanation for WTP-WTA differences in nonlaboratory experiments (table 3.1).

As to our observations of large WTP-WTA differences, this issue is addressed by Randall in chapter 8 wherein he argues that, for a fairly wide range of contingent market designs, one can confidently expect that reported WTP and WTA measures will, respectively, understate and overstate an individual's true valuation. The generality of this conclusion (which we implicitly accepted in chapters 4 and 6) is challenged by Freeman as inconsistent with the "familiarity" issue discussed above: in instances where individuals lack accurate information regarding their preferences—the CVM commodity takes the individual to preference orderings beyond the neighborhood of experienced consumption bundles—indiviuals may make errors in *any* direction, i.e., WTP or WTA may be greater *or* less than values that would result from experience with the new commodity bundles. Along these lines, it is interesting to note that in Bishop and Heberlein's Sandhill study in (chapter 9, tables 9.2 and 9.3) hypothetical WTA values are *less* than cash offers ("true" valuations?) and WTP measures *exceed* cash offers; they also note large WTP-WTA differences in cash offers as well as offers involving hypothetical payment/compensation.

Kahneman strongly supports our "use WTP, not WTA" ROC, but first suggests that it be generalized and second, rationalizes the generalized ROC along different lines. His generalized ROC is: use the CVM only for commodities that have a "transactions structure"; do *not* use the CVM for commodities that have a "compensation structure". A "transactions structure" refers to a commodity-exchange context easily associated with *voluntary* exchange—one pays for a commodity or action which makes him/her better off. A "compensation structure" refers to a commodity-exchange context wherein overtones of *involuntary* exchange are present—how much you must be paid to accept more polluted air. The rationale for Kahneman's suggested ROC is his appeal to "prospect theory" which, in essence, assumes that individuals evaluate gains and losses differently; more specifically, it assumes that individuals value losses disproportionately higher than (identical) gains. Thus, one would expect a subject's valuation of a gain (WTP) to be substantively different from his/her valuation of a loss of identical magnitude (WTA).

We must confess that the link between Kahneman's rationale and his recommended ROC is not perfectly clear. One might appeal to prospect theory as a means for explaining why WTP and WTA measures should be expected to differ, but this would not argue for or against the preferability of one measure over another. It might argue, however, that one must use value functions based on WTP for valuing environmental improvements, but that a *different* value function, based on WTA measures, must be used in valuing (costing) environmental degradations; i.e., one cannot move toward the origin along a "benefit" curve. But this observation could apply with equal force to our conclusion that WTP, not WTA, measures be obtained via the CVM. Our rejection of WTA measures derived with the CVM is, upon close inspection, based on the argument that they are less "stable" than WTP measures; i.e., they are more affected by iterative trials, questionnaire design, etc. We do not make the case that cognivite dissonance, or other psychological/economic factors, are more or less relevant for WTP or WTA measures. Large differences observed between the two measures obtain in CVM studies, and that WTA measures are "high" may be inferred as a motivation for our recommended ROC.

Vernon Smith (chapter 12) casts the WTP/WTA argument in a different light. He asks if we are not confusing WTA/WTP differences for the same individual with such differences among individuals. He notes that such differences among individuals, even if large, should not be disturbing since such differences provide the basis for exchanges—large differences may simply imply a low volume in market trading. In terms of WTA-WTP differences for the same individual, Smith seemingly rejects the assumption of small income effects which underlies the Willig (1976) arugment leading to approximate equality between WTP and WTA. His experiment demonstrates, first, that several subjects persistently reported WTA and WTP that were substantively different; secondly, his experiment demonstrates that, despite differences in WTA and WTP values reported by individuals in the expeiment, when such values are used in a market demand/supply context, the resulting prediction of post-trade market-clearing prices is more accurate than predictions drawn from expected utility theory. Thus, Smith argues that empirical evidence belies the theoretical expectations of "equal" WTP and WTA for individuals—note here the consonance of this observation with those of Kahneman—but that in a market context such differences across individuals can result in accurate pre-trade predictions of actual (post-trade) prices (valuations) at which commodities are traded.

There are some particularly interesting implications of Vernon Smith's argument which warrant further examination. Consider the following data from Smith's experiment given in figure 12.4.

	Measure	Trial: 1	2	3
(a)	Predicted price from the expected utility model	$ 1.25	$ 1.25	$ 1.25
(b)	Predicted price from WTA and WTP	1.25	1.43	1.48
(c)	Actual, post-trading equilibrium price	1.30	1.51	1.52
(d)	Sum of WTA	16.47	10.62	13.86
(e)	Sum of WTP	12.42	10.80	12.24

Smith's experiment suggests a method for addressing accuracy/calibration questions related to CVM measures. For example, for a commodity which is exchanged in the market, a CVM study might be conducted which collects WTP and WTA measures from each subject. Demand (suppyl) curves are estimated from WTP (WTA) measures. Comparison of the resulting predicted price with actual market price has obvious implications for the accuracy of CVM estimates of value. Most importantly, Smith's experiment provides empirical weight for Kahneman's argument that benefits (the area under a WTP-demand curve) attributable to an environmental improvement may be expected to differ from costs (the area under a WTA-supply curve) for an environmental degradation. In this regard, the reader should note the different "areas" (sums) for WTP-benefits and WTA-costs implied from Smith's results given above, particularly values (d) and (e) for the first trial in Smith's experiment.

Related to Vernon Smith's argument is the point raised by Rosen. Rosen argues that WTP/WTA differences may in fact reflect "selectivity" i.e., populations from which WTP and WTA measures are taken are not *homogeneous* populations. In this regard, Rosen points to Brookshire et al.'s earthquake study: those living on a fault may well be expected to value earthquake risks differently from those who do *not* live on a fault.

Based on these interesting exchanges, it would appear to us that the following conclusions are relevant for the WTP/WTA issue. First, we agree with Freeman and Bishop-Heberlein that a compelling case has yet to be made as to the *general* relationship between WTA and/or WTP measures and "true" valuations; certainly our attribution of such differences to cognitive dissonance is little more than an assertion. As is argued below, this implies the need for considerably more attention being given to the collection and analysis of psychological and attitudinal data in future CVM studies. Secondly, we agree with Freeman that the above-discussed "familiarity" issue is relevant for assessments of WTP/-WTA differences; however, the little available empirical evidence does not support the notion that such differences are systematically related to the subject's familiarity with commodities. Referring to table 3.2, WTA/WTP differences ranged from 2:1 to 5:1 in experiments involving private goods (goose permits in Bishop and Heberlein (1979) and a bitter-tasting substance in Coursey et al. (1983). Thirdly, we find Kahneman's "prospect theory" arguments to be, at a minimum, intuitively appealing, and certainly consistent with (if not supported by) considerable empirical findings. The notion that individuals value gains (from transactions structures) differently from losses (from compensation structures) may not, however, lead one to reject CVM applications to the estimation of WTA values; rather, it may suggest particular *uses* of WTP and WTA values: WTP for gains and WTA for losses. Finally, we concur with Bishop-Heberlein (chapter 9) that the "burial" of WTA may be premature and that additional research is required which focuses on explanations of WTP-WTA differences. Meanwhile, it appears to us, our ROC "use WTP, not WTA" may serve as an operationally useful guideline for ongoing research with the CVM.

Attitudes vs. Intended Behavior

In chapter 5, section entitled Attitudes vs. Intended Behavior, the authors reviewed the "attitude versus intended behavior" issue raised by Bishop and Heberlein (1979 and 1983) which focused on the question: do CVM value measures reflect attitudes rather than actual behavior, and to what extent do attitudes correspond with actual behavior? Essentially, we adopted Randall et al's (1983) position that since CVM questions *asked* for intended behavior rather than attitudes, problems of correspondence between attitudes and behavior were likely minimized. We acknowledged, however, the relevance of Ajzen and Fishbein's (1977) design criteria for improving attitude-behavior correspondence (specific targets, actions, context and timing). As an aside, Bishop and Heberlein (chapter 9) may have found our treatment of this subject to be uninformed or shallow, but in light of the major emphasis given results from psychological studies throughout chapter 5, we find ourselves nonplussed by their assertion of our "indifference and hostility" (chapter 9) to the relevance of psychological research for economic inquiry. We confess, however, to understating the importance of attitude-behavior issues in psychology research.

Bishop and Heberlein's elaboration of the attitude-behavior issue in chapter 9, is insightful, illuminating, and we believe, rich in its implications for the state of the arts of the CVM. Their major focus is on attitudes (as they relate to reported WTP) and behavior (actual payment of WTP) and the factors which result in close correspondence between the two. Attitudes are determined by the *interaction* of three components: cognition (dispassionate facts/beliefs), affectation (evaluative/emotional reactions to cognitive information) and intended behavior (intentional "conclusions" derived from affective responses to cognitive information). Interaction between these three components is of primary importance; e.g., an affective change may motivate the individual to acquire more information (a cognitive change) which may then lead to a change in intended behavior. They argue, that a cash offer for a goose/deer license may elicit an affective response, and therefore a behavioral response, that is distinct from the affective response to a hypothetical offer—witness their observed differences between valuations involving real and hypothetical payment. This analogy is consistent with Kahneman's arguments concerning WTP-WTA differences: WTA questions involving compensation structures elicit affective responses that differ from those elicited by WTP questions involving transactions structures.

Of primary interest are the factors which lead to close correspondence between attitudes and behavior. As an example in this regard, define AC (awareness of consequences) as a *measureable* manifestation of the cognitive component of attitudes vis-à-vis a CVM "commodity", and AR (acceptance of personal responsibility) as a *measureable* manifestation of the relevant affective component of attitudes. One can then define design and analytical criteria for assessing the probable correspondence between reported willingness to pay and what a subject might actually pay for a CVM commodity. Design criteria are those proposed by Ajzen and Fishbein (1977) to which we add questions related to AC and AR (see Bishop and Heberlein's examples). In analytical terms, one's assessment of the probable correspondence between attitudes and behavior—which relates to the probable accuracy of estimated values—is based on the values of AR and AC variables. For the commodity in question, the greater is a subject's awareness of consequences (familiarity with the commodity?) and acceptance of personal responsibility, the greater is our expectation of close correspondence between attitudes and behavior (and, therefore, the more accurate the resulting measure of value).

As noted above, Bishop and Heberlein's elaboration of the attitudes-behavior issue allows for sharp focus on the need for attitudinal information for assessments of CVM results as well as for the types of information that would be useful in these regards. While not affecting the weight of their contribution, however, their discussions raise several questions of interest for our broad state of the arts assessment of the CVM. First, in operational terms, we simply note in passing the indexing task implied by their proposed criteria for correspondence between attitudes and behavior; e.g., what constitutes "high" values for AC or AR variables? Secondly, absent from their discussions is the relationship between attitude-behavior criteria and the other psychology-related issues discussed in chapter 5 and reviewed by them. As an example, Bishop-Heberlein's discussion of the three interactive components of attitudes would seem to bear directly on the familiarity issue discussed above. If the cognitive component is empty—subjects are unfamiliar with the commodity, or have little in the way of relevant facts/beliefs—what might we expect in terms of affective responses and formulated behavioral intentions? A response to this question is implied in Kahneman's discussion of starting points (chapter 12): subjects are simply incapable of assigning values to the commodity. Bishop-Heberlein's counterpart to this conclusion would seem to be: low AC values imply divergence between attitudes and behavior and thus (one supposes) inaccurate values.

A third question raised by Bishop and Heberlein's attitude-behavior discussions concerns the conflict between their position on the viability of esimating such things as option and existence values with the positions taken by us and by Kahneman. Appealing to familiarity/experience factors underlying our ROCs 1 and 2, we argue that one can expect *a priori* that such values must involve (using Freeman's model, chapter 9) consumption bundles well beyond the neighborhood of bundles with which the subject has experience; thus, our rejection of uses of the CVM for estimating such values. Kahneman rejects the use of survey methods for valuing all but user values—explicitly excluding option/preservation values—in his discussion of "symbolic demand". Responses to questions related to ideological values, he argues, must reflect the subjects' hierarchy of values which tend to be injected into responses involving political or economic content. While acknowledging, first, that assessments of the validity of existence values via the CVM will not be easy and, secondly, that results from field experiments hold little promise for the use of the CVM in deriving such values, Bishop-Heberlein seemingly take the position that the CVM might indeed be used for estimating option or, particularly, existence values. The relative accuracy or meaningfulness of such measures would be assessed via analyses of the correlation between reported existence values and AC/AR variables. In their acid rain example, high existence values would imply (a) "high" awareness that acid rain damages will affect future generations (an AC variable) and (b) a "high" indication that the subject feels personally responsible for reducing these effects.

In terms of the different positions concerning the use of the CVM for nonuser values described above, we should acknowledge *possible* exceptions to our conclusion that the familiarity/experience ROC's preclude the estimation of nonuser values; but we do not find Bishop-Heberlein's arguments (and the acid rain example) compelling in this regard. "High" AC values, which indicate familiarity with the acid rain problem, and "high" AR values simply do make their case: other values in the affectation "account"—perceptions of how *the subject* is affected in a "user value" sense—are relevant. At issue then is the subject's ability to differentiate between that part of his/her affective reaction to acid rain that is attributable to personal effects (a use value) and, generally, more altruistic affective reactions vis-à-vis future generations. Echoing Kahneman's notion of symbolic demand, it is this latter process, a process with which we expect the subject to have little experience, that we question. We would expect, *à la* Kahneman, that the sum of the user and nonuser parts will greatly exceed the subject's valuation of the whole.

Hypothetical Biases in the CVM: Conclusions

In the authors' view, discussions at the assessment conference were particularly productive in giving perspective and context to the myriad issues concerning hypothetical bias discussed in chapters 3–6. As noted in those chapters, the potential for hypothetical bias in the CVM enters through the hypothetical nature of payment as well as the hypothetical commodity and the institution within which the commodity is exchanged—the contingent market. We now ask, in light of the assessment conference, what *is* the state of the arts of the CVM in terms of the potential magnitude of hypothetical biases?

In terms of hypothetical payment, we view the potential for related biases with a great deal more equanimity than that suggested in the conclusions to chapter 5. In this regard, Mitchell and Carson's arguments as to the weakness of empirical results used by us in arriving at our more pessimistic conclusions are well made. The weight of the "incentives for accuracy" argument must, at worst, be questioned in light of Vernon Smith's experiments, wherein WTP/WTA interrogations were "good" predictors of market outcomes, and the results from comparison studies wherein the CVM generated value estimates that were remarkably close to estimates derived from indirect market methods (holding the question of the accuracy of *any* method aside, for the moment). We concur with Arrow's observation that hypothetical/real payment differences may not be as serious as one might fear: well designed survey instruments wherein the exchange setting is "pseudo-real" may indeed elicit real-like results. This is not to argue that incentives/hypothetical payment issues are not relevant; it is to argue that, first, the jury is still out—it remains an open issue—and, second, that some promise exists for structuring CVM instruments in ways that mitigate, if not eliminate, the magnitude of payment bias.

Within the rubric of "hypothetical bias", we find the most prominent source of bias to arise in instances wherein the CVM commodity, within a contingent exchange setting, is largely unfamiliar to the subject—the subject has no experience in viewing the commodity within the context of trade-offs. In Freeman's terms, the effect of the CVM is to move the individual to areas of his preference orderings that are far removed from neighborhoods of consumption bundles with which the subject is familiar. Our lack of models concerning subjects' behavior in the CVM setting notwithstanding, we see in Freeman's rudimentary modeling efforts, as well as in Kahneman's notion of symbolic demand and Bishop-Heberlein's discussions of the roles of attitudes, the bases for reasserting our contention that, for state of the arts applications of the CVM, (a) participants in the CVM must understand (be *familiar* with) the commodity to be valued (our ROC Number 1) and (b) subjects must have had (or be allowed to obtain) prior valuation and choice *experience* with respect to consumption levels of the commodity (our ROC Number 2).

In terms of learning issues, final state of the arts conclusions concerning the efficacy of iterative bidding processes and laboratory methods/techniques for applications of the CVM must be softened considerably from the tone of earlier conclusions offered in chapters 3–6. We find impressive the substantive effect on bids that result from the iterative bidding process in studies involving, not just the small samples of concern to Mitchell and Carson, but *large* sample sizes. In our view, iterative bidding *does* result in substantively higher bids. Iterative effects notwithstanding, Mitchell and Carson, as well as Bishop and Heberlein, are obviously correct in pointing to the lack of evidence that would support (or reject) the attribution of such effects to the preference research processes as asserted by us in chapters 3–5; moreover, we must acknowledge the substance of Bishop and Heberlein's observation that the parallel between the iterative bidding process and the iterative valuation *trials* used in laboratory experiments, implied by our discussions in chapter 4, is without obvious substance. Nor, it seems fair to say, has the attribution of iterative bidding effects to Mitchell and Carson's "bullying" or "social awkwardness" motives been established. Thus, all that can be said at this point in time is that iterative bidding rather consistently results in higher CVM valuations, but we are unable to explain such differences.

Bishop and Heberlein's lament that economists involved in CVM research are woefully ignorant of research results in the related, and certainly relevant, field of psychology extends with equal force to economists' general ignorance (until only very recently) of developments in experimental economics; the authors concede *their* general ignorance in this area prior to the development of this book. As the novice enters the literature of experimental economics, he/she must be struck with the impressive developments made in that field which relate directly to the most perplexing questions facing the CVM practitioner: how does one establish incentive structures; how do subjects learn; how does one elicit preference revelation? The real "lessons" from experimental economics of unquestionable importance for the development of the CVM are found in two principal areas. First, laboratory methods *can* provide us with a relatively inexpensive and efficient method for conducting experiments concerning design and conceptual questions of relevance for the CVM; examples in these regards are questions concerning strategic bias, WTP-WTA differences, effects of psychological variables on subject valuations, etc. Secondly, and of particular importance, developments in experimental economics may be provocative—challenging—to CVM researchers in terms of stimulating new and imaginative lines of inquiry concerning persistent problems encountered with the method. In these regards, the issue is not, for example, whether or not the Vickery Second Price Auction *per se* will "work" in applications of the CVM; rather, the issue is: can the CVM be structured so as to better provide incentives for true revelations of preferences (as an interesting initial effort in this regard, see Bishop and Heberlein's experiments with a *Fifth* Price Auction in chapter 9). As another example, can we (*should* we) be experimenting with repeated *visits* (repeated "trials") with CVM subjects, with questions designed to help them learn incentive-compatible behavior vis-à-vis a contingent market?

Thus, lessons from experimental economics are clearly relevant for our state of the arts assessment of the CVM: they indicate the lack of substantial progress made in the method's development in important areas concerning subjects' learning/understanding of incentive structures. Such lessons are *not*, however, a panacea for resolving the problems of the CVM. Earlier-noted comments by Conference participants concerning our over-emphasis on the ready transferability of methods/techniques used in experimental economics to applicatons of the CVM for valuing public goods are well made, as are the reminders by Arrow and by Bishop-Heberlein of the important role of field experiments for improving the state of the arts of the CVM.

Turning now to the WTP-WTA issue, relevant state of the arts conclusions were suggested in the closing paragraphs above. V. Kerry Smith's call for theoretical inquiry as to subjects' behavior in the contingent market setting is particularly appropriate for efforts to explain WTP-WTA differences. In this regard, see the contrast between Randall's theoretical model, which relies on subjects' perception that their responses influence policy, wherein WTP (WTA) understates (overstates) "true" valuations, and Bishop-Heberlein's *contrary* evidence as well as Freeman's model which suggests that, for "unfamiliar" commodities, WTP or WTA relationships to true valuations cannot be determined a priori. While we find compelling, on deductive as well as intuitive grounds, Kahneman's argument that subjects value losses differently than gains, we are concerned with the fact that WTA measures appear to vary *much* more than WTP measures in response to such things as iterative trials. Thus, in operational terms, i.e., as we await results from further theoretical and empirical research concerning this question, we maintain our conclusion suggested in chapter 6 which states that WTP, not WTA, measures should be estimated with the CVM.

Finally, the state of the arts of the CVM in terms of our appreciation of the attitude-behavior issue is, in our view, greatly enhanced by Bishop-Heberlein's discussions in chapter 9. Means by which the accuracy of CVM measures, in terms of the correspondence between attitudes and actual behavior underlying reported willingness to pay, are directly implied by the interactive relationships between attitudinal components and behavior. While implementation problems remain for resolution, one can see in Bishop-Heberlein's exposition the essential framework for deriving empirical measures for cognitive and affective components of attitudes and, at least conceptually, their use in deriving indices of attitude-behavior correspondence.

Overview of the "Accuracy" Issue

Recurring throughout Volume I, as well as throughout conference papers and discussions, is reference to a subject's "true" valuation of a public good such as an environmental change. Thus, our standard for accuracy in values derived from the CVM is a subject's reported valuation that reflects a "true" revelation of preferences vis-à-vis the CVM commodity. In this regard, our appeal to market institutions as a framework whose structure we hope to simulate in the process of applying the CVM is motivated by our desire to capture, in applications of the CVM, the *incentives* for preference revelation that our theories lead us to expect from a market context. In the market context, individuals must introspectively balance the utilities foregone as a result of paying for a good with the utilities gained from acquiring the good; to this end, he/she must, however "completely", search his/her preferences for the good in question vis-à-vis *all other* possible goods and their prices (relative to his/her income). Thus as has been extensively argued above, the importance for assessments of the CVM of such themes as the subject's familiarity with a commodity (for the preference "search", or research process) and the credibility of payment and payment modes to the subject (for *meaningful* subjective assessments of implied opportunity costs..

In these regards, we must reiterate our earlier-noted concern with V. Kerry Smith's interpretation of our ROCs related to these themes as requiring that the value derived in the CVM be the subjects' estimation of *market outcomes* as opposed to the subjects' preference revelations; ROCs *per se* are discussed below. ROC-1 requires that the subject have some familiarity with the CVM commodity and ROC-2 requires some *choice experience*, direct or indirect, with respect to consumption levels of the CVM commodity. These conditions then loosely require that, as in Freeman's arguments, the consumption bundles (including the CVM commodity) that the subject is hypothetically evaluating are within neighborhoods of consumption bundles with which he/she has had experience. Thus, our concern with accurate revelations of preferences leads us to require a choice setting which is analogous to a market setting, and which is consistent with the expectation that the subject is capable of meaningful searches of preferences. To require an "informed" choice setting does not, in our view, imply that the CVM application must then elicit the subjects' introspective estimate of solutions of a hedonic market.

Given that our standard for CVM values is the true revelation of a subject's preferences, the primary question becomes: how do we measure that standard? Obviously, if we had a "true" value, assessments of the accuracy of CVM measures vis-à-vis this standard would be straight-forward. The state of the arts relevant to such measures is such that, aside from limited results from laboratory and field experiments involving private goods, these measures are not available. Therefore, in chapter 6 the question of the accuracy of CVM values is addressed in the following indirect and inferential manner. First, we note the literature that suggests that, for ordinary demand studies based on "hard" market data, estimates may involve errors (the range for accuracy might be) on the order of ± 50% or more. V. Kerry Smith (chapter 11) expands on this argument, arguing that much of economist's "hard" data may be subject to the same type of criticism concerning, e.g., hypothetical and reporting biases as those leveled at the CVM. Such errors are generally attributable to such things as assumptions concerning the distribution of error terms and functional forms. Secondly, from these data we then infer that econometric value estimates based on indirect market methods would involve ranges of error no less than those in ordinary demand analyses, i.e., one can argue, at most, that indirect market methods yield value estimates which would encompass "true" values within the range ± 50%. Thirdly, appealing to the concept of "reference accuracy", we note that received studies demonstrate that biases associated with starting points, payment vehicles, information and iterative bidding could result in errors *as large as* ± 50% in CVM studies.

In retrospect, we might well have stopped our arguments here: available evidence suggests that either the CVM or indirect market methods may yield estimates of "true" preference revealing values within a range no better than ± 50%. We carried these arguments a step further, however, in addressing the following question. Noting—uncritically, it must be acknowledged—cited instances wherein economists quite comfortably impute accuracy to market-based estimates of value, we implicitly construct the following strawman: suppose that indirect market methods yield accurate results—"accurate" within the range ±50%; are value estimates from indirect market and contingent valuation methods *different*? We continue by positing that if they are *not* different, then the accuracy of indirect market values implies the accuracy of CVM values. Referring to the fifteen CVM-Indirect Market study comparisons given in table 6.12, and noting that ranges (± 50%) for accuracy of CVM values overlap with those for indirect market methods in 13 comparisons, we then conclude that, for commodities which are amenable to application of indirect market methods (a *caveat* then used to form ROCs), the CVM *may* yield value estimates that are *as accurate* as (the *assumed* accurate) values derived from indirect market methods. It should be noted that any specification for the magnitude of errors associated with the use of the CVM is premature at this time. We choose ± 50% as a means for focusing attention on what is, in our view, an interesting approach for assessing the accuracy of CVM measures.

In many ways our discussions of accuracy achieved their intended purposes: they certainly received the attention of conference participants; most importantly, they succeeded in initiating a dialogue focused on how future research might address calibration and accuracy issues. Constructive criticism of our discussions of accuracy offered by conference participants may be seen as involving the following three sets of issues.

What Is Accuracy?

The first set of issues involves the question as posed by Arrow: what do we *mean* by "accuracy" and what level of accuracy is it reasonable to expect from applications of the CVM? In response to these questions, Arrow offers four observations: (a) referring to hypothetical issues, the reality with which economics (and other social sciences) deal involves counter-factual lines of deduction—statements comparing actions with states that "would" hold, but in fact do not. Our concern is with questions of the form: what would we do if reality were marginally different (e.g., if income were one unit higher)? In virtually, all cases, the "truth" relevant for these questions can never really be known; (b) inaccuracies in real-world efforts to estimate individual preferences via demand analyses based on "hard" data are probably best seen in the fact that half of the "new" products put on the market *fail*. (c) our colleagues in medical and engineering sciences consider, as a matter of course, estimates producing errors on the order of one to ten (one order of magnitude) *to be normal*; (d) therefore, it is not clear that we should be disturbed if our value estimates are thought to be within ± 50% of true values, or +100%. Ranges of error of 3:1 or 5:1 may pale in significance when compared to those reflecting technical ignorance in most environmental fields.

V. Kerry Smith also stresses Arrow's point that we can never *know* "true" valuations. Indeed, in our general scientific inquiry we never *prove* hypotheses, we fail to reject them. Arrow's reminder of the limitations of "hard" data vis-à-vis their use in estimating value is expanded by Smith along interesting and provocative lines. In table 11.1 (chapter 11), he demonstrates the potential for strategic and hypothetical biases (broadly defined) in various sources which are generally thought to produce "hard"—accurate—data.

As an aside, we are compelled to note the contrast between Arrow's and Smith's arguments and the framework for considering the question of accuracy offered by Freeman (chapter 10). Define B as a subject's response to a CVM question and assume that B is a random variable with mean, B′; B* is the individual's *true* valuation. Freeman's suggested approach for analyses of accuracy is then one which focuses on B′–B* and on the variance of e = B–B′. He distinguishes between "biases" B′–B* differences attributable to starting points, information, etc. (the topic of the section above)—and random errors reflected in B–B′ differences, where random errors result from the hypothetical character of the CVM (the substance of the section above). With biases eliminated by questionnaire design, and *assuming* that e is normally distributed with zero mean, large samples (which would result in e = 0) may result in B′ = B*. In the light of our earlier discussions, the application of Freeman's approach involves two major questions, satisfactory responses to which elude the authors. First, on what basis does one argue in a compelling way that the many sources for hypothetical biases are random and, particularly, normally distributed with zero mean? Most importantly, and directly related to Arrow's and Smith's arguments, how does one divine the "truth"—whence comes B* which critically serves as the basis for assessing the effectiveness of questionnaire design in eliminating "biases"? In the scientific literature, the concept of measurement accuracy rejects the notion that "true" valuations can be known, the result of which is a focus on removing demonstrable errors.

Finally, Bishop-Heberlein's arguments have implications for the question: what *is* accuracy? In terms of the accuracy of values derived from the CVM, their discussions would seem to imply that accuracy turns on the correspondence between attitudes and behavior, wherein such correspondence might be in some sense measured by Azjen-Fishbein criteria (vis-à-vis questionnaire design) and by cognitive and affective variables. In passing, we note their second (tongue-in-cheek) criterion for accuracy which was suggested at the Assessment Conference: "good enough for government work", which might (quasi-seriously) be taken to mean that order of magnitude estimates may be regarded as "accurate" for some applications of the CVM.

Reference Accuracy and Public Good Values

In our efforts to couch the accuracy issue in terms of "Reference Accuracy"— accuracy is defined in terms of biases resulting from deviations from Reference Operating Conditions—the approach per se was well received by Conference participants; our exposition of a numerical application of the approach was not. In this latter regard, our ± 50% argument was seen as "weak" by Freeman, as being " ad hoc " by Rosen, and unconvincing by Mitchell and Carson. Referring to the CVM as well as indirect market methods, V. Kerry Smith questions the extent to which *any* error range can be imputed to estimated value measures given the present state of our knowledge. The basis for much of the expected criticism of our (no better than) ± 50% reference accuracy range for CVM measures reflects several related arguments which, we of course concede, are well made. Mitchell-Carson, Bishop-Heberlein and Rosen point to the fact that well-designed CVM studies need *not* include biases resulting from starting points, payment vehicles, infomation and/or iterative bidding. Indeed, our discussions above suggest that payment cards *can* be structured so as to mitigate or eliminate starting point biases; payment vehicle *bias* may be a misnomer— mode of payment may be inextricable from the commodity; and, particularly for "familiar" goods, information issues may be amenable to control by questionnaire design. Thus, these individuals argue, demand studies using the CVM (*or* indirect market methods) are not of equal quality, as is implied by our *general* statement that reference accuracy for the CVM may be no better than ± 50%. To these arguments Mitchell and Carson add the observation that sampling errors, discussions of which were excluded from our assessments of the CVM, must also be considered—sampling errors alone could result in errors of ± 50%.

The Need for Accuracy or Calibration Research

In the physical sciences, Reference Accuracy, based on ROCs, is the accepted practice for evaluating the precision of instruments for measurement. Generally speaking, Conference participants were supportive of our efforts in chapter 6 which were designed to initiate thought and research concerning means by which ROCs might be defined and by which we might measure the error implications of CVM applications wherein one or more of the ROCs are not satisfied. Thus, Arrow calls for more field and laboratory experiments designed to establish conditions under which reasonably defined accuracy in the CVM might obtain, a call echoed by Rosen who, in addition, feels that replications of CVM studies might be useful in these regards. Bishop-Heberlein appeal for research designed to calibrate errors with the extent to which ROC's are satisfied. V. Kerry Smith's insistence on the need for modeling efforts is joined with his observation of our lack of knowledge as to how violations of ROCs affect subjects' valuations.

Of course, the need for standards against which the accuracy of CVM values might be assessed underlies our suggested ROCs. Given the critical importance of ROC's for the use of Reference Accuracy, attention is now turned to an evaluation of those conditions.

The Reference Operating Conditions

There are at least two requirements for estimation and use of Reference Accuracy for the CVM: the specification of Reference Operating Conditions—the conditions or circumstances which limit the accuracy of a measurement tool; and the magnitude of errors which result from failure to satisfy any given ROC.

Consider, first, the problem of specifying ROCs relevant for the CVM. That ours is not the last word on ROCs relevant for the CVM is made clear by ROCs explicitly or implicitly suggested by Conference participants. Referring to table 13.1, ROCs 1 through 4 are those suggested by us in table 6.13; ROC Number 8 was *implied* in our discussions of the ± 50% Reference Accuracy range for the CVM but, for reasons which now escape us, was not explicitly included as an ROC. ROCs 5–7 are those suggested by Kahneman—note the overlap with ROCs 4 and 5. Mitchell and Carson suggest, based on referenda and psychological research, ROC 9 (and concur with ROCs 1, 3 and 4). A *choice* for an ROC Number 10 is implied by the apparently contradictory positions of Randall, who would require subjects to view the CVM process as a real opportunity to influence policy, and Arrow, Freeman (1979a) and, we should add, Rosen, who would view a subject's perception of the CVM process in such a real, nonhypothetical way as possibly inviting strategic responses. Finally, Bishop-Heberlein's discussions imply ROC 11.

It must be acknowledged that the rationale for including *any* of the ROCs in table 13.1, as well as the rationale for excluding other possible ROCs, is weak or nonexistent at this point in time. For example, our suggested ROCs 1 and 2 are justified by, first, the "familiarity" argument and secondly, our observation that in several comparison studies, ± 50% accuracy ranges for CVM values overlap with ± 50% ranges for indirect market methods for valuations of commodities which *we assert* are commodities with which subjects are probably familiar and have some degree of indirect market experience. Obviously, neither argument is immune to challenge. As a further example, in the section above we argue for the abandonment of the "information bias" rubric (ROC 8 (ii)). As a final example, we note that at this stage of the state of the arts, we are unable to even give precise definitions for many of the limits on CVM measures that we believe to be important; e.g., in 9(i), what is a "simple" choice?; in ROC 10, what is a "meaningful opportunity" or a "sufficiently hypothetical" choice?

Thus it is hoped that the combined discussions in this book concerning the potential role of ROCs in providing means by which ranges of Reference Accuracy may be attributed to CVM measures will provoke imaginative thinking and research relevant to the specification of precise and defensible ROCs; in any state of the arts assessment, of course, the immediately preceding disussions establish the infant stage of this process at this point in time.

As is obvious from table 13.1, while we at least can see a place to begin in terms of specifying ROCs, our knowledge is virtually nil in terms of the error implications of not satisfying an ROC. Referring to ROC 8 in table 3, Rowe and Chestnut's (1983) error estimates can be of very limited usefulness for our purposes given our inability to assess the quality of studies used in their samples vis-à-vis *other* relevant ROCs. Of course, this virtual void in our knowledge is

Table 13.1   Alternative Reference Operating Conditions

Reference operating condition	Measurement error when ROC is not satisfied
1. Subjects must understand, be familiar with, the commodity to be valued.	?
2. Subjects must have had (or be allowed to obtain) prior valuation and choice experience with respect to consumption levels of the commodity.	?
3. There must be little uncertainty.	?
4. WTP, not WTA, measures are elicited.	? ± 300%
5. (Kahneman) Valuations must involve transaction structures, not compensation structures.	? ± 300%
6. (Kahneman) CVM values obtained must relate to use, with minimum ideological content.	?
7. (Kahneman) Payment vehicles must be well defined and credible vis-à-vis the CVM commodity; values obtained with one vehicle may not be interpretatively "transferred" to those which we would obtain with other vehicles.	?
8. CVM application must involve:	
(i) No basis for starting points or anchoring;	?
(ii) "appropriate" information concerning the commodity and the valuation process;	?
(iii) initial, noniterated valuations.	?
9. (Mitchell-Carson, from referenda/psychological research):	
(i) Subjects must be given as simple a choice as possible;	?
(ii) outliners should not unduly influence research;	?
(iii) subjects should be permitted to abstain from the valuation process.	?
10. (Implied by Randall Chapter 8): Subjects must view the CVM process as a meaningful opportunity to influence policy via their responses;	?
or	
(Arrow, Rosen and Freeman 1979): Subjects must view questions as being sufficiently hypothetical so as not to provide incentives for strategic behavior.	?
11. (Bishop-Heberlein):	
(i) Azjen-Fishbein criteria for the structure of valuation questions must be satisfied.	?
(ii) "close" correspondence between attitudes and behavior is required.	?

the motivation for the insistence on "calibration" research by almost all of the participants (see, particularly, the comments by Arrow and Rosen in chapter 12, and those by Bishp-Heberlein (chapter 9) and by V. Kerry Smith (chapter 11)).

THE STATE OF THE ARTS OF THE CONTINGENT VALUATION METHOD

In chapter 1 we noted the need for a "reflective pause" in CVM research wherein concerned researchers can take stock of the progress that has been made in the development of the method, and of the major issues which require resolution for further developments. The need for such a pause was made manifest by our review of the myriad "criticisms" of the CVM, all of which pointed to the disarray and confusion amongst CVM researchers attributable to two central facts. First, there has been a lack of consensus among researchers as to the priority issues and hypotheses that warrant empirical focus. Research efforts appeared scattered and diffuse as we repeatedly addressed *asserted* "biases" in the CVM (e.g., starting point, information, vehicle biases, etc.) in the "heuristic" manner described in chapter 3, with seemingly but one basis for accepting or rejecting a "bias": some ill-defined "preponderance of evidence". In large part, this lack of a well-defined, prioritized research agenda for the CVM reflects the *ad hoc*, "chemistry set" approach to CVM research noted by V. Kerry Smith, Bishop-Heberlein, and other Conference participants. Empirical applications of the CVM have outstripped intellectual inquiry—via formal models or otherwise—as to how individuals may behave within contingent market settings and implications for questionnaire design and implementation practices. Secondly, following perhaps from the preceding observations, CVM researchers have been apologetic, or defensive, vis-à-vis the "rest of the profession" due to the pervasive feeling that interrogated responses by individuals to hypothetical propositions must be, at best, inferior to "hard" market data or, at worst, off-the-cuff attitudinal indications which might also be expected to reflect efforts by individuals to manipulate the survey to their selfish ends.

The difficulties involved in efforts to provide some state of the arts context for the controversies surrounding the viability of the CVM for estimating values for public goods are made manifest by the assessment *process* seen in parts I and II of this book. Thus, many of the positions and conclusions presented by us in part I were altered or retracted in this chapter as a result of the focused dialogue concerning priority issues in CVM research between the authors, four other prominent CVM researchers, and leading economics and psychology scholars whose interest in public goods valuation is a step removed from the CVM *per se*. Of course, the reader will judge the success of this process in providing a start of the arts context for the CVM. In this regard, *our* general view of this context is described as follows:

The CVM Without Apology

It is surely time for replacing apologies for the CVM with a positive research agenda to be described below. As a first step in this direction, we must eschew the joys of self-flagellation over our lack of knowledge of the "truth": we don't and won't know it, nor will our colleagues in the "rest of the profession" vis-à-vis *their* value estimates, nor will scientists in other disciplines. Following Arrow's exhortations, we must directly address the question, what *is* accuracy, and then look to calibration methods which provide us with a means to achieve accuracy levels that are reasonable and consistent with those levels obtained in other areas of economics and in other disciplines.

What *is* accuracy in a CVM estimate? It is a subject's valuation of a commodity which "reasonably" reveals his/her preference for the commodity. What does "reasonable" mean? "Reasonableness" is established by criteria—Reference Operating Conditions—which allow us to measure the magnitude of probable errors in any given application of the CVM. Thus, whether resulting ranges for Reference Accuracy associated with applications of the CVM are never better than ± 50% or ± 500%, our focus is on defining the reference accuracy range. As with any other estimates, the "usefulness" of estimates with any range of error is determined by the purposes to which the estimates are to be put.

Conclusions Concerning Accuracy

While perhaps useful in pointing to needed research, the above is little more than a definition of accuracy. Given, as was argued above, that efforts to develop ROCs for the CVM have just begun, and that we are almost totally ignorant of the error implications associated with the few ROC's that seem palatable at this time, must we then agree with V. Kerry Smith's judgement (chapter 11) that no conclusions about the accuracy of CVM measures can be drawn based on research accomplished to date? We think not. At this point of reflective pause in the development of the CVM, one fails to see implications for the accuracy of CVM measures from received research *only* if one's view of "acceptable" implications is limited to evidence that demonstrates some degree of precision—narrow ranges of error. This is to say that while we cannot build the case for ranges of Reference Accuracy for the CVM of magnitudes that would make CVM value estimates of practical use in many cases, at this point in the method's development a "useful conclusion" in the sense of V. Kerry Smith's assertion might well be that the method produces *order of magnitude* estimates—but we think one can argue that error ranges are much smaller.

Before continuing this argument, it is relevant for our purposes to recall V. Kerry Smith's demonstration (chapter 11) of the wide range of potential for hypothetical and reporting errors in "hard" data commonly used, without apology, in economic analyses. Such data are seemingly accepted in total ignorance of ROC's relevant for their collection and the resulting ranges of Reference Accuracy. This observation, when combined with Coursey and Nyquist's findings of potential errors in ordinary demand analysis and Mitchell-Carson's general comments regarding sampling errors, should serve—to paraphrase Freeman (chapter 10)—as a chilling reminder of the limitations of empirical analysis/models in most areas of economic analysis. It seems fair to say that, in the general economics literature, questions of accuracy are not prominent. This is not to suggest a nihilistic approach to CVM research: the whole world is wrong (inaccurate), so why should *we* be concerned with accuracy. We mean to suggest the perspective: economists' typical preoccupation with such things as standard errors, etc., may have misled us into viewing value estimates as "precise" in terms of narrow error ranges, ± 5%, 10% or even 20%. Couched in the broader terms of Reference Accuracy, such "precision" in general economic value estimates may quickly dissipate. Again, that such broader views of accuracy are generally ignored in economics is made manifest by V. Kerry Smith's provocative discussion in chapter 11.

Returning to our discussion of what one *can* conclude regarding the accuracy of CVM measures, we begin by recalling an earlier discussion of the "truth". We do not and will not know it. But something analogous to "truth" may be attributed to values derived from, as examples, *actual* cash trades in Bishop-Heberlein's Sandhill study and in Vernon Smith's laboratory experiments.

Eschewing arguments as to how Bishop-Heberlein's auction formats might have been improved in one way or another, their cash offers/payments are certainly the "truth" vis-à-vis preference revelation in the sense that folks clearly paid (were paid) for a well-defined commodity and then used the commodity. For the limited, most likely nonequilibrium, "simulated" market used by them, we can surely attribute preference revelations to these values. The differences between mean cash and CVM-WTA values was roughly 42%; between cash and CVM-WTP values, differences ranged from about 38% to 124% across their four auction formats (tables 9.2 and 9.30). Do these differences imply nothing vis-à-vis conclusions as to the accuracy of CVM measures? If accuracy is viewed as involving "small" ranges for Reference Accuracy, one would lament the "large" differences, as do Bishop and Heberlein, and concur with V. Kerry Smith that nothing (positive) can be concluded. If orders of magnitude are relevant, one might find Bishop-Heberlein's results startling: CVM and cash offers are virtually the same (see figure 6.1). Our colleagues in environmental engineering may well envy such accuracy. In these regards, we note Bishop-Heberlein's later "surprise" at how well the CVM does work—cash-CVM differences were not "outrageous".

Questions of the transferability of laboratory results to real-world conditions aside, hypothetical responses in Vernon Smith's experiments were consistently within 10% of actual market outcomes. In the Coursey et al. (1983b) laboratory experiment (figure 4.1), differences between values derived from final Vickrey auctions and hypothetical questions were less than 20% for WTP and approximately 100% for WTA. The central point in all of this is apparent, however. In terms of the standard for comparisons of CVM values, we can continually argue as to how well preference revelations are made manifest by Bishop-Heberlein's cash offers, Vernon Smith's securities values, Coursey et al.'s measures related to tasting sucrose octa-acetate, or, moving to public goods, TCM and HPM values derived by the eight sets of authors given in table 6.12. But however well *any* of these measures reflect meaningful revelations of preferences by individuals, *every* piece of evidence that we have demonstrates that the CVM yields value estimates that are indistinguishable from those standards in order of magnitude terms. Indeed, and herein lies the relevance of our ± 50% arguments, in *most* instances CVM values are within ± 50% of values derived from alternative methods for estimating preference revealed values.

Final Remarks

Thus, our *final* (c.f. our stronger, pre-conference, reservations in chapter 1–6, *ad passim*) assessment of the state of the arts of the CVM is generally positive. We find impressive the accuracy of CVM measues inferred by the available evidence at this stage of the method's development. We find encouragement in the Conference results, particularly those reported by Arrow, Kahneman, and Bishop-Heberlein, which suggest that breaking the "hypothetical barrier" in the CVM may not be as hopeless as we and others earlier believed.

"Promise" is not "performance", however, and our assessments given above refer only to the potential promise of the CVM as a viable method for estimating values for public goods. The realization of that promise implies *real* challenges for theoretical and empirical research for those involved with the method's further development. In concluding this book, we now focus attention on critical issues for any research agenda which are relevant for guiding future CVM research.

CRITICAL ISSUES FOR FUTURE CVM RESEARCH

In most general terms, it must be hoped that greater focus can be achieved in future research with the CVM. Both Bishop-Heberlein and V. Kerry Smith emphasize the *ad hoc* character of the bulk of CVM research to date—a characterization aptly described by Bishop-Heberlein as reflecting a "chemistry set" approach. To a large extent, the *ad hoc* quality of CVM research has resulted from the emphasis or priority given empirical results—necessitated in many cases by data needs of the entities providing research funding—as opposed to theoretical and design issues. Results from this empirical emphasis are made manifest by the profession's preoccupation, without resolution, with such operational "biases" as starting point, information and vehicle issues as noted in chapter 3, issues some of which, upon reflecton by Conference participants, may now be viewed as *not* implying biases *per se* but rather implying limits on questionnaire design and the manner in which CVM values are interpreted. Thus, the first critical issue for future CVM research is the metaphorical realignment of the empirical cart and the theoretical horse. There is a critical need for modeling efforts focused on individual behavior in contingent market settings which may serve as a basis for formulating hypotheses for empirical testing. This need for modeling efforts underlies virtually all of the additional issues for further CVM research discussed below.

A second critical issue for future research involves the specification and measurement of Reference Accuracy for CVM measures. In this regard, imaginative and innovative thought is required for defining relevant ROCs (e.g. table 13.1 above) and for calibrating errors with deviations from ROCs. Thus, we must ask questions exemplified by: What *is* "familiarity" or "experience" vis-à-vis a CVM commodity; what is "uncertainty" and what constitutes "ideological content"; what variables may perform best as measures of cognition and/or affectation and how are attitudinal variables calibrated with measures of attitude-behavior correspondence; how can we better structure value questions so as to enhance *a priori* our expectations that preference are obtained which are at least consonant with incentive-compatible revelations in market context? In addressing these issues we will need to profit from and exploit the lessons learned in laboratory and field experiments, as well as in research in other disciplines.

A final critical issue for future CVM research involves our need to resolve the "incentives" question. In this regard, our concern extends beyond the hypothetical payment question. We concur with Arrow's suggestion that question settings that are sufficiently pseudo-real may be expected to result in satisfactorily pseudo-real responses and we are not convinced as to the extent to which one can distinguish between payment effects and those attributed to familiarity and experience questions. Of interest in these regards is the threads of an argument, seem implicity in Randall's paper, as well as in Kahneman's Comments, and explicitly in Mitchell-Carson's paper (appendix), that valuations of contingent changes in provision levels of public goods might be better obtained via processes which attempt to simulate results from institutions *other than* the market institution. In terms of familiarity and experience, the provision of public goods via reliance on market-like transactions valuations is, at best, tenuous vis-à-vis the referendum process which is actually used in this regard. Some sort of preference revelation must surely be inferred by the *act* of an individual's signing a petition which requests a public/social action which the individual generally knows will result in his/her payment of higher taxes. Thus, *à la* Randall, the subject may indeed be motivated by the opportunity to influence policy. Whether such motivation would lead to "strategic" signings of a cost-specific referendum is an important empirical question. Here we simply note the potential appeal for such a variation in CVM applications in dealing with many of the sources of familiarity/experience problems, when market analogies are used in the CVM and its possible use in resolving (or re-casting) the incentives problem.

Appendix:
Some Comments on the State of the Arts Assessment of the Contingent Valuation Method Draft Report

Robert Cameron Mitchell

Resources for the Future

and

Richard T. Carson

Resources for the Future

and The University of California (Berkeley)

ASPECTS OF THE USE OF THE BIDDING GAME FORMAT (Chapter 3)

Starting Point Bias

In our view, the evidence for starting point bias is far stronger than the draft report's review of this literature suggests. Although the authors appear to recommend against the use of bidding games at the point of eliciting the initial bid, presumably because they feel that starting point bias is a real problem, other readers might review the evidence presented in the report and conclude that starting point bias is not a problem with the bidding game format. In what follows, we present a critique of the report's literature review on this topic.

In the first place, the literature review offered in the report includes various items which are extraneous to the issue of starting point (SP) bias but which, nevertheless, appear to be offered as evidence against SP bias.[1]

Second, there are several other studies not cited in the draft report whose findings support the notion of SP bias. These include our reinterpretation of Greenley, Walsh and Young's water benefits study Mitchell and Carson (1984a); the study by Thompson and Roberts (1983) of recreation values for offshore oil platforms which shows a strong effect in a well-designed test; and a forthcoming paper by Boyle, Bishop and Welsh which also shows a strong effect in a well-designed test.

Third, some of the previous tests for SP bias, which are interpreted in the report as showing no SP bias, are potentially flawed because of the *low power* of the tests. It is well recognized that sample size decisions should take into account the size needed to detect a specific difference with a specified power.[2] Hypothesis testing on small samples which have fairly high coefficients of variation face the problem of accepting a finding of "no difference" a large percent of the time when in fact a difference of as much as twenty five percent may be the case.[3] Given the very small samples used in the Los Angeles tests for starting point bias, the likelihood of finding a difference at the .05 or even .10 level was very small. That a few of the tests in that study did find differences should be viewed as a potential sign of strong starting point bias than as evidence that it is rarely found. For the same reason, Desvousges, Smith and McGivney (pp. 64–5) were unable to positively assert that starting points of $25 and $125 caused bias in their study despite the fact that the difference between their means is large and in the predicted direction.[4]

Iterative format

At various points the report emphasizes the importance of using an iterative format in CVM studies. The grounds offered for this recommendation are several. (a) The finding that an initial payment card bid is raised significantly (despite small sample sizes) when respondents are told the amount they originally offered may not be enough to make possible the good's provision; and (b) Laboratory auction results which show that bidding in an auction process only reaches full WTP after a series of iterative learning periods.

Regarding (a), we agree that the initial payment card amount is likely to be a low estimate because people may not initially fully face up to the "all or nothing" character of the situation. This raises the question of how to capture the understated consumer surplus. We do not think the followup bidding game is necessarily the answer. The procedure of bidding the price up in the "would you pay $1 more" manner, runs a strong risk of twisting people's arms to go higher than they would really want to go (or would vote for in a referendum). This is because the followup bidding game procedure places people in the awkward social position of having to say no to the inferred request of the interviewer that they increase their amount by a mere $1 (or whatever the interval is) for a socially desirable public good. One way to iterate with less chance of implied value type biases would be to say something to the effect that "if your amount was not enough to accomplish the change and it would have to be foregone unless more money was available, would you pay anything more?" If the person answered yes, he or she could then be asked to say the maximum additional amount they would pay before they would prefer to forgo the change.

Regarding (b), we agree that CVM scenarios should include iterative elements which permit learning to take place. And the more unfamiliar the good, the greater the need for these elements. We disagree with the notion that using a bidding game or multiple administrations of the instrument in a panel design are necessary to accomplish this end. In the first place, the evidence cited in the draft report that practice round (s) are needed in experiments which use Vickrey auctions is not persuasive because a second price auction is not an intuitive institution for many people. Likewise, their data suggests that a WTA format is also not intuitive. However, unlike either of these formats, the WTP format appears to be simpler and more understandable. Second, as we will argue at more length below, use of a referenda model instead of a market goods model suggests that iteration *of the kind proposed in the report* is not an imperative design feature for CVM surveys.

Thus it does not appear to us to be the case that an extended period of time or numerous iterations of a bidding game format which uses the WTP format are necessary to arrive at the true value. The data presented in the report's figure 4.1 appear to support our contention. In this figure, the experimental iterations made a minor difference at best in the WTP bid compared with very large differences in the WTA bid. We firmly believe, however, that respondents in CVM surveys do need to get into the game, and that scenarios should make every effort to help them to realize how it works. One technique we have found to be helpful (Carson and Mitchell 1984) is to provide respondents with opportunities to reconsider their answers at various points in the course of the questionnaire.

Payment Card

The report says relatively little about the payment card elicitation procedure except to describe some of the experiments which have compared the use of payment cards with several other elicitaton methods. It is important to emphasize that while payment cards formats were designed to avoid starting point bias, payment cards are *not* immune to other forms of bias involving implied value cues. Because of this, decisions about the number of dollar amounts which are displayed in a given card, their range, the size of the increments, and (if used) the nature of the anchors, must take into account the nature of the good and the expected value range. If the appropriate decisions are made, payment card bias can be minimized. If inappropriate decisions are made, the potential for bias is considerable. To take an extreme example, the use of a payment card whose first two numbers are $0 and $25 could lead to a substantial upward bias when valuing a good whose expected value (perhaps determined by in-depth pretests) is in the range of 12–15 dollars. Even when respondents are instructed, as they should be, to pick any number in between the amounts shown on the card, in our experience they tend to limit the choice to the numbers on the card. As a result, respondents who have a true value of $15 for the good may be influenced by the design of this payment card to pick the $25 amount and therefore overstate their WTP amount.

Not enough is known about the effect of changing the various parameters of payment cards and more research is called for. Research which tests the influence of extreme differences in the upper bound is not very informative, however, since different mean WTP amounts are to be expected under this condition. The most useful research would focus on the effect of parameters within the range of reasonable values such as the effect of upper bounds at 3, 5, and 7 times the expected average value.

THE AUCTION ANALOGY (Chapter 4)

This chapter develops an auction analogy for CVM studies which is based on auctions for private goods, where the true price can be established. Since most CVM surveys value public not private goods, the relevance of aucton theory to the provision of collective goods needs to be established, something the draft version of the report does not do.

Second Price Auction

The draft report recommends the second price auction model for CVM surveys. While a second price auction has desirable properties, it is impossible to simulate in a CVM study without greatly complicating the scenario. And the use of increments in an English auction, if they are large relative to the price, make it no longer equivalent to a second price auction (Carson and Foster 1984), thus qualifying conclusion 6 in the draft report.

Putting aside for the moment the collective properties of public goods, CVM surveys might be viewed as analogous to first price auctions in the sense that the respondent, like the bidder in such an auction, believes he or she will have to pay the price if the good is provided.[5] In CVM surveys, such a belief has the desirable property that if it does induce a bias, it is to underestimate the WTP for the good since first price auctions yield prices at or below that of second price auctions. Any difference between a first and a second price (if such a thing could be obtained for a good valued in a CVM survey) is likely to be caused either by strategic behavior or by the respondent's undervaluing the good because of not having faced up to the implications of not receiving it. In both cases, the scenario can help overcome these problems by emphasizing the potential for everyone being excluded from the good if it is not provided.

UTILITY OF LABORATORY EXPERIMENTS

The fact that CVM studies value public goods raises serious questions about the use of laboratory experiments to determine optimal CVM scenario formats such as those advocated in chapter 4. In the absence of a good which can really be sold through a second price auction, *what criterion will such experiments use in order to evaluate various alternative design features?* On the other hand, if the experiments use a good which can be bought and sold (such as Bishop and Heberlein's hunting permits), the direct applicability of these findings based on a private good to situations with public goods is uncertain. Also relevant to the utility of experiments is the fact that CVM surveys normally value goods by interviewing fairly large, random samples. The notion, which the report advocates, of applying a tatonnement voting process, which requires unanimity, to any but a very small group seems highly impractical to us. Quite apart from its impracticality, we fail to understand why unanimity is necessary since the likelihood of strategic behavior in properly designed CVM studies has been shown to be acceptably low.

In our view, what is needed are not experiments aimed at developing mechanisms to simulate second price auctions, which are likely to be unsuitable to the field conditions faced by CVM studies, but laboratory and field work which illuminate the conditions under which certain biases occur in the field and which give us greater understanding of what goes on in people's minds when they answer WTP questions. Desvousges and Smith's use of focus groups is a case in point, as is their work in debriefing interviewers to better understand the responses to their Monongahela survey. Much more work needs to be done on this count. For example, we need to know how people tend to partition environmental goods in their minds in order to better understand the part-whole problem identified by Randall and Hoehn. In-depth interviewing of a few respondents or the debriefing of participants in a relevant experiment can potentially yield insights on this topic which could really make a difference in field applications.

Hypothetical Bias

We believe the use of this term is confusing. Although the hypothetical character of CVM studies has several potential effects, one of which is to increase the likelihood of certain other types of bias (the other is to increase the random quality of the answers), there is no unique hypothetical bias.[6]

Tests of Whether Actual vs. Hypothetical Payment Makes a Difference.

Our review of the literature leads us to question the draft report's conclusions: (a) "The literature abounds with evidence that suggests that... actual vs. hypothetical payment does result in different choices (p. 107, emphasis in the original) and (b)... the quality of empirical measures of value from the HPM per se are far from a level where they might be regarded as accurate, in some sense, estimates for market values attributable to public goods (p. 110)."

The evidence, at least as we read it, is much more equivocal on both of these points. We begin with (a) above. The draft report cites four bodies of evidence in support of this contention, several of which do not support it and others of which support it much less than suggested. The first is Bohm's work whose conclusion that people will act "irresponsibly" where no payment is involved you accept as proved. In our 1981 report, we reanalyzed Bohm's data and showed that this conclusion rested on one outlier. More recently (Mitchell and Carson 1984a), we have further reanalyzed Bohm's findings in light of recent experimental work (Marwell and Ames etc.). Quite apart from our original criticism, which still holds, we now view Bohm's treatment VIb (which is essentially a first price auction where the top ten out of 100 bids were accepted) as representing the closest approximation to the true WTP of all of his treatments. In light of this, it is significant that the mean bid for this treatment is almost identical to the mean bid for VIa, the only hypothetical treatment in his experiment.[7] The second body of evidence is Bishop and Heberlein's original goose hunting study. In this case the draft report accepts our criticism of Bishop and Heberlein's finding. Presuming that our critique of these two important studies is correct, this leaves us with only two pieces of evidence for the draft report's finding that the literature "abounds" with evidence that actual and hypothetical payment result in different choices.

The third study is Coursey et al. 1983, an unpublished experiment. Our reading of this paper suggests that the difference found in this study has to do with WTP vs. WTA and not with hypothetical WTP vs. real WTP. Since the WTA/WTP issue has its own complexity (e.g. Michael Hanneman has shown that the Willig bounds do not hold for discrete choice situations) and since WTP is the format used in most CVM studies, this study is largely irrelevant to the generalization.

The fourth body of evidence are "tests of actual vs. hypothetical payment on decision strategies reported in the psychological literature." The authors' cite

Paul Slovic's 1969 conclusion that real vs. hypothetical gains or losses made a difference in people's decision strategies as "typical" of the findings of these studies (p. 108). Because our understanding of this literature was that it also contained a number of studies, such as Grether and Plott's, which tested certain findings (such as preference reversals) under both conditions with the opposite conclusion, we called Paul Slovic to see what studies we had missed. In our conversation he made the following points: 1) Generally speaking, the literature on this topic shows equivocal findings. 2) Very few studies have examined the effects of hypothetical vs. real payments directly as his 1969 study did. His study was very sensitive to decision strategy in that it looked at gambles. 3) There are a lot of studies similar to Grether and Plott's which find that observed effects hold under both conditions. In the absence of other evidence, we conclude that the matter is less clear than the draft report's presentation would suggest and that Slovic's 1969 study doesn't really support the pessimistic conclusion.

Thus the evidence for actual vs. hypothetical payments making a difference is very weak. What about the other side of the question? According to the report "there is little if any evidence that would support the hypothesis that actual payment = hypothetical payment." It is true that there is very little direct evidence for this hypothesis, just as there is little direct evidence for the reverse hypothesis. Studies which attempt to predict behavior on the basis of measures of behavioral intentions provide some useful indirect evidence on this issue, however. The authors cite one such study—Kogan and Wallach (1968); there are a number of others in the attitude-behavior literature which bear on this question. There is also some relevant work in the market research literature on "concept testing" (Moore 1982). These studies demonstrate that, under certain conditions, surveys can have excellent predictive value.[8]

To summarize, we argue the following: (1) By no means does the literature abound with evidence that actual vs. hypothetical payment results in different choices. The evidence, we find, is very weak on this point. (2) Although there is little direct evidence for the opposite hypothesis, important indirect evidence is available. (3) The essential fact is that the literature simply does not permit an authoritative statement to be made one way or the other.

In making this argument we do not mean to imply that the hypothetical character of CVM studies is unproblematic. Indeed, we believe the greatest methodological problems with the CVM method stem from their hypothetical character. Nevertheless, there are reasonable grounds in the literature to support the idea that carefully designed hypothetical payment situations can approximate actual payment situations with sufficient accuracy to be a useful component of benefit/cost analysis.

We now turn to the draft report's second finding that the quality of hypothetical CVM values "are far from a level where they might be regarded as accurate." Presuming that this means that even well designed CVM studies with good samples and excellent field work are inevitably very inaccurate, this strong statement is simply not supported by the evidence provided in this chapter. Nor do we believe the statement captures the reality of what the past decade of research on CVM has found. To repeat, our own view is that while it is very difficult to obtain unbiased or minimally biased CVM estimates, properly designed CVM studies are possible and they can obtain benefit measures with acceptable levels of accuracy.

POLITICAL MARKETS AND REFERENCE OPERATING CONDITIONS (Chapter 6)

The draft report argues that accuracy in CVM studies can only be measured by the degree to which these studies replicate what is termed the "key reference operating conditions for the market institution." "Market institution" is defined as markets in private goods where goods are traded frequently through a process of competing bids and offers. In such a market, according to the report, people gain information through the process of frequent purchase. The requirements imposed by the market model then determines the first two reference operating conditions (ROC's).

An alternative framework is suggested by the large body of theory developed by economists and political scientists (e.g. Enelow and Hinich 1984; Bergstrom, Rubenfeld and Shapiro 1982; Deacon and Shapiro 1975) on political markets which, after all, are how public goods are supplied. Here the particular form of the political market most relevant to CVM is the referendum. In a referendum, a voter is faced with a one-time (or at best with a very infrequent) choice on a predetermined policy package to which they must vote yes or no before the outcome of the referendum is known. If the particular issue comes up in a subsequent referendum, it is likely to pose a fairly sizable change in the policy package.

The referendum framework suggests a somewhat different set of reference operating conditions. ROC's from referenda and the psychological research which point to distortions in decision processes appear to us to consist of the following:

1. Respondents must understand the commodity to be valued, how it will be provided and how it will be paid for.
2. They should be given as simple a choice as possible.
3. There must be little uncertainty about the provision of the good.
4. WTP, not WTA, measures are elicited.
5. Outliers should not be permitted unduly to influence the results.
6. Respondents should be permitted to abstain from the valuation process.

Items 3 and 4 are identical to those derived from the market model and presented in the draft report. The other items bear some explanation.

Item 1: For a referendum to measure people's true WTP for the commodity, the voters should understand the nature of the commodity, its method of provision and the consequences of its implementation. (In practice, some people make uninformed decisions in referenda just as they do in the marketplace.) In CVM studies, the scenario must be able to accurately convey this information to respondents with widely varying educational attainments and life experience. Understanding is usually made easier if the respondent has had experience with the good. But it is worth noting that experience is not necessarily an advantage since familiarity can interfere with understanding by leading respondents to jump to mistaken conclusions about the scenario's elements. For example, the use of a park entrance fee as a payment vehicle for valuing park amenities is something which many respondents have experienced. Asking for a maximum WTP amount by use of such a vehicle faces the problem that respondents are likely to hold a conception of a "fair" or normative park entrance fee based on their experience. Thus, while they may in fact have a true WTP amount of $13 for a particular amenity, they may bid less than this amount if their view of a maximum fair entrance fee is $10 or $7 or $5 etc.

Item 2: Referenda pose issues in terms of a yes/no decision for a particular level of provision of a good at a given price. CVM scenarios should strive for as simple a choice as possible within the methodological limitations of survey research and modest sample sizes. The potential for yea-saying bias limits the application of a direct imitation of the referenda format as do the large sample sizs required by formats using dichotomous answers to priced levels of the good. Where the choice is complex, respondents should be provided opportunities to change their decisions after they have gone through the valuation process and understand its full implications. Note that referenda are often one-time exercises where voters vote on items about which they may not have had prior valuation and choice experience (e.g. nuclear referenda, water bond issues etc.).

Item 5: Referenda use a majority or 2/3 rule for deciding whether or not a public commodity is to be supplied. In either case a small minority (ie, outliers) do not determine the decision made.

Item 6: Participation in referenda is voluntary. Voters can choose whether or not to go to the polls and once there, they can choose whether or not to vote on particular issues. CVM studies should not "require" answers to the WTP questions from respondents who would prefer not to answer because they are not interested in the valuation exercise, are confused by it, can't determine what value they hold for the good etc. If they do, the quality of the data will suffer. However, in order to obtain a valid population estimate, the effect of nonresponses must be adjusted for by use of scientific sampling and missing data estimation techniques.

ON THE QUESTION OF ACCURACY (Chapter 6)

The report's argument for a fifty percent error range is not convincing. The size of the range appears to be arbitrarily chosen and the statistical properties of the range are not well defined. Is the range, for example, meant to include the sampling variance? We do not think it should. If it doesn't, and sampling variance is added to the fifty percent error range, studies with small samples will be expected to produce very large estimate ranges.

Not all CVM studies in the literature produce findings which are equally valid. Some suffer from severe methodological problems which bias the results. Some have very small sample sizes which affect the statistical tests of differences. To talk about the general accuracy of CVM studies in terms of an arbitrarily chosen and imprecisely defined +/- 50% criterion, ignores this problem and seems to suggest that as long as a study meets the ROC's specified in the report, it will provide a reasonably satisfactory "rough" estimate. Quite apart from our views about whether the ROC's recommended in the draft report are the most appropriate ones, both the report's and ours are too general to be of much help in providing criteria by which a CVM study can be evaluated. The key questions are: How does one tell a "good" study in the sense of a properly conducted CVM study, from a "poor" one? What improvements are needed to increase the accuracy of CVM studies? Which improvements promise the most payoff? These are the kinds of issues which could have been explored to advantage in the report's discussion of accuracy.[9]

The State of the Arts Assessment of the Contingent Valuation Method Draft Report and the conference on this report represent an important milestone in the development of the contingent valuation method.

They addressed a number of the important and difficult issues associated with the methodology, some of which were overdue for attention and others of which have engaged the thought of CVM practioners for some time. These remarks were prepared before the Palo Alto Conference in response to an invitation from the authors for critical comments. We appreciate the opportunity to participate in the debate raised by this stimulating report. What follows are our views on a set of issues where we disagree with the report's presentation. We have revised these remarks somewhat since their original formulation. All page numbers refer to the original draft report.

NOTES

1. Studies such as Walsh and Gilliam (1982), which are cited in the report, appear to be irrelevant to the issue, at least as described.

2. See Desvousges et al. 1983, pp. A-1ff for a good discussion of this topic, but note that the coefficients of variation for given CVM studies in table A-2 are incorrectly estimated and are much too small because they calculated the coefficient of variation with the standard error of the mean instead of the standard deviation.

3. A pretest which we ran in the summer of 1983 illustrates the potential consequence of small sample sizes for hypothesis testing. In addition to pretesting our water quality instrument, we wanted to test the effect of using payment cards with and without anchors. Our usable N's were 37 and 39 for the two treatments and the coefficient of variations were roughly 2.0, a size similar to that found in many CVM studies. If we wished to use standard comparison of means tests to detect a 25 percent or greater difference between the two treatments, with (a) a ten percent chance of rejecting the hypothesis of no difference where there is a difference and (b) a five percent chance of accepting a difference only 5 percent of the time when in fact no difference is present, we would have had to have a sample size of approximately 2000 for each treatment. Expressed another way, given our actual sample size, the mean of the second treatment would have had to have been 75 percent larger (or smaller) than that of the first treatment before we could have rejected the null hypothesis. Because income is a good predictor of the WTP amounts in this case, we were able to assume a log normal distribution which enabled us to use a powerful test of the hypothesis that the medians of the original distribution (mean of the log distribution) were significantly different. (They were not.) In cases where income is not a good predictor, however, such a procedure is not possible and with small samples the deck is potentially stacked against finding a difference.

4. Comparisons of the mean bids for nonusers showed the $125 starting point bids were almost double those for the $25 starting point treatment.

5. The CVM interpretation of a second price auction is that the respondent bids believing he or she will have to pay the average WTP amount if the good is provided. This situation has no known desirable properties.

6. We develop this argument (and some of the others which we mention in this critique) more fully in Mitchell and Carson (1984).

7. Note that subjects participating in VIb had the most "iterative" experience of any of Bohm's subjects, as the same sample also took part in VIa.

8. This assertion is based on an analysis presented in Mitchell and Carson (1984).

9. The draft report does not address these issues and often ignores their implications. For example, table 6.12 presents the mean values obtained by studies which compare CVM and indirect market methods of valuation. Lacking from this table are the studies' sample sizes and standard deviations which, would indicate a) whether the differences are significant and b) whether the imprecision is due to the CVM study, the indirect study or to both methods. Likewise, the issue of sampling is not discussed in the report despite its implications for accurate benefit estimates from CVM data. Many CVM studies in the literature provide no information or very scanty information about the sampling plan and its execution. Errors in aggregation based on faulty sampling could easily be in the 50 percent range. Another type of aggregation problem which the study does not discuss is the sometimes high item-nonresponse rate in CVM studies. A greater number of respondents in some CVM surveys based on random samples fail to answer the WTP questions than fail to answer questions in ordinary surveys. Within limits, this is understandable (WTP questions are demanding) and desirable (better to have don't knows than guesses). In order to derive accurate population estimates from such data, however, the use of approximation techniques is required. Our preliminary work on this topic suggests possible errors due to this factor alone in the 10–25 percent range.

References

Ajzen, I. and M. Fishbein 1977. "Attitude-Behaviors Relation: A Theoretical Analysis and Review of Empirical Research," *Psychological Bulletin*, 84, pp. 888-918.

Akerlof, G.A. and W.T. Dickens 1982. "The Economic Consequences of Cognitive Dissonance," *American Economic Review*, 72(3).

Arrow, K.J. 1982. "Risk Perceptions in Psychology and Economics," *Economic Inquiry*, 20, pp. 1-9.

Arrow, K.J. 1951. *Social Choice and Individual Values*, New York, Wiley.

Banford, N.D., J.I. Knetsch and G.A. Mauser 1977. "Compensating and Equivalent Variation Measures of Consumer's Surplus: Further Survey Results," unpublished paper, Dept. of Economics and Commerce, Simon Fraser University, Vancouver, B.C., Canada.

Bartik, T.J. and V.K. Smith 1984. "Urban Amenities and Public Policy," Vanderbilt University Working Paper No. 84-W18, May.

Batie, S.S. and L. Shabman 1979. "Valuing Non-Market Goods-Conceptual and Empirical Issues: Discussion," *American Journal of Agricultural Economics*, 61(5), pp. 931-32.

Belovicz, M.W. 1979. "Sealed-Bid Auctions: Experimental Results and Applications," in V.L. Smith (ed.), *Research in Experimental Economics*, Vol. 1, Connecticut, JAI Press, Inc.

Bergson, A. 1938. "A Reformulation of Certain Aspects of Welfare Economics," *Quarterly Journal of Economics*, 68(2).

Bergstrom, T.C., D.L. Rubinfeld and P. Shapiro 1982. "Micro-Based Estimates of Demand Functions for Local School Expenditures," *Econometrica*, 50(5), pp. 1183-1205.

Bishop, R. and T. Heberlein 1979. "Measuring Values of Extramarket Goods: Are Indirect Measures Biased?" *American Journal of Agriculture Economics* 61(5) (December): 926-930.

Bishop, R.C. 1982. "Option Value: An Exposition and Extension." *Land Economics*, 58, pp. 1-15.

Bishop, R.C., T.A. Heberlein and M.J. Kealy 1983. "Contingent Valuation of Environmental Assets: Comparison With a Simulated Market," *Natural Resources Journal*, 23(3), pp. 619-34.

Bishop, R.C. and T.A. Heberlein 1984. "Contingent Valuation Methods and Ecosystem Damages from Acid Rain," Agriculture Economics Staff Paper Series, No. 217, Department of Agriculture Economics, University of Wisconsin - Madison.

Blank, F.M., D.S. Brookshire, T.D. Crocker, R.C. d'Arge, R.L. Horst and R.D. Rowe 1978. *Valuation of Aesthetic Preferences: A Case Study of the Economic Value of Visability*, prepared for the Electric Power Research Institute, Inc. (EPRI), Palo Alto, CA, Contract #RP7855-2, October 6.

Blumberg, G.J. 1984. "Application and Assessment of the Contingent Valuation Method for Federal Hazardous Waste Policies in the Washington D.C. Area." Unpublished Ph.D dissertation, University of New Mexico, Albuquerque.

Bohm, P. 1971. "An Approach to the Problem of Estimating Demand for Public Goods," *Swedish Journal of Economics*, 73(1), pp. 55-66.

Bohm, P. 1972. "Estimating Demand for Public Goods: An Experiment," *European Economic Review*, 3(2), pp. 111-130.

Boulding, K.E. 1975. *The Image*, Ann Arbor, University of Michigan Press.

Boyle, K.J. and R.C. Bishop 1984. "Lower Wisconsin River Recreation: Economic Impacts and Scenic Values," Staff Paper No. 216, Department of Agricultural Economics, University of Wisconsin - Madison.

Boyle, K.J., R.C. Bishop and M.P. Walsh, forthcoming, "Starting Point Bias in Contingent Valuation Bidding Games," *Land Economics*.

Bradford, D.F. 1970. "Benefit-Cost Analysis and Demand Curves for Public Goods," *Kyklos*, 23, pp. 775-791.

Brookshire, D.S. and T.D. Crocker 1981. "The Advantages of Contingent Valuation Methods for Benefit-Cost Analysis," *Public Choice*, 36(2), pp. 235-252.

Brookshire, D.S. and R.C. d'Arge 1979. "Resource Impacted Communities: Economics, Planning and Management," paper prepared for the 4th U.S. - U.S.S.R. Symposium on Comprehensive Analysis of the Environment, Jackson, Wyoming, October 21-27, pp. 1-55.

Brookshire, D.S., R.C. d'Arge, W.D. Schulze and M.A. Thayer 1981. "Experiments in Valuing Public Goods," *Advances in Applied Microeconomics*, Vol. 1, V.K. Smith, ed., Connecticut, JAI Press, Inc., pp. 123-172.

Brookshire, D.S. and L.S. Eubanks 1978. "Contingent Valuation and Revealing the actual Demand for Public Environmental Commodities," in *Public Choice in New Orleans*, G. Tullock (ed.), selected paper of the Public Choice Society, New Orleans.

Brookshire, D.S., L.S. Eubanks and A. Randall 1983a, "Estimating Option Prices and Existence Values for Wildlife Resources," *Land Economics*, 59, pp. 1-15.

Brookshire, D.S., B.C. Ives and W.D. Schulze 1976. "The Valuation of Aesthetic Preferences," *Journal of Environmental Economics and Management*, 3, pp. 325-46.

Brookshire, D.S., A. Randall, R.C. d'Arge, L.S. Eubanks, J.R. Stoll, T.D. Crocker and S. Johnson 1977. *Methodological Experiments in Valuing Wildlife Resources: Phase I Interim Report to the United States Fish and Wildlife Service*, USFWS Grants #14016-00009-77-002 and 14016-00009-77-003, November.

Brookshire, D.S., A. Randall, and J.R. Stoll 1980. "Valuing Increments and Decrements in Natural Resource Service Flows," *American Journal of Agricultural Economics*, 62(3), pp.478-488.

Brookshire, D.S., W.D. Schulze, M.A. Thayer and R.C. d'Arge 1982, "Valuing Public Goods: A Comparison of Survey and Hedonic Approaches," "American Economic Review," 72(1), pp. 165-177.

Brookshire, D.S., W.D. Schulze and R. Whitworth 1983b. *An Economic Analysis of the Private Sector Benefits and Potential for Cost Recovery of the National Coal Resources Data Systems*, report to the U.S. Geological Survey, Reston, VA, July.

Brookshire, D.S., M.A. Thayer, J. Tischirhart, W.D. Schulze 1984. "A Test of the Expected Utility Model: Evidence from Earthquake Risks," manuscript, University of Wyoming, Laramie, forthcoming in *Journal of Political Economy*.

Brown, J. and S. Rosen 1982. "On Estimation of Structural Hedonic Price Models," *Econometrica*, 50(3), pp. 765-68.

Brown, W., A. Singh, and E. Castle 1964. *An Economic Evaluation of the Oregon Salmon and Steelhead Sports Fishery*, Oregon Agricultural Experiment Station Bulletin, No. 74, Corvallis.

Buchanan, J. and G. Tullock 1962. *The Calculus of Consent*, Ann Arbor, University of Michigan Press.

Burness, H.S., R.G. Cummings, A.F. Mehr and M.S. Walbert 1983. "Valuing Policies Which Reduce Environmental Risk," *Natural Resources Journal*, 23(3), pp. 675-682.

Carson, R.T. and W.E. Foster 1984. "A Theory of Auctions from the Auctioneer's Perspective," presented at the Econometric Society Meetings, Stanford University.

Carson, R.T. and R.C. Mitchell 1984a. "A Reestimation of Bishop and Heberlein's Simulated Market-Hypothetical Markets-Travel Cost Results Under an Alternative Assumption," Discussion Paper No. D-107 Washington, D.C., Resources for the Future, forthcoming, *American Journal of Agriculture Economics*.

Carson, R.T. and R.C. Mitchell 1984b. "National Fresh Water Quality Benefits: Findings from a New National Contingent Valuation Study," presented at the Association of Environmental and Resource Economists Meeting at Cornell University, August. Discussion Paper No.D-124, Washington, D.C., Resources for the Future.

Carson, R.T. and R.C. Mitchell 1984c. "Non-Sampling Errors in Contingent Valuation Surveys," Discussion Paper D-120, April, Washington, D.C., Resources for the Future.

Cassady, R. 1967. *Auctions and Auctioneering*, Berkeley, University of California Press.

Cesario, F.J. 1976. "Valuing Time in Recreation Studies," *Land Economics*, p. 52.

Chew, Soo-Hung and K.R. MacGrimmon 1979. "Alpha Utility Theory, Lottery Composition and the Allais Paradox," working paper, Faculty of Commerce and Business Administration, University of British Columbia, September.

Ciriacy-Wantrup, S.V. 1952. *Resource Conservation: Economics and Policies*, Berkeley, University of California Press.

Clarke, E.H. 1971. "Multipart Pricing of Public Goods," *Public Choice*, 11, pp. 17-33.

Clawson, M. 1959. "Methods of Measuring the Demand for Outdoor Recreation," reprint No. 10, Washington D.C., Resources for the Future.

Clawson, M. and J.L. Knetsch (1966), *Economics of Outdoor Recreation*: John Hopkins Press, Balliman.

Coppinger, V.M., V.L. Smith and J.A. Titus 1980. "Incentives and Behavior in English, Dutch and Sealed-Bid Auctions," *Economic Inquiry*, 18(1), pp. 1-22.

Coursey D.L., Crocker, T.D. and R.G. Cummings 1984. "On Valuing Deposition-Induced Materials Damages: A Methodological Inquiry," in D.D. Adams and W. Page (eds.), *Acid Deposition: Environmental and Economic Impacts*, New York, Plenum Press, forthcoming.

Coursey, D.L. and V.L. Smith 1982. "Experimental Tests of an Allocation Mechanism for Private, Public or Externality Goods," mimeo, Department of Economics, University of Arizona.

Coursey, D.L. and H. Nyquist 1983a. "Application of Robust Estimation Techniques in Demand Analysis," manuscript, University of Umea, Sweden, October, submitted to *Review of Economics and Statistics*.

Coursey, D.L., W.D. Schulze and J. Hovis 1983b. "A Comparison of Alternative Valuation Mechanisms For Non-Market Commodities," unpublished manuscript, Department of Economics, University of Wyoming, December.

Cox, J.L., B. Roberson and V.L. Smith 1982. "Theory and Behavior of Single Price Auctions," in V.L. Smith (ed.), *Research in Experimental Economics*, Vol. 2, Connecticut, J.A.I. Press, Inc.

Crandall, R.W. 1983. *Controlling Industrial Pollution: The Economics and Politics of Clean Air*. Washington D.C., The Brookings Institution.

Crocker, T.D. 1984. "On The Value of the Condition of a Forest Stock," unpublished manuscript, Department of Economics, Univesity of Wyoming.

Crocker, T.D. and B.A. Forster 1984. "Nonconvexities in the Control of Acid Deposition: Still a Problem," *Journal of the Air Pollution Control Association*, forthcoming.

Cronin, F.J., and K. Herzeg 1982. *Valuing Nonmarket Goods Through Contingent Markets*, Pacific Northwest Laboratory, Richland, Washington, PNL-4255.

Cummings, R.G., H.S. Burness and R.D. Norton 1981. "Measuring Household Soiling Damages from Suspended Air Particulates: A Methodological Inquiry," Report to the U.S. Environmental Protection Agency, R805059010, Washington, D.C., April.

Cummings, R.G., W.D. Schulze, S.D. Gerking and D.S. Brookshire 1982. "Measuring the Elasticity of Substitution of Wages for Municipal Infrastructure: A Comparison of the Survey and Wage Hedonic Approach," manuscript, Department of Economics, University of New Mexico, Albuquerque.

Cummings, R.G., W.D. Schulze and A.F. Mehr 1978. "Optimal Municipal Investment in Boomtowns: An Empirical Analysis," *Journal of Environmental Economics and Management*, 5.

Dasgupta, A.K. and D.W. Pearce 1978. *Cost-Benefit Analysis: Theory and Practice*, New York, MacMillan.

Daubert, J. and R. Young 1981. "Recreational Demands for Maintaining Instream Flows: A Contingent Valuation Approach," *American Journal of Agriculture Economics*, 63(4), pp. 666-676.

Davis, R.K. 1963a. "Recreational Planning as An Economic Problem," *Natural Resource Journal*, pp. 238-249.

Davis, R.K. 1963b. "The Value of Outdoot Recreation: An Economic Study of the Maine Woods," unpublished Ph.D. dissertation, Harvard University.

Deacon, R. and P. Shapiro 1975. "Private Preference for Collective Goods Revealed Through Voting on Referenda," *American Economic Review*, 65(5), pp. 943-955.

Desvousges, W.H. and V.K. Smith 1982. *The Basis for Measuring the Benefits of Hazardous Waste Disposal Regulation*, Raleigh, Research Triangl Institute.

Desvousges, W.H. and V.K. Smith, and M.P. McGivney 1983. *A Comparison of Alternative Approaches for Estimating Recreation and Related Benefits of Water Quality Improvements*, EPA-230-05-83-001, March.

Devletoglou, N.E. 1971. "Thresholds and Transaction Costs," *Quarterly Journal of Economics*, 85(1).

Dubey, P. and M. Shubik 1980. "A Strategic Market Game with Price and Quantity Strategies," *Zeitschrift fur Nationalokonomie*, 40.

Enelow, James M. and Melvin J. Hinich 1984. *The Spatial Theory of Voting: An Introduction*. Cambridge, Cambridge University Press.

Engelbrecht-Wiggans, R. 1980. "Auctions and Bidding Models: A Survey," *Management Science*, 26.

Evans, John S. 1984. "Theoretically Optimal Environmental Metrics and Their Surrogates," *Journal of Environmental Economics and Management*, 11, pp. 18-27.

Feather, T. 1959. "Subjective Probability and Decisions Under Uncertainty," *Psychology Review*, 66, pp. 150-64.

Feenberg, D. and E.S. Mills 1980. *Measuring the Benefits of Water Pollution Abatement*, New York, Academic Press.

Ferejohn, J.A. and R.G. Noll 1976. "An Experimental Market for Public Goods: The PBS Station Program Cooperative," *American Economic Review Proceedings*, 66, pp. 267-273.

Ferejohn, J.A., R. Forsythe and R. Noll 1979a. "An Experimental Analysis of Decision Making Procedures for Discrete Public Goods: A Case Study of a Problem of Institutional Design," in V.L. Smith (ed.), *Research in Experimental Economics*, Vol. 1, Connecticut, JAI Press, Inc.

Ferejohn, J.A., R. Forsythe and R. Noll 1979b. "Practical Aspects of the Construction of Decentralized Decision Making Systems for Public Goods," in C. Russell (ed.), *Collective Decision Making: Applications from Public Choice Theory*, Baltimore, Johns Hopkins University Press.

Ferejohn, J.A., R. Forsythe, R. Noll and T.R. Palfrey 1982. "An Experimental Examination of Auction Mechanisms for Discrete Public Goods," in V.L. Smith (ed.), *Research In Experimental Economics* Vol. 2, Connecticut, JAI Press, Inc.

Fischoff, B. 1975. "Hindsight Is Not Equal To Foresight: The Effect of Outcome Knowledge On Judgement Under Uncertainty," *Journal of Experimental Psychology*, 104(1), pp. 288-99.

Fischoff, B., P. Slovic and S. Lichtenstein 1982. "Lay Folibles and Expert Fables in Judgements About Risk," *The American Statistician*, 36(2), pp. 240-255.

Fischoff, B. 1982. "For Those Codemned to Study the Past: Heuristics and Biases in Hindsight," in *Judgements Under Uncertainty: Heuristics and Biases*, in D. Kahneman, P. Slovic and A. Tversky (eds.), Cambridge, Cambridge University Press, pp. 335-354.

Fishbein, M., and I. Ajzen 1975. "Attitudes Toward Objects as Predictors of Single and Multiple Behavioral Criteria," *Psychology Review*, 81, pp. 59-74.

Fisher, W.L. 1984. "Measuring the Economic Value of Fishing and Hunting: A Conceptual Overview," Paper presented at the Annual Meeting of Omicron Delta Epsilon, Lycoming College, Williamsport, Pa., April 16.

Flinn, J. and J. Heckman 1983. "Are Unemployment and Out of the Labor Force Behaviorally Distinct States?" *Journal of Labor Research* 1, pp. 28-43.

Forsythe, R. and R.M. Isaac 1982. "Demand-Revealing Mechanisms for Private Goods Auctions," in V.L. Smith (ed.), *Research In Experimental Economics*, Vol. 2, Connecticut, JAI Press, Inc.

Freeman, A.M. 1979a. *Benefits of Environmental Improvement*, Baltimore, Johns Hopkins University Press.

Freeman, A.M. 1979b. "Approaches To Measuring Public Goods Demands," *American Journal of Agriculture Economics*, 61(5) pp. 915-20.

Freeman, A.M. 1979c. "Hedonic Prices, Property Values and Measuring Environmental Benefits: A Survey of the Issues," *Scandinavian Journal of Economics*, 81(2), pp. 154-173.

Freeman, A.M. 1984. "The Sign and Size of Option Value," *Land Economics*, 60, pp. 1-13.

Freeman, B. and L. Medoff 1982. "Why Does the Rate of Youth Labor Force Activity Differ Across Surveys," in R.B. Freeman and D.A. Wise (eds.), *The Youth Labor Market Problems: Its Nature, Causes, and Consequences*. Chicago, University of Chicago Press.

Friedman, M. 1953. *Essays In Positive Economics*, Chicago.

Gallagher, D.R. and V.K. Smith 1984. "Measuring Values for Environmental Resources Under Uncertainty," forthcoming *Journal of Environmental Economics and Management*.

Georgescu-Roegen, N. 1958. "Threshold in Choice and The Theory of Demand," *Econometrica*, 26, pp. 157-68.

Gerking, S. and W.D. Schulze 1981. "What Do We Know About Benefits of Reduced Mortality From Air Pollution Control?" *American Economics Review*, 71(20, pp. 228-40.

Gordon, I.M. and J.L. Knetsch 1979. "Consumer's Surplus Measures and the Evaluation of Resources," *Land Economics*, 55, pp. 1-10.

Graham, D.A. 1981. "Cost Benefit Analysis Under Uncertainty," *American Economic Review*, 71, pp. 715-725.

Gramlich, F. 1977. "The Demand for Clean Water: The Case of the Charles River," *National Tax Journal*, 30(2), pp. 183-194.

Green, M.W. 1942. "Sucrose Octa-Acetate as a Possible Bitter Stomachic," *Bulletin of the National Formulary, Pharmaceutical Association*, 10, pp. 131-133.

Greenley, D.A., R. Walsh and R.A. Young 1981. "Option Value: Empirical Evidence From A Casw Study of Recreation and Water Quality," *Quarterly Journal of Economics*, pp. 657-673.

Greenley, D.A., R.G. Walsh and R.A. Young 1982. *Economic Benefits of Improved Water Quality*, Boulder, Westview Press, pp. 164.

Gregory, R.S. 1982. "Valuing Non-Market Goods: An Analysis of Alternative Approaches," unpublished Ph.D. dissertation, University of British Columbia, Vancouver.

Grether, D.M. and C.R. Plott 1979. "Economic Theory of Choice and The Preference Reversal Phenomenon," *American Economic Review*, 69, pp. 623-38.

Groves, T. 1973. "The Incentives In Teams", *Econometrica*, 41.

Groves, T. and J. Ledyard 1977. "Optimal Allocation of Public Goods: A Solution to the 'Free Rider Problem'," *Econometrica*, 45(4), pp. 763-809.

Hammack, J. and G.M. Brown, Jr. 1974. *Water Fowl and Wet Lands: Toward Bio Economic Analysis*, Baltimore, Johns Hopkins University Press for Resources for the Future.

Hanemann, W.M. 1983b. "Welfare Evaluation with Simulated and Hypothetical Market Data: Bishop and Heberlein Revisited," Giannini Foundation Working Paper, No. 276.

Heberlein, T.A. 1975. "Social Norms and Environmental Quality," Paper Presented at the American Association for the Advancement of Science Annual Meetings. New York, January.

Hershey, J.C. and P.J.H. Schoemaker 1980. "Risk Taking and Problem Context in the Domain of Losses: An Expected Utility Analysis," *Journal of Risk and Insurance*, 47, pp. 111-32.

Hey, J.D. 1983. "Whither Uncertainty," *Economic Journal*, (Supplement), pp. 130-39.

Heyne, P. 1983. *The Economic Way Of Thinking*, 4th ed., Chicago, Science Research Associates, Inc.

Hoehn, J.P. and A. Randall 1983a. "Benefit Aggregation and Disaggregation Across Policy Components," University of Kentucky, unpublished paper.

Hoehn, J.P. and A. Randall 1983a. "Benefit Aggregation and Disaggregation Across Policy Components," University of Kentucky, unpublished paper.

Hoehn, J.P. and A. Randall 1983. "Incentives and Performance in Contingent Valuation," University of Kentuck, unpublished paper.

Hori, H., 1975. "Revealed Preference for Public Goods," *American Economic Review*, 65.

Hueth, D. and E.J. Strong 1984. "A Contingent Review of the Travel Cost, Hedonic Travel Cost and Household Production Models for Measurement of Quality Changes in Recreational Experiences," *American Journal of Argiculture Economics*, 66(15).

Hurwicz, L. 1983. "The Design of Mechanisms for Resource Allocation," *American Economic Review Proceedings*.

Issac, R.M. 1983. "Laboratory Experimental Economics as a Tool in Public Policy Analysis," mimeo, Dept. of Economics, University of Arizona.

Jarecki, H. 1976. "Bullion Dealing, Commodity Exchange Trading, and the London Gold Fixing: Three Forms of Commodity Auctions," in Y. Amihud (ed.), *Bidding and Auctioning for Procurement and Allocation*, New York, New York University Press.

Just, R.E., D.L. Hueth and A. Schmitz 1982. *Applied Welfare Economics and Public Policy*, Englewood Cliffs, Prentice Hall, Inc.

Kahneman, D. and A. Tversky 1972. "Subjective Probability: A Judgement Representativeness," *Cognitive Psychology*, 3(3), pp. 430–54.

Kahneman, D. and A. Tversky 1979. "Prospect Theory: An Analysis of Decisions Under Risk," *Econometrica*, 47(2), pp. 263–91.

Kahneman, D. and A. Tversky 1982a. "The Psychology of Preferences," *Scientific American*, January, pp. 160–80.

Kahneman, D., P. Solvic, and A. Tversky 1982b. *Judgement Under Uncertainty: Heuristics and Biases*, Cambridge, Cambridge University Press.

Kazan, N. and M.A. Wallach 1964. *Risk Taking: A Study in Cognition and Personality*, New York, Holt, Rinehart and Winston.

Kleindorfer, P.R. and A. Kunreuther 1983. "Misinformation and Equilibrium is Insuance Markets," in J. Finsinger (ed.), *Issues in Pricing and Regulation*, New York, Lexington.

Kneese, A.V. 1962. "Water Pollution: Economic Aspects in Research Needs," Washington, D.C., Resources For The Future, Inc.

Kneese, A.V. 1964. *The Economics of Regional Water Quality Management*, Baltimore, Johns Hopkins University Press.

Knetsch, J.L. and J.A. Sinden 1984. "Willingness to Pay and Compensation Demanded: Experimental Evidence of an Unexpected Disparity in Measures of Value," forthcoming, *Quarterly Journal of Economics*.

Knetsch, J.L. and R.K. Davis 1965. "Comparsions of Methods for Recreation Evaluation," in *Water Research*, A.V. Kneese and S.C Smith (eds.), Baltimore, Johns Hopkins University Press, pp. 125–142.

Knight, F.H. 1951. *The Economic Organization*, New York, Augustus M. Kelley, Inc.

Kogan, N. and M.A. Wallach 1964. *Risk Taking: A Study in Cognition and Personality*, New York, Holt, Rinehart and Winston.

Kreyszig, E. 1979. *Advanced Engineering Mathematics*, New York, John Wiley and Sons.

Krumm, R.J. 1980. "Neighborhood Amenities: An Economic Analysis," *Journal of Urban Economics*, 7, pp. 208–224.

Krutilla, J.A. 1967. "Conservation Reconsidered," *American Economic Review*, 57(4), pp. 77–86.

Krutilla, J.A. and A.C. Fisher 1975. *The Economics of Natural Environments: Studies in the Valuation of Commodity and Amentity Resources,* Baltimore, Johns Hopkins University Press for Resources for the Future.

Kunreuther, H.L. 1976. "Limited Knowledge and Insurance Protection," *Public Policy*, 24(2), pp. 227–61.

Kunreuther, H.L., R. Ginsberg, L. Miller, P. Sagi, P. Solvic, B. Borkan and N. Katz 1978. *Disaster Insurance Protection: Public Policy Lessons,*, New York, John Wiley and Sons.

Lakatos, I. (1970). "Falsification and the Methodology of Scientific Research Programmers," in I. Lakatos and A. Musgrave (eds), *Criticism and the Growth of Knowledge*, Cambridge, Cambridge University Press.

Lancaster, K.J. 1966. "A New Approach to Consumer Theory," *Journal of Political Economy*, pp. 132–57.

LaPierre, R.T. 1934. "Attitudes vs. Actions," *Social Forces*, 13.

Leamer, E.E. 1983. "Let's Take the Con Out of Econometrics," *American Economic Review*, 73, pp. 31–43.

Lichtenstein, S. and P. Slovic 1971. "Reversal of Preferences Between Bids and Choices in Gambling Decisions," *Journal of Experimental Psychology*, 89, pp. 46-55.

Lichtenstein, S., and B. Fishchoff 1978. "Judged Frequency of Lethal Events," *Journal of Experimental Psychology*, 4(6), pp. 551-78.

Linegard, C.R. 1943. "Acute and Chronic Studies on Sucrose Octa-acetate by the Oral Method," *Bulletin of the National Formulary Committee of the American Pharmaceutical Association*, 11, pp. 59-63.

Linneman, P. 1980. "Some Empirical Results on the Nature of the Hedonic Price Function for Urban Housing Market," *Journal of Urban Economics*, 8, pp. 47-68.

Linneman, P. 1981. "The Demand for Residence Site Characteristics," *Journal of Urban Economics*, 9, pp. 129-149.

Lipsey, R.L. and K. Lancaster 1956. "The General Theory of Second Best," *Review of Economic Studies*, 24(1).

Little, I.M.D. 1952. "Social Choice and Individual Values," *Journal of Political Economy*, 60(5).

Loeb, M. 1977. "Alternative Versions of the Demand-Revealing Process," *Public Choice*, 29, Special Supplement to Spring Issue.

Loehman, E., S. Berg, A. Arroyo, R. Hedinger, J. Schwartz, M. Shaw, R. Fahien, V. De, R. Fishe, D. Rio, W. Rossley and A. Green 1979. "Distributional Analysis of Regional Benefits and Cost of Air Quality Control," *Journal of Environmental Economics and Management*, 6, pp. 222-43.

Loomis, J.B. 1983. "A Review of the Suitability of the U.S. Fish and Wildlife Service 1980 National Survey of Fishing, Hunting, and Wildlife Associated Recreation in National Assessments and Forest Planning," manuscript. U.S. Forest Service, Ft. Collins.

Loomis, J.B. and R.G. Walsh 1982. "An Economic Evaluation of the Benefits and Costs of U.S. Forest Service Wilderness Study Areas in Colorado", Sec. II of *Colorado's Wilderness Opportunity*, American Wilderness Alliance, Denver.

Luce, R.D. 1956. "Semiorder and a Theory of Utility Discrimination," *Econometrica*, pp. 24.

Machlup, F. 1967. "Theories of the Firm: Marginalist, Behavioral, Managerial," *American Economic Review*, 57(1).

Maital, S. 1982. *Minds, Markets and Money*, New York, Basic Books.

Majid, J., J.A. Sinden and A. Randall 1983. "Benefit Evaluation of Increments to Existing Systems of Public Facilities," *Land Economics* 59(4), pp. 377-392.

Maler, K.G. 1974. *Environmental Economics*, Baltimore, Johns Hopkins University Press.

Maler, K.G. 1977. "A Note on the Use of Property Values in Estimating Marginal Willingness to Pay for Environmental Quality," *Journal of Environmental Economics and Management*, 4, pp. 355-369.

Marwell, G. and R.E. Ames 1981. "Economists Free Ride. Does Anyone Else? Experiments on the Provision of Public Goods. IV." *Journal of Public Economics*, 15(3) pp. 295-310.

McCloskey, D.N. 1983. "The Rhetoric of Economics," *Journal of Economic Literature*, 21, pp. 481-517.

McConnell, K.E. and N.E. Bockstael 1984. "Aggregation in Recreation Economics: Issues of Estimation and Measurement," *American Journal of Agricultural Economics*, 66(5).

McConnell, K.E. and N.E. Bockstael 1983. "Welfare Measurement in the Household Production Framework," *American Economic Review*, 73(4).

McMillan, J. 1979. "The Free-Rider Problem: A Survey," *The Economic Record*, June, pp. 95-107.

McNeil, B.J. 1982. "On the Elicitation of Preferences For Alternative Therapies," *New England Journal of Medicine*, 306, pp. 1259-62.

McNeil, B.S., J. Panker, H.C. Cox and A. Tversky 1982. "Patient Preferences for Alternative Therapies," *New England Journal of Medicine*, 306, pp. 1259-62.

Medoff, J.L. and K.G. Abraham 1979. "Can Productivity Capital Differentials Really Explain the Earnings Differentials Associated with Demographic Characteristics? The Case of Experience." Harvard University, Discussion Paper No. 705.

Mellow, W. and H. Sider 1983. "Accuracy of Response in Labor Market Surveys: Evidence and Implications," *Journal of Labor Economics*, 1 pp. 331-344.

Mendelsohn, R. 1980. "The Demand and Supply for Characteristics of Goods," mimeo, Department of Economics, University of Washington, Seattle.

Mendelsohn, R. and G.M. Brown, Jr. 1983. "Revealed Preference Approach To Valuing Outdoor Recreation," *Natural Resources Journal*, 23(3), pp. 607-18.

Milgrom, P.R. and R.J. Weber 1982. "A Theory of Auctions and Competitive Bidding," *Econometrica*, 50.

Miller, G.A. 1956. "The Magical Number Seven, Plus or Minus Two; Some Limits on our Capacity for Processing Information," *Psychology Review*, 63(2), pp. 81-97.

Miller, G. and C. Plott 1983. "Revenue Generating Properties of Sealed-Bid Auctions," in V.L. Smith (ed.), *Research in Experimental Economics*, Vol. 3, Connecticut, JAI Press, Inc.

Miller, J.R. and M.J. Hay 1984. "Estimating Sub-state Values of Fishing and Hunting," *Transactions of the 49th North American Wildlife and Natural Resources Conference*, Boston, MA (in press).

Mitchell, R.C. and R.T. Carson 1981. *An Experiment in Determining Willingness To Pay For National Water Quality Improvements*, draft report prepared for the U.S. Environmental Protection Agency, Washington, D.C., Resource for the Future, Inc., June.

Mitchell, R.C. and R.T. Carson 1984a. "Using Surveys to Value the Benefits of Public Goods:

The Contingent Valuation Method," Draft book manuscript, Washington, D.C., Resources for the Future.

Mitchell, R.C. and R.T. Carson 1984b. "Preliminary Comments on Draft Version of *Valuing Environmental Goods: A State of the Arts Assessment of the Contingent Valuation Method,*" Washington, D.C., Resources for the Future, unpublished paper, June 18.

Mitchell, R.C. and R.T. Carson, forthcoming. "Comment on Option Value: Empirical Evidence From a Case Study of Recreation and Water Quality," *Quarterly Journal of Economics.*

Moore, W.C. 1982. "Concept Testing," *Journal of Business Research*, Vol. 10, pp. 27.

Morgenstern, O. 1973. *On The Accuracy of Economic Observations*, 2nd ed., Princeton, Princeton University Press.

Ness, H.O. 1963. *Market Potential For Selected Fee Hunting Enterprise in New Mexico*, unpublished M.A. Thesis, New Mexico State University, Las Cruces.

O'Hanlon, P. and J. Sinden 1978. "Scope for Valuation of Environmental Goods: Comment," *Land Economics*, 54(3), pp. 381-87.

Palfrey, T.R. 1980. "Equilibrium Models of Multiple-Object Auctions," Unpublished Ph.D. dissertation, California Institute of Technology.

Pashigan, H.P. 1984. "The Effect of Environmental Regulation on Optimal Plant Size and Factor Shares," *Journal of Law and Economics*, 27 pp. 128.

Plott, C.R. 1979. "The Application of Laboratory Experimental Methods to Public Choice," in C.S. Russell (ed.), *Collective Decision Making*, Baltimore, Johns Hopkins University Press.

Plott, C.R. 1982. "Industrial Organization Theory and Experimental Economics," *Journal of Economic Literature*, 20.

Plott, C.R. and S. Sunder 1982. "Efficiency of Experimental Security Markets with Insider Information: An Application of Rational-Expectations Models," *Journal of Political Economy* 90(4): 663-698.

Pommerehne, W., S. Schneider and P. Zweifel 1982. "Economic Theory of Choice and the Preference Reversal Phenomenon: A Reexamination," *American Economic Review*, 72, pp. 569-74.

Pratt, J.W., D. Wise and R. Zeckhauser 1979. "Price Difference In Almost Competitive Markets," *Quarterly Journal of Economics*, 93(2), pp. 189-211.

Rae, D.A. 1981. *Benefits of Improving Visibility at Mesa Verde National Park*, Boston, Charles River Associates.

Rae, D.A. 1983. "The Value to Visitors of Improving Visability at Mesa Verde and Great Smokey National Parks," in R.D. Rowe and L.G. Chestnut (eds.), *Managing Air Quality and Scenic Resources at National Parks and Wilderness Areas*, Boulder, Westview Press, pp. 217-34.

Randall, A., O. Grunwald, S. Johnson, R. Ausness and R. Pagoulatos 1978a. "Reclaiming Coal Surface Mines in Central Appalachia: A Case Study of the Benefits and Costs," *Land Economics*, 54(4), pp. 472-89.

Randall, A., O. Grunwald, A. Pagoulatos, R. Ausness, and S. Johnson 1978b. *Estimating Environmental Damages From Surface Mining of Coal in Appalachia: A Case Study*, report to the USEPA, EPA-600/2-78-003, Contract No. 68-01-3586, Industrial Environmental Research Laboratory, Office of Research and Development, January.

Randall, A., J.P. Hoehn and D. Brookshire 1983. "Contingent Valuation Surveys for Evaluating Environmental Assets," *Natural Resources Journal*, 23(3), pp. 635-48.

Randall, A., J.P. Hoehn and G.S. Tolley 1984. "The Structure of Contingent Markets: Some Experimental Results," forthcoming, *Journal of Environmental Economics and Management.*

Randall, A., B. Ives and C. Eastman 1974. "Bidding Games for Valuation of Aesthetic Environmental Improvements", *Journal of Environmental Economics and Management*, 1, pp. 132-49.

Randall, A., B. Ives and C. Eastman 1974. "Benefits of Abating Aesthetic Environmental Damage from the Four Corners Power Plant, Fruitland, New Mexico," New Mexico State University Agriculture Experiment Station, Bulletin 618.

Randall, A. and J.R. Stoll 1980. "Comsumer's Surplus in Commodity Space," *American Economic Review*, 70, pp. 449-454.

Randall, A., J.P. Hoehn and G.S. Tolley, 1981. "The Structure of Contingent Markets", presented at annual meetings of the American Economics Association, December 30, mimeo, Department of Agricultural Economics, University of Kentucky.

Randall, A. and J.R. Stoll 1983. "Existence Value in a Total Valuation Framework," *Managing Air Quality and Scenic Resources at National Parks and Wilderness Areas*, R.D. Rowe and L.G. Boulder (eds.), Colorado, Westview Press.

Reilly, R 1982. "Preference Reversal: Further Evidence and Some Suggested Modifications in Experimental Design," *American Economic Review*, 72, pp. 576-584.

Ridker, R. 1967. *Economic Costs of Air Pollution*, New York, Praeger.

Robbins, H. 1932. *An Essay on the Nature and Signficance of Economic Science*, London, MacMillan.

Robertson, L. 1974. "Urban Area Safery Belt Use In Automobiles With Starter Interlock Belt Systems: A Preliminary Report," Washington, D.C., Insurance Institute For Highway Safety.

Robinson, J. 1962. *Economic Philosophy*, Garden City, Doubleday.

Ronan, J. 1973. "Effects of Some Probability Displays on Choices," *Organizational Behavior*, 9(1), pp. 1-15.

Rosen, S. 1974. "Hedonic Prices and Implicit Market: Product Differentiation in pure Competition," *Journal of Political Economy*, pp. 34-55.

Rothenberg J. 1961. *The Measurement of Social Welfare*, Englewood Cliffs, Prentice-Hall, Inc.

Rowe, R., R.C. d'Arge and D.S. Brookshire 1980a. "Environmental Preferences and Effluent Charges," Chapter 4 of *Progress in Resource Management and Environmental Planning*, Vol. 2, T. O'Riordan and K. Turner (eds.), New York, John Wiley and Sons.

Rowe, R.D., R.C. D'Arge and D.S. Brookshire 1980b. "An Experiment on the Economic Value of Visibility," *Journal of Environmental Economics and Management*, 7, pp. 1-19.

Rowe, R.D. and L.G. Chestnut 1983. "Valuing Environmental Commodities: Revisited," *Land Economics*, 59(40), pp. 404-10.

Samuelson, P.A. 1954. "Pure Theory of Public Expenditure," *Review of Economics and Statistics*, 36, pp. 387-89.

Samuelson, P.A. 1955. "Diagrammatic Exposition of a Theory of Public Expenditure," *Review of Economics and Statistics*, 37.

Samuelson, P.A. 1958. "Aspects of Public Expenditure Theories," *Review of Economics and Statistics*, 37.

Scheffe, H. 1970. "Practical Solutions to the Behrens-Fisher Problem," *Journal of the American Statistical Association*, 65.

Schelling, T.C. 1978. *Micromotives and Macrobehavior*, New York, Norton.

Scherr, B.A., and E.M. Babb 1975. "Pricing Public Goods: An Experiment with Two Proposed Pricing Systems," *Public Choice*, 23, pp. 35-48.

Schoemaker, P.J.H. and H.C. Kunreuther 1979. "An Experimental Study of Insurance Decisions," *Journal of Risk and Insurance*, 46(4), pp. 603-18.

Schoemaker, P.J.H. 1980. *Experiments on Decisions Under Risk: The Expected Utility Hypothesis*, Boston, Nijoff.

Schoemaker, P.J.H. 1982. "The Expected Utility Model: Its Variants, Purposes, Evidence, and Limitations," *Journal of Economic Literature*, 20, pp. 529-63.

Schulze, W.D., D.S. Brookshire and T. Sandler 1981a. "The Social Rate of Discount For Nuclear Waste Storage: Economics or Ethics?" *Natural Resources Journal*, 21(40, pp. 811-832.

Schulze, W.D., D.S. Brookshire, E.G. Walther, K. Kelley, M.A. Thayer, R.L. Whitworth, S. Ben-David, W. Malm and J. Molenar 1981b. "The Benefits of Preserving Visibility in the National Parklands of the Southwest," Vol. VIII, *Methods Development for Environmental Control Benefits Assessment*, Final report to the USEPA grant R805059010, Office of Exploratory Research, Office of Research and Development.

Schulze, W.D., D.S. Brookshire, E.G. Waltham, K.K. MacFarland, M.A. Thayer, R.L. Whitworth, S. Ben-David, W. Malm and J. Molenar, 1983b. "The Economic Benefits of Preserving Visibility in the National Parklands of the Southwest," *Natural Resources Journal*, 23, pp. 149-73.

Schulze, W.D., R.G. Cummings, D.S. Brookshire, M.H. Thayer, R.L. Whitworth and M. Rahmatian 1983a. "Experimental Approaches to Valuing Environmental Commodities: Vol. II," Draft final report for *Methods Development in Measuring Benefits of Environmental Improvements*, USEPA Grant # CR 808-893-01, July.

Schulze, W.D., R.C. d'Arge and D.S. Brookshire 1981. "Valuing Environmental Commodities: Some Recent Experiments," *Land Economics* 57, pp. 151-172.

Schulze, W.D. et al. 1984. Experimental Methods To Assessing Environmental Benefits. Draft Report for USEPA # CR 811077-01-0, Environmental Protection Agency, Washington, D.C., August.

Schuman, H. and M.P. Johnson 1976. "Attitudes and Behavior," *Annual Review of Sociology*, pp. 161-207.

Scott, A. 1965. "The Valuation of Game Resources: Some Theoretical Aspects," *Canadian Fisheries Reports*, No. 4.

Sellar, C., J.R. Stoll and J.P. Chavas 1984. "Valuation of Empirical Measures of Welfare Change: A Comparison of Nonmarket Techniques," forthcoming in *Land Economics*.

Shubik, M. 1975. "Oligopoly Theory, Communication and Information," *American Economic Review*, 65.

Simon, H.A. 1955. "A Behavioral Model of Rational Choice," *Quarterly Journal of Economics*, 69, pp. 174-83.

Simon, H.A. and A. Newll 1971. "Human Problem Solving: The State of The Theory in 1970," *American Psychology*, 26(2), pp. 145-59.

Simon, H.A. 1979. "Rational Decision Making in Business Organizations," *American Economic Review*, 69(4), pp. 493-513.

Sinclair, W.S. 1976. "The Economic and Social Impact of the Kemano II Hydroelectric Project on British Columbia's Fisheries Resources," Vancouver, Fisheries and Marine Service, Department of the Environment.

Sinden, J. and J. Wyckoff 1976. "Indifference Mapping: An Empirical Methodology for Economic Evaluation of the Environment," *Regional Science and Urban Economics*, 6, pp. 81-103.

Slovic, P. and S.C. Lichtenstein 1968. "Relative Importance of Probabilities and Payoffs in Risk Taking," *Journal of Experimental Psychology*, 78(3, Part 2).

Slovic, P. 1969. "Differential Effects of Real Versus Hypothetical Payoffs on Choices Among Gambles," *Journal of Experimental Psychology*, 80(3), pp. 434-37.

Slovic, P., H. Kunreuther and G.F. White 1974. "Decision Processes, Rationality and Adjustment to Natural Hazards," Chapter 24 in G.F. White (ed.), *Natural Hazards*, Oxford University Press.

Slovic, P., A. Tversky 1974. "Who Accepts Savage's Axioms?" *Behavioral Science*, 19(6), pp. 368-73.

Slovic, P., B. Fishchoff and S. Lichtenstein 1980. "Facts and Fears: Understanding Perceived Risk," pp. 181-216, in R.C. Schwing, and W.A. Albers, Jr. (eds), *Societal Risk Assessment: How Safe is Safe Enough?* New York, Plenum Press.

Smith, V.K. 1983. "Option Value: A Conceptual Overview," *Southern Economic Journal*, 49, pp. 654-668.

Smith, V.L. 1967. "Experimental Studies of Discrimination vs. Competition in Sealed-Bid Auction Markets," *Journal of Business*, 40.

Smith, V.L. 1976. "Experimental Economics: Induced Value Theory," *American Economic Review Proceedings*, 66.

Smith, V.L. 1977. "The Principle of Unanimity and Voluntary Consent in Social Choice," *Journal of Political Economy*, 85, pp. 1125-1139.

Smith, V.L. 1979a. "Incentive Compatible Experimental Processes for the Provision of Public Goods," in V.L. Smith (ed.), *Research in Experimental Economics*, Vol. 1, Connecticut, JAI Press, Inc.

Smith, V.L. 1979b. "An Experimental Comparison Of Three Public Good Decision Mechanisms," *Scandinavian Journal Of Economics*, 81.

Smith, V.L. 1980. "Experiments with a Decentralized Mechanism for Public Good Decisions," *American Economic Review*, 70, pp. 584-99.

Smith, V.L. 1982. "Microeconomics Systems as an Experimental Science," *American Economic Review*, 72(5), pp. 923-55.

Smith, V.L., A.W. Williams, W.K. Bratton and M.G. Vannoni 1982. "Competitive Maket Institutions: Double Auctions vs. Sealed-Bid Offer Auctions," *American Economic Review* 72(1) (March): 58-77.

Sorg, C. and D.S. Brookshire 1984. "Valuing Increments and Decrements of Wildlife

Resources — Further Evidence," report to U.S. Forest Service Rocky Mountain Forest and House Experiment Station, Fort Collins.

Starr, C., R. Rudman and C. Whipple 1976. "Philosophical Basis for Risk Analysis," *Annual Review of Energy*, 1, pp. 629-662.

Stigler, G.J. 1950. "The Development of Utility Theory: II," *Journal of Political Economy*, 63(5), pp. 373-396.

Stigler, G.J. and G.S. Becker 1977. "De Gustibus Non Est Disputandum," *American Economic Review*, 67(2), pp. 76-90.

Strauss, R.P. and G.D. Hughes 1976. "A New Approach to the Demand for Public Goods," *Journal of Public Economics*, 6, pp. 191-204.

Sutherland, R.J. and R.G. Walsh 1982. "Effect of Distance on the Preservation Value of Water Quality," draft, Dep. of Ag. Econ., Colo. State Univ., Ft. Collins, June.

Takayama A. 1982. "On Consumer's Surplus" *Economic Letters*, Vol. 10, pp. 35-42.

Thaler, R. 1980. "Toward A Positive Theory of Consumer Choice," *Journal of Economic Behavior and Organization*, 1, pp. 39-60.

Thaler, R. and S. Rosen 1975. "The Value of Saving a Life: Evidence from the Labor Market," pp. 265-98 in N. Terleckys (ed.), *Household Production and Consumption*, New York, Columbia University Press.

Thayer, M.A. 1981. "Contingent Valuation Techniques For Assessing Environmental Impacts: Further Evidence," *Journal of Environmental Economics and Management*, 8, pp. 27-44.

Thompson, M.E. and K.J. Roberts 1983. "An Empirical Application of the Contingent Valuation Technique to Value Marine Resources," *Transactions of the American Fisheries Society*.

Tideman, T. and G. Turlock 1976. "A New and Superior Process for Making Social Choices," *Journal of Political Economy*, 84.

Tolley, G.S., A. Randall, G. Blomquist, R. Fabian, G. Fishelson, A. Frankel, J.P. Hoehn, R. Krumm and E. Mensah 1984. *Establishing and Valuing the Effects of Improved Visability in the Eastern United States*, final report, #80776-01-1, USEPA, Washington, D.C.

Tversky, A. and D. Kahneman 1974. "Judgement Under Uncertainty: Heuristics and Biases," *Science*, 185(2), pp. 1124-31.

Tversky, A. and D. Kahneman 1981. "The Framing of Decisions and the Rationality of Choice," *Science*, p. 453.

Ullman, E. and D. Volk 1961. "An Operational Model for Predicting Reservoir Attendance and Benefits," *Proceedings of the Michigan Academy of Sciences*, Department of Economics, University of Michigan, Ann Arbor.

Van Nostrand's *Scientific Encyclopedia* (5th ed.) New York, Van Nostrand Reinhold Co. (1970).

Vickery, W. 1961a. "Counterspeculation, Auctions and Competitive Sealed Tenders," *Journal of Finance*, 16, pp. 8–37.

Vickery, W. 1961b. "Auctions, Markets, and Optimal Allocation," in Y. Amihad (ed.) *Bidding and Auctioning for Procurement and Allocation* (New York: New York University Press): 13–20.

Walbert, M.S. 184. "Valuing Policies Which Reduce Environmental Risk: An Assessment of the Contingent Valuation Method," unpublished Ph.D. dissertation, University of New Mexico, Albuquerque.

Walsh, R.G. 1980. *An Economic Evaluation of the General Management Plan for Yosemite National Park*, Technical Report No. 19, Water Resources Research Institute, Colorado State University, Fort Collins, March.

Walsh, R.G., Aukerman and R. Milton 1980. *Measuring Benefits and the Economic Value of Water in Recreation on High Country Reservoirs*, Completion Report No. 102, Colorado Water Resources Research Institute, Fort Collins, September.

Walsh, R.G., R.K. Ericson and D.J. Arosteguy 1980. *An Application of a Model for Estimating the Recreation Value of Instream Flow*, Completion Report No. 101, Colorado Water Resources Research Institute, Colorado State University, Fort Collins, December.

Walsh, R.G., R.K. Ericson, J.R. McKean and R.A. Young 1978a. *Recreation Benefits of Water Quality: Rocky Mountain Nation Park, South Platte River Basin,. Colorado*, Environmental Resources Center, Technical Report No. 12, Colorado State University, Fort Collins, May.

Walsh, R.G., D.A. Greenley, R.A. Young, J.R. McKean and A.A. Prato 1978b. *Option*

Values, Preservation Values and Recreational Benefits of Improved Water Quality: A Case Study of the South Platte River Basin, Colorado, Socioeconomic Environmental Studies Series, EPA-600/5-78-001 U.S. Environmetal Protection Agency, Research Triangle Park, North Carolina, January.

Walsh, R.G., G. Keleta and J.P. Olienyk 1981. *Value of Trees of Residential Property Owners with Moutain Pine Beetle and Spruce Budworm Damage in the Colorado Front Range*, Report by the Department of Economics to the Forest Service, USDA, Washington, D.C., October.

Walsh, R.G., N.P. Millers, and L.O. Gillaim 1982. "Congestion and Willingness to Pay for Expansion of Skiing Capacity," *Land Economics*, 59(2), pp. 195–210.

Walsh, R.G., and J.P. Olienyk 1981. *Recreation Demand Effects of Mountain Pine Beetle Damage to the Quality of Forest Recreation Resources in the Colorado Front Range*, Report by the Department of Economics to the Forest Service, USDA, Washington, D.C., October.

Walsh, R.G., and L.O. Gilliam 1982. "Benefits of Wilderness Expansion with Excess Demand for Indian Peaks," *Western Journal of Agricultural Economics*, 7 (July): 1–12.

Ward, E. 1954. "The Theory of Decision Making," *Psychological Bulletin*, 51 (4), pp. 380–417.

Weinstein, M.C. and R.J. Quinn 1983. "Psychological Considerations in Valuing Health Risk Reductions," *Natural Resources Journal*, 23(3), pp. 659–73.

Weisbrod, B.A. 1964. "Collective-Comsumption Services of Individual-Consumption Goods," *Quarterly Journal of Economics*, 78, pp. 471–77.

Wicksell, K. 1896. "A New Principle of Just Taxation," translated by J.M. Buchanan, in R.A. Musgrave and A.T. Peacock (eds.) *Classic in the Theory of Public Finance*, New York, St. Martin's Press (1967).

Wilde, L. 1980. "On the Use of Laboratory Experiments in Economics," in J. Pitt (ed.), *The Philosophy of Economics*, Dordrecht, Reidel.

Willig, R.D. 1976. "Consumer's Surplus Without Apology," *American Economic Review*, 66(5), pp. 89–97.

Index

Index

A

Accuracy
  auction mechanisms and, 139–41
  bias and, 158
  of bidding, 87
  of cash payments, 233–34
  commodity perception and, 56–57
  counterfactuality and, 184–85, 227–28
  definitions of, 96, 107, 232–33
  of hedonic price method, 95–96, 99–101
  hypothetical payments and, 50–52
  incentives for, 50–52, 155, 156, 211–213
  iterative bidding and, 135–37
  order of magnitude of, 97–99, 157, 161n, 229, 233
  ranges of, 135, 157–59, 174–75, 196, 227, 232–33, 244
  research needs regarding, 229–31
  state-of-the-arts assessment of, 226–31, 233–34, 244
  survey costs and, 151
  time factors of, 155
  of travel cost method, 95, 99–101
  true value and, 226–27
  value comparison assessment of. *See* Value comparison studies
  willingness-to-pay values and, 50–51
Acid rain control, attitude-behavior research regarding, 143–46
Air quality
  loss aversion valuation of, 188
  rent gradient effects of, 90–92
  standards' cost-benefit valuation of, 6–7
  value comparison study of, 90–92
  value measurement of, 163, 176n. 2

Allocation system evaluation
  via auction mechanisms, 39–41
  incentive compatibility and, 38–39
Alquist-Priolo Special Studies Zones Act, 94
Anchoring bias, 192–93, 210
Arrow, Kenneth, contingent valuation method assessment by, 180–85
Asset trading market, 199–204
Attitude(s)
  as behavioral predictors, 5
  components of, 142, 221
  definition of, 141–42
  evaluation of, 170
  vs. intended behavior, 65–67, 142, 143, 221–23
Attitude-behavior research, 141–46, 225–26
Attitudinal bias, 65–67
Attitudinal data, 170–71
Attitudinal information, 171, 222
Auction mechanisms, 39–41
  accuracy and, 139–41
  assessment of, 216, 239–40
  Dutch, 39–40
  English, 39, 140, 240
  fifth-price, 129, 130, 131, 132, 133
  first-price, 39, 40
  iterative bidding and, 178
  learning effects in, 103–4, 198
  oral, 39
  reference operating conditions and, 103–4
  sealed-bid, 39, 40, 48n., 129–30
  second-price, 39, 40, 46–48, 48n., 139–40, 159–60, 238, 240, 245n.
  tatonnement process of, 46–48, 141, 216, 240

of willingness-to-accept/willingness-to-pay discrepancy, 42, 44
Axiomatic behavior, 27–28

B

Behavior, of contingent valuation method subjects
attitudes as predictors of, 5
axiomatic, 27–28
free-ride, 23–24, 121n., 141, 152
intended vs. attitudes, 65–67, 142, 143, 221–23
rational, 5–6, 19, 198
theory of, 115–20
under uncertainty conditions, 18–19, 20n., 44–45
Benefit-cost analysis
accuracy level and, 175
of federal regulations, 6
function of, 71–72
General Possibilities Theorem and, 11–12
social welfare consequences analysis with, 10, 11–13
Benefit estimates, 175
satisfactory estimators in, 119, 120
surveys of, 167–68
Bias, 4–5, 6, 7, 9n., 133–34. See also specific types of bias
accuracy and, 158
empirical research approach and, 115
questionnaire design-related, 28–36
Bidding
accuracy of, 87
auction mechanisms of. See Auction mechanisms
close-ended, 85, 86, 87
factors related to, 4
information bias and, 33–34, 99, 208–9
Iterative. See Iterative bidding
open-ended, 85, 86, 87
subjects' nonparticipation in, 127–28, 152–53, 245n.
zero bids, 152, 153
Bidding game
for hunting permits, 128–33
hypothetical bias and, 54
site substitution method and, 88–89
starting point bias and, 136

state-of-the-arts assessment of, 237–39
willingness-to-pay value and, 54
Bishop, R. C., value comparison study of, 74–76
Brookshire, D. S., value comparison study of, 90–95
Buying-selling discrepancy, 188–89

C

Calibration, of value measures, 135, 182, 229–31
Cash payment
accuracy values and, 233–34
vs. hypothetical payment, 124–28, 134, 183, 211–13, 223–24, 241–42
willingness-to-pay/willingness-to-accept discrepancy and, 128–33
Chavas, J. P., value comparison study of, 81–87
Cognitive dissonance, 35, 58, 104, 159, 217–18
Cognitive psychology, 5–6
Commodity. See also Environmental goods; Public goods
framing bias and, 60–65
heterogeneity of, 102–3
hypothetical, 56–65, 67–69, 182–83
perception of, 56–60, 68–69
starting point bias and, 207
subjects' familiarity with, 49, 155–57, 160, 163, 207, 213–14
Commodity valuation, commodity set description and, 6, 9n.
Compensation structure transaction, 186–89
Conference on Valuing Environmental Improvements: A State-of-the-Arts Assessment of the Contingent Valuation Method, 113–245
description of, 8
overview of, 113
review panel's assessment, 180–204
Consumer Price Index, 165, 168, 177n.
Contingent choice mechanisms, 149
Contingent markets
function of, 3
vs. "real" markets, 116
Contingent Ranking Method, 77, 78, 81, 82–83, 149

Contingent Valuation Method (CVM)
acceptability of, 4–5
accuracy of. *See* Accuracy applications of, 16, 21–36, 197
assessment structure for, 19–20
axiomatic behavior and, 27–28
bias of, 4–5, 6, 7, 9n., 133–34. *See also specific types of bias*
contingent ranking method compared with, 77, 78, 79–81
criteria for, 149–51
criticisms of, 5–6, 9n.
definition of, 3
development of, 3–4, 15–17
efficacy of, 4–5
experimental approaches to, 137–38
experimental economics and, 37–48, 103–4, 216–17, 224–25
future research issues in, 235–36
hedonic price method compared with, 89–95
heuristics and, 18, 49, 55, 215
historical perspective for, 10–20
as market simulator, 72
media and, 6
methodological problems of, 164, 244. *See also types of bias*
nonrandom measures of, 54, 62
objective of, 163
open-ended vs. close-ended forms of, 85–87
operational questions of, 16
psychological research and, 5–6, 17–18
research related to, 17–19
response models of, 173–74
risk and, 18–19, 20n., 56
state-of-the-arts assessment of, 148–61, 180–204, 231–32, 237–45
survey costs of, 151
utility theory and, 6, 19, 27, 28
value comparison studies of, 71–109, 157–58
Cost estimate surveys, 169
Counterfactuality, 184–85, 227–28
Cummings, R. G., value comparison study of, 92–93

D

Data. *See* Value data
Davis, R. K., value comparison study of, 73–74

Decision-making
context effects in, 60–63
under hypothetical conditions, 51, 172
rationality and, 6
sub-allocative, 17
sub-optimal, 116
under uncertainty, 61–63
value information in, 14
Deer hunting permit study
bidding game of, 128–33
design of, 128–29
further research regarding, 131–33
interpretation of, 131–33
preliminary results from, 129–31
willingness-to-accept values of, 128, 129–30, 131–32, 133
willingness-to-pay values of, 128, 129, 130–31, 132, 133
Demand
aggregate, 193–94
elasticities of, 92–93, 181, 196
median, 194
option, 14
symbolic, 190–92, 214
Demand curve, 181–82
ideological loading and, 190–92
Demand equations
estimation techniques for, 99–100
of travel cost method, 81, 84
Desvouges, W. H., value comparison study of, 76–81

E

Earthquake hazards
preference differences and, 195–96
value comparison study of, 93–95, 189
Empirical approach, to value data quality, 114–15
Empirical testing, 176n.
Employment survey, 165, 177n.
Environmental change, perception of, 56–60
Environmental goods
characteristics of, 162–63
description of, 154
preference ordering of, 150, 155–56, 192, 193, 213
required compensation for, 157
subjects' familiarity with, 49, 155–57, 160, 163, 207, 213–14

subjects' perception of, 154
value measures of, 135, 151, 182, 229–31
Environmental Protection Agency regulations
benefit-cost considerations for, 6–7
political economy of, 197
Environmental quality valuation, media and, 6
Environmental safety, benefit-cost valuation of, 6–7
Errors. *See also types of bias*
approximation technique-related, 245n.
order of magnitude of, 97–99, 157, 161n., 229, 233
random, 151, 155–57, 160, 228
ranges of, 135, 157–59, 174–75, 196, 227, 228, 232–33, 244
reference operating conditions and, 230–31
Executive Order 6, 14
Existence values, 144, 145, 146
Expected utility model
attitudinal questions and, 66
efficacy of, 44–45
of self-insurance, 93–94
Experimental economics, 37–48, 216–17
auction mechanisms, 39–41
field experiments, 38
laboratory methods, 41–44
methodological developments in, 38–41
reference operating conditions simulation, 103–4
state-of-the-arts assessment of, 224–25
uncertainty conditions behavior, 44–45
Experimental results transferability, 180–81, 216, 234
Extra-market goods, valuation of, 13–14

F

Familiarity, with commodities, 49, 155–57, 160, 163, 207, 213–14
Field experiments
interpretation of, 38

reliability of results from, 182
subjects' de-briefing in, 240–41
value of, 137, 138
Fisher, W. L., value comparison study of, 89
Fishing fees, value comparison study of, 89
Framing bias, 60–65, 68, 193
Free-ride behavior, 23–24, 121n., 141, 152. *See also* Strategic behavior

G

General Possibility Theorem, 11
Gerking, S., value comparison study of, 92–93
Goose hunting permit study, 124–128
analysis of, 124–26
design of, 124
interpretation of, 126–28
willingness-to-accept values of, 126
willingness-to-pay values of, 125, 126–27
willingness-to-sell values of, 125, 128

H

Heberlein, T. A., value comparison study of, 74–76
Hedonic Price Method (HPM)
accuracy of, 95–96, 99–101, 157
Brookshire *et al.* study of, 90–92, 93–95
contingent valuation method compared with, 89–95
Cummings *et al.* study of, 92–93
development of, 14, 15
elasticity measure of, 92–93
environmental goods value measures of, 151
estimation problems of, 95, 96
hypothetical payment and, 52
limited applications of, 6
property value application of, 90–92, 94–95, 165, 167–68, 173, 176–77n.
rent gradient value of, 90–92, 94, 165
willingness-to-pay values of, 90, 93, 94–95
Hedonic wage model, 168
Heuristics, 18, 49, 55, 215

Household production survey, 168
Hunting permits. *See also* Deer hunt-
    ing permit study; Goose hunting
    permit study
willingness-to-accept/willingness-to-
    pay discrepancy of, 188–89
willingness-to-sell values of, 74–76
Hypothetical bias, 16–17, 49–70, 155–
    57, 223–26. *See also* Payment, hy-
    pothetical vs. real
accuracy and, 50–52
assessment of, 211–26
attitudes vs. intended behavior and,
    16, 65–57
causes of, 16
commodity-related, 56–65
framing bias and, 60–65
of non-contingent valuation methods,
    165
null hypothesis regarding, 67–68
preference research and, 54, 55
proposed solutions to, 53–56
reference operating conditions and,
    134
in referendum-type formats, 206–7
site substitution method and, 88
state-of-the-arts assessment of, 182–
    83, 196, 211–17, 223–26, 241
time-related, 52–56
willingness-to-pay values and, 53–54
Hypotheticality, effects of, 241–42
Hypothetical questions, 185
as contingent valuation method limi-
    tation, 171–73
problems of, 172–73
subjects' response to, 173–74

I

Ideological loading, 190–93, 214
Impossibility Theorem, 12
Incentive compatibility, 38–39
policy evaluation and, 120
of second-price auction, 159
Incentives, 119
for accuracy, 50–52, 155, 156, 211–13
future research regarding, 235–36
models of, 117–18
state-of-the-arts assessment of, 211–
    13
for strategic responses, 5, 117–18,
    165–66, 173, 236

Indirect market methods
accuracy of, 227
evaluation of, 174
sampling distribution of, 177n.
Indirect market values
reference accuracy and, 100–102, 105
reference operating conditions and,
    107, 108–9
Information
attitudinal, 171, 222
sensitive, 166, 170
Information bias, 33–34, 208–9
bidding effects of, 99
commodity perception and, 59–60
policy evaluation and, 120–21
state-of-the-arts assessment of, 184
    209–9, 210–11
time factor-related, 53–56
types of, 153–54
Information processing, 55–56
commodity perception and, 59–60
questionnaire pretests and, 209, 210
time factors in, 53–56, 156
Intrinsic values, 144–46
Iterative bidding, 37, 38, 215–27
accuracy and, 135–37
auction mechanisms and, 178
learning effects, 218, 238
payment cards, vs., 135
as preference-researched bidding, 54
random error and, 160
starting point bias and, 178
state-of-the-arts assessment of, 224,
    238–39

K

Kahneman, Daniel, contingent valua-
    tion method assessment by, 185–94
Knetsch, J. L., value comparison
    study of, 73–74

L

Laboratory experiments, 41–44
assessment of, 216
limitations of, 137–38
objective of, 38
uncertainty conditions behavior and,
    44–45
utility of, 240–41

Learning effects, 215–17, 218
  of auction mechanisms, 103–4, 198
  of iterative bidding, 218, 238
  state-of-the-arts assessment of, 215, 224
Loss aversion, 187–89
Love Canal, 6, 18

M

Market
  definition of, 102
  political, 243–44
  reference operating conditions of, 102, 103–6
  simulated, 124–34
  survey respondents' awareness of, 171
Market institutions
  contingent valuation method as substitute for, 72
  definition of, 243
Market prices, as social welfare measures, 10, 12–13
McGivney, M. P., value comparison study of, 76–81
Media, contingent valuation method values and, 6
Model, of contingent valuation method, 173–74
Municipal infrastructure, value comparison study of, 92–93

N

Nonrandom measures, 54, 62
Nonrespondents, in contingent valuation surveys, 127–28, 152–53, 245n.

O

Opinion polls, 3
Option demand, 14
Option value, 20n.
  definition of, 144
  ideological loading of, 190
Order of magnitude, of accuracy, 97–99, 157, 161n., 229, 233

P

Pareto-improvement, benefit-cost estimation and, 119, 120
Pareto Optimality, 12–13
Payment
  bias related to. See Vehicle bias
  description of, 193–94
  framing bias and, 64
  hypothetical vs. real, 50–52, 66–67, 69, 124–28, 134, 183, 211–13, 223–24, 241–42
Payment card, 29–31, 37
  iterative bidding vs., 38, 135
  starting point bias and, 207, 208, 210
  state-of-the-arts assessment of, 239
Payment card bias. See Vehicle bias
Perception
  of environmental changes, 56–60
  of environmental goods, 154
  of hypothetical commodities, 56–60, 68–69
  of risk, 56
Policy evaluation, information bias and, 120–21
Pollution control, cost data for, 165–66, 177n.
Preference(s)
  differences in, 195–96
  methodological procedure sensitivity of, 183–84, 193
Preference ordering, 150, 155–56
  coherent, 192, 193
  commodity familiarity and, 213
  market behavior and, 192
Preference research, 53, 54
  bidding-like trials and, 28
  hypothetical bias and, 54, 55
  issues of, 211–17
Preference reversal, 44
Price elasticity estimation, 100
Price index measures, 168
Pricing, of public goods, 22–26
Property values, hedonic model of, 90–92, 94–95, 165, 167–68, 173, 176–77n.
Prospect theory, 187–89, 219
Psychology, contingent valuation method and, 5–6, 17–18
Public goods
  allocation of, 21–22
  individual valuations of, 22

market institutions for, 72
pricing of, 22–26
theory of, 193–94
Public goods valuation
auction mechanisms and, 40–41, 103–4
for extra-market goods, 13–14
historical perspectives for, 14–15
reference accuracy and, 229
social welfare and, 13–15
by survey, 13–15
Purchase structure transactions, 186–90

Q

Questionnaires
bias related to, 28–36
design of, 177n.
evaluation of, 175
framing bias of, 60–65
information bias and, 33–34
open-ended vs. closed-ended, 85–87
pretests of, 209, 210
quality of, 166
starting point bias and, 28–31
vehicle bias and, 31–33
Questions, hypothetical, 171–73, 185

R

Random errors, 151, 155–57, 228
iterative bidding and, 160
Rational behavior hypothesis, 5–6
criticisms of, 19
direct decision responses and, 198
Reagan, Ronald, 6
Recreation participation models, 167
Reference accuracy, 96–102
bias sources and, 99
definition of, 96–97
of demand equations, 99–100
future research in, 235
indirect market values and, 100–102, 105
order of magnitude of, 97–99
public goods values and, 229
ranges of, 100–102, 233

reference operating conditions and, 97, 102, 103–6, 107, 108–9, 229–31
of significant digits, 97
Reference operating conditions (ROC), 97, 102, 103–6, 107, 108–9, 226
auction mechanisms and, 103–4
commodity choice experience and, 104, 105, 106, 156, 171
commodity familiarity and, 104, 105, 106, 213, 214
evaluation of, 229–31
generalized, 186–90, 219
hypothetical bias and, 134
indirect market values and, 107, 108–9
of market, 102, 103–6
measurement errors and, 230–31
reference accuracy and, 97, 102, 103–6, 107, 108–9, 229–31
for referendum, 243–44
relevant, 104, 107
state-of-the-arts assessment of, 185–94
subjectivity of, 108
Referendum
hypothetical bias and, 206–7
reference operating conditions for, 243–44
strategic behavior and, 236
Rent gradient, of hedonic price method, 90–92, 94, 165
Repetitive valuation trials. See Iterative bidding
Reservation values, 190
Risk, 18–19, 20n., 56
Rosen, Sherwin, contingent valuation method assessment by, 194–97

S

Sales tax, as payment vehicle, 32–33
Sample size, 160, 166, 238, 244, 245n.
Scaling, 181, 182
Schulze, W. D., value comparison study of, 90–95
Scientific method, social science applications of, 7
Securities trading market, 199–204
Selectivity effects, 197, 220
Self-reporting bias, 114
Self-selection bias, 152, 153, 154, 196

Seller, C., value comparison study of, 81–87
Significant digits, 97
Site substitution method, 87–89, 149, 160n.
Smith, Vernon
  contingent valuation method analysis by, 197–204
  value comparison study of, 76–81
Social arrangements, of payment vehicles, 193–94, 209, 211
Social sciences, scientific method applications in, 7
Social welfare
  benefit-cost analysis of, 10, 11–13
  definition of, 11
  market price measures of, 12–13
  public goods valuation and, 13–15
Starting point bias, 28–36, 207–8
  bidding and, 28–31, 99, 137
  commodity unfamiliarity and, 207
  control of, 153, 207, 208, 210
  evidence for, 207, 237–38
  payment cards and, 207, 208, 210
  preference order and, 192
  questioning format and, 178
  random error measurement and, 158–59
  sample sizes and, 238, 245n.
  site substitution method and, 88
  state-of-the-arts assessment of, 207–8, 237–38
Stoll, J. R., value comparison study of, 81–87
Strategic behavior
  definition of, 5, 116
  incentives for, 5, 117–18, 156–66, 173, 236
  information bias and, 34
  referendum and, 236
  second-price auction and, 159
  true value and, 115
  willingness-to-pay and, 117–19
Strategic bias, 14, 16, 21–26, 152–53, 206–7
  avoidance of, 152
  bid distribution of, 24–26
  computerization and, 197
  control of, 119
  importance of, 210
  state-of-the-arts assessment of, 183, 196, 206–7

  tests for, 24-26
Subjective phenomena, scaling of, 181, 182
Subjects
  behavior of. See Behavior, of contingent valuation method subjects
  bidding accuracy perception of, 87
  commodity familiarity of, 49, 155–57, 160, 163, 207, 213–14
  debriefing of, 240–41
  decision basis of, 120
  nonresponse by, 127–28, 152–53, 245n.
  response conservatism of, 127
  response model of, 173–74
  tasks requested of, 170–72
  value formation by, 115–16, 121–22n.
  value reporting by, 116–19
  value theory and, 27–28
Surplus, seller vs. total, 202, 203
Survey respondents. See Subjects
Surveys, 13–15
  cost of, 151
  design of, 175
  employment, 165, 177n.
  uncertainty and, 18–19
  underidentification in, 38
  usefulness of, 162
  as valuation device, 3
  wage information, 166, 177n.

T

Tatonnement process, 46–48, 141, 216, 240
Thayer, M. A., value comparison study of, 87–89, 20–92, 93–95
Three-Mile Island, 6, 18
Time factors
  accuracy and, 155
  hypothetical bias and, 52–56
  information bias and, 53–56
  information processing and, 156
Travel Cost Method (TCM), 6
  accuracy of, 95, 99–101, 157
  contingent valuation method compared with, 72–89
  demand equations of, 81, 84
  development of, 14, 15
  environmental goods value measures of, 151

goose hunting permit study of, 124, 125–26, 127
site substitution method of, 87–89
value comparison studies of, 73–89
visitor values vs. travel cost in, 95
willingness-to-drive values of, 73–74
willingness-to-pay values of, 73, 74, 75, 76, 78, 81, 87
willingness-to-sell values of, 74–76
True value
  accuracy and, 107, 226–27, 228
  auction mechanisms and, 40
  definition of, 150
  estimation of, 163, 174
  hedonic price method and, 96
  strategic behavior and, 115

U

Uncertainty
  behavior under, 18–19, 20n., 44–45
  decision-making and, 61–63
  expected utility model and, 44–45
  mental account partitioning in, 55–56
  value theory and, 45, 48n.
Underidentification, in survey evaluations, 38
Utility bills, as payment vehicle, 31–32
Utility theory, 6, 19
  value theory and, 27–28

V

Value(s)
  ideological, 190–93, 214, 223
  uncertainty and, 45, 48n.
  willingness-to-accept. See Willingness to accept
  willingness-to-drive. See Willingness-to-drive
  willingness-to-pay. See Willingness-to-pay
  willingness-to-sell. See Willingness-to-sell
Value comparison studies, 71–109
  assessment of, 157–58
  of Bishop and Heberlein, 74–76
  of Brookshore et al., 93–95
  of contingent ranking method, 77, 78, 79, 81, 82–83
of Cummings et al., 92–93
of Desvouges, Smith and McGivney, 76–81, 178–79
of Fisher, 89
of hedonic price method, 89–95
of Knetsch and Davis, 73–74
results of, 95–102
of Seller, Stoll and Chavas, 81–87
of Thayer, 87–89
of travel cost method, 72–89
Value data
  attitudinal, 170–71
  noncontingent valuation, 164–70
  quality of, 114–15, 119
Value formation, 115–16, 121–22n.
Value function, hypothetical, 187, 188
Value judgements, in social welfare function, 11, 12
Value measures, 151
  of air quality, 163, 176n.
  calibration of, 135, 182, 229–31
Value reporting, 116–19
Value theory, 27
  uncertainty and, 45, 48n.
Vehicle bias, 31–33, 99, 135, 209–10, 239
  bidding effect of, 99
  definition of, 154
  social arrangements of, 193–94, 209, 211
  state-of-the-arts assessment of, 183–84, 209–11
Vickrey auction. See Auction, second-price

W

Wage information survey, 166, 177n.
Water quality
  benefits assessment of, 76–81
  value comparison study of, 76–83
Willingness-to-accept
  abandonment of, 138–39
  of asset trading market, 199–202
  auction evaluation of, 42–44
  of hunting permit studies, 126, 128, 129–30, 131–32, 133
  hypothetical vs. real, 41–44, 51
  iterative bidding and, 238, 239
  laboratory evaluation of, 41–44

measures of, 35–36
order of magnitude of, 98
overstatement of, 116, 120, 139, 157
purchase structure transactions and, 186, 188–90
state-of-the-arts assessment of, 186, 188, 189, 190, 198–202
survey instrument construction for, 45–48
upward adjustment of, 44
value formation and, 115–16
Willingness-to-accept/willingness to-pay discrepancy, 35–36, 38, 48n., 122n., 138–39, 198–202, 217–21
cash payment and, 128–33
cognitive dissonance in, 35, 159, 217–18
of hunting permit studies, 128–33, 188–89
hypotheticality in, 241
individual differences in, 219–20
laboratory evaluation of, 41–44
selectivity of, 220
state-of-the-arts assessment of, 217–21, 225
Willingness-to-drive, 73–74, 149
Willingness-to-pay, 27–28
accuracy incentives and, 50–51
aggregate, 193–94
of asset trading market, 199–202
auction evaluation of, 42–44
axiomatic behavior and, 27–28
bidding game and, 54
cognitive dissonance effects, 159
commodity perception and, 59
of hunting permit studies, 125, 126–27, 128, 129, 130–31, 132, 133

of hedonic price method, 90, 93, 94–95
hypothetical bias and, 53–54
hypothetical vs. real, 41–44, 50–51
iterative bidding and, 238, 239
laboratory evaluation of, 41–44
measures of, 35–36
missing values of, 161n.
optimal strategy for, 117–19
order of magnitude of, 97–98
overstatement of, 239
payment mechanisms and, 64
purchase structure transactions and, 186, 188, 189, 190
question framing for, 60, 63–65
as reference operating condition, 104, 107
referendum measures of, 243, 244
social arrangements of, 193–94
starting point bias and, 29, 30
state-of-the-arts assessment of, 186, 188, 189, 190, 198–202
strategic bias and, 22–23, 25
of travel cost method, 73, 74, 75, 76, 78, 81, 87
understatement of, 116, 119, 120, 127, 132, 157, 240
upward adjustment of, 153
value formation and, 115–16
vehicle bias and, 31–33
Willingness-to-sell
of hunting permits, 125, 128
of travel cost method, 74–76

Z

Zero bids, 152, 153